FIONN MAC CUMHAILL
IMAGES OF THE GAELIC HERO

Do Chaitríona agus An Chlann

Acknowledgments

The author wishes to thank all who assisted in his research for this book, either by advice or discussion. Special thanks are due to the following: Bo Almqvist, Séamas Ó Catháin, Pádraig Ó Fiannachta, Pádraig Ó Héalaí, Proinsias Mac Cana, George Eogan, Liam P. Ó Caithnia, Charles Doherty, Éamonn Ó hÓgáin, Donald A. MacDonald, John McInnes, Nessa Ní Shéaghdha, Mainchín Seoighe, Diarmaid Breathnach, Gabriel Cooney, and Michael Kelleher. Any errors are the sole responsibility of the author.

Dáithí Ó hÓgáin
Lá Bealtaine 1987

DÁITHÍ Ó hÓGÁIN

Fionn mac Cumhaill

Images of the Gaelic Hero

Gill and Macmillan

Published in Ireland by
Gill and Macmillan Ltd
Goldenbridge
Dublin 8
with associated companies in
Auckland, Delhi, Gaborone, Hamburg, Harare, Hong Kong,
Johannesburg, Kuala Lumpur, Lagos, London, Manzini,
Melbourne, Mexico City, Nairobi, New York, Singapore,
Tokyo

0 7171 1532 1
Print origination in Ireland by Galaxy Reproductions Ltd
Printed in Great Britain by
The Camelot Press, Southampton

British Library Cataloguing in Publication Data
Ó hÓgáin, Dáithí
Fionn mac Cumhaill: images of the Gaelic hero.
1. Finn Mac Cool – Legends – History and criticism
2. Goidelic literature – History and criticism
I. Title
891.6 PB1197
ISBN 0-7171-1532-1

Contents

Introduction

The purpose of this book is to examine the Gaelic lore concerning the hero Fionn mac Cumhaill from its origins down to recent times. Few characters have held the stage in both literary and oral story-telling for so long, and so it is necessary to trace the development of the tradition and the alterations which it underwent from epoch to epoch. All the more significant stories, themes, and images concerning Fionn are included in the analysis, which thus covers the entire corpus of Fionn narrative. The various strands of the tradition are interconnected and yet can be viewed as distinctive, having survived through extremely long periods.

In order to facilitate the identification of various strands, the chapters are arranged in a broadly chronological sequence and the material is divided into generally phenomenological sections within each chapter. The intention is to place each item of lore in its historical context by dating, and in its narrative context by deciding its relationship to other aspects of the lore. For a millenium and a half accounts of Fionn and of his adventures have fascinated Irish audiences, and so the material is found in texts belonging to the Irish language at various stages.

Old Irish is the term used to designate the form of the language from when it was first committed to writing, at the end of the sixth century, to the early tenth century. The phase of transformation from then until the fourteenth century is known as Middle Irish, after which the modern linguistic period begins.

Scottish Gaelic and Manx had sprung from Irish just before the literary tradition began, but a very influential learned caste kept the three branches of the language in close relationship to each other by standardised literary and official forms.

As will be seen, it was during the Middle Irish period that the lore of Fionn spread to Scotland and to the Isle of Man. But the divisions of linguistic history do not satisfactorily reflect the full nature of the lore's development. Several items appear as almost identical in quite different textual forms of the language, while there can be great discordance between items of lore within a single period. The problem of such resemblances and discrepancies can only be solved through studying the growth of each particular item, but in general it can be said that what historians term the 'Middle Ages' was a time of transformation in Gaelic literature and story-telling as in other European cultures.

Thus it is often found suitable in this book to use the term 'mediaeval' in discussing the chronology of development. By 'early mediaeval' is meant the period coinciding with Old Irish, while 'late mediaeval' refers to the phase of transition from Middle to Modern Irish, i.e. about A.D. 1150 to 1450.

The orthographical forms of personal names and place names employed in this book are made to accord with this latter period, which is taken to represent most clarity *vis-à-vis* ancient and modern morphology because of its medial position. Toponymics are given in Gaelic form when they occur in direct quotation, but in anglicised form elsewhere.

The material discussed in the final chapters represents a new flowering of the whole narrative tradition in free-flowing literary and oral media – that is in the final four centuries before our own time. A new epoch had brought new tastes to the fore and the fabric of tradition was accordingly being re-designed. To the tellers of tales at all periods, however, and more especially to their listeners, all such 'historicising' of the Fionn tradition was superfluous and without real meaning. Most people believed – as many still do – that Fionn had really lived, but the literati and the annalists never troubled themselves overmuch to provide conclusive proof.

Fionn, as a wise man and a great warrior, invited exploitation for social and political purposes, but in the long run what was most relevant was adventure. Every known story was valued, each idea concerning him and his company which could be the occasion for new fancies in the mind.

1.

A Celtic Denizen

Many of the characters who occur in early Irish literature have attributes which lead us to suspect that they were originally deities, or at least preserve characteristics of gods whose identities have been lost in the dim and distant past. Of all these, Fionn is one of the most interesting to study, though also one of the most complicated, for there is no substantial early text completely devoted to a portrayal of him. In terms of anecdotes and individual traditions, however, he is probably the character whom we encounter most often in Old Irish literature.[1]

Name and Origin of **'Fionn'**

References to this hero, and stories about him, are found in the literature of the Irish language at all periods. The Old Irish form of his name was *Find*, and the first clear mention of him occurs in a text which may date from the dawn of Irish writing in the sixth century. In translation this reads: 'Find, Tulcha, and Caílte, a tribe of heroes – they shook the fierce sea-surface with waves from barks – three descendants of Baíscne, a victorious company, best among warriors, three descendants of Nuadhu Necht.'[2] Here the outline of Fionn's identity, as known to later tradition, is already clear. Baoiscne was his ancestor, Nuadhu the patriarch of the family, Tulcha his half-brother, and Caoilte his nephew and faithful comrade. A more strictly genealogical text from the same early period again mentions him in association with Baoiscne and Nuadhu Necht. It further refers to Tréanmhór, who traditionally was his grandfather, and calls Fionn 'the son of Umall' [*fer Umaill*].[3] Down through the ages, in both literature and folklore, this is given – generally in its later forms of Umhall and Cumhall – as the name of Fionn's father. From these two texts we can conclude that Fionn was, in the sixth and seventh centuries, being portrayed as a historical character. It is also apparent that he was a figure in narrative at that time.

The earliest surviving examples of such stories are found in texts of the eighth century, and the variety of these attests to the existence of a thriving corpus of this kind of oral tradition. There can be no doubt but that Fionn was a well-known character in the spoken lore for a considerable period before the language was committed to writing.

The historicity of Fionn, however, becomes very doubtful when the evidence is examined. First of all, there are references in early Irish tradition to other characters with similar names – characters with enough similarities to him to make us suspect that they are emanations from the same basic personality. These others are mythical characters. They include an imagined Leinster king called *Find File* [Fionn the Poet], and a fictional seer and judge called *Móraind.* This latter name is derived from *Mór-Fhind*, which means Great Fionn.[4]

Wisdom, in ancient Irish culture, was expressed in the form of poetry and magical knowledge and, as we shall see, these gifts were primary aspects of Fionn's image. It is significant that the epithet *fionn*, meaning brightness, was often attached, in early Irish literature, to wisdom and to the craft of poetry.[5] Furthermore, the name of a character with magical powers in mediaeval Welsh literature was Gwynn, which name is cognate with Fionn.[6] We will be referring in due course to other seer-characters whose names reflect that of Fionn, but for the moment it is sufficient to say that the combination of such references indicates that our hero is a character of great antiquity whose name has been important enough to develop several by-forms in ancient lore.

The name Fionn occurs in genealogical god-names.[7] It is significant also, considering the fact that the names of Celtic deities were often employed in referring to Ireland, that a common poetic appellation for the country was 'the Land of the Three Fionns'.[8] Triplication of deities was a noticeable aspect of ancient Irish tradition, as indeed of the tradition of the Celts generally.[9] Given, then, that the Irish evidence suggests that Fionn was originally a divine figure, we must enquire if any vestiges of him can be traced in Continental Celtic sources.

A god-name Vindonnus was indeed found among the Gauls, and the first element here is cognate with our *Find*. This Vindonnus was equated by Latin writers with their own Apollo, and dedications to him have been discovered at several wells.[10] An apparently more standard form of his name was Vindos,[11] and many places in different parts of Europe have the element *vindo* contained in their names. Most striking are the many places called *Vindobōna*, the best-known of which is Vienna in Austria.[12] This could mean ‘the white town‘, but ‘the town of Vindos’ is a much more likely interpretation. There are many examples of ancient Celtic placenames which contain the personal name of a deity as their first element.[13] The Celtic word *bōna* signified a collection of buildings, and we find it joined to personal names in Romanised toponymics, such as Augusto*bōna* and Iulio*bōna*.[14] So the possibility of Fionn having had so high a profile in antiquity prompts us to ask the questions, what does his name really mean and what seems to have been his role in primitive Celtic belief.

The Continental, Welsh, and Irish forms – *vindo-*, *gwynn*, and *find*, respectively – come from a postulated Celtic word *u̯indo-*, meaning white or bright.[15] This has led some scholars to regard his name as an epithet describing the appearance of the deity. The adjective *u̯indo*, however, derives from the present stem of an Indo-European verb which covered a range of meaning connected with the process of cognition. Derivatives of this stem are found in several languages of Indo-European origin, denoting wisdom, insight, and discovery.[16] In Irish these words include *fios* [wisdom], *fionnadh* [illumination or revelation], and *fionn* [white or blond]. This type of terminology suits exactly the image of Fionn himself in the whole corpus of lore concerning him, for in both literature and folklore he is portrayed as a fair-haired seer who has unique access to mystical knowledge. So, persistent Irish tradition bears out the original connotations of his name in remote antiquity, and the suggestion is that

Vindos, was, in effect, a personification of wisdom.

This gives rise to questions about the nature of Celtic myth and, in particular, about deities connected with knowledge and the arts. Statues from throughout the ancient Celtic world represent a male figure with three heads, and there is good reason for supposing that the image intended in these statues was a god of knowledge.[17] Irish literary tradition has early and recurring references to a group called *na trí dé dána* [literally, the three gods of art or the three gods of knowledge].[18] Although these three characters have no connection with Fionn in the sources, they do parallel the idea of 'the three Fionns' and could well have originally been related to him. A consideration of the general body of evidence for ancient Celtic mythology leads one to the conclusion that the deities were rather an amorphous lot, easily confused with each other due to a common set of ideas concerning the supernatural. What real distinction there was between them had principally to do with function, and in the present context the function we are examining is that of knowledge.

Triple-headed and triple-faced figures were used in many cultures to symbolise omniscience, the notion being that full knowledge can be gained by gazing on all sides at once.[19] Such simultaneous vision of three different planes accords well with ancient Irish ideas of deep or 'true' knowledge. The poets, who were most associated with this, could see without effort into past, present, and future. The very word for a poet in Irish, *file*, is related to words which refer to vision and originally had the actual literal meaning of 'seer'.[20] It, therefore, comes as no surprise that Fionn is said in early sources to have had the gift of poetry, and that a character called Fionn File appears, as we have said, as a duplicate of him.

Several of the Continental tricophaloi have attributes, (such as a ram, a he-goat, a tortoise as companion), which identity them with the polytechnic Celtic deity whom Latin writers referred to as Mercurius.[21] Such a polytechnic deity appears in Irish tradition with the name Lugh, and the same name survives on the Continent in the many toponymics derived from *Lugudunon* [fortress of Lugos]. These include

Lyon, Laon, Laudun, Leiden, and Lauzun. In Ireland, Lugh was the patron of one of the four great festivals of the year – the harvest-festival of August [*Lughnasadh*]. As well as a rich portrayal in mediaeval Irish literature, he also occurs – under the form *Lleu* – in British placenames and Welsh tradition.[22] There are certain indications that this cult of Lugos was introduced into Ireland and Britain from the Continent in the not too remote pagan past. Irish descriptions have him entering the company of the gods (the *Tuatha Dé Danann*) in a dramatic, but nevertheless belated, manner. When the Tuatha Dé Danann are preparing for the final battle with their demonic foes, the Fomhóire, Lugh arrives at the last moment to take command of their army.[23] It seems clear also that the name of his festival *Lughnasadh* replaced an earlier name, which appears in the literature in the forms *Laithe mís Troghain* and *Brón Troghain*. This word *trogan* or *troghan* is used with the meaning of 'the fertile earth', which accords well with its function as a festival of ripening fruit and crops.[24]

If, then, Lugh is a relative newcomer to Irish myth, where does this leave Fionn? Perhaps we can best approach this question by comparing their nomenclature. The more conventional derivation of Lugh's name connects him with light, such as in Latin *lux*, and this leaves him with an image similar to the 'brightness' of Fionn. On the other hand, it has been argued that his name is related to a Celtic word **lugio* meaning 'oath', and that he may have been a patron of sworn contracts.[25] This would entail the idea that he was a kind of supervisor or divine witness to human affairs. We come close here to the function of Fionn as a seer and repositor of wisdom, except that Lugh's role would be a more specific and social one. In the same way, the general portrayal of Lugh as patron of skills and trading constitutes a far more practical and social context than the mystical knowledge of Fionn.

The only plausible way in which the two could be connected with each other is to regard them as playing different roles which belonged to one original deity. Given the tendency towards diffusion within Celtic myth, this might have been the case. If the tricophalic figures signify the god of knowledge, we would expect them to be closely related to Vindos, and this would not prevent some such figures on the Continent from being associated with Mercurius or Lugos. In so far as one can rely on the evidence of toponymics and dedications left behind them by the Continental Celts, however, the distinction between the two appears to have been clear. It might well be that they, in common with other Celtic deities, had their distinctive provenances depending on regional variations between Celtic communities. Their distinctiveness is very clear in insular Celtic tradition.

Nowhere in Irish lore are the characters Lugh and Fionn confused, and this is reflected also by the occurrence of Lleu and Gwynn as quite separate personalities in Welsh literature. There is every reason to believe, therefore, that their cults reached Ireland from different sources and at different stages. If we accept sometime around the first century A.D. for the introduction of Lugh, we must postulate that the cult of Fionn was established in Ireland for a good while prior to that.

Influence of Lugh

According to the story of which we have several versions in Irish literature, Lugh led the Tuatha Dé Danann to victory against the Fomhóire in a mythical battle at Moytura (in Co. Sligo). This story is based on an eighth- or ninth-century text, now lost, which doubtlessly reflects much older tradition. There are two basic levels of plot involved. One is the struggle between two supernatural races – the divine Tuatha Dé and the demonic Fomhóire. This parallels the conflict between the Devas and Asuras in Vedic myth, and that between the Aesir and Vanir in Norse myth; so there is reason to regard such a struggle as an antique theme. The second plot, inserted into this, concerns Lugh and his special foe Balar.

On the eve of the battle, Lugh arrives as a stranger at the assembly of the Tuatha Dé and gains admittance because he can perform every art and skill. He is entrusted with the command of the army, and when the battle is joined he uses his magic powers – moving around the enemy host 'on one foot and with one eye closed' while chanting a spell.

Finally he confronts Balar, who has a venomous eye which when exposed in battle can destroy thousands. Lugh casts a stone from his sling and drives the eye back through the tyrant's head, with the result that Balar's own host falls victim to its venom and they are routed.[26]

The basic motif here is that Lugh came to the Tuatha Dé Danann in their hour of need and overcame a monstrous foe who possessed destructive power in his eye. We have a story of Fionn which parallels this in a general way. It occurs in a twelfth-century text, and scholars agree that it is a rather corrupt version of what was then a current folktale.[27]

The text tells us that when he was ten years of age, Fionn arrived at the court of the High-King at Temhair [Tara] for the feast of *Samhain* [November]. The king was desperate, for every year on that night the citadel was burned by an otherworld being called Aillén. This Aillén used to arrive playing magical music which put everyone to sleep, and then used to blow fire from his mouth to affect his purpose. Fionn undertook to face the burner, was given a shield and spear, and stood on guard:

> Before long he heard the magical music, and he placed the sharp point of the spear to his forehead. Aillén was playing his harp to put everybody to sleep as usual, and then he released a blaze of fire from his mouth to burn Temhair. Fionn saw that, and he placed his purple-fringed cloak before the blaze and made it fall from the air.
>
> When Aillén saw that his magic had been overcome, he turned back towards the otherworld fort of Fionnachadh on top of the Mount of Fuad. Fionn followed him to the Cairn of Fionnachadh, and as Aillén was passing in by the door of the fort Fionn put his finger in the cord of his spear and gave it a strong accurate throw. It struck Aillén high in the back, putting his heart out through his mouth as a dark mass of blood.

As a result of his feat, Fionn was given command of the Fianna troop. The latter position had accordingly to be relinquished by the incumbent commander, who was called Goll [literally, one-eyed].[28] The text has Goll resigning with good grace, but we must not forget that this is a late and rather worked-up redaction.

There are several points of resemblance between these respective stories of Lugh and Fionn. Both of them arrive at a great assembly on the eve of a great event, are given an all-important commission, and play a messianic role in delivering the people from a monstrous being. The spear which Fionn used to keep himself awake and to kill his foe is of relevance here also, for it is believed that Lugh's sling is a substitute and that a special spear was his proper weapon of triumph over Balar.[29] Furthermore, there are parallels between the hostile beings themselves. It is clear that the imagery has been confused and scattered in the case of Aillén, who does not wreak havoc with his glance but rather with another magical body function – his breath. It is significant, though, that Fionn outdoes a man whose name means 'one-eyed' and, although it is never stated in the old literature that Balar had only one eye, it was a single eye of his which had the baleful power.

In one account of the battle of Moytura, in fact, Lugh also killed a leader of the Fomhóire called Goll, and it seems reasonable to assume that this figure was a duplication of Balar. More recent folklore recensions state that Balar was indeed one-eyed and that the eye withered things and set them on fire.[30] This imagery is quite logical, and it could well be that, in this case, folklore preserves the more logical and more original formulation. Balar would then have been a one-eyed fiery foe – an embodiment of the sun in its more sinister aspects. In Fionn's case, we find the hostile being subdivided into his two constituent functions – the one-eyed Goll and fiery Aillén.

The fact that Fionn killed the burner Aillén at the feast of *Samhain* is of importance, for that was the Celtic feast of the dead, coming, as it does, at the onset of the winter season. So, if Fionn was understood to have overcome the spirit of winter, why did that spirit reign immediately after its defeat? There is obviously a dichotomy involved here, which can only be explained by supposing that an original Fionn-myth was influenced by a myth of some other personage and thereby put out of focus. The confusion can be unravelled if we accept that Fionn was a victor over the world of the dead and that a harvest myth of Lugh was superimposed onto this image.

Lughnasadh, the harvest-festival of Lugh, has survived in Irish folk custom down to our time. All the evidence points to the conclusion that a particular myth was once central to the celebration of the festival, and that this myth related how Lugh overcame the burning summer and thus saved the harvest for his people. It was accordingly the blazing eye of the sun, personified in Balar, which was being conquered by the advent of Autumn; but the drama of this was such that it overshadowed the next great Celtic festival – that of November – and the imagery of sun and heat was rather incongruously transferred into the latter context.[31]

A desire to preserve the sun would, of course, have made the borrowing easier, particularly since Fionn's name suggested brightness; but this was not the main reason for the borrowing, for the triumph over fire by Fionn would, in that case, be self-contradictory. We shall see (pp. 46-7) that lore of Fionn opposing fiery figures was well established by the eighth century, so it is clear that this influence from the Lugh myth must have taken place in quite early times. The attempt to determine how early will require some further examination of Lugh's contest with Balar.

A striking aspect of the myth is that Balar was in fact the grandfather of Lugh. Folk tradition relates that it had been prophesied to Balar that a son of his daughter Eithne would kill him, and so the tyrant tried to ensure that no man would visit his daughter. The warrior Cian gained access to the maiden, however, and so the prophesied child Lugh was born. Although the prophecy motif is not expressly stated as part of the plot in the mediaeval literature, it is clear that it was part of the story in its original form. The story, in fact, has several parallels in ancient myths of the eastern Mediterranean. The best-known of these is the myth of Perseus.

According to this, an oracle declared that Danae, the daughter of king Acrisius, would give birth to a son who would kill his grandfather. Acrisius had Danae shut up in a tower or, alternatively, in an underground apartment, but notwithstanding his precautions she was made pregnant and had a son, Perseus. Acrisius ordered the mother and child to be exposed on the sea in a chest, but they were rescued.

Perseus grew up and performed great feats, and the oracle was fulfilled when he killed his grandfather by accident.

Classical writers also relate versions of the story concerning the Persian hero Cyros and the Babylonian hero Gilgamesh. We have a possible reference to it in a Babylonian inscription dated about 2,800 B.C., and scholars are of the opinion that the myth lies behind the Exodus account of the birth and youth of Moses.[32] All of this leads one to believe that the plot-structure was circulating from antiquity among the peoples of the eastern Mediterranean and that they were accustomed to applying it to some of their greatest heroes. These were crop-cultivating peoples, and it is feasible to assume that the Celts borrowed the myth from them and related it to their own harvest-god Lugh.

It is an obvious inference from this that the story in question was being told concerning Lugh among the Continental Celts. When his cult was introduced into Ireland, we can postulate that it met with the myth of the conflict between rival sets of supernatural beings associated with the *troghan* festival; and from this combination resulted the story of the battle of Moytura, probably in the early centuries A.D. The influence of Lugh on Fionn would occur later still.

Victory over a Foe

Mediaeval Irish literature tells of how a druid called Tadhg (son of Nuadhu) had a beautiful daughter called Muirne. The girl was wooed by a warrior called Cumhall, but her father refused to let him have her. Then Cumhall carried her off by force and kept her for a year. Tadhg went to the King of Ireland and had him declare war on Cumhall. At the battle of *Cnucha* [Castleknock in Co. Dublin] Cumhall's forces were routed and he himself killed. However, shortly before the battle he had begotten a child on Muirne. When Tadhg saw that his daughter was pregnant, he intended to kill her, but was restrained by the king who sent her to Cumhall's relatives for protection. Thus she gave birth to Fionn, 'the man of good fortune' [*fer an ratha*]. When Fionn grew up, he challenged Tadhg to single combat or else to pay compensation for Cumhall's death. The grandfather had no choice but to give up his fortress of Almhu, which became Fionn's principal residence ever after.

Although the earliest recension of this story which we have cannot be older than the tenth century,[33] we can safely say that the kernel of it is much more ancient, for it is obviously patterned on the Lugh myth we have been discussing. A later prose version, indeed, preserves the basic motif of the myth – that of the prophesied grandson who would displace the current incumbent of power. Tadhg, we are told, rejected Cumhall as a son-in-law 'because he knew that it would be through him that he would be divided from Almhu'. Moreover, some other references help us to trace the background to the narrative. The man who killed Cumhall in the battle of Castleknock, we are told, was Goll son of Morna.

That the Lugh myth is the ultimate source of this story is underlined by the only detail of the battle which is mentioned, apart from Cumhall's death. According to it, 'Luchet wounded Goll in his eye, and hence it is that [the name] Goll attached to him'. A stanza, which seems to be of earlier date, is quoted to the same effect. This describes how Goll's first name was Aedh [fire] and that Luchet wounded him with a heavy lance.[34] This type of weapon typically belonged to Lugh, and the name Luchet is, in fact, a diminutive variant of Lugh.

So this story concerning Fionn contains a direct echo of the combat between Lugh and his fiery-eyed foe, although in a very truncated form. It is also in a quite distorted form, for we are told that Goll then killed Luchet. For such a reversal of the incident to take place would, presumably, require a good passage of time and a complete blurring of the original. Other distortions and accretions also suggest that the borrowing from Lugh took place at a date long preceding our tenth- and twelfth-century texts. The grandfather is a druid and understands the future, all of which must be a development of character based on the original motif of the prophecy. Then Fionn does not kill his grandfather, but in a somewhat moderated manner takes his property instead. Finally, the grandfather, Tadhg, has had his function subdivided with Goll.

This latter development is especially interesting, since we have met the same type of duplication in the story of how Fionn saved the citadel of Tara from Aillén. Obviously, the problem of the influence of the Lugh myth is tied up with the origin of the character Goll son of Morna himself. There are several examples in the early literature of single characters being known by both these names, Goll and Aedh, which indicate that solar imagery was operative for a long time.[35] There are indications also that this solar imagery spread into tradition from the Lugh myth. In a seventh-century biography of St Patrick, written in Latin by an Irishman, the saint is represented as contending with a champion of paganism called MacCuill. This name means Son of Coll – Coll being an early form of Goll and the 'son' idea an accretion. So here we have another Goll character opposing a hero. 'This man', the biography states, 'was a fierce and wicked ruler, so much so that he was named Cyclops.'[36] This reference in the Patrician lore can be taken to derive from the Lugh myth. Lugh's victory over his foe presented a very suitable pattern for an epical description of the triumph of the new Christian religion, and so in folk tradition the festival of *Lughnasadh* is always said to commemorate the victory of Patrick over a pagan potentate.[37]

The potentate in question is called Crom Dubh in folklore, and we are told that he gave the saint the gift of a great cauldron. In the seventh-century biography cited above this potentate is called Dáire [suggestive of *daighre*, i.e. flame].[38] The great cauldron was an attribute of the Celtic deity, the Daghdha, in his role as patron of agriculture;[39] and so this Dáire appears to be an echo of the ancient god of food and plenty. Lugh's opponents, the Fomhóire, are also represented as agriculturalists,[40] and so we can see the outlines of the harvest-myth which is here reflected in an early Irish Christian source. We have, therefore, two opponents of the archetypal hero as early as the seventh century with the names Goll and Dáire, both of them demonstrably the same personage.

To return to the mediaeval texts which have Goll son of Morna as Fionn's rival, we find that Goll's father is stated to have the additional name of Dáire. Again the evidence suggests that Fionn's original foe was none other than the fiery-eyed one of Lugh, which had become a model for opponents of heroes generally in the Old Irish period. But in Fionn's case the foe has become far removed from the harvest myth which was the real context of Lugh's triumph over the solar deity.

Balar was Lugh's maternal grandfather, and his name originally meant a flash,[41] so it is easy to see why a character called Dáire or Daighre could be synonymous with him. Again, in a text of the early ninth century, the father of Fionn's mother is stated to have been called Dáire.[42] The attribution of such a maternal ancestry to Fionn must be somewhat older than this text, the early literature often coupling the name Dáire with Dearg [red] for characters connected with our hero. Again, in the bricolage of mediaeval Fionn lore, we find several mentions of characters called Dáire Dearg, from which we may assume that in this context Dáire and Dearg were one and the same personage.[43] Our texts describing Fionn's contest with the fiery burner and with the tyrant grandfather belong to the period from the tenth to the twelfth centuries, but we must allow for some previous generations of existence for these narratives – so, how far back to the original Lugh source?

The many traces in nomenclature and direct echoes of Lugh which survive in the Fionn versions underline the fact that the borrowing occurred in a distinctly Irish setting. The scattered effect of the episodes in the Fionn context, however, suggests a good passage of time before the texts were written. The other characters called Goll, who are referred to in the early sources, were not necessarily exclusive of an embryonic lore – deriving from the Lugh myth – which would be making a particular Goll the opponent of Fionn. This would have been occurring perhaps through the fifth and sixth centuries, and would have led to an increasing warrior profile for Fionn. As the Goll figure crystallised into the martial image of Goll son of Morna, its fiery and tyrannical attributes were discarded and left to form such diffuse characters as the fiery burner of Tara – Aillén on the one hand, and the maternal grandfather Tadhg or Dáire on the other.

Knowledge Obtained

What were the reasons for the myth to be transferred to Fionn, or what impulses caused the transfer? We have already suggested that Fionn had connections with the realm of the dead and that the lore concerning the harvest-festival overshadowed that concerning the November festival of the dead. But, more specifically, certain correspondences must have existed between the lore of Fionn and the Lugh plot – grandfather versus prophesied youth. We have seen how in tenth- to twelfth-century texts Fionn's maternal grandfather is said to have been Tadhg son of Nuadhu. Both of these characters, the texts tell us, were druids. But we have also seen how genealogies which stretch back to the sixth century enumerate one Nuadhu Necht as the ancestor of Fionn on the paternal side. It is, therefore, clear that Nuadhu was switched onto the mother's side of the family in order to facilitate the plot of the tyrant-grandfather story, and that this alteration was not convincing enough to impose itself on the Leinster genealogists.

The question of Nuadhu's original relationship to Fionn is a very confused one, and several scholars have argued that the occurrence in Welsh tradition of a character called Gwynn ap Nudd testifies to a Celtic connection between the two anterior to Irish culture.[44] The evidence for this is not sufficiently clear, however, and the attribution of a father called Nudd to Gwynn could be a borrowing from Ireland by a Welshman who knew that the names Fionn and Gwynn had the same meaning.[45] The real explanation may be that Nuadhu was superimposed on the figure of Fionn in the Boyne valley in antiquity. His name is cognate with that of the British Celtic deity Nodons and probably signified 'catcher of fish'.[46] We shall see presently that Fionn was often portrayed as a gainer of wisdom from mystic waters, and this would have attracted the figure of Nuadhu to his context.

The nomenclature of Nuadhu and Fionn is united in quite early literary sources. The former is sometimes, in fact, called Nuadhu Find or more explicitly Nuadhu *Éices* [the seer]. A combination of the two designations occurs in 'Nuadhu Finnéices'[47] This same Finnéices is the name of a character in a twelfth-century text with whom Fionn has dealings in the process of acquiring wisdom. He was cooking a 'salmon of knowledge' in order to gain wisdom, but Fionn accidently tasted it before him and thus took the prowess from his grasp.[48] When we recall that Nuadhu was portrayed by the Leinster genealogists as the ancestor of our hero, we can gather that Fionn was understood as having gained mystic insight from a predecessor for whom Nuadhu has been substituted.

The evidence multiplies, for in the same twelfth-century text Fionn goes to learn the craft of *éicse* [seer-poetry] from a certain Cethern son of Fintan.[49] The name of Fintan seems to be derived from primitive Celtic **Vindo-senos*, which means 'the old Vindo-'.[50] Elsewhere in Irish literature Fintan is a wise man who has lived for over five and a half thousand years and can thus relate all kinds of ancient history. He has spent various periods in the form of a salmon, an eagle, and a hawk.[51] Such an old Vindo- would be an archaised version of the seer-figure Fionn himself – in other words, a projected ancestor-seer from whom Fionn obtains knowledge.

The world of the ancestors is the realm of the dead, and in Irish tradition the ancient ones were believed to live on in the *sí*-barrows, that is, the remains of prehistoric constructions which dotted the Irish landscape and were particularly evident in the Boyne valley. Several mediaeval accounts, which we shall discuss in later chapters, have Fionn entering these mounds and receiving the drink of wisdom therein. So we assume that in archaic Irish lore Fionn had the function of visiting the realm of the dead in order to gain knowledge. This is a shamanic practice which is well-documented among primitive peoples, and Irish tradition itself furnishes much evidence of it. This includes the rituals engaged in by poets, such as composing in the dark and near mounds and raths, as well as the wide antiquarian knowledge which the true poet was expected to possess.[52]

One reference which is especially pertinent in this context comes from a ninth-century text which describes a disputation between two poets. One of the two, Ferchertne [whose name means, literally, man of the poetic craft] states that he has got his mystical gift from *síd mná Nechtain* and from *rig mná Nuadat*. These two sources are 'the mound of Nechtan's wife' and 'the forearm of Nuadhu's wife'.[53] Nechtan is the same personage as Nuadhu Necht, and thus another name for Nuadhu Find,[54] so here again we have wisdom being gained from sources which involve an eponymous ancestor of Fionn. The well of Nechtan, situated within a mound, was said to be the source of the river Boyne, and the forearm of Nuadhu's wife is a kenning for the same river. The Boyne itself [*Bóinn*] originally was *Bó Fhind*,[55] that is 'cow of illumination', 'white cow', perhaps even 'cow of Fionn'. This was a metonym for the river, with its waters the flowing milk. But poetry was also the flowing milk of a mystical cow, and so early Irish texts tell us that wisdom could be gained by drinking the water of the Boyne at certain times.[56] Elsewhere the early literature tells us directly that Nuadhu, called *Elcmhar*, 'the Envious', was the spouse of a lady named Bóinn,[57] thus showing that the introduced Nuadhu had taken over Fionn's female consort. The imagery of a white cow's milk for seer-poetry occurs in a quite diffuse way in Old Irish texts,[58] and from what we have said it is logical to regard the concept of Fionn and the Boyne as its fountainhead.

The Divine Child

Having worked backwards through different layers of superimposed material in the search for the basic Fionn, we can now discuss certain other features of the early tradition in support of our hypothesis. The plot structure of the Lugh myth requires that emphasis should be placed on the birth of the prophesied descendant. We find recognition of this necessity in the eighth- or ninth-century text of the battle of Moytura where, in explaining the hero's birth as grandson of Balar, Lugh is called a 'glorious child' [*gen búadha*].[59] In so far as Lugh is concerned, this is the only context in which tradition emphasises his youth.

In the lore of Fionn, however, youth is a recurring theme and covers a much more general range of narrative. So his youth, as opposed to the age of his ancestor, must have been central to the reason why he was a suitable character to borrow the Lugh myth. We can illustrate this by quoting a little story which is found in a Munster genealogical tract which was compiled around the ninth century. It concerns a character called Noíne, whose name in its older form *Noende* is found in the mythological parts of the genealogies. The story goes as follows:

> Dáire son of Dedha took the kingship. Before he died his daughter bore a son, that is Noíne. The druid had told him that when his daughter gave birth to a son he would himself die. So he kept watch over her. Nevertheless, Mac ind Óc made her pregnant, as the girl went through delirium out of the fortress.
>
> The druids watched her womb for nine years, that is nine months by nine, until the son was born – a child of nine sayings, which is nine sayings he gave immediately after being born. He was born with locks the length of two hands, and with a curly beard. Then Dáire son of Dedha died when Noíne was born.[60]

Mac ind Óc, who appears to be an intruder into the story, is a character worthy of note. His strange ungrammatical name is supposed to be a corruption of 'Maccan Óc', and he was also called 'in Mac Óc' – all of which signifies a youngster.[61] This echoes the name of the child Noíne [older forms, Noende and Noíndiu], which seems to be a corruption of *noídiu* [infant]. Mac ind Óc is featured in eighth-century stories. According to these, he was born after the Daghdha took advantage of the absence of Elcmhar [i.e. Nuadhu] to dally with his wife Bóinn, and when he grew up Mac ind Óc got possession of the famous mound of Brugh na Bóinne (Newgrange) from Elcmhar by a trick.[62]

Judging by the image of youth in his name, Mac ind Óc could well have had some ancient connection with Fionn. At any rate, the motifs of an elderly opponent being outwitted would have allowed his name to be given to the father-figure in the Noíne version of the tyrant-grandfather myth. The true name of this father figure is suggested by an entry in another Munster genealogical tract, where Noende is said to have been the son of Umall. As we have seen, this Umall or Umhall was the father of Fionn, so there is a strong likelihood that the story of Noíne is a survival in Munster tradition of a narrative concerning the birth of Fionn.[63] If so, we are dealing with a petrified example of the transfer of the myth from Lugh to Fionn at a primitive stage.

This theory seems to hold when we dissect the elements of the Noíne story. Dáire is there, that fiery grandfather figure of the Lugh complex, whom we have already met in an artificial role as maternal grandfather of Fionn. Also, similar to the Lugh complex, the grandfather is not himself a prophet but is a king who has had the prophecy made to him. However, the switch to Fionn is already under way, and the story definitely stresses the possession of wisdom. The child is born with mature physical features as if to underline mental maturity, and he mouths nine maxims. The stress on the number nine here must refer to the nine months (or nine years!) parturition, that is to say the stages of his full mental development have been achieved before birth. Perhaps most revealing of all is the hesitancy which the narrative shows as regards the final twist in the plot. The child does not actually kill Dáire, but the grandfather dies instead in a rather contrived way. In other words, his role is being taken over rather than his power conquered. This accords well with what we have been saying about the old Fionn bequeathing his wisdom to the young Fionn.

There are other strong indications that such a birth-story of Fionn was current in antiquity, and that due to a confusion of the word *noí* [nine] with the designation Noíne, the number nine was habitually stressed in it. A tenth-century poem states that Fionn was conceived nine hours before his father's death in battle.[64] Equally relevant is another mediaeval text, which appears to reflect quite old tradition and has the seer Móraind pronouncing nine wise judgements after his birth. A spirit, we are told, appeared to the mother after she gave birth, saying that the child would be called Móraind, which he explained as a compound of *mór* and *find* [great fairhaired one].[65] As we have said, this Móraind is etymologically related to Fionn and may well have originally been a duplicate of him, meaning Great Fionn. It is clear that the spirit making an annunciation to Móraind's mother is an intrusive element in this story, having derived from the

Christian Gospel account of Jesus' birth, but it is related to another more native motif. The latter we find in a variant of the Noíne story, where a phantom from the sea impregnates the daughter of Dáire and thus causes the child to be born.[66] This motif is apparently used to suggest that water is the source of Noíne's wisdom, and we find it again in an eighth-century account of the birth of Mongán.

This Mongán is identified as a king of Dál nAraidhe in east Ulster who died in the year A.D. 625, but the early legends concerning him have obviously been influenced by tradition of another, more mythical, character with the same name.[67] Mongán is represented as a great seer, and we can assume that this portrayal of him owes much to his mythical namesake. According to his birth-story, he was conceived after the sea-spirit Manannán visited his mother during her husband's absence. Mongán was a 'wonder-child' [*amre in mac*], and when he grew up he showed amazing knowledge of past, present, and future.[68] The name Mongán means 'the little hairy fellow', which reminds us of the child Noíne who was born with hair and beard. It appears from this that 'Mongán' might have been a descriptive appellation given to a child-seer who was better known by another name, but how the king of Dál nAraidhe came to be christened with such a nick-name is not clear. Whatever about the technicalities, the issue itself is settled for us, for the ancient compiler of the Mongán lore tells us directly that Mongán and Fionn were one. As if baffled by the different traditions he is trying to reconcile with each other, he says: 'That Mongán was Fionn, though he would not allow it to be told.'[69]

Although shamanic ritual required that Fionn should be portrayed as dependent on the ancestor world for his know-ledge, as an actual figure symbolising wisdom he must have primacy in himself. As in human culture generally, from magic to epistomology, it is the concept of knowledge which has initial stress. The most natural image to express primacy is, of course, that of a child, of the initial stage in our lives; and so we can expect to find Fionn represented by this image. Myths placing deities in the role of a primordial child were common among the ancient peoples of Europe. Describing the god as an orphan child, open to all the threats of the world, but surviving them, was a way of emphasising his primacy and his invincibility.[70] We shall see in chapter 4 that the abandoned and threatened youth of Fionn was of great and longstanding importance in his traditional biography.

Again, the divine child in several Indo-European mythologies was depicted as emerging from, and floating on, primal waters. These waters reflected the pre-natal phase of existence, and so the frequent image of the child, emerging from an aquatic realm, represented his coming into being. We can mention in particular in this context the Hindu Vishnu, the Greek Dionysus, and the Germanic Scyld.[71] Fionn, too, is closely associated with water. We have seen how his wisdom was associated with the river Boyne, but his connections with the aquatic world have a physical or corporeal context also. In folk traditions concerning his birth it is said that he fell into water, or was thrown into it, immediately after he was born. He did not drown, but emerged holding an eel in his hands.[72]

This legend of him seems to be very old, for a version of it – probably borrowed from Fionn – is told of the mythical king Conchubhar mac Neasa in a mediaeval text.[73] It was through a water-adventure in his youth that Fionn got his name, according to his twelfth-century biography. The scene was the plain of the river Liffey in Co. Kildare:

> The boys were swimming in a lake nearby, and they challenged him to put them under. He jumped into the lake then to join them, and he drenched nine of them in the lake, and he himself returned to Sliabh Bladhma after that.
>
> 'Who drenched the boys?', asked everyone.
>
> 'Fionn [the fairhaired one]', they said.
>
> On account of that, the name stuck to him.[74]

What is being said here is that a new life began for the hero with that episode, the social life in which he had a name. Other traditions, in fact, have him called Fionn since birth,[75] so this can be viewed as an elaborated account of an earlier birth-in-water motif.

Another twelfth-century text connects him even more

dramatically with water. It states that a spring on top of Slieve Bloom overflowed and it threatened to flood the whole province of Leinster. 'It was then that Fionn performed the best, strong deft exploit that anyone ever did before or after it' we are told. He collected a variety of magical helpers and 'they sucked up that wavy chilly lake'.[76] The overflowing spring which makes a lake is a motif found in the mediaeval place-lore of Ireland,[77] and there is no reason to regard it as very ancient in the context of Fionn. The magical helpers are also a mediaeval introduction into the Fionn lore, as we shall see in chapter 6. But the basic idea, lying at the core of the story, is that Fionn had some sort of prodigious expertise in aquatic matters.

He is again strikingly associated with water in a story which is related in late mediaeval prose and poetry. According to this, Fionn came one day to the shore of Lake Gullion in Ulster, where he met a beautiful lady lamenting her two golden brooches which had fallen into the lake. She asked him who he was, and when she learned that he was Fionn she demanded that he get the brooches for her. He took off his clothes and plunged into the lake. He recovered the brooches without difficulty, but when he reached the bank he found her gone, and he himself had been turned into an old man by the water. Meeting his followers again, he had difficulty in persuading them that he was Fionn. Eventually they went to a nearby *sí*-mound, into which the strange lady had gone, and they forced her to give him a rejuvenating drink from a magic goblet. He was thus restored to his usual appearance, except for his hair. He wished that to retain the colour it had got from the water – silver on one side and golden on the other.[78]

The narrative here is not of early date, but Fionn's ability to recover treasure through his mystical knowledge is already mentioned in an eighth-century text,[79] and the kernel of the story must be older still. This kernel is that he gained his bright hair-colour, and concomitantly his name, from the water. In fact, the experience as related in the story itself constitutes a rebirth into a new stage of maturity – into the 'old' Fionn. It, therefore, reflects the story of Noíne, whose birth expressed maturity in the form of his hair and beard. In the figure of wisdom, that is the maturity of knowledge, the young and the old are one – the old Fionn and the young Fionn. And his brightly coloured hair, which is at one with his name, is the outward sign of wisdom.

An ancient Sanskrit story describes the god Vishnu as a boy, 'amidst a cluster of enraptured staring children'. He had luminous features and was 'radiant with the lustre of wisdom'. This boy explained to the god Indra the secrets of past ages and of the many dissolutions and recreations of the universe through which he had lived.[80] This reminds us of the Irish tradition of the reincarnations which Fintan [old Fionn] had gone through and the great historical knowledge he had as a result. This metamorphosing is significant. We read in an eighth-century text that Mongán, who was identified with Fionn, lived for ages in the shape of a deer, a salmon, and a swan, and as a result was able 'to reveal secrets to men'.[81] The strong implication is that the archaic Fionn, as a personification of wisdom, practised shape-shifting as a means to fulfil his function.[82] Before the literary evidence becomes available to us, however, this means had been delegated to his ancestor [the old Fionn], because the deity was believed to have undergone the transformations at a pre-natal stage.

Since the birth of mature knowledge is the beginning of wisdom, the Fionn-child is a symbol of his whole life-span. His most characteristic act, and the earliest attested of him, is the sucking of his thumb to gain knowledge. This is, of course, a typical pose adopted by a child, but it continues as his own peculiar mystical rite at all stages of his life. As we shall see in chapter 3, various stories were used by writers from the eighth to the twelfth centuries, and by the oral tradition generally, to explain the origin of this unique capability of his. The capability itself was stressed, as a matter of course, in stories concerning him in both ancient and modern times. It is appropriate to enumerate here the earliest descriptions of how he used the rite.

In a ninth-century text a corpse is identified in the following way: 'Fionn put his thumb in his mouth and he sang through *teinm laída*.' What he sang was an obscure rhetoric, making the identification.[83] This *teinm laída* has not been conclusively explained, but the most likely meaning is 'the shining of intellect'. In a slightly earlier text, he recognises a stranger by the same process: 'Fionn put his thumb in his mouth. When he took it out again, his *imbas* illumined him and he sang an incantation.' Again we have an obscure rhetoric naming the person.[84] The term used here, *imbas*, is a compound of *fios* and means 'great knowledge'.[85]

Perhaps the earliest evidence for Fionn's rite is provided by a carving on a stone cross-slab in Co. Donegal, dated to the eighth century. This comprises two figures on the arms of the cross, each of them a man sucking his thumb. Scholars are of the opinion that they represent Fionn as a prophet foretelling the coming of Christianity.[86] If our interpretation of the youth-themes concerning him is correct, then the thumb-sucking image of him as a child-seer could be almost as ancient among the Celts as the name *Vindo-* itself. That this would not be an incongruous portrayal of a deity is suggested by a parallel in the iconography of ancient Egypt, which often had the child-god Horus sucking his thumb.[87]

To summarise, then, although hampered by the scantiness of evidence for Celtic beliefs in antiquity, we can formulate the following theory regarding the origin of Fionn: He was a divine figure symbolising wisdom among the ancient Celts and, being knowledge originalised, he was represented as having been already a seer at birth. Thus, the typical thumb-in-mouth gesture of a child was portrayed as his practice when gaining knowledge of any particular situation.

The idea of pre-natal waters, associated with divine-child figures, was especially stressed in Fionn's portrayal because it was believed that in water resided the source of mystical inspiration. Since his name in adjectival form signified bright or fair-haired, the lustre of wisdom – showing itself in his person – was expressed in terms of his blond hair. Due to the shamanic ideas of actual practising seers, Fionn was mythically described as entering the realm of the dead in order to gain knowledge from an ancestral double of himself.

When introduced into Ireland by some incoming Gaelic group in antiquity, he and the symbolism attached to him became associated with the Boyne river. He was early confused with the cult of another Celtic deity Nuadhu who was also annexed to the Boyne. He was further confused with the harvest-myth of Lugh, which was introduced later still. This caused Fionn to be portrayed as an opponent of a one-eyed tyrant figure.

The idea of youth predominates throughout all these motifs. Expressed in various narrative patterns, the motifs comprise the earliest layer of distinguishable tradition concerning Fionn. On this basis, a rich and multifaceted heroic cycle was in the process of developing when the Irish language was first committed to writing, that is in the sixth and seventh centuries.

2.

Warrior and Hunter

Fionn mac Cumhaill is portrayed in Gaelic tradition as the leader of the Fianna, a troop of warriors famed for their skill at hunting and fighting. One mediaeval source tells us that Fionn was 'the leader and head of exiles and paid soldiers and every fighting band'.[1] How this whole tradition of his dual character as seer and great military leader came about has never been fully explained. It is a complex question, and can best be approached by examining in piecemeal manner all the earliest mentions of Fionn and his adventures.

A Local Symbol

The importance of the hill of Tara stretches far back into prehistory. The Gaelic people, finding many neolithic remains there in the surrounding Boyne valley, located their gods in the region and made it a centre of their mythology.[2]

We have argued that Nuadhu was associated with the area at an earlier stage than Lugh and that there are indications that Nuadhu himself was preceded by Fionn. It is clear from the old literature that the great festival of Tara [*feis Temhro*] was celebrated at *Samhain*,[3] the November feast of the dead, and this makes sense when one considers the several great cemeteries in the vicinity.[4] What we have said of Fionn as a seer-figure fits well into this picture, for a tenth-century poem states that there was at Tara a 'Mound of Fionn' [*Duma Find*].[5] This is immediately followed in the poem by reference to a 'Mound of Druids' [*Duma na nDrúad*] in a manner which might suggest the identity of the two barrows. At any rate, it is significant that a mound, which usually in Old Irish literature has connotations of a burial place of the ancestors, should bear Fionn's name and should be situated at Tara.

Some archaeologists believe that the ramparts of Tara were erected as much for ritual as for military purposes, and several allusions in the early literature have these ramparts as defences against otherworld forces.[6] So it would have been natural to have the protection of that great citadel at Halloween assigned to the archetypal seer Fionn who was envisaged as an expert in otherworld affairs. We have argued that, with the passing of time and inevitable change in perceptions, he was invested for this quasi-martial purpose with what was considered appropriate imagery from the Lugh myth. Thus, we have the legend of Fionn defending Tara against a fiery otherworld being at the festival of Halloween. It follows from this that it was in the context of Tara that the Lugh/Balar narrative influenced the lore of Fionn. Examination of the texts (pp. 12ff) has led us to assume that this influence occurred in or about the fifth century.

This was the period in which an incessant struggle was taking place for the possession of Tara itself in real life. The citadel, together with the Boyne valley, had long been held by the *Laigin* [Leinstermen], but the rise of Niall Naoighiallach and his sept (which became known as Uí Néill) was to change all this. Niall himself took Tara from the Leinstermen sometime around A.D. 430, but control of the area seems to have oscillated between the Uí Néill and the Leinstermen throughout the remainder of the fifth century.[7]

The Leinstermen placed great emphasis on the mythology of the Boyne valley – a mythology which they themselves had probably inherited from local septs conquered by them in previous centuries. This emphasis is illustrated for us by the fact that, whereas Labhraidh Lorc was their own mythical ancestor, they adopted Nuadhu into the same role and accommodated him in their genealogies as the ancestor of their more recent line, relegating Labhraidh Lorc to the dim and distant past.[8] They also adopted Fionn. In his case they even changed his dwelling to their more secure territories by associating him with one of the ancestral sites of their kingship, the hill of Ailleann [Knockaulin in Co. Kildare], which was a ceremonial site.[9]

The Fionn cult there became historicised so that Leinster genealogies make much of a fictional seer-king of theirs called Find File. To this seer are attributed several verses on the ancient history of Leinster.[10] Since Ailleann, as an archaeological site, dates from the early Iron Age, the superimposition of the Fionn cult from the Boyne valley onto it could well have occurred at an early date – perhaps third or fourth century A.D. The lack of any familiar Fionn lore in connection with this Find File – apart from the image of a seer – suggests that the borrowing took place when Fionn was a deity of knowledge only and not yet a martial hero. The suggestion is strengthened by the fact that the genealogists never confused Find File with the great Fionn mac Cumhaill of tradition. This early emanation of the god Find became a petrified historical character, while 'the real Fionn' underwent a dazzling series of character developments.

In order to delineate these developments, we must again cast an eye on the political scene in the struggle between the Leinstermen and the Uí Néill, their northern foes bent on expansion. The Annals tell us that in A.D. 483 a Leinster sept called the Uí Garrchon attained to the kingship of the province and held it for about fifteen years. The outcome of several battles fought on the northern frontier was a strike by the Uí Néill king, Cairbre, into the heart of the Uí Garrchon territory around the year 501. This devastation was so great that the Uí Garrchon were totally uprooted and forced to retreat eastwards into the mountains of Wicklow.[11] Ailleann was in their territory, the focus of their kingship, and this must have been the occasion of its final desertion, thus consigning both the site and its myth of Find File to the realm of past history and genealogical fancy. The lines against Uí Néill pressure were now being held by another sept who dwelt to the west of the Uí Garrchon, at the juncture of present-day Counties Offaly, Kildare, and Laois.

This sept, the Uí Fáilghe, had already suffered the loss to the Uí Néill of much land to the north and west of them, and at the time of the Uí Garrchon collapse were led by one Fáilghe Berraidhe. The Uí Fáilghe claimed that this Fáilghe Berraidhe was a direct descendant of Cathaoir Mór, reputedly the last Leinster king of Tara.[12] This shows that the sept at the time regarded Tara as rightly theirs. The river Boyne had its source in the territory they still held; and naturally the lore of both Nuadhu and Fionn, as well as the latter's protective function against otherworld forces, would be a vibrant part of their culture. Their hopes ran high, and in the year 510 – according to the Annals – Fáilghe Berraidhe inflicted a stunning defeat on the Uí Néill at Frevin in Co. Westmeath. The Uí Fáilghe held the stage in Leinster for a while, but in 516 Fáilghe Berraidhe suffered a crushing defeat at the hands of the old foe.[13] After this the sept was on the wane, and the leadership of their province passed from them to other more southern-based kin.

The Uí Fáilghe are important to our investigation for three reasons. They were the Leinster sept most pre-occupied with the affairs of the Boyne valley, they fought a very courageous campaign against superior Uí Néill strength, and in the nucleus of their territory was an ancient cultic site at Almhu [the hill of Allen]. Each of these three points is reflected in the mediaeval literature concerning Fionn mac Cumhaill. Firstly, regarding the Boyne valley, Fionn is represented as acquiring or practising his magical knowledge in the vicinity of the Boyne and as protecting Tara in its hour of need. Secondly, regarding the Leinster contest with the northern foes, one mediaeval text claims that he fought and won a great battle for that province against the Uí Néill.[14] And thirdly, the literature portrays Fionn as having his dwelling and headquarters on the hill of Almhu – all of which indicates that the Uí Fáilghe, when that sept were in the vanguard of the struggle against the Uí Néill at the turn of the sixth century, had the figure of Fionn as a symbol of their aims and aspirations. The lack of early direct evidence linking Fionn to the Uí Fáilghe makes it impossible to describe the precise nature of such a process, but the weight of evidence in the whole surviving literary tradition makes it feasible to raise the level of informed speculation to that of theory. Conclusive proof is lacking, but we come tantalisingly close to such proof when we examine some references in mediaeval sources which claim that Fionn mac Cumhaill was of the Uí Tairsigh, a sub-sept to the Uí Fáilghe who inhabited the area north of the Curragh of Kildare.[15]

Judging by the confidence with which it is made, the claim seems to be well-based. One twelfth-century text is direct and straightforward, putting the question:

'Of whom was Fionn mac Cumhaill?' and giving the answer: 'Of the Uí Tairsigh of Leinster'. Again, to the question: 'What place in that area?' – the text answers: 'From Glaise Bolgain'.[16]

This place is unidentified, but another mediaeval source says that it was on Sliabh Guaire, which appears to have been in the vicinity of Almhu.[17] So we can be reasonably confident that the image of Fionn as a war-leader comes from an Uí Fáilghe hero-cult of the late fifth and early sixth centuries – this cult being based on ancient Fionn lore from the Boyne valley but now centred on the hill of Almhu in the immediate jurisdiction of the Uí Tairsigh.

As we have said (p. 3) the earliest literary mentions of Fionn date from a century later than this. These mentions are in Leinster genealogical tracts, and they state him to have been a patrilineal descendant of Nuadhu Necht. This is the old tradition, which the genealogists still followed in preference to the newer Lugh-like structure already in existence at the time (see pp. 8ff). The actual lineage attributed to Fionn in these tracts is as follows: Son of Cumhall, son of Tréanmhór, son of Sualt, son of Eltan, son of Baoiscne, son of Nuadhu Necht.[18] How this system, with several named ancestors between Fionn and Nuadhu, came about, must now be explained.

It seems that the name of Fionn's father, Cumhall or Umhall, does not belong particularly to the Leinster context, but that it preceded the fifth- to sixth-century Uí Fáilghe developments. The origin of it has never been satisfactorily accounted for. Some scholars have claimed that the character is one with a Gaulish war-deity called Camulos;[19] while conversely it has been argued that Umhall was another name for Nuadhu.[20] It might, however, be possible to trace the name along different lines.

In a mediaeval story a character called Umhall from an otherworld fort is said to have been father of a fairy woman Rothniamh, who gave prophecies to a poet called Fíngen at

Halloween.[21] Fíngen means 'wine-birth' and was a reasonably common name in the old literature.[22] It may have been suggested to this context, however, by an original form *Finngen* and, if so, could represent the child Fionn. The Halloween allusion could also have come from the myth of Fionn the seer, whereas encounters with female figures of wisdom from raths were commonplace in the mediaeval lore of Fionn, as we shall see in future chapters.

Another text from around the same period gives Umhall as a name of a servant of the sage Fintan mac Bóchra,[23] whom we have already (p. 17) associated with Fionn at an early stage. These two texts mentioning Umhall come from about the tenth century, and the mythological allusions in them are obviously remnants of some more logical narrative units. So we may have echoes here of Umhall as a father figure in the otherworld realm of wisdom. This is little more than speculation, but a few other points might also be added.

One early manuscript gives the name of Fionn's father as Camall [i.e. Camhall],[24] which, if correct, would suggest that *Amhall* was the original form (assuming that, like in *Umhall*, the initial *c* comes from the preceding *mac*). *Amhall* was a rare word with the meaning 'visit'.[25] It is, therefore, possible that the name might have derived from Fionn's visit to the otherworld to gain knowledge, with tradition, in time, altering the significance of the word from the function to a personification.

In one of the early genealogies Fionn is called *fer hUmaill* [literally, the man of Umhall].[26] Could this be a petrified phrase which originally meant 'the man of the visit'? Possible, but hardly probable. A more likely explanation would be that *fer hUmaill* means, as intended in the text, simply son of Umhall, and the visit being referred to is that of the hero's father to his mother which caused the conception against the wishes of the tyrant grandfather. This is the plot of the Lugh-myth, and so it would mean that Fionn was first given a father called Amhall or Umhall after the influence of the Lugh-myth had occurred, i.e. about the fifth-century.

The name of Fionn's father, at any rate, can be taken to predate the conscious and deliberate Leinsterisation of the lore. The names of the other inserted forebears were later inventions, and it is clear that they have been invented in an off-the-peg manner to dramatise Fionn as a martial character. *Tréanmhór* means simply big and strong; *baoiscne* means great tree or stalwart; *sualt* seems to signify virtuous; and *eltan* having troops.[27] So, owing to the expropriation of his lore by the Uí Fáilghe in their struggle, Fionn was in the course of the sixth century being cast in an increasingly military role and was being accepted as a military symbol of Leinster in general. He was being portrayed as wise and courageous, possessing the dual complex of skills which Gaelic culture held in highest regard – verbal and martial dexterity. But he also had the image of youth, thereby holding a certain fascination for the young. This made him an ideal figure for practical education, a medium of lore through which young men could be trained and prepared for the function which invariably fell to them – that of defending in arms the interests of their sept and province. In short, Fionn was being portrayed as the warrior-hero *par excellence*.

The ordinary word for a warrior in Old Irish was *fian*. The life and the ideas shared by young warriors of the time, however, gave several other connotations to the term. These connotations, in turn, made the lore of Fionn undergo a whole new series of developments.

The Great 'Féinnidh'

The original form of this word for a warrior was *fían* (nominative singular). In time it came to be written as *fiann*. The original form of the nominative plural was *fíana*, which was later written as *fianna*.[28] One mediaeval glossarian claimed that the word is cognate with Latin *venatio* [hunting],[29] and this is the generally accepted view of modern scholars. Both Irish and Latin forms apparently come from **ueiená-*, with an original meaning of gaining, hunting, or fighting.[30] A survey of the contexts in which the word *fían* and its derivatives are used in early Irish literature shows that it involved a group of roving warriors who were more or less independent of outside authority. Yet they were not mere marauders. A legal text from about the eighth century describes fianna groups as a good and necessary institution, provided they acted 'without overbearing'; and a prophetic text of the same time claims that the cessation of the institution would be a sign of social disintegration.[31] An individual member of a fianna band was called a *féinnidh*, and the ancient law tracts refer to 'permissible acts of plunder' which could be carried out by such a person.[32] On the same lines, a somewhat later mediaeval source rates the *féinnidh*'s right to distraint on a par with the ecclesiastical rights of the clergy and with the right of a king to take hostages.[33] So it is obvious that fianna bands were a social reality, and that they had an accepted function.

Yet, the evidence is somewhat ambiguous. The Christian authorities were not always favourable to them, and the Alphabet of Piety, which dates from about the eighth century, is quite scathing towards their practices [*fíanas*]. This text lists four ill effects of *fíanas*: 'It oppresses territories, it increases enmity, it cuts off life, it lengthens torments.'[34] The latter reference is to damnation, which shows how hostile to the institution this ecclesiastical writer felt. His statement, in fact, echoes clerical denunciations of another type of activity which was current in early Ireland – that of *díbherg* [reaving], the practitioners of which were termed *díbhergaigh*. These are described as small groups of pagan brigands, marked with 'the sign of the devil'.[35] The portrayal given to them is obviously biased and, whatever the actual reality behind it, it is clear that the *díbhergaigh* were social outlaws, desperate men who preyed on society and who organised themselves into groups in order to pursue their purposes.

In the sixth and seventh centuries, the growing power of the Church was linked to the political status quo, and in such circumstances it is to be expected that clerical writers would look with a jaundiced eye on those outside the political and religious establishment. This explains the special antipathy shown to the *díbhergaigh*, who were still pagans and who must have been largely composed of members of 'unfree' or subject septs. Given their own particular mode of existence, the fianna groups would have a good deal of contact with *díbhergaigh*, and we can suppose that some co-operation would take place between the two sectors. So the fianna would also be regarded with a degree of suspicion by churchmen. It was, after all, a period of much religious and political confusion in Ireland, as a number of leading septs carved out new spheres of influence for themselves and Christianity jostled with paganism in every realm of life.

Although the word *fían* could be used to signify any type of fighting men, and sometimes even robbers, it is clear that in its basic and restricted sense it was applied to a particular institution of social life. So the question arises, who were these rather independent groups of warriors whom we find portrayed for us as an accepted social institution but who could in some cases be confused with mercenaries and outlaws? Only one answer suits the portrayal, and that is that *fíanas* was the general term to describe the training of young men to be warriors. The nature of this training would, of course, have varied from context to context, given the turbulence of the times, but we can presume that the idea of an initiatory period in the life of young men was a basic part of ancient Irish culture. We can trace similar systems in connection with many other peoples.

Among the ancient Greeks and among the Germanic peoples, as in warrior societies generally, tolerated forms of brigandage were a means of training for young warriors.[36] It would, of course, be a logical type of preparation for formalised and officially-directed war, and, therefore, such initiation into the martial life would have been a necessary process in social life. The activities proper to groups of this kind would involve hunting, athletics, and survival in the wilderness, as well as actual fighting. This type of life peeps through the references to fianna.

One very early source – perhaps seventh century – describes *oaic féine* [fían youths], as 'wandering on the mountain';[37] while another early text, written as instruction for noble youths, states that 'everyone is a *féinnidh* until he obtains a household'.[38] When war broke out, of course, these young men – strong, agile, and energetic, and with no social dependents – would have to carry out most of the raiding and bear the brunt of the fighting. Indeed, the adjective *óc* [young] was often used in Old Irish as a nominal substantive to designate a warrior.[39] As if to deliberately exemplify the process, we have an old compound word for a youth, *óclach*, being re-interpreted by mediaeval writers as *óc-laoch* [young warrior].[40] The word *laoch* itself is of interest. It is a seventh-century derivation from the Latin *laicus*, which was the ordinary equivalent employed by Irish writers in Latin for a *díbhergach* [reaver].[41] Here again we see the complex of fighting and raiding associated with young warriors.

It is important to note that all of these tableaux of the youthful *féinnidh* are found with great vibrancy in the narratives which developed throughout the Middle Ages concerning Fionn's fianna. Fionn himself, and his men, are said to have been great hunters, athletes, fighters, and they continually tested young aspirants for entry into their company. On the principal that ritual retains its basic outlines when its elements become transformed into narrative tradition, we can regard all of this as emanating from the sixth century promotion in Leinster of Fionn as the ideal warrior-figure. The original deity, of course, was an archetype of youthful ambitions to inherit the knowledge, and consequently the social authority, of the seniors. He would, therefore, have been an attractive deity in the eyes of the young *féinnidh*, and those in authority would encourage his cult since it contributed to the defence of the province and helped to ritualise martial training. The ritual and therefore socially stabilising heritage of Fionn served another purpose which must have been in the minds of the elders, that is to prevent the influence of *díbhergaigh* and other social outcasts from having a detrimental effect on fianna groups. Given the energy and mental independence of youth, a certain antipathy to the authority of the older generation could be expected among such groups, and so cultural symbolism was all the more necessary for social control. We can expect, therefore, to find in the image of Fionn a reflection of conflicting ideas – of the ideas of the elders who wished to stabilise tradition on the one hand, and the ideas of the young fianna themselves on the other hand with their adolescent longing for independence.

This uneasy synthesis was the basis of the Fionn warrior-lore which was launched onto the narrative stream and which developed gradually from within itself. The basic contrast between the young and the old, which was part of the Fionn myth from antiquity, was thus strengthened by the very conditions which gave rise to the new martial development.

The culture within which this development was initiated in early sixth-century Leinster was, of course, a pagan one, but within a few generations everybody of any social importance in the province was a Christian, at least nominally so. The Church would have had no real reason to object to the Fionn tradition as it then was. After all, Fionn had been a pagan deity and was now being unconsciously reduced from that status to the role of a pseudo-historical hero. The only potential point of conflict with Christian teaching was his prophetic knowledge, his ritual of thumb-sucking which was so basic to his image and the memory of which survived persistently in popular tradition. That the ecclesiastics came to early grips with this problem is clear.

A short poem in Irish, dating from the sixth century, has a pagan druid foretelling the coming of Christianity, which is personalised as St Patrick with his crozier [adze-head].[42] There is every reason to believe that this druid was soon transformed in Leinster preaching into the figure of prophecy *par excellence* – Fionn himself. The idea, as we have seen (p. 25), is represented on a stone-cross carving from as far away as Co. Donegal as early as the eighth century. This carving has a figure with a thumb in his mouth sitting under a bishop who holds a crozier in his hand.[43] The clearest literary attestation of the idea is in a twelfth-century text, which has Fionn's friend Caoilte saying the following words to St Patrick:

> We never had knowledge of heaven until Fionn sat on this rock and put his thumb under his tooth of knowledge, so that heaven and earth were illumined for him, as well as the faith of the gilded true God, and your coming to Ireland, o Adze-Head.[44]

Similar prophecies of Christianity and of individual saints made by Fionn are referred to on three other occasions in the same text, which show that the tradition was strongly established. In other mediaeval texts he is claimed in at least seven other instances to have prophesied the coming of celebrated saints. It is interesting to note that most of these are Leinster saints.[45] There is less certainty that the figure of a hunter, which is portrayed on several Christian crosses dating from the eighth to the tenth centuries, is meant to represent Fionn but, if it does, it offers further evidence of ecclesiastical concurrence with Fionn as a symbol of fianna.[46] So, the introduction of Christianity did not hinder, but seems to have actually helped, the growing lore of Fionn in sixth- and seventh-century Leinster.

The Adapted Lore

A Leinster tract from around the year A.D. 700 is entitled 'The Genealogy of Fionn mac Umhaill'. Besides giving the usual names for his predecessors, the tract refers to some other interesting personages. These are the three Fothadhs [*na trí Fothad*], who are listed as relatives of his. This connection is contrived, the Fothadhs, Find File, and Fionn himself being listed as all second generation descendants of three fanciful sons of Nuadhu Necht.[47] No doubt the compiler thought it appropriate to tie things neatly together. These three Fothadhs represent a triplication of some important mythical personage, and the name Fothadh may in fact be derived from Celtic **Vo-tádos*. *Tádos* meant 'father', and Fothadh was apparently a designation of an ancestor deity of some septs who had fallen from prominence in ancient Ireland.[48]

The lore of the Fothadhs seems to have been borrowed by the Leinstermen from the province of Connacht, and we are told that Fothadh Canainne was 'a leader of fianna among the men of Connacht'.[49] A whole mini-cycle of stories, some of which have survived in manuscript, described his feats and his escapades,[50] and it is obvious that he too was a deity who enjoyed cultic importance for some fianna group or groups. Notwithstanding the attempt by Leinster genealogists to make Fothadh Canainne one of their own, the early literature portrays him as a bitter enemy of Fionn. This is understandable. The young Leinster fianna, after all, must be taught to oppose the Connacht forces in preparation for whatever military hostilities might occur. A text which appears to be as early as the eighth century retains some evidence for this state of affairs. Fionn, we are told, was for a long time without a woman. Being in the east Munster area, he crossed the river Suir and carried off the daughter of a herdsman from Cahir. Badhamair was the maiden's name, and she became his wife. However, a certain warrior of Leinster called Cuirrech Life, with whom Fionn was at hostilities, cut Badhamair's head off, and Fionn beheaded him in revenge. The account continues:

> Cuirrech was a son of the mother of Fothadh Canainne. Now he [Fothadh] lay in ambush for Fionn until they made peace. Fionn prepared an ale-feast for Fothadh, and invited him to it. Fothadh said:
>
> 'I may not drink ale unless it be drunk in the company of white faces!'
>
> 'That is indeed not easy to arrange', said Fionn, 'for there is a statute of Cormac in Ireland that nobody shall be slain until seven years have passed. However, there are places where the slaying of a man is fully allowed', Fionn added, 'Slighe Miodhluachra, Áth Fhir Diadh, Áth Cliath, Belach nGabhráin, Áth Nó at Cnámhchoill, Conachlaidh, Dá Chích Anann'.
>
> Then Fionn went to Dá Chích Anann in order to kill a man.
>
> 'Let us go', said Téite, Mac Niadh's daughter and sister of Fothadh Canainne. 'We shall have the ale-feast which Fionn is preparing for my brother. Let us go and drink it!' she said to her husband Finn mac Reghamhain. The two of them come eastwards in their chariot, the woman behind and he in front of her.
>
> As they go past Fionn, the descendant of Baoiscne, he casts the lance at them so that it is in the breast of the man, having gone through the woman. It seemed to the man that it was the woman who had killed him. Then he said:
>
> 'A cold blast is the blast which has come to me from you, woman!'

'Blind is the charge you have made against me', said the woman. 'I shall die, man, for it is because of me that this reached you, the moment of death! Cut my head off, warriors', she said, 'for that is the purpose for which you have come!'

'What we have done', said Fionn, 'we regret!'

Evil resulted thereupon from the ale-feast, so that after it the slaughter of the fianna of Ireland occurred between them. Each of them, Fionn and Fothadh Canainne, was lying in ambush for the other from then on as long as they lived.[51]

It is obvious that this story has become somewhat diffuse in this telling. The accretions include the wider geographic setting which brings the action from Leinster to Dá Chích Anann [the Two Paps of Anu] near Killarney in Co. Kerry, as well as claims that slaughter threatened all the fianna of Ireland as a result of the savage feud. The reference to king Cormac mac Airt in this context can hardly have originated before the eighth century (see chapter 4), and must, therefore, be an accretion. The location for the action of the story is in the east Munster area, but the narrative itself betrays the Leinster origin.

The personal name of Cuirrech Life [the Curragh of the Liffey] is a direct adaptation of that placename in Co. Kildare. The plain of the Curragh, within a few miles of the hill of Allen, was claimed by the Uí Fáilghe, but was taken from them and settled by their Leinster rivals, the Uí Dúnlainge, in the sixth century.[52] This explains why the character, Cuirrech Life, would be portrayed as hostile to Fionn. It is just another step to make Currech a relative of Fothadh Canainne, who was the ancestor deity of Connacht septs, the Uaithne and the Aradha, which had settled in present-day north Co. Tipperary,[53] that is on the western flank of the Uí Fáilghe. In other words, different opponents have been grouped together in the Cuirrech/Fothadh complex.

The third member of this hostile family, Téite, is represented as living with her husband at the Paps of Anu, i.e. in the territory of the Eoghanacht of Loch Léin and the

Eoghanacht of Raithlinn. This is obviously a Munster inclusion, reflecting rivalry between the Eoghanacht of Cashel in the east and the western branches of that same leading sept. The actual introduction to the story has Fionn operating from a base in *Cend Cuirrigh* [Kincurry, a townland just across the river Suir in Co. Waterford], and stating that this place got its name from the severed head [*cend*] of Cuirrech Life. This is contrived, but it does show that, to the redactor of the story, Fionn was on the side of the east Munstermen.

The Eoghanacht records tell us that Feidhlimidh mac Tighearnaigh, leader of the Eoghanacht Raithlinn from the west, became king of Munster for a few years towards the end of the sixth century. He was not allowed, however, to reign from Cashel, so he had a fortress dug instead at Badhamair near Cahir. After his death the kingship reverted to the eastern Eoghanacht.[54]

These developments explain why the story has Fionn raiding in the Cahir area and carrying off a woman called Badhamair. It was probably on account of shared political interests with the Uí Fáilghe that the Fionn lore was first adopted by the eastern Eoghanacht, but ecclesiastical sources might also have played a part.[55] Behind a whole stratum of Munster adaptation, at any rate, the Leinster outlines of this story can still be deciphered. Basic to it is a tradition of rivalry between Fionn and Fothadh Canainne.

That these were regarded as leaders of distinctive fianna bands is shown by a poetic enumeration of such bands:

> The Fianna of Fionn, worthy and without cowardice,
> Of the descendant of Baoiscne, they speckled spear-points;
> The fianna of Foilnge, a famous crew;
> The fianna of Fothadh Canainne.[56]

Foilnge must have been another leader of fianna, but we know nothing further of him. Both Fionn and Fothadh were mythical, so their reputed rivalry was symbolical of conflicting interests which was, basically, conflict between Leinster and Connacht. The story of their feud has Fionn exacting vengeance, since it reflects the Leinster point of view. Admittedly, the revenge is savage, but the eye-for-an-eye philosophy in it would be less than repellent to the minds of the warring chieftains of the time. And, to lessen the crudity of the story, we have Fionn giving an air of tragic destiny to the proceedings by saying that he regrets the extreme to which he was driven. The great, after all, are carried along helplessly by their fate – a theme of tragedy which was quite popular in ancient Irish hero-lore.

Another mythical leader of fianna who occurs in early tradition was Mac Con. A seventh-century biographer of St Patrick has a giant who was raised from the dead by the saint relating his own story thus:

> I am the son of Cas son of Glas. I was the swineherd of Lugar, king of Hirota. The *fian*-youths of MacCon slew me in the reign of Coirpre Nia Fer.[57]

The full name of this fianna leader was Lughaidh Mac Con, and his floruit was put down by the traditional historians to the third century A.D., to which they also relegated Fionn mac Cumhaill.[58] In early mediaeval texts we find both heroes brought into the same ambit. In the ninth-century *Scéla Moshauluim*, 'Find descendant of Baoiscne' is represented as being among the host of Mac Con in Munster after Mac Con had decided to leave the company of the provincial king, his own foster-father Ailill Ólom. Ailill sent the warrior Ferchess on the track of Mac Con in order to slay him:

> It was then that Fionn said through his *imbas forosnai* [great knowledge of enlightenment]:
>
> 'A man in pursuit!'
>
> 'Warriors would be glad against a number', said Mac Con.
>
> 'A man in pursuit!' said Fionn.
>
> Ferchess prepares an ambush, with his spear in his hand, across the glen from the east, behind them. . . . Ferchess launched the spear from his hand and it pierced Mac Con in his chariot, and his memorial stone is there to this day.
>
> Fionn descendant of Baoiscne went on the track of Ferchess to avenge Mac Con, for Fionn was his *féinnidh*. And he killed him at the end of seven years at the Pool of Ferchess on the Bandae (river), when he found the wood-shavings that Ferchess had loosed upon the stream.

> Others say that it was in the Waterfall of the Máigh that Ferchess was killed. Seven years afterwards to the day Fionn killed him.[59]

A companion text from the same period, *Cath Cinn Abrad*, claims that Fionn was a first cousin to Mac Con, their mothers having been sisters. Fionn's mother is here stated to have been Fuinche, daughter of Dáire.[60] Since these are Munster texts, the Dáire in question must be Dáire son of Dedha, an ancestor figure for many Munster septs. We note that this was the tyrant maternal grandfather of Noíne, who appears in the Munster genealogies and whom we have identified with Fionn (pp. 19f).

The import of all this is that the Dáire pedigree for Fionn was seized upon and given special development in Munster. The *Cath Cinn Abrad* text also calls Fionn the 'king-féinnidh of Ireland',[61] thereby making it clear that in the lore of Fionn, known to ninth century Munster, he had achieved an advanced status. Having borrowed the lore from Leinster sources, Munster tradition had begun to portray the hero, not any longer as a provincial figure, but as a wise warrior whose memory should rightly belong to the whole country.

Feuding and Womanising

Another ninth-century text also shows Fionn in his dual aspect of seer and fighter. The surroundings here are the original Leinster, and the account gives further insight into the environmental and social life of the young men called fianna:

> Fionn descendant of Baoiscne had as jester Lomhna the fool. There was a woman of the Luaighne [sept] with Fionn, for in every mountain and every forest which Fionn and his fianna frequented there was a particular woman awaiting him in every territory.
>
> Fionn once came into Tethbha with his fiann and went on a hunting expedition, and Lomhna stayed at home. As he was walking about he saw Coirpre, a féinnidh, lying with Fionn's woman in secret. The woman thereupon begged Lomhna to conceal the matter, but he thought it grievous to betray Fionn.

Fionn returned afterwards, and Lomhna carved an inscription on a foursquare rod. What was on it was:

'An alder stake into a fence of silver. A poisonous lily amid edible plants. The husband of a lewd woman is a fool among the educated fianna.'

Then Fionn understood the matter, and he was disgusted with the woman. She knew that it was from Lomhna that he knew. She sent a message then to Coirpre, so that he came and killed the jester and cut the head off him and took it with him. Fionn came to the hunting-booth in the evening, and he saw the dead body.

'Here is a body without a head!' says Fionn.

'Let us discover', said the fianna, 'whose body it is!'

Then Fionn put his thumb in his mouth, and he sang through *teinm laída* [shining of intellect]:

'Nícon ruba dóine, nícon arlaig, níco topaig nais, nícu derg raigi, nícon ruba torc, nícon fornae, nícon torgrae, nícu rarbarrt a lighe Lomnae.

This is the body of Lomhna,' Fionn said, 'Enemies have taken his head from him!'

They slip the hounds and put them on the track. Fionn went upon the track of the warriors, and he found Coirpre in an empty house cooking fish upon a stone, and Lomhna's head was on a spike by the fire. The first set which was cooked on the stone Coirpre divided among his thrice nine persons, and he put no morsel of it into the mouth of that head. There was a prohibition on Fionn against doing that. It was then that the head said to him:

'A speckled white-bellied salmon bursts forth from spawn under the sea!'

The second set, then Coirpre divided again in the same way as the first, and something was heard from the head:

'You have divided a share at the second division. A better division would be made by a drunken servant. I would like a piece of the stomach. The fianna will hate the Luaighne for this!'

'Put out the head, though it be wrong of me to say it!' said Coirpre. And something was heard from the head outside:

'The stake relates that a champion was running with his

battle-spear at their first coupling. Ye will be like many pieces or several fragments. Fionn will light the Luaighne with much fire!'

At that Fionn approached Coirpre and killed him.[62]

This story shows the strength of the raw fianna perspective in the early martial lore of Fionn. We can, indeed, regard the retributive morality and the hostility to the Luaighne sept as emanating from Leinster war-lore of the sixth century. The Luaighne were vassals to the Uí Neill and played a leading role in the Uí Néill armies. They lived just north of the Uí Fáilghe, who thus often found them stern opponents in battle.[63] Another rendering of the above story states that Coirpre, as well as Fionn's woman, was of the Luaighne,[64] so it is obvious that the narrative reflects official Leinster feelings of hostility for their foes. Ancient warrior lore is encapsuled in the decapitation motif. The Celts were head-hunters, and the practice is stressed in several early Irish sources.[65]

The taste and colour of this narrative, however, is very much that of unruly adolescents. The almost dismissive savagery of Coirpre and of Fionn must owe much to the real gory life of apprentices to a martial career, and the same situation emerges even more clearly in the cause of the bloodletting. Jealousy over women would naturally have been a large contributory factor to feuds among young undisciplined warriors and, if this lore is to be credited, the fianna bands had quite a libertine attitude to liaisons with women. The above text includes a striking reference to women whom Fionn had in each territory. The writer of the story, by way of explanation, adds that there were 'female hosts' and that 'they were good to support the fianna, for their relatives were spread over the territories, so that nobody dare do them harm'.[66] This rather confused sentence apparently means that a recognised system existed according to which young unattached warriors were allowed to have sexual relations with women of different areas without danger of reprisal. The suggestion is that the women's relatives would even take pains to protect this privilege of the fianna. One can hardly imagine the ecclesiastical party upholding this system, nor would the lay elders be entirely happy with it, so it is obvious that in the synthesis which occurred the influence of these parties did not succeed very well in taming the ideas of the youths themselves.

That the lore of fianna bands placed strong emphasis on sexual prowess is exemplified by the cycle of stories concerning that other great *féinnidh*, Fothadh Canainne. As we have suggested, this personality was a hero of fianna lore in a different area and at a demonstrably earlier period than was Fionn. One story made Fothadh the object of the love of the Hag of Beare, who was a version of the earth-goddess.[67] Another story describes an amorous adventure of his with a woman called Lethderg; while yet another has him carrying off the wife of a rival fianna leader, Ailill Flann Bec, which escapade brought about his death and beheading.[68]

We have seen that this theme of woman-stealing was much to the fore in the early lore concerning Fionn himself. Here is another eighth-century narrative, with the same east Munster setting as we encountered in a previous story:

> The fianna carried off captive women from Dún Iascaigh [Cahir] in the territory of the Dési. A beautiful maiden was taken by them. Fionn desired this woman for himself. She set her mind on a servant who was with them, that is Derg Corra son of Daighre's descendant. For this was his custom: While food was being cooked by them the servant used to leap to and fro over the hearth. It was because of that that the maiden loved him, and she asked him one day to come and lie with her. Derg Corra did not accept that on account of Fionn, who desired her as a wife. She brought accusations against him to Fionn and said that he had raped her. Then Fionn said to him:
>
> 'Begone from my presence. You shall have a respite of three days and three nights, and after that beware of me!'
>
> Then Derg Corra went into exile and dwelt in the forest, and he used to go about on shanks of deer (*si verum est*) he was so light.
>
> One day when Fionn was in the forest searching for him Fionn saw a man on the top of a tree with a blackbird on his right shoulder and a bright bronze vessel in his left hand, with water in it, in which was a leaping trout. And

a stag was at the foot of the tree. And what the man was doing was cracking nuts, and he was giving half the kernel of a nut to the blackbird on his right shoulder while he himself ate the other half. And he would take an apple out of the bronze vessel in his left hand and divide it in two, and throw half to the stag at the foot of the tree. He himself would then eat the other half. And he would wash it down with a sip of water from the bronze vessel in his hand, so that he and the trout and the deer and the blackbird were drinking together.

Then his company asked Fionn who he in the tree was, for they did not recognise him because of the cloak of concealment which was about him. Fionn put his thumb in his mouth. When he took it out again, his *imbas* [great knowledge] illumined him and he sang an incantation and said:

'*Con fri lon lethcno contethain cotith in dithraib Dercc Corra comól fri hich ni ba filliud fabaill a uball fín mblais cona fricarbaith mac úi co dedail Daigre.*'

'It is Derg Corra son of Daighre's descendant,' he said, 'who is in the tree!'[69]

The Lore Expands

We notice that the theme of Fionn's amorousness in this early text has attracted the international motif known as 'Potiphar's Wife'. This motif has a woman making advances to a man and, when disappointed, accusing him of trying to force her. It was very popular in different ancient cultures,[70] but this is the earliest example of it in Irish literature. Since it, although an intrusive motif, is already well-knit into the texture of this story concerning Derg Corra and Fionn, the basic tradition of a conflict between the two characters must be quite older. We have argued (pp. 14f) that the occurrence of foes of Fionn called Dearg and Dáire owes much to the Lugh/Balar myth. The story here, however, has a definitely fianna-atmosphere as the setting for the conflict, with themes, such as the expropriation of women and man-to-man struggles. in the forest environs. This leads us to believe that the reformulation of the Fionn versus Dearg conflict in fianna terms took place in the sixth or early seventh century. The other types of evidence we have considered also suggested this as the period in which the synthesis of Fionn lore and fianna practices was effected.

The strange appearance of Derg Corra in the forest needs to be commented on. The portrayal of him as a cowled figure in a tree, surrounded by different kinds of wild creatures, parallels several figures which are depicted in Celtic iconography on the Continent. One of these figures preserves the name of the god Cernunnos, which means 'the horned (or peaked) one', an interpretation which can also be put on Derg Corra's name [literally, the red peaked one]. Furthermore, Cernunnos-type figures on the Continent often have a stag engraved with them.[71] The deity himself has an antlered head, which brings to mind the strange deer-like deportment of Derg Corra in the forest. The writer of the eighth-century text found it difficult to make up his mind on this tradition, '*Si verum est*', he says, 'if it be true!' To go about 'on shanks of deer' [*for luirgnib oss n-allta*] could mean as fast as a deer or, more strikingly, possessing the actual legs of a deer; but whichever the interpretation it is clear that Derg Corra is being given a cerval significance.

The reason why vestiges of an ancient animal deity should resurface in a story concerning fianna seems obvious, for hunting wild animals would have been a primary aspect of the life of such young warriors in the wilderness. This all the more so since the deity in question had the attributes of a stag and since deer were the principal quarry of hunters in early Ireland. It is as if the hunters treated the deity as a symbol of their quarry and yet feared to meet him in his lonely retreat, where he would be a threatening protector of their victims. Such a rather sinister figure in the imagination of young fianna was seen to coincide with Fionn's otherworld enemy, Dearg [Derg] or Dáire [Daighre]. Therefore, this name of 'Derg Corra son of Daighre's descendant' was given to him. The strange ritual engaged in by Derg Corra – that of leaping to and fro over the cooking-hearth [*léim ocus doléim tarsin n-indiu*] – is apparently due also to the Fionn lore, for *daighre* means flame and this type of jumping is an attribute of a blazing fire.[72]

The plot of the whole story is quite illogical. A servant with whom Fionn quarrels ends up, without any proper progression or explanation, as an enigmatic figure in the forest. The narrative has all the hallmarks of varying elements being jumbled together, and the writer of the text was clearly at a loss to make sense of what had come down to him, being fianna traditions of womanising, mythological remnants in hunting lore, offshoots of the story of Fionn, and a version of the international folktale motif known to scholars as 'Potiphar's Wife'.

But the outline of yet another narrative element can be detected, involving a dispute between Fionn and a member of his band. Little can be said about this element, since it has become so confused with the imposition of the 'Potiphar's Wife' motif on top of it. The very fact, however, that the story is built upon such a dispute suggests to us that already in the seventh or eighth century there was a living lore concerning Fionn and other distinctive members of his fianna. We have already referred (p. 3) to mention in very early Leinster genealogical sources of Caoilte, who was one of the most famous characters of Fionn's fianna in later tradition. His name and fame did not take long to spread further afield, and we find him mentioned as fighting alongside Fionn in southern surroundings in the Munster text *Scéla Moshauluim* two hundred years later.[73] That he was known also in Ulster is clear from a ninth-century text from that province, in which he is called 'Caílte, the foster-son of Fionn' and where it is claimed that he killed Fothadh Airgthech in a conflict between that warrior and Fionn.[74] So the name of this particular comrade of Fionn, at least, was known throughout the country by the end of the eighth century. There is evidence also that another of Fionn's men had a celebrated part in the tradition at an early date, for one text of that same period concerns Oisín. This Oisín (called in the text Oiséne) was the son of Fionn, and the story goes as follows:

> Fionn descendant of Baoiscne was seeking his son throughout Ireland. Oiséne had been a year without his whereabouts being known. He had hostile feelings towards his

> father. Then Fionn found him in a very great wilderness. Oiséne was cooking a pig. Fionn turns upon him and gives him a blow. Oiséne seized his weapons and his accoutrements. He did not recognise him at first. But Fionn said it was foolish for a young warrior to fight against a grey-headed man.

The two heroes then argue with each other in poetry and are reconciled.[75]

Oisín, as we shall see in later chapters, was to become one of the leading figures – in some ways the pivotal figure – of the whole cycle. Here, however, his character is given no distinctive marks apart from his being Fionn's son and one of the actors in an early Irish version of an international folktale. The plot of this folktale, known from antiquity in European and Asiatic sources, has an aging hero killing his unrecognised son.[76] The softening of the plot here from a physical to a verbal duel must reflect a pre-existing knowledge that Fionn and Oisín got on quite well together, and Oisín's year long absence in a pique appears contrived in order to make the narrative possible. So we can assume that Fionn as a fianna leader must have had sufficient time for his image to age, and to father a son, before this text was written.

By the eighth century, then, Fionn was being accompanied in the lore by fianna followers and sub-heroes, like Caoilte and Oisín. The list must have been longer. We have seen (p. 3) that in an early Leinster genealogy another companion of his, called Tulcha, was mentioned. We have no surviving stories concerning this character, but a twelfth-century source describes him as a half-brother of Fionn.[77] We also have, of course, Goll. This figure, as already said (pp. 9ff), was well in the process of developing into Fionn's great rival *féinnidh*, the Goll mac Morna of the mediaeval literature, of whom much more will be said.

In summarising the material dealt with in this chapter, we find the lore of Fionn in a state of rapid development from the fifth to the eighth centuries. The Boyne valley cult of Fionn as god of knowledge had made a strong impression on the Leinstermen and, after they lost control of that area, the Uí Fáilghe sept in particular began to associate the figure of Fionn with their hope of regaining Tara. Fionn was a suitable symbol for this on account of the myth of how he had rescued Tara from oppression by a destructive foe. His youthful imagery rendered him attractive to aspiring young warriors, and this interest in him on the part of their fianna was cultivated by the Uí Fáilghe elders. The result was that Fionn son of Umhall [later, Cumhall] was given an important role in the genealogy and topography of sixth-century Leinster.

The synthesis of a god of knowledge with the life of martial apprentices gave rise to a series of simple stories concerning Fionn and his struggles with other warriors, especially regarding women. This primitive form of the new cycle was quite uniform, and a hunger for new motifs is demonstrated by the rather facile and loose adaptations of floating narrative motifs.

Already by the seventh century, Fionn was being associated with other fianna leaders, and was being given a special set of warrior comrades of his own. Such synthetic lore of him and his fianna band was, due to its origins, rather diffuse from the beginning, but the perennial themes were his thumb of knowledge, his struggle against an otherworld foe, his life in the forest, and his feuding with rivals and associates.

3.

The Narrative Core

We have discussed the basic elements which go to make up the Fionn tradition: his images as god of knowledge, the influence of the Lugh lore, and the manner in which Fionn was made a symbol of fianna bands. All of these elements belonged to the pre-literary period; and so it is to be expected when we enter the earliest phase of the written language, called Old Irish, that they would be found in quite developed forms. They also would have attracted some materials related to them as individual elements, and would be in the process of developing these and reconciling them to each other.

The Special Act

Fionn gained insight into hidden things by placing his thumb in his mouth and sucking it. This indicates that he was envisaged in ancient times as a child deity, and we have seen in chapter 1 how many vestiges of this archaic portrayal of him have survived. The magical knowledge of seers and poets was known as *fios*, which is the root used to designate Fionn's gift, as well as to describe his celebrated 'thumb of knowledge' [*ordóg feasa*].[1] In fact, the word *fios* comes from the same Indo-European root **u̯i* as does the name Fionn itself, and has connotations of 'discovery' and 'finding out'. Just as Old-Irish *find* [modern, *fionn*] is cognate with Germanic *finden* and Latin *videre*, so Old-Irish *fiss* [modern, *fios*] is cognate with Germanic *weise* and Latin *visere*'.[2] Fionn's gift then, the magical power of *fios*, is synonymous with his very name. His typical action and his own personality are one – he sees and is a seer, he knows and is a symbol of knowledge.

With the passage of time, Fionn's character underwent development and diversification, and he became a hero-figure for warriors and hunters as well as a seer-figure for poets. He became more humanised, invested with more of the traits of a genuine living character. This meant that his thumb of knowledge tended to be envisaged in a naturalised way as a real part of the body of the warrior-hero Fionn mac Cumhaill. That such a character would have preserved the childish trait of sucking his thumb became a rather awkward notion. The metaphoric image of a child-seer representing knowledge originalised was being replaced by more concrete ideas, and it was untypical of an adult hero to behave like a child. It was necessary, therefore, to stress that there was something unusual about Fionn's thumb. Emphasis was shifted from the sucking of it onto the thumb itself. Fionn, now an epical hero, could be envisaged as having a special magical attribute – as such heroes often had – and in his case the attribute resided in a specific part of his body. It accordingly became necessary to explain the origin of this attribute, and narratives developed to describe how his thumb first got its inherent power.

The first such account of which we know is in an eighth-century text, and it goes as follows:

> When the *fianna*-band was at Badhamair on the bank of the Siúir river, Cúldubh the son of Ua Birgge came from the *sí*-fort on Femen and took their cooked food [*fulacht*] from them. For three nights he did thus to them. The third time, however, Fionn knew and went before him to the *sí*-fort on Femen. Fionn caught him as he entered the *sí*-fort, so that he died over there. As he [Fionn] stretched his hand towards him, a woman met him with a wet vessel in her hand after distributing drink just before. And she closed the door on the *sí*-fort, and Fionn inserted his finger between the door and the post. Then he put his finger into his mouth. When he took it out again he began to chant. The *imbas* illumined him, so that he said:
>
> '*Tair Femen fuigial formuig meis mui muic cetson sirchrand sirlúath laith find sra aulad Cúlduib chanmae.*'[3]

The location here is in east Munster, and the story is part of the corpus of early Fionn lore found in that area. That this corpus is a borrowing from Leinster we have already suggested (pp. 39ff), and this becomes clearer when we examine the present item. Fionn's opponent Cúldubh [literally, black-haired] is found in another story where he is called *mac Déin* [son of Swift] and is said to be 'flame-red' [*daigderg*]. This story, in the twelfth-century metrical 'Place-Lore', tells of how Cúldubh was killed in a Leinster bog on the first day of November by a warrior called Gae Glas, who wielded a special magical spear.[4] The name Gae Glas, in fact, means Green Spear and must properly refer to the weapon. In later mediaeval texts we are told that Fionn mac Cumhaill was also called Glasdic – a compound based on this same word *glas*.[5] The special spear and the November-tide recall Fionn's killing of the burner Aillén at Tara (see p. 9). So all the indications are that the death of Cúldubh at the hands of Gae Glas in the twelfth-century text is a confused version of Fionn's victory over his archetypal foe at Halloween.

That differing versions of that story were current is proved by another twelfth-century text. Here Fionn is described as killing by a spear-cast a hostile underworld warrior called Aedh [literally, fire] son of Fidach as that warrior, also carrying cooked meat, enters a *sí*-dwelling at Halloween. Another source gives Fidach as father of the Cúldubh whom Fionn killed, and Fidach was also stated to have been father of the Tara burner Aillén, thus showing the common base for all these narratives.[6]

The Cúldubh story from east Munster, then, is really another version of Fionn's contest with the fiery otherworld foe, onto which a new interpretation of the thumb-motif has been attached. We have a further version from east Munster – this one dating from the ninth century. According to it, Fionn was in Cend Currigh, where 'it was customary for him to be'. One morning when Oisín was cooking a pig, it was snatched from him and taken away into the *sí*-fort of Femen. The same happened next day when Caoilte cooked a pig. On the third day, Fionn decided he would have to prepare the food himself:

He went to cook it, his spear-shafts in his left hand, with his other hand turning the pig on the points of the fork. It stuck fast. Fionn made a thrust at him [the robber], but only the point of the spear reached his back. Thereupon he left the belly [of the pig] at Magh Tarra in Éile at Cill Íochtair, the whole side at Toirb Muice. Seven times he leaped across the Siúir river.

'Open', he [the robber] said, 'before it!', at the top of the hill. 'Open', he said, over the length of the mountain.

'Here is something from me!' said Fionn. He made a thrust at him as he entered the *sí*-fort, so that his back broke thereby. His hand stuck fast against the door-post as the door was closed on his thumb, and he put it into his mouth. It is thus that some people say that Fionn had knowledge, for it was the part of his finger which entered the *sí*-fort that he used to put in his mouth. Their [the *sí*-dwellers] wailing was heard.

'What is that?' everybody said.

'Cúldubh has been killed!'

'Who killed him?'

'Fionn descendant of Baoiscne.'

They all wail. It was then that he [Fionn] said:

'*Bind berlai bind bee nimgnae buiriud tairb coi coistecht fria Femen furlae. Mai muiced son dar Femen fugiath sir-chrand sir-luth laitho Find fri ulaid Cul Dub.*'

He carried his pig in his bosom and apportioned it among his people.[7]

Here the meaning of the episode becomes clearer. The thumb is a carrier of knowledge because it was the only part of Fionn's body which gained access to the otherworld dwelling, and he put it into his mouth because it had been hurt by the slamming door. The idea of Fionn entering the otherworld is in the background. This is the older tradition – the visit to the world of the dead at Halloween – which survives only obliquely within the narratives of his contest with the fiery foe.

The Salmon of Knowledge

Once the notion that Fionn had got the power of knowledge

by hurting his thumb gained currency, further interpretations of the motif became possible. The most striking of all these interpretations developed around the tenth century and quickly achieved wide popularity. Narratives of the slamming door did not survive long in tradition, but this new interpretation was destined to become the best-known of all folk stories about Fionn and versions of it have been circulating in folklore all over Ireland and in the west of Scotland down to recent times.

The earliest version of it which we have is in the twelfth-century youth-biography of Fionn called *Macgnímartha Find* [Boyhood Deeds of Fionn]. The text tells us that the hero was first known by the name Demne, and, when seven years old, he went to learn the craft of poetry from a character called Finnéices, who lived by the Boyne river:

> For seven years Finnéices had been on the Bóinn seeking the salmon of Féc's Pool, for it had been prophesied to him that he would eat the salmon of Féc and that nothing would remain unknown to him after that.
>
> The salmon was caught and was entrusted to Demne for cooking, and the poet [*file*] told him not to eat anything of the salmon. The lad brought him the salmon after it had been cooked.
>
> 'Did you eat anything of the salmon, lad?' said the poet.
>
> 'No', said the lad, 'except that I burned my thumb and then put it in my mouth.'
>
> 'What is your name, lad?' said he.
>
> 'Demne', said the lad.
>
> 'Fionn is your name, lad', said he, 'and it is to you that the salmon was given to eat, and you are the Fionn truly!'
>
> The lad then ate the salmon. That is what gave the knowledge to Fionn. When he used to put his thumb into his mouth and sing through *teinm laída*, and that which was unknown to him would be revealed to him.[8]

The reference here to 'the Fionn' [*in Find*] is important, for it has resonances of the original meaning of the name, 'Knower' (see pp. 5, 52 above). It is also apposite in the sense that the statement is attributed to Finnéices, who thus concedes that his own name properly belongs to the other character. It is as if 'the old Fionn' is admitting that he is merely an extension of 'the young Fionn' (see p. 17). It is clear that the nomenclature and the Boyne setting belong to ancient tradition. We have already seen that *Finnéices* [literally, Fionn the seer] is an epithet given to a god of the Boyne, Nuadhu. The form of this deity's name in Celtic Britain was Nodons, who is represented on an engraving from Gloucestershire in the act of hooking a fish.[9] Nuadhu (under the name Elcmhar) is also associated with a Boyne salmon in a mediaeval story concerning the hero Cúchulainn,[10] so it is obvious that the cult of Nuadhu involved such a fish. In fact, we have a good deal of background information on this salmon.

Mystical tradition had it that the well of Seghais at the source of the Boyne was surrounded by nine hazel-trees, from which nuts fell into the water. These nuts, full of *imbas* [great knowledge], floated up the river and were consumed by the 'salmon of knowledge' [*eo fis*].[11] The source of the Boyne was also metaphorically known as the *Sídh* [otherworld dwelling] of Nechtan.[12] Nechtan was another name for Nuadhu (see pp. 17f), and so the wisdom-bearing salmon has close connections with the realm of Nuadhu himself. It is obvious that we are dealing with a series of ideas belonging to the esoteric lore of poets and seers, who through such imagery rationalised the wisdom-gaining power of their own deity Fionn. The salmon of the Boyne was consumed by the young Fionn, who thus took from Nuadhu Finnéices – a substitute for the old Fionn – the secret treasure of knowledge.

We have already taken this text as a repository of seer-lore (pp. 16f), and have referred to another striking detail in it. According to this, after eating the salmon, 'Fionn then went to Cethern son of Fintan to study the craft of poetry further with him'.[13] This character's first name means simply 'kerne' or 'warrior'. Its generalised nature suggests improvisation, but the element Fintan is more significant.

One mediaeval text tells of a certain Fintan who spent hundreds of years in the form of a salmon at the falls of Assaroe in Ulster, and in Welsh literature we read of the magic salmon of Llyn Llyw which was the most knowledgeable creature in the world.[14] There are good reasons for regarding both these wise fish as being derived from their counterpart of the Boyne. The Assaroe salmon is called by names, such as Aedh, Goll, and Ruadh – all of which can be taken as loose fragments from the myth of Fionn's fiery foe; while the Welsh text which refers to the salmon of Llyn Llyw shows heavy Irish influence. It can hardly be doubted that this fish was envisaged as a kind of mediator in the transfer of knowledge from the ancients to Fionn, swimming upwards from the nether regions and thus providing an apt symbol in the lore of practising poets and seers. We can postulate a longstanding tradition connecting Fionn with this salmon – a tradition which belonged to the Boyne Valley cult among the early Gaelic inhabitants of that area, and it was part of the antiquarian lore which was avidly preserved by the Leinstermen.

The actual structure of the story as we have it, however, is clearly an innovation. Since the narrative is based on the idea of a hurt thumb, we may assume that it postdates the slamming-door motif which we have discussed above. This would put down the story of Fionn and the salmon of the Boyne – in the form known to posterity – to an origin in or about the tenth century. The plot has the hero eating magical food which was intended for another, and comes from international folklore. This structure is known to folklorists as the story entitled 'The White Serpent's Flesh', and examples of it have been collected from living oral tradition throughout Europe and further afield. It is clearly of some antiquity, probably having a central European source and predating mediaeval times. The basic features of this international folktale plot can be summarised thus: A man is put in charge of cooked meat by a wizard. The man discovers that it is the flesh of a white serpent, and when he gets an opportunity he eats it. Immediately he gains the ability to understand the speech of birds, who tell him hidden facts, and in this way he becomes a seer.[15]

There are, however, some distinct differences between this international plot and the story of Fionn. The clearest of these concerns the hero's intent and the manner of gaining the power. Unlike the international plot, Fionn unintentionally performs the act of tasting the flesh, for he burns his thumb and puts it into his mouth as a natural reflex.

That special format is also found in a mediaeval Norse tradition concerning the hero Sigurd. The best version of this is in an Icelandic poem written around the year 1100. It describes how Sigurd killed a dragon and was asked by a comrade, called Regin, to roast the dragon's heart. In the process, Sigurd burned his thumb on a spurt of blood coming from the heart and, putting the thumb into his mouth to relieve the pain, he found that he could understand the speech of birds. They warned him that Regin intended to harm him, and so Sigurd killed Regin first.[16]

The accounts of Fionn and Sigurd obviously constitute a special oecotype of the international story, and it can hardly be doubted that some influence has passed between them. The precise nature of that influence, and in which direction it occurred, are matters which have never been satisfactorily unravelled. The Sigurd story did not survive in later Norse folklore, but we know that it had some currency in the Middle Ages. Several carvings of it, dating from the tenth to the twelfth centuries, have been found over a wide area in Scandinavia, northern England, and the Isle of Man.[17] This geographical spread makes a direct contact between the Sigurd and Fionn variants likely, but it does not solve the question as to which tradition influenced the other.

It appears that the influence was not simply a once-off affair, but that both traditions affected each other for a continuous period. We can speculate that, in Norse tradition prior to the tenth-century, Sigurd was reputed to have killed a dragon and to have burned his finger by accident in its broth. Finding that this gave the finger a horny covering, he smeared himself with it so as to acquire invulnerability. This narrative format is, in fact, evidenced by a late mediaeval ballad concerning the German hero Siegfried, who is based on earlier Norse lore of Sigurd,[18] so it is plausible to consider it as the basic pattern of the Sigurd story. The idea of gaining a gift from the dragon's broth would have attracted the international plot of the white serpent's flesh, and the resultant confusion would have settled down to a story-pattern which had Sigurd gaining knowledge of bird's speech after he burned his finger and tasted the dragon-broth.

Meanwhile, in Ireland, Fionn had a sore thumb. But the same thumb was the source of his knowledge [*imbas*], and that knowledge was associated with the salmon of the Boyne. It is probable that there was a tradition that he had, in fact, eaten the salmon. But the clearest point of similarity between these two heroes was the burnt finger of Sigurd and the hurt thumb of Fionn – both injuries connected with magical knowledge. The close contacts between Norse and Gaelic cultures in the ninth and tenth centuries would have enabled this parallel to be noticed, and in such a situation the influence could work in both directions. Sigurd's finger would be transformed into his thumb due to the Fionn imagery, while Fionn would borrow the outline of the Sigurd variant of the international plot. Thus Fionn's salmon of the Boyne would be given a role based on the cooking heart of Sigurd's dragon. The motif of bird-language would naturally be discarded in Fionn's case, because the Irish tradition of seer-poetry was so strong as to blot out any alternative ideas in its context.

There is an additional reason for considering this explanation as the proper one. We recall that in the Sigurd story the hero was warned against his false friend Regin, and as a result killed him. This motif is endemic to the Irish and Scottish folk versions of the Fionn story – Fionn, on gaining the knowledge from tasting the salmon, realises that the fisherman intends to kill him, and so decides on a pre-emptive strike against the (unnamed) rival. The writer of the twelfth century text omitted this, apparently because he considered it unsuitable to the Leinster genealogical use of both Nuadhu and Fionn. The ancient seer-lore of Fionn winning knowledge from the ancestor, which had been reshaped by the Lugh myth into a mortal combat with the grandfather, had existed for centuries in uneasy tension with that learned genealogical system. Now the dramatic theme of conflict between the two characters was prevailing in sub-literary tradition, assisted by the Sigurd influence. And so in mediaeval oral narrative, as in the folklore of our own time, we can assume that the fisherman was one-eyed and echoed the imagery of the time-honoured fiery foe.

Rituals of the Dead

We have noticed, in the accounts from the old literature of how Fionn's thumb became a source of wisdom, that he immediately after the event began to utter rhetorics. We have also (pp. 44ff) seen him doing the same thing after he deliberately put his thumb into his mouth to gain knowledge. It is obvious that these rather unintelligible speeches are verbalisations of his *imbas*. The rhetorics given in our texts are, in fact, little more than jumbled words put together by the writers to give them the appearance of antiquity, but there is no doubting the basic integrity of the idea. This is that Fionn spoke in the difficult and esoteric language of a seer when delivering his oracles.

There are, in fact, many examples in early Irish literature of seer-poets delivering wise statements in obscure speech. This was called *dorchacht* [darkness] – a cryptic language which the poets used in talking to each other.[19] Another term for it was *iarmbérla*, which the ninth-century Glossary of Cormac mac Cuilennáin explains in the following way:

> It is called that because of the dimness of the language and because of its darkness and its condensation, so that it is not easy to decipher it.[20]

Obviously, it was a kind of meta-language and, given the magical powers attributed to poets and poetry in ancient Ireland, it was understood to belong to the otherworld. Respect for this special language is a very ancient thing, with parallels in other Indo-European cultures.[21]

The text concerning Fionn and the Boyne salmon tells us that thereafter he had 'the three qualifications of a poet', and it names these as *imbas forosna*, *teinm laída*, and *díchetal di chennaib*. This triad of skills is mentioned in a variety of Old Irish sources, but none of these sources seem to understand the precise meaning of them. Cormac's Glossary has a long tract on them, and claims that St Patrick forbade the practice of *imbas forosna* and *teinm laída* because they were incompatible with Christianity. With regard to *díchetal di chennaib*, however, the glossator says that the saint allowed that because it comes from ordinary human creativeness and 'no offering to demons is necessary'. This phrase is a typical one for a Christian writer to use when referring to pagan rituals, and it suggests that these aspects of the poetic craft had such a nature. The glossator indeed gives a description of what he claims the rite of *imbas forosna* involved:

> It discovers whatever thing the poet wishes and which he desires to enlighten. This is how it is done. The poet chews a morsel of the red meat of a pig, or a dog, or a cat, and puts it then on a flagstone behind the door. He chants an incantation over it, and offers it to idol gods, and calls them to him, and does not abandon them on the morrow. He chants over his two palms, and calls again idol gods to him lest his sleep be disturbed. He puts his two palms on his two cheeks and sleeps. And he is watched lest he turn over or lest he be disturbed by anybody. Then is revealed to him that for which he was seeking.[22]

This description is rather fanciful and has been patched together by the glossator from different traditions of which he had an uncertain grasp. The reference to the poet's palms on his cheeks comes from a mistaken etymology of the word *imbas*, which the glossator takes to mean 'palms about' but which in fact means 'great knowledge'.[23] Also, the undisturbed trance-sleep is based on dim memories of a ritual – elsewhere described in the old literature – by which a poet slept on the hide of a bull or other animal in order to have a prophetic dream.[24] One section of the description, however, does have connections with Fionn lore. This is the process of chewing meat and then placing it on a flagstone behind the door. There are no parallels to this in Irish literature, and it seems very likely that the glossator is here using the story of Fionn and Cúldubh (perhaps the actual text we have quoted on p. 53) for his purpose. He has kept the image of meat inside the door, but has replaced Fionn's thumb-sucking with a supposed ritual of chewing raw meat. We note also his use of the word *mír* [morsel], which recalls Fionn's *mér* [finger] in the eighth-century version of the Cúldubh story.

If we are right in assuming that the glossator made primary use of Fionn material, then such material must have been to the fore in the surviving seer-lore of the time. The frequency with which the three terms *imbas forosna*, *teinm laída*, and *díchetal di chennaib* were applied to the mystic wisdom of Fionn also suggests that – whatever their precise meaning – they had long been associated with him. His technique of knowledge is called *imbas forosna* twice in the Ferchess text, and the same term is used indirectly in the first Cúldubh text (*fortnosmen imbas*, [i.e. the *imbas* illumined him]). In the Lomhna story the technique is called *teinm laída*, and he chants as a result. The word used for this chanting has the root *can*, the verbal noun of which was *díchetal*. This term *díchetal* is in fact used with *imbas* in the first Cúldubh text; and in the story of Derg Corra, Fionn chants a *díchetal* as a direct result of his *imbas*. It is clear from all of this that the eighth- to the ninth-century writers regarded each of the three terms as appropriate to Fionn's magical wisdom.

Old Irish sources insist that the test of a 'true poet' [*fírfhile*] was the ability to compose extempore,[25] which was, indeed, how Fionn produced his rhetorics. When the true poet was composing, he was giving verbal expression to knowledge which was drawn from the depths of his being, from the mystical reservoir within him. Thus we have, in early sources, terms such as *díchetal di chennaib colla* [chanting from the extremities of the body], *cetal na haisnéise* [chanting of prophecy], and *aisnéis di chennaib cnáme* [prophecy from the tips of the bones].[26] It is clear that behind these types of phrases lies the term *díchetal di chennaib*, the meaning of which had grown obscure but which translates, literally, as 'chanting from heads' or figuratively, as 'chanting from points'. We suspect that originally some ritual was involved but that the term was rendered acceptable to Christian culture through the rather innocuous interpretation of 'extempore composition'. But what was the basic ritual?

The compiler of Cormac's Glossary, in referring to 'prophecy from the tips of the bones,' appears to have envisaged *díchetal di chennaib* as poetic speech uttered over the tips of the practitioner's fingers. This strange posture seems to have some traditional warrant, for we read in an early ninth-century text that, as part of a charm against illness, one should 'insert the two fingers that are next to the little-finger into your mouth, each of them apart'.[27] It is difficult to say precisely what the relation is between such finger-posturing and Fionn's thumb, but it might be that ancient seers mimicked Fionn's characteristic act in this way. Perhaps this also explains the stress placed in some of the relevant texts on morsels of fish. Common measures used for such morsels were *ordu* [a thumb] and *mér* [a finger].[28] We recall that in the Lomhna story (p. 44) the severed head complained in rhetoric at not being given a morsel [*mír*] to eat when the fish was being divided.

A story written within a hundred years later is based on this, but it tells of the severed head of Fionn himself. According to it, after the hero's death, two fishermen of the Boyne took his head with them and were partaking of a meal of fish. Fionn's head spoke and demanded a portion [*mír*].[29]

Elsewhere in the old literature, we find heads of various dead warriors being hosted at feasts and chanting in verse – an Irish tradition which apparently had antecedents among the Continental Celts.[30] These latter, we are told by classical writers, valued and preserved the heads of slain enemies.[31] That all of this was part of ancient Fionn tradition seems very likely. We have already mentioned (p. 39) the instance of Fothadh Canainne telling Fionn that he could not attend an ale-feast without dead heads in his presence. Another account of the same Fothadh Canainne has his own severed head, after his death, chanting a poem.[32] These two examples in connection with Fothadh Canainne suggest a deeper significance to the motif, for in his background lie ideas concerning ancestry and the world of the dead (see pp. 38, 46). So was there once a ritual which involved seeking knowledge from the dead through use of heads?

Although never stated directly in our sources, there are certain indications that this was the case. Mediaeval Norse literature also has mentions of speaking heads, the best known being in the Ynglinga Saga. The god of wisdom Mímir, we are told, was killed by his enemies and his head was returned to his friends. Odin preserved the head, and it spoke to him relating much secret lore. Odin was, like Mímir, a figure closely associated with knowledge and poetry, so there is a parallel here between Germanic gods of wisdom and Fionn playing both roles – that of severed head and of its preserver. Scholars believe that this Norse lore of speaking heads was borrowed from the mantic tradition of the Gaelic people, and so the parallel may be no coincidence.[33]

There are other significant pieces of evidence also. A ninth-century Irish text describes how the head of a poet called Donn Bó was placed on a pillar at a feast held by his victorious foes. When asked to recite, the head 'turns its face to the wall of the house, so that it would be dark to him'.[34] This reference to darkness is at one with the long-standing custom of Gaelic poets seeking inspiration in dark surroundings – a custom which the Norse also encountered among the Gaelic people and borrowed into their own lore.[35] The dark surroundings are very likely the physical expression of the 'darkness' [obscurity] of the poetic speech itself, since the same word *dorcha* is used in both contexts. Donn Bó's action was typically that of a seer-poet, echoing ancient ideas of wisdom and inspiration.

It was natural to portray the head as the source of wisdom, and so it was a part of the poet's anatomy which was especially stressed in the old literature. One mediaeval Irish text has the mythical poet Amargen claiming that he is of the essence of all things, including very inspiration itself, 'the god who gives sense to the head'.[36] We have referred (p. 6) to the many instances of the Celts representing a deity by sculpted heads – this one part of the body standing for the whole on account of the function in question.

A ninth-century text has the mythical king Conn making prophecies concerning his successors – the original meaning of his name was 'sense', 'reason', or 'head'.[37] A vestige of a similar tradition is found in Welsh literature in a twelfth-century text, telling of the hero Pwyll, whose name meant 'sense' or 'reason', and who is described as *penn Annwvyn* [literally, head of the otherworld].[38] Of special relevance is a passage from another Welsh text of the same period. This tells of king Bendigeidfran, how he made prophecies and how his severed head was displayed for years at feasts. The head was as good company as ever he had been when alive, and as a result his court became known as 'the Hospitality of the Wondrous Head' [*Ysbydawt Urdaul Benn*].[39]

The motif here is more likely to be a direct borrowing from Irish tradition than a survival of indigenous Celtic lore in Wales. But, at any rate, the account echoes what may be the basic import of the idea, that is that the head of the all-knowing god presides over an otherworld feast, and that ritual participation in this feast could be achieved through fêting a dead head. The seers' purpose, of course, was to gain knowledge, and so a severed head, having access to the world of the dead, could be seen as an ideal oracle.

It appears, therefore, that the various mantic elements found in early Fionn lore can all be traced to archaic ideas concerning inspiration and wisdom – ideas which must have been associated with Fionn as personification of knowledge. Scattered elements of these survived into historical times, although, of course, deprived of their function by Christianity. These were elements, such as the thumb-sucking by the child deity, the fish swimming up from the nether regions, the ritual composition in darkness, the otherworld feast, and the speaking head. Such fragments could be joined together to form new narratives suitable to the portrayal of seer-poets, and so we have, in the first few centuries of Fionn literature, a combination which results in a severed head uttering rhetorics when it consumes a 'finger' or 'thumb' of fish. Fionn typified the ritual visit to the world of the dead ancestors in search of knowledge. So it is logical that he – originally the Celtic god of knowledge and in Irish tradition the ideal seer – could be represented equally as the speaking head and the communicator with that head.

Entering the Otherworld

The seers of ancient Ireland, like their counterparts in other cultures, sought inspiration from otherworld agencies. These agencies could make themselves present to the practitioner, either within himself or close at hand, and thus be the source of his art. Such an understanding is represented by Fionn's practices to generate insight, by his obscure but penetrating utterances, and, strikingly, by the voices which he is able to hear speaking inside the raths. Side by side with this subjective analysis, however, mantic ideas tend to situate the otherworld in some faraway place, to which the seer must go on a mystic journey. This is the ideology which lies behind the experience of trance, which is felt to be the means of undertaking the journey.

In Irish tradition, the otherworld-realm is that of the *sí* (usually translated as fairy-people, but a more accurate meaning would be the communal spirit world). It is obviously these spirits who are meant by the references to 'idol gods' in Cormac's Glossary. We have seen in the accounts of the tussle with Cúldubh how Fionn was supposed to have got wisdom by having his thumb for an instant inside a *sí*-dwelling. The word, in fact, was originally *side*, and referred both to these spirits and to the barrows in which they dwelt.[40] The *sí*-people are perennially associated with antiquity and with inspiration. They are also associated with the world of the dead.

The early Gaels found the country dotted with burial mounds of earlier inhabitants, and they tended to connect their own Celtic deities with these sites. This is particularly evident, as we have said (pp. 27f), in relation to the Boyne valley. So to the Irish the *sí*-people embodied both the world of the dead and the world of the gods, and were very suitable actors in the complex of ritual and narrative relating to Fionn. The notion that wisdom could be obtained by frequenting old burial mounds was common to many civilisations,[41] and there are good examples of it in the Celtic context. Welsh tradition has the hero Pwyll, whose name symbolises intelligence, sitting on a mound in order to make contact with the otherworld.[42] More appositely, we have mention in a ninth-century Irish text of a mound at the source of the Boyne. This mound, to which poetic inspiration is attributed in the text, is called 'the barrow of Nechtan's wife' [*síd mná Nechtain*].[43] Since Nechtan is another name for Nuadhu, this brings us back to the role of that deity in connection with Fionn. Nuadhu himself was said to have dwelt in the great barrow of *Brugh na Bóinne* [the Hostel of the Boyne], now known as Newgrange, and it is no surprise to find that the Pool of Féc, in which the salmon of knowledge resided, was situated in the Boyne river beside this very barrow.[44]

Nuadhu is referred to in some mediaeval sources as Nuadu Find *Feimin*, i.e. 'of Feimhean'. This Feimhean [earlier, Femen] was the name of an area in south Co. Tipperary and was the location of Fionn's adventure with Cúldubh. So it seems that when east Munster borrowed the Fionn lore from Leinster in the seventh to the eighth centuries, that lore still strongly connected Fionn with Nuadhu.[45] As we have said above (p. 54), the Cúldubh narrative itself is derived from a Leinster tradition which was already reshaped by the otherworld-foe motif, and so the hostility between Fionn and *sí*-beings was a persistent theme thereafter. Vestiges of the older idea of his visit to the otherworld in search of knowledge lived on side by side with the idea of conflict, however, as we have seen from the Cúldubh story itself.

The figure of a male-ancestor [old Fionn] as source of the knowledge had receded by the beginning of the literary period, and in his place we find other symbolic figures. One such is the *sí*-lady who has a goblet of mystical liquid to distribute. This type of figure for poetic inspiration was well-known in ancient cultures. We recall the Muses at the well of Aganippe, and Odin seeking a drink of mead from the giantess Gunnloth.[46] In the Fionn context, the image may have been derived from a native and co-existing stream of lore concerning inspiration, but it seems more likely that it was part of quite ancient seer tradition of him. There are even indications that women, as symbols of inspiration, were associated with Fionn at a time when he was still overtly identified as a god of wisdom.

These indications are linguistic. The epithet *fionn* is often used in the literature in connection with otherworld women. We might take this to mean 'fair-haired', but the same epithet is repeatedly used with the meanings 'sacred', 'poetical', and 'mystical';[47] so when we find the phrase 'words of fair-haired women' [*briathra ban bhfionn*] to describe poetry in one mediaeval text, we must assume that otherworld women were regarded as the givers of wisdom which had the quality *fionn*.[48] That this concept is ancient is shown by the name of Nuadhu's wife Bóinn [i.e. the river Boyne], which contains the idea of wisdom being given as a special cow [*bó fhind*] gives milk.[49]

In an unrelated mediaeval text *Inis Bó Finne* [the Island of the White Cow] off the west coast of Ireland is said to have been the location where a Munster seer Corc Duibhne was reared. He was washed each morning 'on the cow's back' [*for druim na bó*].[50] Again, we have the name *Bé Fhind* [fair lady] for a daughter of Bóinn and her husband Elcmhar [i.e. Nuadhu]. This Bé Fhind was, according to a twelfth-century text, accompanied by 'three times fifty fair women' [*trí caogaid findbhan*] in a *sí*-dwelling.[51] It is, therefore, logical to assume that Fionn himself, as the personification of wisdom and of the adjective in question, very likely had a long association with tutelary goddesses of this type. We find such a lady mentioned in the eighth-century version of his encounter with Cúldubh. When he came to the *sí*-dwelling of Feimhean, 'a woman met him with a wet vessel in her hand after distributing drink'.[52]

The mountain on which this otherworld dwelling was situated was known as *Sliabh na mBan bhFionn* [the Mountain of the Fair Women', now anglicised as Slievenamon].[53] Nor can there be any doubting that the vessel contained the drink of inspiration. A common metaphor in the old literature for poetic skill was 'fair stream' [*find-shruth*],[54] and it was claimed that flowing water could contain inspiration – particularly the water of the Boyne. Other sources tell us that the waters of the Boyne were impregnated with *imbas* at special times, so that those who drank from the river could gain wisdom.[55] A twelfth-century text has Fionn prophesying his own death after drinking from a well in his native territory:

> Fionn went on from Almhu until he reached Adharca Iuchbha in the Uí Fáilghe. He found a spring in the mound, and he took a drink from the spring. And he put his thumb under his tooth of knowledge, with the result that he sang through *teinm laída.* The approaching end of his time and his life was manifested to him.[56]

This is a late redaction, as evidenced by the stress on his 'tooth of knowledge' [*déd fis*]. The tooth is first mentioned in twelfth-century sources, and was an innovation based on the image of chewing – the source of knowledge being transferred from the thumb to it.[57] The idea that Fionn got an otherworld drink, however, appears to have long predated the text, for the writer has Fionn reciting a poem in which he refers to drinks he had received from various women. Among these is one Sadhbh daughter of Bodhbh, the otherworld ruler of *Síd ar Feimean* [i.e. the cairn on top of Slievenamon] into which Cúldubh ran from Fionn.[58]

One is somewhat bemused at the variety of themes relating to the manner of gaining wisdom in all this lore. The variety can best be explained by referring again to the original function of the lore and its context in seer-craft. Fionn is, in these narratives, a projection of the seers' own aspirations onto a personality; and the mystical perspective can accommodate a broad range of fanciful ideas without seeing them as contradictory. The central idea is that Fionn was the *mór-shaoi* [great sage],[59] and around that all other related imagery falls into place. A curious aspect of these developments is the actual poetry which was attributed to the hero.

We have mentioned the obscure rhetorics which the earlier accounts claim that he uttered after placing his thumb in his mouth. We have, however, no examples of poetic compositions as such being ascribed to Fionn prior to ninth- and tenth-century sources. The number of poems put in his mouth by these sources strongly suggests that it had been customary to do so for some time before that, although it is difficult to be specific on the question. The most antique kind of verse connected with his name is seasonal poetry. Five poems in all – these are believed to have been composed in or about the ninth century – became ascribed to Fionn at some time within the following two hundred years. They are gnomic in tone, comprised of short lines with a tendency for each line to describe an individual scene. The earliest (which might, in fact, be quite older than the ninth century) describes May Day and the coming of summer. There are fourteen quatrains in all, a good example being:

> The harp of the wood plays music,
> Melody provides complete peace;
> Colour has settled on every hill;
> Haze on the lake of full waters.[60]

Another poem is also in praise of summer. It contains seven quatrains, including the following:

> The hardy blackbird sings a strain,
> To whom the thorny wood is a heritage;
> The sad turbulent sea sleeps,
> The speckled salmon leaps.[61]

The other three poems describe winter. Two of them have four quatrains each, the other having only one. The most striking of these winter poems is quoted in a ninth-century gloss on a sixth-century text in praise of St Colmcille. The gloss is a reference to sea-tides and states the following:

> *Ut dixit Finn* [As Fionn said]
> I have a story for you –
> The stag bellows,
> The winter snows,
> The summer has gone.
>
> Wind high and cold,
> The sun low,
> Short its course,
> The sea running high.
>
> Very red the bracken –
> It has lost its shape,
> Sung as usual
> Is the wild goose's cry.
>
> Cold has seized
> The wings of birds,
> Icy season –
> That is my story.[62]

These season-poems, in their direct statement and pantheistic simplicity, resemble the verses attributed to the mythical Amargen when he arrived in Ireland (see p. 65). It seems as if they were put in the mouth of Fionn because of the impression of mystical insight inherent in them, and it is possible that they were attracted to this context by other (now lost) versification more intimately connected with the mantic lore of Fionn. Perhaps we have an echo of such lore in the attribution to Fionn of riddles in the tenth-century text concerning his courtship of Ailbhe, which we shall discuss in chapter 4.[63]

A second stratum of verse ascribed to our hero was being composed from the eleventh to the fourteenth centuries. In all, nine such poems survive.[64] They are long narratives, and deal with place-lore, with the exploits of his Fianna, and with prophecies. The seasonal poems probably provided the precedent, but there were additional reasons for the attribution to Fionn. Knowledge of history, description of habitat, and foretelling of the future were three functions of the Irish sage and were, therefore, appropriate to Fionn. As well as this, the versifying aspect of his wisdom was strengthened by the survival of the name of the mythical Leinster king Find File [originally a duplicate of the deity Fionn. (See pp. 28-9)]. The learned would have noticed the name Find File mentioned in the Leinster genealogies. Late mediaeval Fianna lore, indeed, created a new character from the name, a personage called Fionn File who was one of Fionn mac Cumhaill's retainers.[65] So the writer of one eleventh-century text had good precedents, and plenty of reasons, for enumerating our hero [*Find hua Baiscne*] among the twelve great poets of Ireland.[66]

Peripheral Worlds

Another *sí*-woman mentioned in the old literature is a certain Mongfhind or Mongfhionn [meaning, fair-haired]. She had, we are told, died at Halloween, and hence that tide was 'by the common people called the Festival of Mongfhionn, for she was powerful and a magician while alive, so that women of the rabble addressed petitions to her at Halloween'.[67] Her name, containing the word *fionn*, is redolent of our hero, and it is not surprising to find her connected with him in the literature. An eleventh-century text gives her name to Fionn's foster-mother, while another text written a century later mentions Mongfhionn as his wife and says that she reared eight hundred fianna warriors.[68] These are obviously fragments of an earlier portrayal, and it seems that she may have originally been an emanation from the deity Fionn. Her association with Halloween is significant, for several sources stress that festival in Fionn's context.

We have seen (p. 9) how he was believed to have saved the citadel of Tara from an otherworld foe on this, what was, in fact, the date of Tara's festival.[69] Perhaps of equal importance are references – in thirteenth-century sources, but doubtlessly based on earlier tradition – to prophecies which Fionn is supposed to have made at Halloween. One of these, made at the *sídh* of Éadar [i.e. Howth near Dublin], foretold St Patrick's coming and that some of his own Fianna would live to see it. Another, made at a place called Iubharghlenn foretold the end of the Fianna.[70]

The festival of *Samhain* (Halloween) marked the end of the old Celtic year and heralded in a new one, hence it is not surprising to find prophecies being made at this time. But the significance of such prophecies goes deeper, for this was the great festival of the otherworld when seers could play an intermediary role. 'The *sí*-dwellings of Ireland', we are told, 'were always open at *Samhain*, for nothing could ever be concealed in the *sí*-dwellings at *Samhain*.' This reference occurs in the mediaeval biography of Fionn (see chapter 4), and is in the context of a visit he made to such a dwelling.[71] A ninth-century text has him being presented with a stone and a chain of gold by the eponymous female spirit of the Shannon river at Ballyleague, Co. Longford. This account was told as a sequel to the battle of *Samhain*, fought between the kings of Ulster and Munster, with Fionn on the side of the latter.[72] Mention of *Samhain* in such contexts must be a petrified element from the old functional connection with Halloween.

So Halloween has shrunk into the background, and it is not specified as the time for the many contacts with the otherworld which are attributed to Fionn in the developed lore. Nevertheless, indications of his dealings with the world of the dead persisted in diffuse ways. For example a text dating from the tenth century, but now lost, was variously entitled *Uath Derce Ferna* and *Echtra Fhind i nDerc Ferna*.[73] This referred to an adventure [*echtra*] which Fionn had in the cave [*uath*] of Dearc Fearna, now known as the Cave of Dunmore in Co. Kilkenny. This is an enormous prehistoric cavern, and was reputed to be 'one of the three darkest places of Ireland'.[74]

It is clear from what we have been saying that the basis for Fionn's otherworld visits lies in the wisdom lore, but there can be no doubt that the perspective on such visits became very much altered with the passing of time. The more hostile atmosphere of the otherworld derives mostly from the fiery foe myth, but the definitely uncanny sense which attaches to the latter mediaeval accounts seems to come from the fianna context into which Fionn was fully domiciled.

These fianna groups consisted of young men living for a few years outside of normal society, and their peripheral social existence meant that the aura of adventure and of the bizarre attached to them. They lived in the wilderness, and were thus in contact with the animal world and the spirit world. They would gain a deep and intimate knowledge of the landscape and of the secrets it contained and was believed to contain. Thus a strong tradition of nature poetry and of onomastic lore became associated with Fionn and his Fianna, and the influence of this is found in almost all the literary texts concerning him from the Middle Ages onwards. General popular imagination played a large part in this development, but there must also have been an input from fianna groups themselves.

Fionn was the adopted symbol of such groups, and they would have projected their own esoteric imagery onto him. Several aspects of this imagery found permanent niches in the tradition. The many allusions to life in the wilderness and to hunting which we read in the literature of Fionn have an authentic ring to them. These allusions begin early. The eighth-century story of how the hero found his son Oisín after a year's separation (pp. 49f) has the scene set 'in a great wilderness' with Oisín 'cooking a pig'. The second version of the Cúldubh story has a pig being cooked for Fionn as his day's ration, when Cúldubh snatches it away from the *sí*-dwelling. Some other texts – outside the ambit of Fionn lore – also have the cooking of a pig as a contact point between the physical world and the otherworld. Boars, with stags, are portrayed as the favourite quarry of Fionn and his men, and there is a preternatural significance to some of this. An early eleventh-century text refers to a wonderful boar which came from Druim Leithe in present-day Co. Sligo and which wandered as far as Magh Lí in Co. Derry:

> Fionn was unable to do anything about it, until it fell in Magh Lí by a peasant who was kiln-drying. So that Fionn said:
>
> 'Not well have we fed our hounds,
> Not well have we driven our horses,
> Since a little peasant from a kiln
> Has killed the boar of Druim Leithe!'[75]

The ninth-century story of Lomhna (pp. 43ff) refers to the hunting-booth [*uarbhoth*] of Fionn. A much later (thirteenth-century) writer gives a minute description of how these booths were prepared, and this can be taken to reflect traditions about fianna practices:

> They went through the glen, and they got a secluded place beside the waterfall, and they made a beautiful booth, and they placed a brace with a ridge-pole on it, and a shelter over it. And Feargaire spread heather and fresh rushes on the floor, and he made a bed for every two of the Fianna and a bed for each hound.
>
> And while the servant [*giolla*] was making the fiann-booth they went hunting. The servant made a gravel-sided cavity in the ground beside the stream, and he let the stream in. And he kindled a fine fire, and he reddened stones in the fire so that everything would be prepared for his people.
>
> These returned from the hunt, and they made a cooking [*fulacht*] and a spitting [*inneonadh*]. And they bathed themselves and ate a meal after that.[76]

Earlier forms of the three key-words from that description [*gilla*, *fulacht*, *indiu*] are used for the open-air cooking of the fianna in the eighth-century story of Derg Corra (p. 46) – a factor which adds weight to our conviction that the details are of some antiquity. The remains of ancient cooking-pits, called *fulachta*, are found in many parts of Ireland.[77] They consist of a horseshoe-shaped mound of burnt stones, with the opening connected to a stream by a wooden trough. The method of cooking was to heat stones in a fire and drop them into the water in the trough so as to bring it to the boil. Cormac's Glossary, from the end of the ninth century, mentions the term *fulacht fian* and explains it as a cooking site used by fianna.[78] It may be that the glossator had the Fianna of Fionn in mind, for a twelfth-century text dealing with Fionn and his men describes how they brought many different types of meat and other foodstuffs to be cooked at *fulacht Féinne*, which clearly is intended to mean a cooking-apparatus of this particular fianna band.[79]

The historian Seathrún Céitinn, writing in the seventeenth-century, tells of how Fionn's men when out hunting used to make pits in the yellow clay of the heath, place the meat in these, and then put heated stones in the water on top of the meat to cook it.

> 'And these fires were so large', he says, 'that their sites are today in Ireland burnt to blackness, and these are now called *fulacht Fiann* by the peasantry.'[80]

Here, then, we have an aspect of outdoor life in ancient times which has become crystallised in tradition as an exclusive trait of Fionn's men.

Cormac's Glossary refers to another aspect of life in the wilderness under the word *esnad*. This was, the glossator writes, 'the name of the music that the fianna made at the *fulacht fian*'. The actual process he had in mind was probably a type of chant, and it seems to have had some ritual significance.[81] In several mediaeval texts there is mention of the *dord fiansa* or *dord fiann* in which Fionn's men are said to have engaged. This was a kind of hummed refrain, sometimes accompanied by the sound of their spearshafts clashing together. In the later mediaeval literature it is said to have been made by nine men until Fionn's time, but by thirty-one after that; and we are further told that it was made by drawing the lips together, that it had the power of lulling people to sleep, and that it was struck up by members of the Fianna, who were in danger, so as to call their comrades to their assistance.[82] Here again we can see the expropriation by the Fionn lore of an ancient hunter's custom, and of its development in an exclusive context.

In effect, whatever general connotations attached to the

word fianna in ancient times became concentrated in the mediaeval literature to mean Fionn's troop, and them only. So, to the lettered and unlettered alike, the only fianna who were of any importance were that increasingly formalised band – the Fianna of Fionn mac Cumhaill. Certain definite images and even certain aspects of life became, to the story-tellers and story-writers, the stuff which was proper to the realm of Fionn and his men and to them only. Thus a tendency arose to typify the tradition, almost on the lines of a modern cataloguer of folklore or researcher into literary themes.

We have referred above to the bedding prepared for the Fianna in the wilderness, according to a thirteenth-century text. Four hundred years later, Céitinn could write of this in an even more rounded-off manner:

> And when they had eaten their meal they used to start building their fiann-booths and arranging their beds, so that they prepared for sleep in that way. Of three things each one of them used to make a bed for himself. That is, the folliage of trees, moss, and fresh rushes – the foliage underneath on the ground, the moss over that, and the fresh rushes on top. And it is these things which are called in the old books 'the three tickings of the Fiann-band'.[83]

Similar tendencies can be noticed as regards the emphasis put on deer as quarry of the Fianna. That the imagery of deer-hunting had affected the fabric of the lore at an early date is shown by the names of certain Fianna heroes themselves. The twelfth-century biography of Fionn states that he was also called Demne in his youth. This name appears to be a corruption of *damne* [a little stag < **dam-nijo*].[84] Fionn's son was called Oisín [little fawn]; while Oisín's son was called Oscar, which name may mean deer-love.

As to how this close association with deer came about, two ideas are likely to have played major parts. One is the idea in early Irish myth that deities could go about in the shape of deer. The other is that hunters would assume the characteristics of their quarry as a magical means of gaining success in the hunt – possibly they also disguised themselves with antlers and hides for the practical purposes of getting within spearing range of the deer. Both ideas, indeed, are reflected in the strange story we have discussed (pp. 46ff) concerning Derg Corra, a figure redolent of the otherworld who has deer-like qualities and wears antlers.

The case of Oisín illustrates well how the imagery of deer-hunting could give rise to whole new narratives within Fianna lore. Originally his name was a simple diminutive or pet form of the word *os* [fawn], which was not unusual as a personal name but which very likely was suggested in this context by cerval imagery.[85] In time, the name was re-interpreted within the special perspective of Fionn tradition and against the specific background of the hostile otherworld foe called Dearg, of whom the deer-like Derg Corra himself was a derivative. Thus an eleventh-century verse tells us that the mother of Oisín was called Blái Derg:

> Blái used to come in the shape of a doe
> And join the *díbherg*-band
> So that Oisín was thus begotten
> Of Blái Derg in the shape of a doe.[86]

This motif may have been well-developed at the time, and there are some indications of what the actual narrative was like. The mother's full name was Blái of Derg, which suggests that she was understood to be the daughter of Dearg. The story of Oisín's birth may, therefore, have been an adaptation of the story of Fionn's own birth, but put in the context of his supposed deer-nature. Dearg, a stag-like figure, would thus have been the tyrant grandfather, and Fionn himself the lover of Dearg's daughter and by this means the father of Oisín.

We must depend on late folklore recensions of the story for its colouring. These, collected in the last two centuries from Ireland and Scotland, tell of how Fionn had a beautiful wife who was transformed by a jealous rival into the form of a deer. While in that form she gave birth to Fionn's son and raised him in the wilderness. Then one day while out hunting the hounds of Fionn chased a doe. The doe escaped, but she left behind her young boy. Through talking to him, Fionn discovered who he was, and he gave him the name Oisín.[87]

There is some variation in these oral tellings. Most versions say that it was a jealous fairy lady who turned Fionn's pregnant wife into a deer, but some others have it that Fionn begot Oisín on her when she was already a deer. One such Scottish version – collected in Mull in 1871 – states that a certain woman laid injunctions [*geasan*] on Fionn that he must marry the first female he met, so he fell in with the doe.[88] An Irish poem, written in Co. Clare in 1778, describes how the hounds of the Fianna hunted a beautiful bright-coloured doe. The description is put in the mouth of Oisín.

> Fionn caught the doe in time –
> Her fur and hair were fine –
> And he did not allow her to be hurt or injured
> By the tooth of a hound or the hand of a warrior.
>
> Having calmed the doe of her terror
> He was seized by a male urge,
> A scandalous story to tell
> That he put her in the role of a woman.

Oisín then goes on to relate how Fionn released the doe towards the mountains, and how she wandered from covert to covert until she reached 'Crumlin of the branches' (in Co. Dublin).

We translate again:

> When pregnancy reached its fruition thus
> And her parturition and her time came
> She bore me instead of a calf
> Amongst the branches and the trees.

The doe suckled the child, and he grew up strong and very athletic, until Fionn discovered him one day while hunting.[89]

It has been claimed that these latter versions, which entail bestiality, are more primitive. There are, however, indications that this is not so and that the transformation of the woman into a deer is the original motif. A twelfth-century poem tells of a maiden called Aige [literally, hind] being put in the shape of a deer by 'otherworld sprites' [*siabra side*] and being killed while in that shape by a fianna band,[90] so the idea of an innocent woman being thus transformed by hostile forces is old in Irish tradition. On the other hand, the eleventh-century reference to Blái Derg becoming Oisín's mother reveals that she deliberately assumed the form of a doe.

Gaelic lore constantly represents deer as associated with otherworld beings or as disguises for them, and so this would have been an obvious way for an otherworld woman to make advances to Fionn the great hunter. A text of about the fourteenth century has such a woman putting herself into the form of a doe in order to lure him to a lonely place and then reassuming her role as a beautiful lady and beseeching him to recover treasure from a lake for her. She did this in order to turn him into an old man by magic (see p. 23).

There are several accounts in the mediaeval literature which describe the daughter of Dearg as hostile to Fionn and his Fianna,[91] so that there was a tradition of Fionn having to contend with such a female otherworld foe, and we can see how this lore brings us back to the hostile figure of Dearg. That idea, interconnected with the tyrant-grandfather myth, would naturally attract the plot of amorous involvement with the daughter of Dearg. We notice that the lady's hostility towards Fionn – a complication in this extension of the tyrant-grandfather myth – had not entirely disappeared in mediaeval tradition, though it has in later folklore.

The story of the deer-mother, a rationalisation of Oisín's name, thus provides us with an early example of a process which is repeated again and again in Fianna tradition, that is that certain basic plots and motifs are continually recast in new moulds. The combination of narrative elements, which were formed into a unit in the Old Irish period, provided a rounded and identifiable figure of Fionn, with enough dramatic content to ensure the tradition's survival. Its development also, was assured.

Radiating out from this dominant core through the Middle Ages are concentric circles, ever-widening and drawing into their vortex new ranges of narrative.

4.

The Hero's Life

It is clear from what we have been saying that a definite series of adventures were coming to be associated with Fionn in early mediaeval Irish story-telling. So it is not surprising that the idea of compiling a general account of the great hero gained vogue. One such account was already developing towards biographical form in the tenth century, for from then we have a poem which tells of how he was born and grew up to gain possession of Almhu [the Hill of Allen in Co. Kildare].[1] From the early twelfth-century we have a mixed prose and poetry text of great importance, called *Macgnímartha Find* [the Boyhood-Deeds of Fionn].[2] And finally, from around the year 1200, we have a third text, which is, in fact, a conflation of the foregoing two. This is called *Fotha Catha Cnucha* [the Cause of the Battle of Castleknock].[3]

Once a standard portrayal of our hero's life until manhood was established, his personality became more rounded and the need was felt to fill out further details of his career and, indeed, of how his life would end. So we find many such details described in texts from the same period, details of which, when put together, build up into something approaching an integrated account of Fionn, the pseudo-historical champion.

Begetting and Destiny

The Almhu poem, of twenty-two quatrains, occurs in the large compilation known as the 'Metrical Placelore'. Its purpose is, therefore, to explain the history of the Hill of Allen. That hill was situated in the Uí Fáilghe territory, and was stressed in various early texts, so it is obvious that it was a location of some importance to Leinster culture. The first line of the poem calls the place 'a fort of the Fianna' [*les na Fían*]. Originally, we are told, it belonged to a druid called Nuadhu the Great, and he painted his fortress white with alum [*almhu*], whence the name. This strange motif of bright colouring connects the hill with Fionn's divine grandfather Nuadhu Find and suggests that the place was really a cultic centre of the deity Fionn himself. We have seen (p. 28f) that a different hill in Co. Kildare, Knockaulin [*Ailend*] was associated with Find File, so the likelihood is that the Hill of Allen was the Uí Fáilghe site of the cult – their particular Find being, of course, Fionn mac Cumhaill.

The poem goes on to tell us that the druid Nuadhu left the fortress to his son Tadhg. Here again the Uí Fáilghe origins of the lore surface, for we are told that this Tadhg was the druid of Cathaoir Mór, an ancient Leinster king who had controlled Tara and who was claimed by the Uí Fáilghe as belonging to their line.[4] Tadhg, at any rate, had a daughter called Muirne. She was demanded by Cumhall, but Tadhg refused him, and then Cumhall carried her off by force and possessed her for a year. Tadhg, heartbroken, went to Conn 'of the Hundred Battles' and got a banishing order against Cumhall. As a result, the abductor found himself engaged in the battle of *Cnucha* [Castleknock in Co. Dublin], against Conn's forces. In this encounter Cumhall was killed, but,

> Nine hours before the battle was fought
> Was begotten the man of good fortune,
> On the daughter of Tadhg the bright-sided
> Fionn the true *féinnidh* was begotten.

After the slaying of her lover, Muirne came to Almhu, but her father now threatened to kill her before she gave birth. She was protected by Conn, to whom she came at Tara; and he had her escorted to Cumhall's sister Bodhmhall, who lived with her husband Fiacail Fí son of Conchenn at Temhair Mairge [a peak of the Slievemargy hills between Cos. Laois and Kilkenny].

Thereafter was born Fionn the honoured,
King of the Fianna – great his valour –
For nine years precisely
Was he the king-*féinnidh* of Ireland.

Fionn demanded of Tadhg of the towers
A price for killing great Cumhall –
Battle without respite, without delay,
Or to get single combat.

Tadhg, since he could not face battle
Against the true prince,
Abandoned to him – it sufficed him –
As it was all Almhu.

We can see from this how the original myth of the tyrant-grandfather (pp. 8ff) has been transformed and conditioned by the passage of time. Nuadhu, properly the grandfather, has been replaced by his son Tadhg, which is obviously a corruption of the tradition. Secondly, Fionn does not, in fact, kill the grandfather (see p. 20 above), but merely takes his possessions from him. And thirdly the mythic Uí Néill king, Conn of the Hundred Battles, has intruded into the narrative. We notice that he reigns in Tara, but this conciliation of the Leinstermen's tradition with their deadly enemies can hardly have taken place long before the text was written. It is difficult to imagine how Leinster ambitions to regain the Boyne Valley would have waned sufficiently prior to the ninth century in order to allow such a formulation to be accepted. In fact, although the prose text on the battle of Castleknock [*Fotha Catha Cnucha*] is much later in date,[5] its author was aware of the unsuitability of the situation, and he tried to reverse it.

In accordance with earlier Leinster sources, he has Cathaoir Mór in the kingship of Tara and Conn occupying 'the territory of a prospective king' [*ferand rigdomna*]. Again, this text is more precise regarding the basic plot, saying of Cumhall:

> He also like everybody else was seeking the maiden. Tadhg gave him a refusal, because he knew that it was through him that he would be divided from Almhu.

Even this writer, however, cannot escape from the Uí Néill contamination of the story, for he says that Cumhall was 'the king-*féinnidh* of Ireland under Conn's control' and that 'Cumhall and Conn's father had the same mother'. The text adds somewhat to the drama of the narrative. Cumhall's arrogance is softened by having him vainly offer 'everything in compensation saving only the woman'. On the other hand, it darkens the portrayal of Tadhg, saying that after Cumhall was killed he wanted his people to burn his own pregnant daughter. But he feared Conn. After the latter had sent Muirne to Bodhmhall and her husband Fiacail Fí at Temhair Mairge, she gave birth to Fionn:

> The boy was reared by them after that, until he could make raids on everyone who was a foe to him. He then proclaimed battle or single combat against Tadhg, or else the full honour-price of his father to be given to him. Tadhg said that he would allow him his [Fionn's] own judgement therein. The judgement was given, and this is the judgement: that Almhu as it was be ceded to him in forfeiture, and Tadhg to leave it.

So Tadhg went to live in another territory of his, while 'Fionn went to Almhu, and he dwelt in it, and it was his principal fortified residence for as long as he lived'.

This text, as we have said, is a conflation of the tenth-century Almhu poem and the twelfth-century Boyhood-Deeds. The account of the actual battle given in it is wholly borrowed from the latter source and should thus be discussed in that context. The Boyhood-Deeds is a text comprising about 2,500 words,[6] but less than a fifth of it (the opening portion) is concerned with the hero's conception and birth. The most striking aspect is the fact that the grandfather-plot is excluded. There is no mention of Tadhg mac Nuadhat, and a quite different explanation is given for the cause of the battle of Castleknock. Cumhall son of Tréanmhór, we are told, was of the Uí Tairsigh sept, and he was married first to a lady called Torba and then to Muirne. Rivalry developed between him and a champion of the Luaighne sept called Uirghriu 'concerning the fianna-affairs [*fianaigecht*] and the chief-stewardship of Ireland'. This is obviously the indigenous

Leinster lore concerning Uí Tairsigh support for the Uí Fáilghe in their struggle against the Luaighne – a martial sept connected with the Uí Neill – which we have already discussed (pp. 30f, 45). The reference to the stewardship of Ireland, of course, must reflect a later stage in the lore, when the scope of Fionn's Fianna was extended to cover the entire country.

So, according to this text, the battle of Castleknock was fought between the forces of Cumhall and those of Uirghriu. Prominent in the latter's army was a character called Dáire Derg (whom we are told was also known as Morna) and his son Aedh. A warrior called Luchet destroyed one of Aedh's eyes in the fighting, and so Aedh became known as Goll [one-eyed]. Goll then killed Luchet. We recognise the *débris* of the Lugh myth. But this is a very diffuse reflection of that myth – an echo of the one-eyed burner recension such as would develop in oral transmission. As we have seen, the Almhu poem has a more direct version of the grandfather-plot, along the Nuadhu lines and clearly based on learned Leinster redaction. The Leinster genealogists moderated the plot deliberately, removing the cyclopic imagery of the grandfather because it would compromise the good name of Nuadhu, who was an essential prestige-figure in the genealogical system.

The text also tells us that 'Cumhall fell in the battle by Goll, son of Morna, who carried off his spoils and his head, on account of which there was a hereditary feud between Fionn and the sons of Morna'. Then seven quatrains, which 'the *senchaid* [reciter of lore] sang' concerning the battle and the feud, are quoted. These quatrains seem to predate, and to be the basis for, the prose-description. On the question of the feud, they state that Fionn and Goll later made peace and that this peace lasted until a quarrel arose over a pig (see p. 161 below).

Returning to Fionn's conception, the text of the Boyhood-Deeds continues:

> Pregnant it was that Cumhall left his wife, Muirne, and she bore a son, and a name was given to him, that is 'Demne'. Fiacail, son of Conchenn, and Bodhmhall the druidess and

> the Grey One [Liath] of Luachair came to Muirne, and they took away the boy, for his mother dared not keep him. Muirne afterwards slept with Gleor Red-Hand, king of the Lamhraighe, whence is the saying 'Fionn son of Gleor'. Bodhmhall, however, and the Grey One, and the boy with them, went to the forest of Sliabh Bladhma. The boy was reared there in secret. That was indeed necessary, for many was the sturdy bitter youth, and many the venomous hostile *féinnidh* of the Luaighne warriors and of the sons of Morna who were searching for the boy.

Coming of Age

The whole sweep of Fionn's youth is covered in the Boyhood-Deeds. While threatened by his foes, we are told, he was reared by the two female *féinnidh*s Bodhmhall and the Grey One. At the end of six years, his mother came to visit him, since she had heard that he was in that place and was afraid of what the sons of Morna might do to him. In the forest of Sliabh Bladhma [Slieve Bloom in Co. Laois], she found him asleep in a hunting booth [*fianbhoth*]. 'And then she takes the boy in her bosom and presses him to her'. She recited quatrains to him, of which the opening line only is quoted, 'Sleep in the slumber of tranquillity'. She departed then, leaving him in the charge of the woman-warriors until he learned to hunt. A colourful little scene follows:

> The boy went out alone another day, and he saw ducks on a lake. He hurled a dart at them which cut the feathers and the wings off of one, so that she fainted. And then he seized her and took her with him to the hunting-booth. And that was Fionn's first chase.

The author of the Boyhood-Deeds was in no doubt regarding the Leinster provenance of Fionn lore, and he situated the main actions in the Midland area. The forest of Slieve Bloom is where the hero finds refuge in his youth. This mountainous terrain was the most apt area of wilderness contiguous to the Uí Fáilghe lands, and so when Fionn went through his period of estrangement from society this is where he lurked. The area might also have been a favourite one for the fianna or *Männerbunde* of ancient Leinster, so there could well be a double reason for situating the young Fionn there. There are indications, indeed, that the Boyhood-Deeds is dealing in some respects with a more original form of the tradition than that found in the Almhu poem. We have no mention here of Conn or any other Uí Néill overlord. Some scholars have opined that the Boyhood-Deeds belong to a period earlier than the twelfth century, which is the conventional dating. The most likely explanation is that it is, indeed, a compilation of that period, but that it incorporates some passages which were written down perhaps as early as the ninth or tenth century. These may entail prose narratives as well as verse ones. For example the next episode is cited from Fionn's youth:

> He went with craftsmen while a fugitive from the sons of Morna, and was with them around the Crotta [i.e. Galtee Mountains in Co. Tipperary]. These were their names: Futh, Ruth, and Regna of Magh Feadha, Teimheal, Ailbhe, and Roghein. A disease came over him then, so that he became mangy, and so he was called Demne the Bald. There was a reaver among the Leinstermen at that time. He was Fiacail son of Codhna. This Fiacail happened upon the craftsmen in Fiodh Gaibhle, and he killed them all except Demne alone.

We are then told that Fionn spent some time with Fiacail in the reaver's house at Seiscenn Uarbheoil, a Leinster marsh – probably in present-day Co. Wicklow.[7] His two female guardians went south to that place, and took him back to Slieve Bloom. The strange character, here presented as a reaver, we have met before. In the Almhu poem he was described as son of Conchenn and husband of Fionn's aunt Bodhmhall. He lived at Slievemargy, and the present text makes it clear that his residence at Seiscenn Uarbheoil was a temporary one.

The passage itself, with its reference to Fionn's mange, is so cryptic as to lead us to suspect that the writer had read it somewhere and had failed to grasp its meaning. First of all, it is significant that the young Fionn was in the company of craftsmen [*aes cerda*] – a usual designation for members of the poetic profession. Secondly, the fact that a list of definite names is given to these six poet-like figures suggests that the story predates the text. Thirdly, such sudden baldness is mentioned as being inflicted on other characters in mediaeval Irish literature as a result of contact with the otherworld. Fionn's nickname 'the Bald' [*Mael*] is, in fact, a common epithet applied to druids in the old literature, and reflects the practice these men had of tonsuring their heads.[8] All the indications, therefore, are that here again we have a ritual of ancient seers being personified in the figure of Fionn. To the compiler of the Boyhood-Deeds the meaning of this narrative was obscure, which was why he could only give it in garbled form.

So in this case a druidic baldness was taken to reflect Fionn's contact with the otherworld, just as his fair hair did. In fact, he has his name changed from Demne to Fionn on account of the colour of his hair in a passage just a few lines further on. According to this, he went alone on three consecutive days to the plain of the river Liffey and overcame all the youths who were hurling there. The youths asked him his name and he told them it was Demne. They reported this to the man who owned the fortress there, and he told them to kill the stranger, if they could. But they said that they were unable to do that:

> 'What does he look like?' said he.
> 'A handsome and fair *finn* [fionn] youth', they said.
> 'So Demne's name is Fionn', he said.
> On account of that the youths used to call him Fionn.

Next day he came again and joined in their game. They flung all their hurley-sticks at him, but he charged them and knocked seven of them to the ground before returning to Slieve Bloom. At the end of a week he came to a 'lake' there on the plain of the Liffey,[9] and, when challenged by the youths, he drenched nine of them in the water. After he had gone back to Slieve Bloom again, everyone was enquiring as to who drenched the boys. 'Fionn,' the youths said. And so the name stuck to him.

We have already discussed this passage (p. 22) and have argued that the motif of naming in it pertains to the original function of Fionn as a character symbolising knowledge and showing the mark of the otherworld in his shining hair. It may be that, together with the practice of tonsuring, the druids ritually dyed their hair white.

The account of how Fionn overcomes the rival boys is one of several parallels with another Irish biography of a hero's youth – the deeds of the young Cúchulainn.[10] The latter also blocks a hail of hurley-sticks which are flung at him, and then lays low a large number of his opponents on the field. Such parallels might indicate that the author of the Boyhood-Deeds of Fionn was under the influence of the ninth-century text concerning Cúchulainn. But the numerous differences in detail between the description of Cúchulainn and that of Fionn suggest that the texts are independent of each other and derive separately from a genre of lore about heroic youths.

The next episode in the Boyhood-Deeds concerns how the young Fionn, accompanied by his two female guardians, saw a herd of wild deer on the slope of Slieve Bloom. One of the women regretted that they could not capture a deer. Fionn said that he could do it, 'and he ran after them and caught two of the deer and brought them with him to the hunting-booth [*fianbhoth*]'. After that he used to do the hunting for the two women. This account again resembles the Cúchulainn text, where the hero captures a wild stag and leads it home tied to his chariot.

The Boyhood-Deeds of Fionn now describes how his guardians told him to leave the area as he was in danger from the sons of Morna. So he headed southwest and arrived at Loch Léin [the large Lake of Killarney in Co. Kerry]. There he entered the service of a local king. He was so great a hunter that his employer began to suspect his real identity, and so he departed from there and went to another king in Kerry. One day, when that king was playing chess, he was prompted by Fionn and as a result won seventeen consecutive games. The king enquired who he was, and Fionn answered untruthfully that he was 'the son of a peasant of the Luaighne of Temhair'. The king, however, saw through this deception and realised that Fionn was hiding behind the names of his own enemies.

'No,' said the king, 'you are the son whom Muirne bore to Cumhall!'

He then ordered Fionn away, fearing that the youth would be killed while under his protection.

The series of separate adventures continues. Coming to Cullen [in Co. Tipperary], Fionn arrives at the home of a celebrated smith called Lóchán. The smith has a beautiful daughter called Cruithne who falls in love with the hero and sleeps with him. Then he asks the smith to make two javelins for him, and takes his leave. Lóchán tells him to avoid the road where lurks a savage pig which has ravaged the centre of the province of Munster. But, despite the warning,

> The lad happened to go on the road where the pig was. The pig attacked him then. He made a cast of his javelin at it, so that it [the javelin] passed through it and left it lifeless.

Hence a place in Munster, the text tells us, was called *Sliabh Muice* [the Mountain of the Pig]. Fionn brought the pig's head to the smith in compensation for the daughter's honour, and then went his way.

Using a particular placename, the author has written this episode to a preconceived pattern of how the hero must kill a monstrous creature as his first great feat. The presentation here lacks high drama, however, and it appears quite flat when compared to Cúchulainn's killing of the great hound, the leash of which takes nine men to hold and which comes at night upon Cúchulainn as a little boy. It is difficult to avoid the conclusion that the author of the Boyhood-Deeds was trying to fill out, and work up, into an epical narrative an amount of scattered traditions which he had heard about Fionn.

The young hero next sets out for Connacht, seeking Criomhall, the brother of his father Cumhall. On the way he meets a woman shedding tears of blood and vomiting blood. She explains to him that her only son has been killed by a huge warrior. The son was called Glonda, and we are told that certain place names are based on his name. Similarly, *Áth mBéldeirge* [the Ford of the Red-Mouthed One] is called after that woman. 'Fionn then went after the warrior, and they fought, and he slew him.' The defeated warrior was called the *Liath Luachra*, and he was the one who had dealt the first wound to Cumhall at the battle of Castleknock. On that occasion he had also taken a treasure-bag belonging to Cumhall, and Fionn now recovered that bag.[11]

The name of this hostile warrior presents a problem, as it is the same as that given to one of Fionn's female guardians on Slieve Bloom. This is a clear illustration of how the author was trying, and not quite succeeding, to assemble diverse elements into an integral text. In this case the mistake seems to be in applying the name to the female guardian, for the Liath Luachra is mentioned several times as a male warrior inimical to Fionn in other mediaeval texts.[12] His name means the Grey One of Luachair, that is, the Logher area in west Cork and south Kerry. This region belonged to the western Eoghanacht sept who were at odds with the eastern Eoghanacht in the seventh to the eighth centuries. The latter, as we have said (p. 41), adopted lore of Fionn from the Leinstermen, and this is the probable explanation of why a warrior from Logher should be portrayed as a foe of Fionn.

After a brief visit to Criomhall, who is lying low in the Connacht forest with the remnants of Cumhall's fianna band, Fionn heads east to the Boyne river in order to learn the craft of poetry. 'For he dared not to remain in Ireland unless he undertook poetry, for fear of the sons of Uirghriu and the sons of Morna.' This reference is to the sanctuary from injury which poets enjoyed because of their sacred profession.[13] The idea is that Fionn wished to become a poet for his own security, but we can be sure that the real background to this reference lies in the image of Fionn as being himself a great and ideal seer. The episode of the salmon of the Boyne follows, which we have already discussed (p. 56). Again, and now for the third time, his name is changed from Demne to Fionn. The author was obviously experiencing some confusion in his efforts to bring various fragments together.

Having learned the three qualities of a poet (see p. 61), Fionn went on to another sage, Cethern son of Fintan, to study the craft of poetry further with him. An interesting, but quite complicated, story ensues.

A beautiful otherworld girl called Éile resided in Sídh

Éile [now the hill of Croghan in Co. Offaly]. Many of the men of Ireland had come to woo her at *Samhain* [Halloween] when the otherworld dwellings were always open, but a misfortune had befallen every wooer, that is one of his company would be slain by an unknown agency. Now Fionn becomes involved in this mystery:

> Cethern the poet went to woo the girl, like everyone else. Fionn, however, thought it a bad idea for Cethern to go on that undertaking. They formed three bands to go on the wooing, with nine in each band. When they went to the *sí*-dwelling a man of his company was slain in their midst and it was not known who had slain him. Oircbhél the Poet was the name of the man who was killed there – the Grave of Oircbhél in Cluain Fota is called after him. They disbanded then, and Fionn departed from them and he did not return.
>
> This incident was grievous to Fionn and he thought it a great disgrace.

Next, Fionn goes to the home of Fiacail son of Conchenn at Slievemargy. This character we have met already in the Almhu poem as a protector of Fionn's mother before the hero was born, and in this text he has occurred as a reaver from Leinster whom the boy Fionn had encountered in Munster and had stayed with for a while. Fionn now explains to Fiacail how the man had been slain at Sídh Éile. Fiacail tells him to go and sit down between the mountain peaks in the territory of Logher which are known as *Dá Chích Anann* [the Two Paps of Anu]. We notice that this is in the hostile west Munster region, and we are told that on each of the two peaks was an otherworld stronghold:

> When Fionn was there between them at Halloween he saw the two *sí*-dwellings opened around him, that is the two fortresses – their magic mists [*fé fiada*] having dissolved. He saw a great fire in each of the two fortresses, and he heard a voice from one of them which said:
>
> 'Is your sweet food good?'
>
> 'Good indeed', said a voice in the other *sí*-dwelling. A question:

'Shall anything be brought from us to you?'

'If that be given to us, something will be brought to you after that.'

While Fionn was there he saw a man come from the *sí*-dwelling, with a kneading trough in his hand and a well-done pig on it, and a cooked calf and a bunch of wild garlic for that Halloween. The man went by Fionn towards the other *sí*-dwelling. Fionn made a cast of the spear of Fiacail son of Conchenn. He had brought it south from Sliabh Mairge. Fionn then said:

'If the spear from us has reached anyone, even if he live after it, I think this is vengeance for my comrade!'

He fled, and at once heard lamentation and great cries from the *sí*-dwelling, saying:

By the javelin Biorgha on the Berbha [river Barrow]
Aedh son of Fidach has fallen,
By the spear of Fiacail son of Codhna
Fionn has slain him outside the dwelling!

Fiacail comes to Fionn at the Paps of Anu and brings him back to Leinster. Fionn then goes to Sídh Éile and seizes a woman from there to hold as a hostage for the return of the javelin. He allows her to return to the *sí*-dwelling after she promises to retrieve it for him. She recites a verse on the venom of the javelin, saying that, unless it is returned, the land will be seized by plague. So it is thrown out to Fionn. He brings it back to Fiacail, who tells him to keep it because of the feat he has performed with it. Fiacail further says that the man whom Fionn has slain was the killer of those who used to come to woo Éile, 'because he himself loved her'.

This episode represents a type of Fionn story which has him killing by a spear-cast a hostile otherworld being at Halloween. This story-type must have been circulating rather freely in the mediaeval lore, for there are great divergencies between it and other versions (see pp. 53ff). Originally a borrowing from the Lugh myth, it had attained a maximum degree of independence in the narrative stream and the circumstances surrounding the feat could vary greatly.

Fiacail has arranged to meet a fianna group at Inbher Colptha [the estuary of the Boyne], and Fionn decides to go with him.

> Twelve balls of lead were around the neck of Fiacail so as to check his speed, he was so fast. He would drop one ball of them at a time, and Fionn collected them. And Fiacail was running no faster than Fionn was running. They reached Inbher Colptha, and Fionn gave him his leaden balls, the twelve, and he was pleased.

The method which Fiacail had of allowing others to keep pace with him is striking and is, no doubt, based on some humorous motif from the popular culture of the time.[14] It provides a good backdrop against which to describe the great swiftness of Fionn; and one is reminded again of Cúchulainn, who in his youth travelled on a journey casting his javelin into the air and catching it always before it touched the ground. As in the other examples, the resemblance seems to be patterned by tradition rather than by direct derivation.

When the fianna group encamps at Inbher Colptha for the night, Fionn is put on watch [*foraire*]. He is told to wake a *féinnidh* if he notices anything out of place. An impressive scene now materialises:

> When Fionn was there for a period of the night he heard a shriek from the north. But he did not wake a *féinnidh*. He went alone towards the shriek, to Sliabh Slángha [Donard Mountain in Co. Down].
>
> When Fionn was there in Ulster at the hour of midnight he came upon three women before him, at a green mound, with horns of *sí*-women. As they were crying on that mound they used to all put their hands upon the mound. They fled into the *sí*-dwelling before Fionn then. Fionn caught one woman of them as she was going into Sídh Slángha. Fionn snatched her brooch out of her cloak. The woman went after him and besought him to give her the brooch of her cloak, and she said that it was not fit for her to go with a blemish into the *sí*-dwelling. And she offered a reward.

The text breaks off here, and we are left speculating as to the outcome of the particular episode, and, more importantly, as to the manner in which the author would have Fionn become leader of the Fianna and thus regain his father's position. It is hard to imagine that the text would not have included some version of the saving of Tara from a burner by Fionn – the event which is portrayed so dramatically in *Acallamh na Senórach*, an anthology from the same period (see p. 9 and chapter 5).

The Intrinsic Youth Narrative

In order to put the Boyhood-Deeds text in its proper context, reference must be made to some other sources which deal with the youth of Fionn. We have suggested that the text's author was selecting various data from the living oral tradition of his time and trying to make these consistent with each other. This is further indicated by a few verses which predate the Boyhood-Deeds text and may, indeed, have been source material for it:

> By Caoilte the swift-footed and chariot-like
> Fothadh Findairgdech fell;
> Aedh son of Fidach by the hand of Fionn,
> By the spear of Fiacail son of Conchenn,
> Due to the love – I conceal nothing –
> Which he gave to the maiden of Brí Éile;
> By the same spear Fionn killed Cúldubh –
> Cúldubh son of Fidgha the very fair;
> By that spear was killed long ago
> Fair Deicill the Vassal of the Érainn.[15]

Two of these events we have already referred to – that concerning Caoilte (p. 49) and the Cúldubh story (pp. 53ff). The episode which the author of Boyhood-Deeds selected – that of Aedh son of Fidach – is a variant of the fiery foe tradition and, therefore, is a double of the killing of Cúldubh. The story of Deicill, now lost, might also have been a variant.

Since we do not have the full text, we cannot say whether the author deliberately selected just one version of the story-type or whether he would accommodate other versions in his narrative. It is clear, at any rate, that he was rather discriminating in practice. We have seen that he gave a secondary explanation for the cause of the battle of Castleknock, omitting the grandfather theme and replacing it with a contest between Cumhall and Uirghriu for the leadership of the Uí Néill king's army. Here the less ancient tradition takes precedence. But, conversely, he edited aggressive aspects out of the Boyne salmon story, as then current, in order to keep it in line with the older Nuadhu tradition. Both of these cases suggest that the author disliked the idea of hostility between Fionn and his grandfather and that he re-arranged his narrative accordingly.

Furthermore, his packing together of disconsolate elements stands in contrast to his omission of some details which appear to have been very popular in oral tradition at the time. For instance, we have a poem composed in the twelfth century by a certain Gilla an Choimdhedh,[16] which diverges in certain respects from what is said in the Boyhood-Deeds.

Gilla an Choimdhedh first states that the hero's original name was Glaisdíge and that it was the sons of Morna who called him Fionn. His mother's name is here given as Torba, daughter of Ech of the Érainn of Cermna. He spent the first seven years of his life as a refugee in Connacht, and his first feat was to run around the circle of that province in one day. His first hunt was at Slieve Bloom, where the quarry was seven deer. Then, at eight years of age, he went to Tara and slew Aillén who came with fire and music:

> 'A timbrel for sleep!' said everybody,
> At each Halloween was the usual deed,
> Every year, continual provocation,
> The candle was burning brightly.

We are told that the reason why Fionn went to learn poetry from Cethern mac Fintain was 'for fear of Conn the sword-fierce'. Then we are told that the fianna brought Fionn to avenge the death of Oircbhél at Brí Éile, and that he did so at the Paps of Anu when he killed the grandson of Fidgha with the spear of Fiacail mac Conchenn. Halloween was also the date of this encounter. He then ran a race with Fiacail to

Inbher Colptha and went to Sliabh Slángha in Ulster, but we are told nothing of his adventure there except that a *sí*-woman gave him 'a vessel all of gold and silver'. In all, this version tells us little besides what we know from the Boyhood-Deeds text, but it does show that there was some variation in the stories referred to.

This variation becomes clearer when we examine a lay composed a little before the year 1400.[17] It contains eighteen quatrains and gives a potted version of Fionn's birth and upbringing. He was born to Muirne, a daughter of Tadhg the Great son of Nuadhu, and was called Glaisdíge. His foster-mother Bodhmann took him away to a secret hill and he was nursed 'in the hollow of a tall ivy-covered tree'. Therefore, he was nicknamed 'the Lad of the Hollow' [*Giolla an Chuasáin*]. One day, when left alone eating pork, he had a dangerous experience:

> A polecat passed by the side of the wood and came near to the hollow. It came towards the smell of the slice (of pork), which caused the child no small terror. He closed his grip on the polecat – it was a great portent of courageous encounters – he remained choking the polecat from early morning to eventide. Bodhmann came to inspect the child, like any doe unwearied. When she found the polecat choked, Bodhmann thought the first feat was good.

The polecat is skinned then and its hide put about Fionn as a good augury of the chase. He is nursed by Bodhmann until nine years old, and then brought by her to the fair of the king Conn at Tailtiu (Teltown near Tara). There he plays 'three games of the loop [hurling]' amongst the boys there. Conn asks, 'Who is that little fair-haired fellow [*fionn*] who is winning the goal against the handsome youths of Ireland?'

Bodhmann tells the king that he is 'Fionn himself, descendant of Baoiscne' and that he is 'the prophesied one of old who has come to you from the hunting-booth [*fianbhoth*]'. The young hero then has to race away from the fair, pursued by sword-edges, and does not stop until he reaches Fiodh Gaibhle [the ancient forest of Feeguile near the Hill of Allen].

The topography here seems to be the proper one for the story, and it accords strikingly with what we have been saying of the early Fionn tradition. He comes to Teltown, clashes with the retainers of the Uí Néill king, and then has to go for sanctuary to the territory of the Uí Fáilghe.

Redactions of the youth biography of Fionn have been collected from all over Ireland and Gaelic Scotland in the past two hundred years.[18] The basic plot in all of these shows remarkable consistency, focusing, as it does, on a number of definite episodes. It is prophesied to a certain tyrant that if his daughter gives birth to a boy-child, that child will take his power from him.

The warrior Cumhall gains access to the girl and she becomes pregnant by him. The tyrant causes a great battle to be fought against Cumhall, in which that warrior is killed. The tyrant then has his daughter watched, but when the child is born, an old nurse spirits it away to the wilderness. She asks a brother of hers to cut a large hole in a tree, and when he has done this she kills the brother lest he might disclose their whereabouts. She and the child live in the tree until he is big enough to hunt. Then she brings him to an assembly where his foes are, and he overcomes all the boys there at the game of hurling. 'Who is that fair-haired [fionn] fellow?' asks the king, thus giving him his name. The nurse then tells that the child – hitherto un-named – is the son of Cumhall, and they have to flee immediately.

She carries the boy on her back for a long way, but then she tires and Fionn reverses the positions. He races through forests and thickets, and when he has finally left the pursuers behind he discovers that only the shin-bones of his nurse remain on his shoulders, because the protruding branches have decimated her in the heat of the chase. Fionn then travels on until he meets a huge one-eyed man cooking a salmon. He takes the first taste of the salmon by accident, after he burns his thumb on it, gets knowledge and understands that the fisherman intends to kill him. He kills the fisherman, and sets out for the court of the king. There he kills a hostile being who comes at night to either burn or knock down the court, and as a result the king makes him head of the Fianna

There are a few aspects of these folk tellings which merit special attention.The manner of death which the grandfather intends for the child is usually drowning, and some Irish versions state that the child was thrown into water but emerged holding an eel in his hand.[19] This is a rough parallel to the polecat episode (p. 97), the polecat having been put in place of the eel by some mediaeval writer. Swimming activities in general seem to have played an important part in early Fionn stories (see pp. 21ff), even though the later lore tends to minimise them. Witness the swimming feat by which he overcomes the hostile youths in the Boyhood-Deeds, a story which may have given rise to the particular name Glaisdíge [meaning 'backwash' or the like]. This motif has dropped out of later oral versions since the hurling contest fulfils the function satisfactorily on its own.

Two rather peculiar episodes are found in folk versions from both Ireland and Scotland and must, therefore, be of some antiquity. These are the killing by Fionn's nurse of her helpful brother, and the death of the nurse herself while being dragged through the branches on Fionn's shoulders. Since both motifs are concerned with the nurse, an investigation of her and her function is necessary. The late ninth-century Cormac's Glossary refers to a mythical lady called Buanand, who is described as 'the nurse of the fianna'. The glossator derives her name from *buan* [good] and *Anand* [the genitive of Anu, which was the name of a goddess]. 'Just as Anu was the mother of the gods,' the glossator says, 'so also was Buanand the mother of the fianna.' And he adds that this Buanand was 'a good mother who taught feats to the fianna'.[20] It appears, then, that the fianna had a special version of the goddess for themselves as a kind of tutelary 'nurse'. It is significant that Buanand is identified with Anu. This may be incorrect, but the glossator obviously applied a similar function of nourishment to both figures. Anu was conceptualised in the mountain peaks known as her 'Two Paps' [*Dá Chích Anand*].[21]

We have found these peaks occurring in the lore as early as an eighth-century Munster adaptation, and they occur again in his biography. Although the basic reason for such a west Munster location is political (see pp. 39ff), the selection of the two peaks must have been helped by the idea of a goddess as nurse to the fianna. An earth-goddess would be particularly apposite, given the life of young fianna in the wilderness. In the folklore of how Fionn's nurse was decimated, place names in the respective areas from which the versions come are explained as deriving from the various parts of the nurse's body as they fell off. That such an aetiological method of explaining place names belonged to ancient Irish tradition is witnessed by an episode in the Ulster epic *Táin Bó Cuailnge*, in which the parts of a mangled bull give rise to various toponymics.[22] The folklore accounts of the nurse's decimation would, therefore, appear to have come from fianna lore of the earth-goddess.

This interpretation connects also with the rather distinctive way that the nurse hides the child Fionn within the trunk of a tree. The fourteenth-century lay, referred to above, agrees with later folklore in this detail. It further mentions that the baby was covered with the skin of a polecat as an augury for the chase. We have already referred to hunter rituals in the formation of fianna narratives (pp. 77f), and it is easy to imagine that hiding within trees and the covering of oneself with animal skins would be part of such hunter lore. In other words, the fostermother is fulfilling the function of a hunting tutelary goddess in these matters. In support of this reasoning, we can mention the fact that, whereas the general outline of Fionn's threatened youth corresponds to other Irish epical sources and, indeed, to international patterns, these motifs are special to the Fionn context. This suggests that they are an input from the lore of indigenous fianna bands.

The compiler of the Boyhood-Deeds could hardly have been ignorant of such imagery embedded within the tradition. He himself portrays the nurse Bodhmann as a female *féinnidh* who nurses and teaches the young Fionn, and the likelihood is that he deliberately omitted some motifs because he regarded them as outlandish.

The most startling motif in the folklore versions is the treacherous killing by the nurse of her helpful brother. After he has made the hollow in the tree, she asks him to correct a fault in his work and when he has his back thus turned to her she cuts his head off. The only parallel-character to him in the mediaeval literature is Fiacail, described in one text as Bodhmhall's husband and in another as a mere acquaintance of hers. Fiacail's helpful act is to give a great spear to Fionn. This is the weapon with which Fionn kills his archetypal foe – a feat which has become somewhat confused in the Boyhood-Deeds.

Apart from Fiacail in that text, for instance, we have a smith making a sword for Fionn with which the young hero kills the fierce pig. The feat had, in fact, developed several duplicates in the mediaeval tradition – in different literary recensions the spear kills otherworld characters called Aillén, Cúldubh, and Aedh. Each of these is described as a son of Fidach, which name signified 'venom' or 'sorcery'. The idea that Fiacail was the bestower of the weapon is old. In a manuscript of an eighth-century story, which we have discussed (pp. 39f), it is called *carr Fiaclach* [the spear of Fiacail].[23] Again, in the twelfth-century account of how Fionn saved Tara from the burner Aillén, it is clear that the victorious spear was given to him by Fiacail son of Conchenn or Codhna, even though his name appears in corrupted form as Fiacha son of Conga.[24]

Quite obviously, then, Fionn's helper was not killed by the nurse in the story, as known in mediaeval times. The most plausible theory is that, since hiding in the tree was part of the story, the notion developed that the nurse could employ a carpenter to fashion the hollow. It would be a natural, though rather incongruous, extra development to make that carpenter her brother and to have her killing him in order to protect the secret. Since the extra development is an integral part of Irish and Scottish folk versions, this implies that the surviving oral recensions of Fionn's youth biography must derive from a prototype which postdates the twelfth century. So the question of when the youth biography of Fionn first came into being can be faced.

We have argued at length in chapter 1 that the tyrant-grandfather plot had been part of Fionn lore since the fourth or fifth centuries, but the combination of different adventures in the biography is obviously much later in date. The geographical references in the Boyhood-Deeds text show that the material used by that compiler was patterned after the eighth- and ninth-century lore associating Fionn with east Munster. Another important indicator is the fact that all versions of the youth biography presuppose that Fionn became leader of an Uí Néill king's troop and this can hardly be earlier than the ninth century. Furthermore, the story of how he accidentally gained knowledge from tasting the salmon must postdate Norse influence, a proposition which gives a date in either that or the following century. Taken all in all, it is safest to ascribe the development of a standard traditional account of Fionn's childhood and adolescence to a period sometime in the tenth century. Leinster would obviously have been the area where it developed, and it would not have taken long for the new oral epic to spread to other areas. The prototype of modern oral versions, which we have discussed above, was probably the vehicle through which it gained widespread popularity in the Gaelic world.

Fionn's Adult Life

A leader of a fianna group was known as a *ríghfhéinnidh*, that is a chief or 'king' *féinnidh*, and this designation was naturally applied to Fionn. As emphasis on this role of his increased, the royal-sounding term would invite comparison with the Uí Néill kinship, and so a synthesis had to be found. Thus the idea that Fionn was commander of the fianna forces attached to the Uí Néill kings developed in the eighth or ninth century. This resolution was achieved through making the fall of the warrior Cumhall, on account of Muirne's wooing, synonymous with a fall from the position of commanding Conn's forces. It was, therefore, Fionn's destiny, according to the synthesis, to regain his father's position. The tenth-century Almhu poem goes so far as to make Cumhall a step-uncle of Conn, but this is to overstrain the point. The new synthetic plot had a far more pressing issue to be sorted out. This concerned Goll, Fionn's archetypal one-eyed foe, killer of his father Cumhall, who had to be accommodated in a suitable role. Thus Goll was now portrayed as the man who, after killing Cumhall in the battle of Castleknock, had taken the leadership of the high-king's fianna.

The earliest clear expression of how Fionn was supposed to have recovered his father's old position is found in the twelfth-century text, *Acallamh na Senórach*. There we are told that, after he had killed the burner Aillén at Tara:

> Then the men of all Ireland gathered around the king on the green of Temhair where Fionn was.
>
> 'You see there, o king', said Fionn, 'the head of the man who used to burn Temhair, and his pipe and his timbrel and his musical melody, and I consider that Temhair has been spared along with its trappings.'
>
> Then the place was filled with them, and advice was taken, and the advice that was decided on was to give the chief fianna position of Ireland [*ríghfhéinnidhecht Éirenn*] to Fionn.
>
> 'Now, indeed, o son of Morna', said Conn of the Hundred Battles, 'take your choice, to leave Ireland or to put your hand in the hand of Fionn.'
>
> 'Upon my word', said Goll, 'my hand will be put in the hand of Fionn!'
>
> Then the charm and the fortune came to fruition, and the three battalions of the Fianna came and put their hands in Fionn's hand, and Goll son of Morna did it first so that the shame would be less for anyone else of the Fianna to do it.[25]

Fionn's status as a martial commander was much stressed in the literature. A tenth-century poem, enumerating great heroes, refers to him as 'the *ríghfhéinnidh* whose name was Fionn, leader of the fianna'.[26] Eleventh-century texts call him a 'prince of the fianna', a 'fianna king', and even a 'high-king'.[27] The synchronisers of history, of course, realised that the high-king Conn, who was made contemporary with Cumhall, could hardly be expected to outlive Fionn also; and so we have Conn's grandson and successor Cormac usually playing the part of Fionn's overlord. This was the great Cormac mac Airt, legendary king and symbol of the Uí Néill power. An eleventh-century text claims that Cormac appointed three times fifty fianna chiefs 'and he gave authority over them all as well as the chief-stewardship of Ireland to Fionn descendant of Baoiscne'.[28] From the same time comes a similar description:

> Fionn mac Cumhaill was the household leader and the head of every exile and every mercenary and every troop under Cormac, so that the common people used to refer to them as the Fianna of Fionn [*Fianna Find*].[29]

Given that Fionn was by this time looming large in popular culture, and that he was believed to have directed a kind of national volunteer force called Fianna, one would expect a particular portrayal of such a militia to be current, and we do, indeed, have a suitable account in a twelfth-century source.

In all, we are told, there were one hundred and fifty divisional commanders, and each of these commanders had three times nine warriors under him. None of these warriors was allowed to plunder cattle, to refuse gifts or food to anybody, or to flee before nine warriors. When a volunteer was accepted into the Fianna his family undertook not to avenge him if he should be killed in that service, and likewise they were not held responsible for his acts while he was in the Fianna. This stipulation sounds like an echo from genuine fianna regulations of ancient times (see p. 45). The account continues with a hyperbolic list of necessary qualifications. The applicant must know 'the twelve books of poetry', and he must be a supreme athlete:

> A large hole was made which reached to the fold of his girdle and he was put into it with his shield and an arm's length of a hazel rod in his hand, and nine warriors against him with nine spears, and ten ridges between them, and they would target him together, and if he were wounded from that he was not accepted into the fianna profession.
>
> And, also, a man was not accepted until his hair was braided and he was set running through the woods of Ireland with them all coming after him intending to wound him, and with only one branch between them. If he were caught he was wounded, and he would not be accepted then. If a branch of the wood affected a braid in his hair

> he was not accepted either. If a dead branch cracked under his foot he was not accepted. If he did not jump over a branch as high as his forehead and bend under a branch as high as his knee he was not accepted. And if he did not draw the thorn from his foot with his nail without slackening his pace he was not accepted into the fianna profession.[30]

The race through the protruding branches of the forest is reminiscent of the flight of Fionn and his nurse which we have discussed above, and it may be an echo of some real initiation test among ancient fianna bands. Given the nature of the tests as described here, however, it is not surprising that the writer of the account is loud in his praise of Fionn's standards:

> Good was the man who had these Fianna, for he was the seventh king in Ireland – that is, the five provincial kings, the king of Ireland, and he the seventh king.

The anomolous social position of Fionn as a fianna-king helped to preserve in mediaeval tradition the ancient tension between him as a Leinster hero and the Uí Néill high-kingship. Vestiges of the old Leinster feeling itself survived, for in a twelfth-century text we are told that Fionn 'the *ríghfhéinnidh* of Ireland' defeated Cormac's son Cairbre Lifeachair in a great battle at Camross in Co. Laois, so as to free Leinster from tribute.[31]

This in-built tension between Fionn and the high-kings proved a very fertile theme for dramatic narrative, and it appears that the hero's new role as commander of the high-king's Fianna was not long established when a special kind of such narrative became prominent. This had Fionn wooing a daughter of Cormac. Two stories based on this idea were already current in the late tenth century. Of one, *Aithed Gráinne* [the Elopment of Gráinne], we have mere mentions and a few fragments;[32] and the earliest intact version which survives is much later in date and general structure (see chapter 6). It concerns how Cormac's daughter Gráinne was betrothed to Fionn but eloped instead with Diarmaid descendant of Duibhne.

The other tenth-century text survives in full. It is called *Tochmharc Ailbhe* [the Wooing of Ailbhe], and in its introduction reference is made to the previous romance:

> There was hostility between Cormac descendant of Conn and Fionn descendant of Baoiscne, and the reason for the conflict was that Gráinne gave her hatred to Fionn while she gave love to Diarmaid descendant of Duibhne. Fionn was banished on account of that and the Fianna were separated from him.

Then the action of the Ailbhe story commences. Peace, we are told, was made by Cormac with Fionn, and 'the soldiers and the household and the hound-keepers and the command of the hunt' were restored to Fionn. Furthermore, the king gave his permission to any of his daughters who wished to go with Fionn.

One of these daughters, Ailbhe 'the Freckle-Cheeked' [*gruadbric*], went to the druid Cithruadh to enquire of him who her husband would be. The druid told her that she would see that man in a dream that night, and next day he would appear on the green of Tara.

Next day was, in fact, the beginning of the great fair of Tara, and Fionn and his men came to the green outside the citadel and began to play their fianna melody [*easnad fianso*] with their spear-handles. Ailbhe was embroidering her father's helmet when she heard the melody. Cormac sent a messenger to Fionn to enquire what art he brought with him to Tara. Fionn said that he was good at 'ancient words and proclaiming banter'.

'That is regarded by us as an art of youths and girls', said Cormac.

Fionn said that he had made 'three times fifty wooings until now of princes' daughters in Ireland and Scotland' and that all the maidens were obtained for members of the Fianna, so that he alone was left without a mate.

'Then ask for yourself', said Cormac, and admitted him to the quarters of the princesses.

Fionn then began to ask riddles, all of which were answered by Ailbhe. He spoke a poem proposing marriage to her, reciting in it the beauties of the fauna and flora among which the fianna spent their lives, and she accepted his proposal. Three wonderful things, we are told, happened to Fionn when Ailbhe came to him.

> He slept on the stream of Sadhbh; a white-purple pimple came on his breast with the brightness of a carbuncle-gem; his hair became yellow, so that it was as yellow as the red-gold shine of a gem, and a curled braid was made of it around from the back of his head, which was as round as a ball of bronze, and which was not loosened during his life.

Ailbhe bore three sons to Fionn. They were called Raighne, Iollann, and Caoince, and we are told that they gave their names to three places – Raighne in Ulster, Sliabh Iollainn in Leinster, and Cruach Chaoince in Connacht.[33]

A little anecdote survives from a century or so later, which is a by-product of the same basic idea. According to it, another daughter of Cormac, called Sodhelbh [good appearance] slept with a man called Glanghresach. But a rival girl used magic to turn Sodhelbh against her lover, so that he felt it necessary to seek Fionn's protection.

Once when Glanghresach was in a smithy with Fionn and Fionn's foster-daughter Ailelbh, a young man called Mogh Smaile was working there. When Mogh Smaile raised his head from his work and saw Ailelbh he immediately fell in love with her. Fionn noticed this and remarked on the matter. Then Mogh Smaile asked to be allowed a running-test with the Fianna in order to gain her. Fionn agreed, and Mogh Smaile took the girl by the hand and outran all the Fianna with her. He got the girl, and Fionn accepted him into his troop. Glanghresach and Cormac's daughter Sodhelbh were also reunited.[34]

The garbled nature of this latter story shows that the theme of love was being utilised in various ways in the Fionn lore of the time and was being seen as an integral part of that lore. From the eleventh century, we have two lists of the women in Fionn's life.[35] These are stated to have been Badhamair, daughter of the fisherman Lughair; Smirnat Mhongfhind, daughter of Fothadh Canainne; Gráinne, daughter of Cormac; and Ailbhe, daughter also of Cormac.

And these lists are not complete. The woman of the Lomhna story is not mentioned, for instance, nor is Blái Derg, nor Cruithne the daughter of the Munster smith. We have seen that Fionn, as a fiann, was quite a capable womaniser (p. 43), but the proliferation of wives and lovers in mediaeval lore owes less to memories of libertine fianna life than it does to the growth of varying narratives.[36] In other words, there was an increasing demand for narratives based on the theme of love. This development of amorous interest in the tradition continued, and we shall meet yet more women presently.

The Death of Fionn

The same curiosity which we encounter concerning the hero's birth, upbringing, profession, and private life, is to be found also regarding his death. A ninth-century text states as a curiosity that Fionn, like his uncle Criomhall, died on a Wednesday.[37] This mention is in a list of famous warriors arranged according to the days of the week on which they died, and it is relevant to us only in that it shows that lore of Fionn's death was already in vogue at the time.

The earliest tradition, it seems certain, derived from the Uí Fáilghe's martial opposition to the Luaighne of Tara (see p. 45) and had it that he was killed by treachery at the hands of these Uí Néill vassals. The poet Cinaedh ua hArtacáin – who died in the year 975 – tells us that in a battle fought at *Ferta na Fáilend* occurred 'the death of Fionn by the fierce fianna of Luaighne'. In another poem, Cinaedh states that 'by the fianna of Luaighne was the death of Fionn at Áth Bréa on the Bóinn [i.e. the river Boyne]'.[38] In some manuscripts an extra quatrain is added to this poem:

> Fionn was killed then, Fionn was killed,
> It was by javelins – without a hero's wound –
> Aichlech son of Duibhriu cut off
> His head from the son of Muirne of the [beautiful] Neck.[39]

Other sources state that Aichlech was accompanied by 'the sons of Uirghriu' when he beheaded Fionn. A poet called

Gilla Coemháin, writing in 1072, refers to the hero's death as follows:

> Seven and fifty years without a doubt
> From the battle of Mucraimh of the champions
> Until Fionn was killed by them – though it was treachery –
> By the spear points of the three sons of Uirghriu.[40]

Uirghriu had been the rival of Cumhall as described in the Boyhood-Deeds (p. 84), so it is not surprising that his sons would be portrayed as hostile to Fionn. We have a text from the eleventh century, citing the quatrain which was added to Cinaedh's poem, and giving the attribution 'as the historian says'. The text, therefore, represents a development on what is said in that quatrain. It claims that, when old age came on Fionn, his men persuaded him to remain at home. Nine men stayed with him to keep him company, but one of these left to join the rest of the fianna on their adventures each day until only one man remained:

> 'So it is true', he said. 'It is age the men notice on me! I will know about that from my running and my leaping, for it is in the east that my "Leap" is, on the Bóinn, and I will go to its bank.'
>
> So he set out from the west of the Highway of Gabhrán [Gowran, Co. Kilkenny] towards Maistin [Mullaghmast, Co. Kildare]. There in Maistin he found a woman making curds.

The manuscripts are corrupt here, but the damaged portions seem to refer to how the woman gave him a drink from a horn, and then reminded him of a prophecy that he would die from drinking thus:

> 'True, o hag', said he. 'Here is my brooch for you!'
> Thereupon he went east along the Bóinn until he reached his Leap. He then fell between two rocks so that his forehead struck a rock, and his brains were all over it, and he was dead between the two rocks. Fishermen of the Bóinn found him. There were four of them, three sons of Uirghriu and Aichlech son of Duibhriu. These found him, and Aichlech cut off his head. And the sons of Uirghriu

slew him [i.e. Aichlech]. They brought his [i.e. Fionn's] head with them to an empty house, and boiled their fish, and divided it in two. His head was in front of the fire.

'Give a morsel [*dantmír*] to it', said a dark evil-jesting man, 'since Aichlech does not live!'

The fish was divided in two three times, and there were three portions still.

'What is this?' said one of them. Then said the head from before the fire:

'It is this that causes the third division
With you, without any flattery –
That I am not given at meal
By you my morsel [*mír*] like the others!'[41]

This new twist to the tradition, which has the sons of Uirghriu killing Aichlech for beheading Fionn, is referred to also in a twelfth-century verse:

Fionn was beheaded –
He was a strong man –
By the warrior-son of Duibhriu.
The head was taken off him
By the lustrous sons of Uirghriu.[42]

This strange idea – that Fionn's enemies would avenge him – has its origin in a misunderstanding. The genuine tradition was that Aichlech had beheaded Fionn, aided by Uirghriu's sons.

The two above texts themselves give a clue as to how the confusion came about, i.e. Aichlech was misunderstood to be the 'him' referred to in the second mention of decapitation. An account of Fionn's death from the twelfth-century, although late, is undoubtedly more accurate as regards the part played by Uirghriu's sons. This account says that Fionn was,

The chief of household and of mercenaries, and the keeper of hounds for Cormac, for the best soldier of the king of Temhair was always his keeper of hounds.

Fionn, we are told, was surpassing as a warrior and as a host, and he was a king among fianna, so that 'it is with Fionn that every champion [*rígnia*] is compared from then to today'. Then his ending is referred to:

> It was in Almhu that Fionn's abiding was after decrepitude and old age came to him, Cormac also being dead. Smirghat the daughter of Fothadh Canainne was Fionn's wife. She was a prophetess and a wise woman. It was she who told Fionn that when he drank a draught from a horn that that would be the end of his life. Which was the reason why he did not drink a draught from horns, but from goblets always.

The episode of his taking a drink from a well in Adharca Iuchbha (see p. 69) follows. The name of this place means 'the Horns of Iuchbha', and so Fionn unintentionally fulfils his prophecy of doom:

> Then he went on until he reached Druim Bregh. The people were hostile to him in that area, since it was by him that Uirghriu of the Luaighne of Temhair fell.
>
> There gathered then the Luaighne of Temhair and the three sons of Uirghriu and Aichlech son of Duibhriu – that is, the son of the third one of Uirghriu's sons. A great ruthless battle was fought between them, manly, fierce, courageous; so that everybody remembered there the hostility against each other, whether remote or immediate. Áth Bréa on the Bóinn, that is where that battle was fought, and they were struggling for a long time, till the destruction on each side was great.
>
> The battle went against Fionn, and he perished in that battle. Aichlech son of Duibhriu, it was by him that Fionn perished, and it was he who beheaded him.[43]

The story of his fatal leap seems to have been a folkloric development, and the idea that he was killed by his enemies the older and more learned tradition. But there were still other accounts, as is clear from a mention in the Colloquy of how he met his death at the Cliff of Broc in Luachair Deaghadh [i.e. the area of Slieve Logher in Co. Kerry].[44] This was also hostile territory for Fionn (see p. 91), but the notion of his dying there is rejected by a later source which stipulates that 'it was by Aichlech son of Duibhriu that Fionn was killed at Áth Bréa on the Bóinn, and not in Beola Broghóige in Luachair!'[45] Such literary men were continually pointing out that the ancient and 'proper' tradition concerned Uirghriu's sons and Aichlech. But it is clear that this tradition itself was open to fluctuation in detail.

A long and very stylised text from the fourteenth century, for instance, makes the episode follow on a great boar-hunt and an invitation that Fionn received to spend the night feasting at the house of a certain Fer Taí, who is described as grandson of Goll mac Morna and chief *féinnidh* of the Luaighne. Fer Taí's son treacherously attacked Fionn's men, and could only be dissuaded from killing the hero himself by the arranging of a great battle, to be fought between their respective armies on the banks of the Boyne next day. Great numbers are slain in that battle, including Fer Taí's ally Aichlech son of Duibhriu, and Fer Taí himself falls at the hands of Fionn. The text lacks an ending, but this is the final paragraph which survives:

> That was when the five sons of Uirghriu came upon the scene, and they set their faces on Fionn. When Fionn saw those inveterate enemies attacking him he did not avoid them. And each man of them stuck a spear in the *rígh-fhéinnidh*. And he replied to the five champions in like manner, dealing them wound for wound.
>
> When the children of Uirghriu saw that the champion had been gashed in the preceding combats which he had fought against Fer Taí and his son Fer Lí, and that he was weak from the loss of his blood. . . .[46]

It is clear that the author had read one of the earlier references to the killing of Fionn by the sons of Uirghriu, and that he was reproducing that scenario in his elaborate text.

As this chapter demonstrates, Fionn was, during the Middle Ages, being increasingly seen as a great warrior with a definite life-span and a marked (and reasonably consistent) career. The historians had even found agreement on the question of chronology. Fionn had lived, they claimed, in the reigns of the high-kings Conn, Cormac, and Cairbre. By the eleventh-century, an annalist could confidently place him in the third century A.D. and claim that he had died, having been beheaded by Aichlech and the sons of Uirghriu, in the year 283.[47]

Conflicting items of lore concerning details of his life were reconciled as best they could be, and he was set in a narrative framework which allowed for any amount of new stories to be invented about him and his Fianna. And a great number were being invented. In story-lists used by professional raconteurs of the tenth century we have mention of a mere handful of adventures involving him,[48] but within two hundred years all that had changed. So much so that Gilla an Choimdhedh, writing towards the end of the twelfth century, claims that 'six times twenty stories of the fianna could be recited by every genuine poet'.[49]

5.

The Hero's Character

When discussing the image of Fionn in late mediaeval narratives three basic sources must be referred to repeatedly. The first of these is the long compilation called *Acallamh na Senórach* [the Colloquy of the Old Men].

This text is written to a framework which has the Fianna heroes Oisín and Caoilte surviving the demise of their fellows, meeting St Patrick when he was in Ireland, and relaying to him a large amount of stories and onomastic lore concerning the doings of Fionn and his band. Most of the talking is done by Caoilte. The Colloquy was written about the year 1175, but the full original text is lacking. What we have is an incomplete – but almost complete – copy of it (nearly 90,000 words in length) which was made in the beginning of the thirteenth century. From that same century we have an additional text in which Oisín is the main speaker – apparently written by someone who thought that extra material was required. It is in length less than a tenth of the first text. Then, in the fourteenth century, a new version was written, uniting the foregoing two and adding a little more.[1]

The second major source is even more diverse in nature and scope. This is the corpus of narrative poems or lays composed about the Fianna in a period from the twelfth to the fifteenth centuries. These lays – written in the standard literary language common to Ireland and Scotland – were highly prized by the literati of both countries, and the evidence suggests that they were sung aloud as entertainment at feasts in the houses of nobles.[2]

The third source is a text of about 16,000 words written in or about the fifteenth century, called *Feis Tighe Chonáin* [the Feast at Conán's House]. It is copied from the structure of the Colloquy, but instead of Caoilte or Oisín talking to Patrick it has Fionn himself, telling various adventures which befell him, to Conán, the lord of a *sí*-dwelling where the hero finds shelter for the night from inclement weather. This is a valuable source in respect of several traditions, but it is coloured somewhat by its writer's taste for phantasy and ornamentation.[3]

Fionn the Person

A good deal of scattered detail is found in these sources which shows that their authors were speculating and theorising with the material. Taking up the image of Fionn as a champion youth coming to save Tara from the burner, the first Colloquy text portrays him rather exaggeratedly as a mere boy:

> He was plundering and reaving [*ar díbheirg*] until the end of his ten years, and in the tenth year Conn of the Hundred Battles held the feast of Temhair. And when the men of Ireland were drinking and enjoying themselves in the great House of Midhchuarta they noticed nothing until a handsome young boy arrived there. He sat in the presence of Conn of the Hundred Battles and of Goll son of Morna.

No hostility was allowed for the fortnight's duration of that feast, and so Fionn told his name, was made welcome, and then undertook to save the citadel from the burner Aillén.[4] Thus he became leader of the Fianna at that tender age, and the subsequent tradition accepted this chronology.

A Munster account, written about the year 1300, varies matters to suit its own interest and tells us that he became the *ríghfhéinnidh* of that province 'at the end of nine years' and had to wait a further fifteen years for the command of the whole country.[5] Political considerations aside, the notion of him as a prodigious youth did allow for freedom in descriptions of him. In *Feis Tighe Chonáin* Fionn is quoted as saying:

> My first name was Glas Díge, and my name after that was the Lad of the Hollow [*Gilla an Chuasáin*], and it was at

the Well of Crithirlinn on the side of the mountain of Smól son of Eighleachar that I had my first swim. And it was at Dún Brocna that I did my first ever plundering – that is, the swift duck with her twelve ducklings. . . .

The first day that I departed from my nurse Bodhmann, after she had been killed by Morna's progeny, I took a wandering path until I reached Luachair Deaghadh in the south. And I was a young silly unwise boy then, with no clothes on me but a covering from the skin of a young wild deer.

Fionn tells how he then saw a group of men on one hill-top and a group of women on another. Between the two hill-tops was a great gulf, and the women told Fionn that one of their number, Athnait daughter of Dáire from a *sí*-dwelling, had demanded that her suitor leap across to her. That suitor was the son of a local king, and he had been coming annually to the cliff-edge for several years but had always withdrawn before he jumped.

Fionn himself took the jump over and then back again. Seeing this, Athnait gave him three kisses and fine clothes to wear.

And I went along with her to her house that night, and I rose early next morning. She came to me and made a morning request of me, that is to do that leap each year, and I granted that to her. She put prohibitions [*geasa*] on me, the year I would not do it that I would get death and demise.'[6]

Later on in the same text the motif is used again, with another set of circumstances. Fionn says that when he was at Magh na Céide [probably between Cos Westmeath and Offaly] he saw a beautiful maiden, who told him that she was seeking a man who could jump over a particular rock in that place. Fionn did this, but then she demanded that he repeat the jump holding on his palm a slab of stone of his own size:

As soon as I heard that, I put the slab on my palm and did the leap in that manner; and I scarcely ever performed a feat on land which I found more difficult than doing that leap.

> 'Éadaoin of Sliabh Caoin is my name', she said; and she put me under prohibitions to go with her to her dwelling that night. I went, and she was my bed and sleeping partner that night.

Again, before he leaves next morning, this lady enjoins on him to repeat the jump each year, else he will die.[7]

These accounts exemplify a general trait of the Fionn-lore, i.e. certain basic motifs recur in new narratives without altogether losing their original flavour. From meaning 'the *fiann*-profession' the word *fiannaigheacht* was acquiring the sense 'narratives of Fionn's Fianna', but the original foundations were so solid as to allow freedom of redaction within a perennial tradition. It is as if there was a continual return to the source imagery. This is perhaps symbolised by a thirteenth-century lay which accords with earlier sources by saying that Fionn was born in Almhu, goes on to say that he met his death at a place called Broc, and then returned to Almhu where, it states, he was buried.[8]

We have seen (p. 111) that the author of the first Colloquy mentioned the tradition that Fionn met his death at the Cliff of Broc in Kerry. Given the above references to his cliff-jumping – one of them in that very area – we can be sure that the variant mediaeval idea of his death in Logher was derived from the earlier tradition of how he died as the result of a fatal leap on the Boyne. The repeated tendency to connect our hero with topography is worthy of attention.

As early as the eighth century, as we have seen, he was being associated with place names in Munster and Ulster, as well as in Leinster. The impetus for such onomastic lore of Fionn was two-fold: the new narratives being created required a multiplication of venues and, conversely, his fame had so grown that to associate him with a place meant an increase in that place's prestige. As usual, adaptable floating motifs were grist to the mill. An eleventh-century poem on places in south Kerry, for instance, makes use of a well-known narrative formula for delivering a covert message.

After Cuirrech Life had been killed by Fionn (p. 39), we are told that Cuirrech's wife Sengharmain looted and burned the homes of many of Fionn's associates, including his foster-mother Mongfhind and her fianna apprentices. Sengharmain's band then hid from Fionn in an underground cave beside a well in Logher, which they fortified.

One day they saw Oisín alone and took him as hostage into the cave. Oisín embarked on a ruse to alert Fionn. Given a spearshaft to pare, he cut shavings from it and cast them into the well, from which they flowed into the river Feale. Fionn was at a ford down-river. He caught the shavings and recognised Oisín's handiwork. Whereupon he gathered his warriors, went to the source of the river and, raiding the cave, slaughtered and routed his enemies. Hence the place was known as 'the Well of Sengharmain'.[9]

Another poem from the same period concerns a place called Druim Den in the midlands near the Shannon river. Here, we are told, Fionn had a fortress. But, after he had won a battle against the forces of a certain Uinche, the latter went and destroyed the fortress. Discovering it quite denuded [*fornocht*], Fionn with Oisín and Caoilte set out on the trail of Uinche. They fought and killed him and his thrice seven men at Hallow-tide – a usual date for Fionn's triumphs. The fort of Druim Den was hence known as Fornocht [today Farnagh in Co. Westmeath].[10]

The ancient seer-lore could be refurbished in more direct ways and made to support tenuous connections with places. Thus Cnámhros [probably Camross in Co. Laois] was explained in the mediaeval literature to have got its name from how Maer, wife of one Barnsa, fell in love with our hero. She sent a messenger with love-nuts [*co cnóib seirce*] to him when he was at that place. These were nine nuts from the Well of Seghais (see p. 57), but Fionn rejected the charmed present, saying that they were 'nuts of ignorance' [*cnói amruis*]. Hence this – clearly contrived – derivation of the place name Cnámhros, which is elsewhere more convincingly explained as 'the Wood of Bones'.[11]

Tying more directly with his reputation as a seer-poet, we even have poems on place-lore, native lore, and history attributed to Fionn himself.[12] Not surprisingly, much praise is lavished on our hero on account of his supposed traits of pesonality.

'He had a good mind,' says Caoilte in the Colloquy, 'and

he was never seized by fear of any person by day or by night.' In a more expansive mood, Caoilte delivers the following eulogy:

> All who ever came of the host of Banba (i.e. Ireland),
> Including kings and aspirants to kingship,
> Fionn was better than them all –
> The great warrior of Almhu!

And he continues:

> If there were seven tongues in my head and seven rhetorics of wise men in each tongue, I would not manage to tell half or a third of Fionn's goodness. For Fionn never refused a person who had but a head to wear something and legs to move.

And again in versified form:

> He whom nobody would allow into his house
> Fionn the true judge would allow in;
> And as well as that he would keep him
> For as long as he lived!

These praises of Fionn occur in the context of Caoilte trying to persuade St Patrick that Fionn, although a pagan, was a man of great merit. In such passages, the Colloquy author succeeds in 'living' the part of Caoilte, and then his own attachment to the Fionn-perspective rivals his attachment to that of Patrick. The resultant tension accounts for the, at times, high artistic achievement. Perhaps the most succint statement of praise for Fionn is contained in one striking quatrain:

> If the russet leaf were gold
> Which the wood casts aside,
> If the bright wave were silver,
> Fionn would have given it away![13]

This idealising of Fionn, in its full force, must have been something of a novelty in the twelfth century. In the earlier tradition, he was a celebrated seer, a character of high adventure, and a heroic warrior, but the pure ethics which are attributed to him here owe much to the picture of a good man which the author had. His portrayal of Fionn is, in fact, a synthesis of the ideal Gaelic prince and the good Christian leader, and it found its own niche in the tradition.

Thus, according to a poem of around the thirteenth century:

> He was a poet and a prince,
> He was a king over every king,
> Fionn the Fianna prince,
> He was a king over every country!
>
> He was a great whale on the sea,
> He was agile on the trail,
> He was a dexterous hawk in the wind,
> He was a wise man in every skill!
>
> His skin like chalk,
> His cheek like a rose,
> Clear and bright was his eye,
> His hair like the gold![14]

His generosity in particular accords well with Gaelic ideals. In the Colloquy we are told that,

> he left no woman without bride-price, and he left no servant without his fair due, and he left no man without his wages, and he promised nothing at night which he would not fulfil in the day, and he promised nothing in the day that he would not fulfil in the night![15]

These accounts are, in fact, according him royal status, and this is obviously connected with the notion that he was a type of fianna-king (see pp. 102ff).

The Colloquy author had in many ways a discerning mind, but this quality did not affect his hyperbole. Fionn had, he informs us, no less than ten hundred poets in his employ. Nor does it prevent him from telling some things which represent the hero as falling far short of a paragon of virtue. Fionn, for instance, tries to give the hand of his daughter Aoi Arduallach to the king of Scotland against the girl's wishes.[16] Such over-assertiveness is shown again in an incident concerning a chess-game between Fionn's servant Guaire and a member of the Fianna called Fionn Bán son of Breasal.

When Guaire loses he flies into a temper and grossly insults his opponent, whereupon Fionn Bán deals him a mortal blow. When Fionn hears of this, he decides that Fionn Bán should be put to death immediately, and is only dissuaded from this by the earnest representations of Oisín. The hero's final verdict is more chastened and, in the context, more realistic: 'A strong word deserves a strong blow', he remarks.[17]

Whether intentionally or not, the Colloquy author has hit upon a dichotomy which often recurs in the tradition and helps to heighten the drama of many narratives, i.e. that Fionn is capable of not only great magnanimity but also of great pettiness. It is probably this more than anything else which guaranteed that the lore of him remained so popular through the ages, for it echoes a paradox at the core of human nature itself.

A strong curiosity regarding things connected with Fionn was also growing at this time. His weapons were given names and, to a certain extent, characteristics of their own. The sword he wielded was called An Chraobh Ghlasach [the cold champion];[18] and his shield, An Seancholl Snidheach [the strong ridged hazel]. This shield had a long history, having been previously in the possession of the sea-deity Manannán and of the Daghdha [good god], and eventually of Fionn's tyrant-grandfather Tadhg mac Nuadhat, from whom it was taken by Cumhall when he abducted Muirne.[19]

Weapon-history of this type was inspired by the lore of Cumhall's crane bag (see p. 91), which was also owned at different times by various heroes including Manannán. This strange bag contained items such as Manannán's shirt and knife, the girdle and hook of Goibhniu (a mythical smith), the king of Scotland's shears, and the king of Scandinavia's helmet. Clearly the crane-bag is an eleventh- to twelfth-century fabrication; and it is likely that it, the *corr-bholg*, originally meant 'sharp javelin'. This would make it an alternate name for Fionn's great spear Biorgha, which was the most celebrated weapon in his armoury (pp. 93, 101).[20] The *Feis Tighe Chonáin* text elaborates further on his weapons. Here we are told that he also had a short sword called 'Mac an Luinn' [son of the fierce one], and that his shield shrieked out a warning when its owner was in dire straits.[21]

Parallels to some of these motifs can be found in other

epical traditions, and the Fionn tradition undoubtedly was being influenced by lore of Cúchulainn and even that of non-Gaelic heroes in the late mediaeval period.[22] There was also an amount of pure invention. One description says that Fionn's house was seven-sided, with a shield hanging on each side; and in late texts we are told of his banner, called 'Dealbh Gréine' [sun-shape] which was composed of sixteen cubits of pure white satin.[23]

Neither did Fionn's household servants go unnoticed. A poem from around the year 1200 gives an elaborate list of his retainers with readily-invented names for all. It includes triads of clowns, jugglers, horse-grooms, comedians, butlers, and doorkeepers, as well as 'Maċ Samhain his just judge', 'Aodh of the blue nails his candle-bearer', and his poet Fearghus Fíonbhéil – the only character in the list to enjoy wider mention in the cycle.[24] Fionn's dealings with his servants must have had some popularity as a theme. In a twelfth-century document, one of the poems on winter which was attributed to the hero is put in the context of an altercation between himself and a gillie called Mac Lesc [lazy boy].

One night, we are told, when they were separated from their comrades at Slieve Gullion (in Co. Armagh) Fionn sent this gillie to fetch water. Mac Lesc complained that it was too cold for that work.

> They say, however, that he had perforce to go and fetch the water, and Fionn bound him stark naked till morning to the standing-stone of Colt. And nobody in the Fiann-band of Fionn was quicker or more untiring henceforth.[25]

Even though its connection with the winter-poem must have been rather new, there is much of the earlier rough-and-ready Fionn in that account. What motivated the Colloquy author, on the other hand, was a desire to make him a delectable chieftain.

This is instanced by the picturesque account in the Colloquy of a little harper of the Tuatha Dé Danann called Cnú Dearóil, from the otherworld fort on Slievenamon:

> Envy and jealousy towards him seized the entertainers of the Tuatha Dé Danann because he excelled them all, and

they banished him from the *sí*-dwellings and forbade him to visit them forthwith.

He went away from the *sí*-dwelling with his melodious sweet-stringed timbrel on his back. On that very day Fionn went west to Sídh Ban bhFionn [Slievenamon] for the hunt and the chase, and he sat on the sodded hillock there. He then looked around and saw the little man tuning and deftly playing his harp on the ground beside him. He had long bright fair hair growing down to his two thighs, and when he saw Fionn he approached him and took his hand in his hand – for he was the first person he had met after he came out of the *sí*-dwelling.

He continued playing his harp in Fionn's presence until the Fianna came. And when they arrived they heard the entrancing *sí*-music. They were mystified and asked whence he had come, and Fionn told them the story exactly. . . . And he was with Fionn until he died.

Cnú Dearóil measured 'four fist-sizes of Fionn', and the hero decided that the dwarf musician would need a wife of appropriate size. So he sent to the House of Donn [*Tech Duinn*] – the otherworld rock off the coast of Kerry – where a beautiful little maiden called Bláthnait lived. She was five fists tall, and the members of the Fianna contributed an ounce of gold each as bride-price for her. So Cnú Dearóil and Bláthnait were married, and we are told that Fionn was accustomed to take the little couple under his cloak to shelter them when it rained.[26]

Fionn the Hunter

Several stories which blossomed in the mediaeval period are based on indigenous fianna tradition but have been refashioned and expanded according to the current taste. The clearest examples of this are provided by the narratives of Fionn's hunting exploits.

We have already discussed some motifs which reflect the genuine culture of ancient hunters, particularly the assimilation of Fionn and his men to their deer quarry. A similar, but technically different, development was taking place with regard to hunting hounds. We have few mentions of such hounds in connection with Fionn prior to the twelfth-century, and it seems certain that they were not part of the indigenous hunting lore of fianna groups. There are indications that hound-imagery was connected with such groups in other ways, however. *Cú* [a hound] is a metaphor which occurs frequently for a warrior in early Irish literature, and the name Conán [little hound] is given to several different characters in the Fianna of Fionn.

It was customary in many ancient civilisations to compare warriors, particularly young apprentice warriors, to fighting hounds, and we can view this type of nomenclature in Irish tradition as a reflection of the same process.[27] It is easy to imagine that the hardy young fiann would have been perceived as showing the qualities of a hound in battle. Such striking pictures tend to develop from the metaphoric function into narrative motifs, and so it is not surprising to find a close connection between Fionn's Fianna and dogs. The connection can be so close as to cause a blurring of human and canine nature. We have several redactions of a story, of which this thirteenth-century version is the earliest:

> Uirne Úirbhél daughter of Tadhg mac Nuadhat was the mother of Bran and Sceolaing, and Iomchadh king of Dál nAraidhe their father. And the way in which they were conceived was that Iomchadh requested her from Fionn, and Fionn did not give her to him until he got Lughaidh Lágha's guarantee that the wife of the king of Dál nAraidhe would not harm her.
>
> The wife of the king of Dál nAraidhe paid no heed to that protection of Lughaidh Lágha, and she struck Uirne with a wand and put her into the shape of a hound. And she had to be put into her own shape again. But it was not possible to put the two pups out of their hound-shapes, since it was not they who had been struck.
>
> Lughaidh Lágha set out then and killed the king of Dál nAraidhe to avenge his honour. And he himself had Uirne, and she bore him three sons. . . . So that in the one womb were the three sons of Lughaidh Lágha and Bran and Sceolaing.[28]

The Uirne of this story was said to have been a sister of

Fionn's mother Muirne; so Bran and Sceolaing, the two most famous of Fionn's hounds, were made out to be his cousins. Of the many hounds of the Fianna to whom names are given, these two always have precedence in the narratives. In fact many of the other dogs are nothing more than names, thus forming another illustration of the late mediaeval writers' tendency towards empty expansion of texts. But there is no doubting the affection which Fionn had for good dogs – this trait being a genuine part of several narratives.

The first Colloquy tells of 'a beloved hound' [*cú ghrách*] which he had, called Adhnuall [great barking], which was 'the third best hound that Fionn ever got'. This Adhnuall went astray and searched Ireland three times over for its master, finally dying from its loneliness.[29] Even more graphically, we are told of another 'beloved hound'.

> Cú Bheag was its name, and the deer at which it was set would find no shelter in Ireland. And no hound lay in the same bed as Fionn except it.[30]

Like dogs, horses are mentioned very rarely in the earlier Fianna lore, and their prominence in late mediaeval texts is definitely a novelty. It is significant that the Colloquy author gives precedence to dogs over them in an attractive story.

According to this, a young prince from Britain called Artúir mac Béinne Bhrit was in the Fianna, with twenty-seven men under his command. One day, when Fionn was hunting at Beann Éadair [Howth, Co. Dublin], this Artúir was positioned to keep the stags from escaping by swimming across the harbour. He saw the three fine hounds, Bran, Sceolaing, and Adhnuall approaching and decided to steal them. So he and his twenty-seven men sailed quietly away from Howth with the hounds and crossed to Britain.

When the hunt was concluded, Fionn noticed that the hounds were missing. He had a vessel brought, in which he washed his hands and face, and then put his thumb under his tooth of knowledge. The truth was revealed to him, and so a group of leading Fianna warriors set out for Britain. They were Diarmaid, Goll, Caol, Oisín, Oscar, Feardhomhan, Raighne, Caoince, Glas, Mac Lughach, and Caoilte. Finding the thieves, they killed all except Artúir himself, whom Oscar seized with his bare hands and took prisoner.

> And when Goll gave a glance around he saw a vigorous dark-blue steed with a gold-plaited bridle, and looking to the left he saw an evasive brown steed with a fine bright bridle of beautiful tempered silver with golden bits.

Along with Artúir and the three hounds, they took this stallion and mare back to Fionn in Ireland:

> And of their progeny were all the horses of the Fianna-band, for they were not accustomed to horses until then. And the mare had eight parturitions, and by each parturition eight foals. And these foals were given to the ranks and to the nobles of the Fianna-band.[31]

So Fionn was being provided with the full paraphenalia of a mediaeval chieftain or king. His sphere of relevance, too, was being greatly expanded. This is not the only Britonic prince who is mentioned as a member of his troop in the Colloquy, and the theme of warriors coming from abroad was well-known to early Irish literature.

The name of this particular prince, however, betrays an influence from the Arthurian lore. There are indeed many similarities between Fionn and Arthur, and it was easy for not just names but also motifs to be exchanged between the Irish and Welsh story-tellers. It may be that the use of hunting-hounds and horses in the late mediaeval tradition of Fionn owes something to Arthurian influence, for such imagery had been attached to Arthur from at least the eighth century.[32]

The imagery of hounds contributed much to narratives concerning great hunts carried out by Fionn – hunts which provided the authors with the opportunity to out-stylise one another. In the earlier tradition, as we have seen (pp. 74ff), hunting of stags and boars was an activity performed by Fionn either on his own or accompanied by a small group. Now they became great undertakings, planned and organised with military precision. This again – allowing for exaggeration – accords with the practices of great mediaeval lords and kings rather than with genuine fianna tradition.

The first Colloquy does portray hunting as a pastime of Fionn and his men as well as a food-necessity, but is sparing enough in its descriptions of the magnitude of *la chasse*. It mentions the hunting of particular stags, and other twelfth-century sources tell of similar chases of great solitary stags and boars. Typical of these is a lay about a magic pig which was chased by the Fianna at Luachair Deaghadh (in Co. Kerry). This pig wrought havoc among its pursuers, killing many men and hounds, until Fionn hurled a spear at it and laid it low.[33]

These chases may be of great length, such as from Slieve Bloom in Co. Laois to Howth in Co. Dublin, or from the Knockmealdown Mountains in Co. Waterford to Slemish in Co. Kerry.[34] But this is well in keeping with the earlier tradition, such as the case of the boar at Druim Leithe (see pp. 74f). On the other hand, the Colloquy author makes a quite inflated reference to,

> a bountiful chase which Fionn and the three battalions of the Fianna got – that is, a stag for every two men of the Fianna of Ireland and three stags for Fionn.[35]

It is clear that in the twelfth century Fionn's hunts were being envisaged as planned affairs with several members of the Fianna acting in consort and with their hounds wearing down and even killing the quarry. Central to these narrative tableaux is the idea that Fionn himself supervised the proceedings from some elevated part of the landscape, waiting to make the decisive thrust downhill.

Already in the first Colloquy we have reference to a hilltop called 'Suidhe Finn' [Fionn's Seat] in a favourite hunting area at Formoyle in Co. Galway. It is unlikely that the author invented the place name, but this particular kind of topographical association with Fionn need not have predated the text by very long.[36] The designation Suidhe Finn in time became very popular for hill and mountain-tops (see chapter 8), and the elaborated hunting techniques became accepted as the general custom of the Fianna.

The *Feis Tighe Chonáin* text, in a rhetorical passage, describes how a clamour was created to rouse deer, hares, foxes, and badgers, which were slaughtered by both hounds and warriors.[37] This is from around the year 1400, and another prose-text from the same time, *Seilg Shliabh na mBan*, follows a similar pattern, with wild pigs, hares, wolves, badgers, and deer the prey, and with traps being used as well as hounds and spears.[38] An unrelated poem with the same title *Seilg Shliabh na mBan* was composed about a century later, and this has no less than three thousand hounds being used in a chase which bagged double that amount of deer. But even this was not all, for a thousand of the hounds were killed by one hundred boars, which were in turn speared by the warriors. No wonder this poem has Oisín exclaiming:

> Never in my time did I see in the east or the west a single day's hunting greater than that by the Fianna of Fionn![39]

It is very likely that this notion of great hunts was strengthened by Norman influence and by the customs of these great foreign lords. Arthur, whom the Normans had expropriated from Welsh tradition and made into a symbol of their own power, would have been an important model. Actually, Arthur's own skill in the chase seems to owe much to older lore of Fionn the great individual hunter.

In the twelfth-century Welsh text *Culhwch ac Olwen*, Arthur hunts a giant magical boar called Twrch Trwyth, which had 'destroyed a third of Ireland' and which haunted a place called Ysgeir Oervel before it swam over to Wales.[40] This place is the marsh of Seiscenn Uarbheoil in Leinster which we have already encountered in the Fionn lore (p. 87), and there can be little doubting that this Twrch Trwyth is a borrowing from Irish tradition.

The earliest Welsh reference to it is in a Latin text [*porcus Troit*] of the early ninth century, where Arthur is said to have hunted it.[41] We have allusion in Irish literature of the same period to 'the fair of Torc Triath' [*oenach tuirc thréith*], which suggests that the pig in question had some ritual importance. The original borrowing from Ireland must, therefore, have occurred as early as the eighth century and, given the close association between the cooking of pig-meat and Fionn's entry to the otherworld in search of knowledge, that ritual would appear to have involved some form of seer-craft.

In Cormac's Glossary (late ninth century), a variant form Orc Tréith is mentioned and is immediately followed by a Fionn story – that concerning Lomhna (pp. 43ff). Although the glossator does not say that it was the name of a pig, we suspect that he should have done so and that his explanation of *orc* as 'a name for a salmon' is a clumsy attempt to fill a gap in his information. In fact, both words, *torc* and *triath*, had the clear meaning of 'boar' in Old Irish.[42] An extended form of the latter word was *tréithirne*; and the compendium of mythology, *Lebor Gabála*, tells us that Torc Triath was 'king of the boars, from whom is called the Plain of Tréithirne'.[43] This plain was situated in Co. Tipperary in the vicinity of Cullen, where Fionn according to the Boyhood-Deeds killed a great pig (p. 90). The conclusion suggests itself that this pig was in fact Torc Triath and that Fionn was reputed to have hunted the enormous boar.

There is another parallel also, for Twrch Trwyth was said in *Culhwch ac Olwen* to have been a prince transformed into that shape. We can take it that this idea was borrowed from Irish tradition along with the name. Cormac's Glossary might be referring to the same motif when it states that Orc Triath was 'the name of a king's son'. At any rate, such transformations were very popular in mediaeval Irish story-telling and we have already discussed an example in an eighth-century Fionn story, the stag-portrayal of Derg Corra (pp. 46ff). The origin of this lies in early Irish ideas about how divine figures could take on animal form.[44] In *Culhwch ac Olwen*, Twrch Trwyth was changed into a boar against his will, but a related Irish example from the twelfth century preserves the more basic idea of deliberate metamorphosis.

This describes how a great hunt was held by Fionn in Leinster, and he encountered a 'huge pig, horrid, hideous, rugged' with 'its colour purple and brindled black'. The savage beast killed many of the Fianna's hounds, and their spears merely glanced off it. Then Fionn began to incite his hound Bran, reminding it of all the boars it had killed. The boar fled at the approach of the great hound. Fionn and his men gave pursuit and ended up in an otherworld banqueting-hall. There the boar re-assumed human form, being the son of the ruler of that *sí*-dwelling, and he gave gifts to the Fianna before they departed.[45]

Another twelfth-century story shows the newer construction. This tells of how Donn, an important figure among the Tuatha Dé Danann, was turned into a stag by a jilted lady and in that shape gained a fearful reputation. Eventually Fionn went to hunt him, and a tremendous tussle ensued, with the stag killing a hundred men of the Fianna before he himself succumbed.[46]

The transformations could assume more grotesque dimensions. The Colloquy has Caoilte relate the following concerning Glendalough in Co. Wicklow:

> Fionn had an otherworld lover, Uaine daughter of Morn. And he refused her wooing because of the number of different shapes she used to take, as there was no beast the shape of which she would not assume.
>
> The Fianna came one day to the cairn over that lake, and a deer went out onto the lake. We followed it on the lake, and a worm rose up before us and killed a hundred hounds and a hundred men of us.

Caoilte asked Fionn would the Fianna kill the monstrous worm. Fionn put his thumb under his tooth of knowledge and realised that it could not be killed until St Patrick came to Ireland; whereupon one of the saint's disciples, Caoimhghein of Glendalough, would perform the feat.[47]

Such lake-monster lore – very common in Irish tradition – derives ultimately from Christian preaching on the Apocalypse, and it occurs in the Fionn context as a borrowing from hagiographical legends.[48] The writers realised the dramatic value of fights with extraordinary beings. A poem from the fourteenth century tells of Fionn that 'he left no worm in a lake nor horror in a cave which he, the wise nobleman, did not kill'.[49] A longer poem from the same period has Oisín describing how he organised a great hunt at Sliabh Truim (Bessie Bell in Co. Tyrone).

> I never thought the cries of battle more dreadful, though in many battles I had before been, than the cries of hounds and deer when the pack came at the herds!

A multitude of deer, boars, badgers, and hares were killed. Then the Fianna set out for Loch Cuain (Strangford Lough), and found a huge worm in the lake there.

The monster spoke to Fionn, demanding either food or

battle. A ferocious fight ensued, with the monster swallowing men and beasts in its massive maw. Then it swallowed Fionn himself, but the hero cut his way out of its stomach and released the rest of his men. A list is then given of reptiles and monsters which Fionn is said to have slain in lakes and valleys throughout Ireland.[50]

When the killing of these massive beings is not just literary convention, but forms actual narratives, the accounts are on a par with the hunting of great boars and stags, with large numbers of men and hounds involved. A quite late (fifteenth- or sixteenth-century) lay tells of the great worm of Lough Derg, which killed two thousand of the Fianna in one single day. When the fray was in progress, Fionn rushed at the monster, seized one of its joints, and knocked it over on its back. Then his son, Dáire, jumped into the huge maw and cut his way out of its stomach. Those warriors who emerged from the monster's interior were all hairless as a result of their ordeal.[51]

This motif is borrowed from the myth of Heracles[52] – a fact which is betrayed by having a son of the King of Greece to the fore in the poem. This, and the Sliabh Truim lay, proved very popular when they passed into oral tradition, and many resultant versions of them have been collected from folklore. One of these, quite appropriately, has the hound Bran biting the monster while Fionn hacks away at its inside.[53] For, aside from all added detail and ornamentation, the hunting lore of Fionn always has at its core the hero himself and his two faithful hounds, Bran and Sceolaing. The latter's name means 'news-bringer', which suggests that its function was to discover the whereabouts of the quarry. But in reality Sceolaing plays little part in the narratives, being little more than a comrade or double of Bran. Of all animals, Bran is the nearest to Fionn in the whole tradition.

The appellation given to it was quite usual as a personal name in Irish literature. The story of the hound's semi-human nature, which we discussed above, was hardly in existence prior to the tenth or eleventh century, but it is based on older canine imagery of warriors. The fact that its name is Bran [literally, raven] might indicate that the hound had a special background of its own, for ravens were portrayed as symbols of both hunting and knowledge in Celtic myth; but it is unlikely that it was a companion animal to Fionn since early times.[54] Once the connection between them was made, however, the mediaeval writers found Bran's close association with the hero an attractive and worthy theme. Fionn and Bran, we are told, used to 'make great voice' together at drinking-sessions, the master claiming that 'no deer or boar ever travelled a plain' which that hound would not overcome.

In this context the role of Bran in a psychological range between man and beast invites pathos, and a lay from about the thirteenth century makes artistic use of this potential. Put in the mouth of Fionn, the lay describes what a magnificent hound Bran was. The tallest of the Fianna's dogs would pass under its groin without stooping and its head was as high as Fionn's shoulder. It had two white sides, a purplish haunch, four bluish feet, and 'a fierce eye in its shapely head'. A stupendous hare-catcher, if the Fianna had spent a futile day hunting, Bran 'would bring their meal from the wood'. Fionn laments that he once struck this beautiful dog to keep it from baying at the deer:

> I gave him a blow of a yellow leash with rings of bright bronze, the golden circlet entered his head – alas for him who did the cruel deed!
>
> He wondered at being struck by me, for a while he stared at me, and then showers of tears poured from his piercing eyes. He jerked his leash from me suddenly, breaking the silver collar, and quickly fled along the mountain until he plunged with a swift leap into the lake.

Fionn says that the dogs of the Fianna used to raise three cries every morning seeking Bran, and that he himself was heartbroken:

> I never heard the voice of a hound hunting, on plain or bog or great slope, since I parted with my brave hound, but that my heart was overcome by woe![55]

Not surprisingly, this lay passed easily into oral culture, and many versions of it have been collected in both Ireland and Scotland.[56]

Fionn and the Otherworld

The belief that Fionn was a poet survived through the Middle Ages, but this aspect of his personality was not stressed as directly as in the early sources. The late mediaeval literature tends to confine his compositions to verse of a prophetic nature. This appears to be a direct result of the use of his name to prophesy the coming of saints in eleventh- to thirteenth-century documents. These saints include Patrick himself, Ciarán of Clonmacnoise, Fionnchua of Brigown, Caoimhghein of Glendalough, and Maodhóg of Ferns.

In one thirteenth-century poem Fionn is made to declare: 'I believe in the King of heaven, I am the best prophet under the sun.' He is also quoted as foretelling the coming of foreign conquerers, saying that 'it grieves me that I cannot come when the shout of the foreigners will be raised', but he promises their final defeat.[57] A poem dated to the fifteenth century has him covering the sweep of Irish history by foretelling the Norse raids and the Norman conquest, as well as prolonged oppression by the English. Such patriotic prophecies ascribed to Fionn had much vogue, and several others were composed down to the eighteenth century.[58]

The narratives describing the seer-craft of Fionn, however, did not undergo a comparable development. The account of how he had tasted the salmon of the Boyne was well remembered, but its detail was settled and non-variable and provided a standard explanation for his perennial use of the thumb and tooth of knowledge. The only late divergent accounts of how he gained wisdom are found in the *Feis Tighe Chonáin* text. In one of these, the givers of wisdom are three otherworld maidens who guard a well in the *sí*-dwelling of Carn Fhearadhaigh (Cahernarry in Co. Limerick). Fionn relates as follows:

> I happened one day to be hunting on this plain, where there were many deer, and I came to the summit of Carn Fhearadhaigh, with only Diorraing mac Doghair and Mac Reithe in my company. We were not long there when we saw the door of the *sí*-dwelling open before us, and we went towards it without delay.
>
> When the three daughters of Beg mac Buain saw that,

> they went quickly to close the door. They put their hands all together to the inside of the door to close it, and we put our shoulders and hands together to the outside to open it against them. Céibhfhionn [i.e. one of the three maidens] at that time had a vessel full from the well in her hand and, as she closed the door against us, a large measure of that drink spilled into our mouths, so that truly wise knowledge remained with us from then hence.[59]

Another account in the same text has Fionn, along with Oisín, Caoilte, Mac Lughach, and Diarmaid coming to the summit of Cahernarry and seeing a churl carrying a pig on a fork there. The churl was accompanied by a beautiful young woman. The five Fianna follow them into the dwelling, where they find – among many strange things – two wells with vessels beside them. Fionn takes a drink from each well.[60]

It is not expressly stated here that the drinks gave him knowledge, but the general context leaves no doubt as to the motif. A third narrative in the text is a version of a story already discussed (p. 23), which has Fionn becoming an old man after swimming in a lake at Slieve Gullion in Co. Armagh. The Fianna lay siege to the neighbouring *sí*-dwelling, and Fionn is given a drink from a golden cup by the lord of the dwelling. This drink restores him to youth and gives him wisdom.[61]

The combination of health and wisdom as gifts gained from the otherworld well has precedents in early literary sources. A lady called Bé Fhind from the Boyne, for instance, was giver of a healing drink, and her name can be connected with that of Fionn.[62] It is significant, too, that in the first Cahernarry story above the leader of the three maidens is called Céibhfhionn [literally, the fair-haired] and thus doubles Fionn's own name and imagery. Though these accounts in *Feis Tighe Chonáin* are late, it is clear that they reflect several elements found in earlier seer-lore of our hero (see pp. 53ff and pp. 67ff). They show that, in the literary sphere at least, some echoes of Fionn's otherworld journey in pursuit of knowledge survived.

In the general tradition, however, the search for knowledge

has disappeared as rationale for these visits of his. Instead he is portrayed as entering otherworld dwellings more or less by accident and meeting with fantastic adventures in them. These adventures fit into two basic categories: visits to the Tuatha Dé Danann, who are a divine people and whose life is in many ways a mirror of human society; and visits to a grotesque underworld, the inhabitants of which are horrendous and demonic. Of the first category there are several examples.

The Colloquy describes how Fionn with five warriors – Caoilte, Diarmaid, Oisín, Oscar, and Mac Lughach – hunted a young deer from the north of Ireland all the way to Slievenamon. Reaching there, the deer put its head into the ground and disappeared. A heavy fall of snow followed, 'which made a withy knot at the top of the forest', and they were forced to seek shelter.

Looking about, Caoilte saw a dwelling all lit up and entered it. Inside he found twenty-eight warriors with their ladies, and a gentle maiden playing beautiful music on a harp. On hearing that he was not alone, the maiden instructed Caoilte to bring in his comrades also. When they came in, they received the best of food and drink, and Fionn asked who his hosts were. Their leader was called Donn, and he told Fionn that the warriors were all brothers – grandsons of the Daghdha – and had had to leave Newgrange on the Boyne when their uncle Bodhbh Derg was made king of the Tuatha Dé. Three times a year the forces of Bodhbh Derg came to Slievenamon to do battle with them, and they had in this way lost all of their army.

The deer which had brought Fionn and his men to them had been one of their number metamorphosed, for they needed the help of the Fianna in the next contest with their foes.

The guests decided to stay and help them for a year, and in the ensuing battles Fionn and his men – though suffering terrible wounds – routed the forces of Bodhbh Derg. Oscar and Diarmaid were in a critical condition, so two of Donn's brothers went with Caoilte to Newgrange to kidnap the leech of the Tuatha Dé to heal them. Meanwhile, the feast of Tara was held by king Cormac mac Airt and a conference convened there to replace Fionn as chief of the Fianna, since he had disappeared from the physical world without trace. The druid Cithruadh, however, insisted that he was alive.

'On the last night of the feast of Temhair', he said, 'Fionn the prince will be seen drinking!'

And so it was. Fionn and his men returned, and the difficulty was resolved.[63]

Another story from the Colloquy is even more explicit concerning relations between the Fianna and the Tuatha Dé. According to this, Fionn and his men visited the *sí*-dwelling of Beann Éadair [Howth] and, after feasting there, a marriage was arranged between the daughter of the *sí*-lord Aedh and Fionn's grandson Oscar. The maiden's name was Étaín Fholtfhind [the fair-haired], and she was a faithful wife to Oscar until she died of a broken heart on observing his wounds after a terrible battle.[64] Fionn himself was the lover of several women in *sí*-dwellings.

A lay composed around the year 1200 tells of how a great boar, being hunted by Fionn and a few companions, led them to a *sí*-dwelling where they found a brilliant company of the Tuatha Dé. The boar was in fact a handsome youth, son of the *sí*-lord Énna. The visitors were royally entertained there, and many treasures were given to them. Énna gave his daughter Scáthach, who excelled all earthly women in beauty, to Fionn as wife. But she played magical music, which put the Fianna to sleep, and when they awoke in the morning they were back in the ordinary world. Only the treasures remained of the night before.

This is in fact a version of a well-known international fairy legend – that of the 'dream-visit' – which had been adopted here into the Fianna lore.[65]

The whole structure of the text *Feis Tighe Chonáin*, of course, is based on a visit by Fionn to a residence of the Tuatha Dé. There he conceives a passion for Findearbh (nicknamed Findchiabhach [fair-haired]), the daughter of his host Conán, and eventually he is allowed to sleep with her. A marriage feast is arranged for a month hence, and Fionn returns to his own residence at Almhu, where the Fianna greet him with a homecoming feast. While they are eating, Cairbre Lifeachair, son of king Cormac mac Airt, arrives and room is made for him and his retinue. It so happens, however, that two of the Tuatha Dé are among those displaced from their seats to accommodate the royal guest and, becoming incensed, they go next morning to Fionnbharr – an otherworld wooer of Findearbh – and incite him against Fionn.

When the hero and his men accordingly go to Conán's residence for the marriage feast, they find themselves surrounded by Fionnbharr's forces. A tremendous battle takes place, with Conán and his people fighting bravely to defend their guests. Goll mac Morna plays a leading part in the fighting in support of Fionn, and the enemy is routed. But the slaughter on all sides has been massive, and there is no further mention of the hero's proposed marriage to Conán's daughter.[66]

So it is clear that, no matter how good the relations with the otherworld appear, there is always a hostile element present. This reflects the general pattern of Irish stories from ancient to modern times; and it is strengthened in this context by the idea that Fionn was a surpassing mortal, who would because of his precocity be regarded as a threat to their position by divine beings.

The second category of visit is to underground dwellings inhabited by grotesque beings. These represent the dark side of the supernatural realm, and are always portrayed as inveterate enemies of Fionn. A story which belongs to the eleventh century, and which we have in both verse and prose, provides a good illustration of this. Horse-racing was being held at Clochar (near Manister in Co. Limerick) and a black horse proved far superior to all its competitors. After the racing, the animal was presented to Fionn by Fiacha, a prince of Munster. Having feasted there for three days, Fionn and his two comrades Caoilte and Oisín went west over Logher on their horses. He dashingly rode his brilliant new black horse on a long gallop from the strand of Berramhain (near Tralee) to a hillock called Bairneach south of Killarney. He and his comrades drew rein there and, as night was falling, they looked about for lodgings.

He saw a house in the glen which he had never seen before, and decided that they should spend the night there. But they soon discovered that it was not a pleasant place. A grey churl seized their horses and fastened the door of the house with iron hooks.

'Welcome, o Fionn of fame', said he, 'it took you a long time to come here, o son of Cumhall of Almhu!'

Within the sinister place were a three-headed hag and a headless man with one eye protruding from his breast. The churl called for music, and nine bodies and nine separated heads came forward to perform. These joined with the hag and the other grotesque beings in a chorus of terrible shrieks. Then the churl killed the visitors' horses, and offered the raw flesh as a meal. Fionn stoutly refused this, saying he had never eaten uncooked meat. He and his two men seized their swords, and a fierce hand-to-hand fight ensued.

Driven into a corner by the foes, they fought desperately all night until the sun rose in the morning. Then their attackers melted away and the whole house disappeared. Their horses were there again safe and sound, and none of their own wounds remained. Fionn put his thumb under his tooth of knowledge and realised that they had been dealing with 'the three phantoms of Iubharghlenn' who had been seeking revenge for the death of their sister Cuillenn 'of the Wide Maw' at the hands of the Fianna.[67]

This story, like some of the others mentioned before it, is concerned with a dream-visit to the otherworld, which disappears with the dawn. The repeated occurrence of such a story pattern in the context of Fionn is significant, and is best explained by taking it as an echo of ancient trance-practices of seers (see pp. 61ff). Fionn, once the ideal seer, continues to visit the otherworld, but in these mediaeval stories his function has become that of a warrior-hero.

The two categories – the Tuatha Dé on the one hand and the demonic world on the other – can now be seen as no more than the intrusion of general lore from outside the specifically Fionn context. The tradition of Fionn, we have argued, had basically to do with gaining wisdom from the ancestor-world and in its development was open to various interpretations which could be put on that world. The combination of the ancestor Nuadhu who belonged to the Tuatha Dé, with the image of the tyrant-grandfather, allowed for easy confusion between positive and negative perspectives on the otherworld in the lore of Fionn. Thus we have seen, in adventures which entail the acquisition of knowledge, raths belonging to the Tuatha Dé Danann as residences of Fionn's otherworld foe whom he kills with his spear.

In mediaeval Fianna lore the important thing was drama rather than esoteric philosophy, and so the known elements of the tradition were combined in whatever ways were felt suitable for narrative.

Fionn the Commander

The desire for detail and systematisation which characterises the late mediaeval lore is witnessed also by references to the Fianna, now seen as a volunteer force of first-class warriors under Fionn's command.

The author of the first Colloquy repeatedly refers to the force as organised in three battalions [*trí catha*], and he tells us that each battalion comprised three thousand men.[68] In other words, numerically as well as in function this author saw the Fianna as a national militia. We have met, in another source from the same period, with a comparably large host of men (pp. 103f), but here the organisational structure is different. The more clumsy earlier descriptions of many small units has given way to a clear-cut triadic arrangement.

This change indicates a new kind of perspective within the lore, for the 150 divisional groups smack more of original loosely-connected fianna bands, whereas the three straightforward battalions represent a standing army. The first Colloquy author calls them 'the Fianna of Ireland' [*Fianna Éirenn*], and states that the force had four chief centres – Temhair Bhregh [Tara in Co. Meath], Temhair Luachra [in Co. Kerry], Almhu [the hill of Allen in Co. Kildare where Fionn lived], and Cuillenn [Cullen in Co. Tipperary]. In the latter place, Fionn used to inspect the three battalions each year and select replacements for those who had been killed.[69]

We have several long lists of names of leading members of the Fianna, but we are not told in the Colloquy who the specific commanders of the battalions were, and it is apparent that the idea of three battalions was in itself little more than a numeric device to give the impression of a regular army.

Despite the efforts of those writers who wished to present a neat and synchronised picture, the tradition tended to re-assert its own untrammelled nature. Fionn's ambiguous role as 'king' of Ireland's Fianna, for example, makes his subservience to Cormac mac Airt a matter of some doubt. In the first Colloquy, we are told that at the fair of Tailtiu (Teltown, Co. Meath), Fionn sat on one side of the king, with Cairbre son of Cormac on the other side, and Oisín beside Fionn.[70] The protocol here suggests that Cormac and Fionn were in a sense equal kings, with their two sons as crown princes. Later on in the text, when Fionn is missing (see pp. 135f), it is Goll who sits beside Cormac at the fair of Tara.

The compiler of the third Colloquy text uses the opportunity which such a situation gives to describe the actual ranks of the Fianna. He says that they would sit in seven groups at the fair of Teltown, with seven hundred warriors in each group.[71] This is yet another new system for arranging and enumerating the Fianna, and it was this system which gained currency in the literature from the fourteenth century onwards.

In *Feis Tighe Chonáin* we read of 'the seven battalions of the established Fiann-troop' [*seacht gcatha na gnáth-Fhéinne*],[72] and this became the conventional reference.

The historian Seathrún Céitinn, writing in 1633, elaborates on the command structure through rationalisation of his own. He tells us that the ordinary force kept in his employ by Fionn consisted of three battalions, with three thousand warriors in each; but in times of need this was increased to seven battalions. Céitinn envisages the Fianna as corresponding to armies as he himself knew them:

> There were several high chiefs of the Fianna under Fionn – that is a battalion leader over a battalion, as a colonel is over a regiment; a commander of a hundred-man group, as a captain is now; a chief of fifty like a lieutenant; and a chief of three nines, like a corporal; and a chief of nine, as the Romans had a decurio.
>
> And when the hundred were divided into ten units or ranks, there was an officer over each rank, and it was he who was called a chief of nine.

Again, however, the imagery of Fionn's followers refuses to be straight-jacketed, and the old anarchic life of genuine fianna bands peeps through. Céitinn, despite his purpose of making their whole existence legalistic and orderly, has to allow them a half of their time to roam freely:

> The Fiann-troop used to be kept by the men of Ireland from November to May, with the duty of defending justice and preventing injustice for the kings and lords of Ireland, and also to protect and guard the harbours of the land against the violence of foreigners, and performing every other function which the king of Ireland asked them to – that is, preventing theft and having taxes paid, preventing reavers [*díbheirgigh*] and every other evil that used to occur in the land at that time. And they got a definite payment for that. . . .
>
> From May to November, however, the Fiann-troop had to depend on their own hunting and chasing for upkeep and for earnings under the king of Ireland. That is, the meat as food for them, and the hides of the wild animals as wages.[73]

Regardless of the writers' efforts at historicisation, the main impetus for the Fianna lore has always been the drama of its narratives. For this impetus the martial tactics and military formations were of no importance, but the individualised heroes were. This is indeed admitted, though indirectly, in the first Colloquy when five warriors are singled out, not for their official position, but for being 'the five men of greatest valour at the one time in Ireland'. They are named as Fionn, Lughaidh Lágha, Oscar, Goll, and Caoilte.[74] The pre-eminence of five or six great warriors was – as we shall see in subsequent chapters – a recurrent feature of Fianna lore; except that, instead of Lughaidh Lágha, Oisín and Diarmaid were usual members of the select company.

The special perspectives of the literary men could, however, add valuable extra dimensions to the tradition. For example, the writer of *Feis Tighe Chonáin* succeeded, in several of his passages, to cull drama from the very detail itself, and in so doing gave something of a social perspective to the Fianna company. He lists members of the troop who surpassed their fellows in particular attributes. Fionn was the best person by way of honour, Leargan Luath the fastest person, Daolghus mac Duibhdhoiligh the tallest person, and Mac Méin the smallest.

Not all other sources would agree with these selections, but it would be difficult to defeat the following for graphic description. As usual in this text, Fionn does the talking:

> Deardubha Duibhshléibhe is the worst person in the Fianna of Ireland – that is, a female courier whom I have and who travels throughout the lands and peoples of the world on my business; and nobody ever wishes but to criticise anyone who talks to her, and each person who sees her at breakfast-time benefits nothing from that day.
>
> Liphthe the Lazy, the fire-attendant of the great cauldron at Almhu is the slowest person in the Fianna of Ireland, since it takes his best effort on a Summer-day to come from the well which is at the door of Almhu as far as his own bed in the kitchen.[75]

The contrived setting does not here lessen the humorous effect. In another list, the author draws on a series of contrasts to give life to a variety of extravagant ideas. The result is to present the Fianna as an incongruous kind of allegorical society:

> A deaf warrior who is in the Fianna troop, and no poem or recitation has been made which he does not know as clear learning and by rote.
>
> Another wonder in the Fianna is a man with a wooden leg, and he leaves all the Fianna – hound or horse or man – behind him running.
>
> Another wonder in it is a blind man who never made an inaccurate cast by day or indeed by night.
>
> Another wonder in it is a woman whom I myself have, and she is dead every night and alive every day, and I hold no woman I ever had in greater affection than her.
>
> Another wonder in it is a warrior who is on alternate years a woman and a man, and he bears children when he is a woman, and children are borne for him when he is a man.

Another wonder in the Fianna troop is a spear which I have – that is, the spear of Fiacha mac Croinghind [*sic*]. When it is hurled handle-first it moans and is damaging to the person or beast at which it is hurled, and when thrown point-first it does neither harm nor damage to the person or beast it is thrown at.[76]

Fionn at War

As with the personnel of the Fianna, we have several pseudo-learned lists of battles which were fought and won by Fionn and his warriors. One such list, dating from as early as the eleventh century, cites ten great battles: fought at Cuillenn, Cliath, Cumar Trí nUisce, Muigh-Inis, Sliabh Mis, Luachair, Sídh Feimhin, Fea, Crionna, and Sídh Dá Bholg.[77] Although accounts of some of these battles may have been current, it seems that most of them have been invented spontaneously for the list.

Other series of battles are given in later sources, with no doubt the same principles of composition involved. A twelfth-century poem states, concerning the battles won by Fionn, that 'it would be difficult to number them', and then goes on to mention no fewer than forty-four places where such engagements were fought. The poet says that he is not reckoning 'indoor fights and duels with hard swords', but is not deterred from saying that Fionn fought thirty-two battles outside of Ireland, eight in Leinster, sixteen in Ulster, thirty in Munster, twelve in Connacht, and twenty-five against the Tuatha Dé Danann![78] We have actual narratives concerning only a small number of these contests, however, and there were hardly many more in existence.

Mediaeval portrayals of the Fianna at war focus mainly on the battles of Cnucha (Castleknock, Co. Dublin), Fionntráigh (Ventry, Co. Kerry), Ollarbha (Larne, Co. Antrim), and Gabhair (Gowra, Co. Meath). The oldest accounts of the battle of Castleknock we have already discussed in chapter 4, but it maintained its popularity and there are several references to it in the subsequent poetry and prose. The great heroism and mighty fighting of Fionn's father, Cumhall, and his tragic death in that battle were subjects which could always evoke interest. A poem from around the year 1200 stresses how, at the end of the contest, Cumhall stood alone and fought stubbornly with 'all the men of Ireland' wounding him. Garadh mac Morna tells Fionn in the poem that sixteen men of his own Morna clan thrust spears into the side of 'Cumhall the champion'.[79]

Perhaps the most colourful account is given in a lay of the fifteenth century or so, which has Garadh telling of the frightful slaughter which Cumhall caused to the Morna clan, and describes his great enemy's death in revealing terms:

> When the man was without any warriors
> It was easier for us to kill him;
> There were none of them on yonder mound
> Around him from Cumhall's clan.
>
> We made a run which was not slow
> To the house where Cumhall was;
> We, each man of us, dealt a deep wound
> To the body of Cumhall with our spears![80]

There is a brief, but significant, description of another battle in the Colloquy. This, it is stated, was fought at Tráigh Rudhraighe (now Dundrum Bay in Co. Down). Fionn, with his three battalions, was on a great hunt in that area. He left the two sons of the king of Connacht, Art and Eoghan, on sentry-duty by night, and these went with four hundred warriors and four hundred servants to the strand.

They were not long there when two Norse kings, Conus and Conmhael, arrived with many ships and a huge force of men. These Norse kings were seeking revenge for Fionn's killing of their father in the battle of Druim Derg in Scotland. The Connacht princes engaged the invaders, and the battle went on from nightfall to midnight.

Meanwhile, Fionn was sleeping in his camp, and he had a vision of two grey seals drinking from his breast. He asked his poet, Fearghus Fíonbhéil, what this meant, and was told that foreigners had attacked the Connacht princes. He rose with his forces and went to the strand, and there found all the Norsemen slain. Only the two Connacht princes survived the battle, but they too were mortally wounded. They died soon after, and were buried by a disconsolate Fionn along with their two great spears, the Órlasrach [lightning-gold] and the Muinderg [red-neck] which he himself had given them.

The story, the Colloquy tells us, was 'a speciality from among the specialities of the Fianna-lore' [*tallann do thallannaib na fiannaigechta*].[81]

The fictional battle illustrates the effect that the memory of Norse raids had on the Fianna tradition. The place where the action is situated is in the north-east, where raiding Vikings might be expected to land. But the specific choice of Loch Rudhraighe seems to be on account of an association between it and the theme of slaughter.

A story from about the eighth century told of how a warrior called Ferghus mac Léti killed a water-monster there, and that as a result the water was red for a month.[82] This latter idea is based on a pseudo-etymology of *Rudhraighe*, of which the first element is taken to be *ruadh* [red]. This was a common conventional explanation in early Irish narratives to represent great slaughter. It was often taken as half of an equation – the other half being that the lake was beforehand called Fionnloch [*White Lake*].[83] This *fionn* terminology in itself would tend to attract elements of the story to the great character called Fionn.

Very likely we can date the composition of this Fianna story by its use of the particular Loch Rudhraighe situation, for the tenth-century poem by Cinaedh ua hArtacáin which describes Fionn's last stand (p. 108) also cites the Ferghus mac Léti story in cryptic form. The poem gave a potted history of heroic endeavours and was highly valued as source-material, so a writer of Fianna tales would not hesitate to cull imagery from it. This explanation would leave us with a composition-date for the battle of Tráigh Rudhraighe around the eleventh century. And this is what we would expect, given the Norse theme and the portrayal of Fionn as halfway between an ordinary hunter and a leader of a national army. In the story Fionn posts sentries to guard his hunting camp, the aggressors are personal enemies of his, but the net effect of the battle is to protect Ireland from foreign invaders.

Once the Tráigh Rudhraighe story gained currency, and since the name of the place was etymologised as meaning reddened by blood, the question of such a strand's previous name would naturally arise. The name would have to be *Fionntráigh* [White Strand] or a certain variant of that. And so some Munsterman, who read or heard the Tráigh Rudhraighe story, conceived the idea of a similar battle being fought at the Fionntráigh which he knew – that is, Ventry in Co. Kerry. Such a battle would, on the Tráigh Rudhraighe pattern, make the strand of Ventry the site of a great clash between an invading army and the country's Fianna protectors. In this Munster story, the leader of the invading army was called Dáire Donn – a name which was very popular in the southern province for Fionn's archetypal foe (see p. 43), and Fionn himself was accordingly given a more central part in the action.

In time, this battle of Ventry became regarded as the greatest ever fought by Fionn. First composed towards the end of the eleventh century, it had already achieved prominence when the first Colloquy was compiled. Several references to it are found in that text, as well as in other twelfth-century sources,[84] but the original version has not come down to us. For a full recension of the story, we are dependent on a fifteenth-century text, which is based on the original but is definitely an amplification. The following is a synopsis of the main actions in this recension:

Fionn was once in banishment from Ireland and was a mercenary in the employ of the French king. While he was in France, the king's wife and daughter eloped with him. This was the reason why Dáire Donn, the king of the world, decided to invade Ireland, for the foreign nobility sought vengeance on Fionn.

When a man called Glas mac Dreamhain was banished by Fionn, he offered to guide the invasion force to Ireland. It was a massive army, with contingents from many countries. Glas first brought the fleet to the island of Skellig Michael, and from there to Ventry. Fionn, however, had received a prophecy that the country would be invaded, and had watchmen posted at every harbour.

The watchman at Ventry, Conn Crithir, had fallen asleep, and when he awoke he saw the soldiers of the Spanish king plundering and burning the countryside. He immediately went to attack them, and on his way met three women who had fallen in love with him and, therefore, promised him magical help to protect the area until Fionn arrived. He killed the Spanish king and many of his men; and Dáire Donn, who was watching from his ship, sent Glas ashore to talk to him. Glas told Conn that he wished to be reconciled to Fionn, but in fact he intended to spy for Dáire.

Soon after, a strong man of the Fianna called Taistealach arrived. This Taistealach overcame Dáire's champion wrestler and was then sent by Conn to raise the alarm. He alerted the Tuatha Dé Danann, who came and held the front for the moment. Fionn was swimming in the Shannon river when Taistealach arrived. Hearing the calamitous news, he immediately gathered his forces and headed for Ventry.

When they reached there, Oscar went to reconnoitre, but since he was exhausted from the forced march he began to slumber. Wakened by the sound of a hostile group coming ashore, he seized a broken club and a sword and slew all of them.

Hearing of this, the French king came ashore with another force, determined on revenge, and was wreaking havoc on Oisín until Oscar intervened. Terrified by Oscar's ferocity, the French king raced away demented from the field.

A great warrior called Dolar Durba then came ashore and performed wonderful tricks with a hurley and ball. He did this several days running, but none of the Fianna dared to compete with him. A young Ulster prince arrived with twelve other boys to help the Fianna, and he attacked the exultant Dolar. All day long they fought, and on into the night, so that when morning came they were found dead on the shore locked in each other's grip. The Ulster prince was buried by the Fianna with great honour and sadness.

Fionn's poet, Fearghus Fíonbhéil, had meanwhile gone to seek the assistance of the high-king, but Cormac mac Airt refused to come since he saw the possibility of being rid of Fionn. Cormac's son Cairbre Lifeachair, however, became ashamed of this policy, so he gathered his forces and set out for Ventry, where he got a great welcome from Fionn. Other help also came, including magical weapons destined to kill Dáire Donn, which were presented to Fionn by his uncle Labhraidh Lámhfhada, son of Tadhg mac Nuadhat. But the incessant fighting had reduced the Fianna to just one battalion, and they decided on one last great effort.

Urged on by Fearghus the poet, they made a savage attack on the full enemy host. The leader of the Ulster Fianna, called Druimdherg of the Rughraidhe clan, killed the Norse king with a great spear called Cró Derg; and, as Fionn directed the onslaught, Fearghus relayed to him all the tidings of the struggle.

Coming face to face in fierce combat with Dáire, 'Fionn divided the head and trunk of the king of the world from each other'. In another terrific struggle, Goll mac Morna slew Conmhael, the son of Dáire.

Fionn was now exhausted and covered with wounds, and he was attacked by a ferocious female warrior, Órarmach daughter of the Greek king, but he beheaded her also. The two sides continued to fight each other to a standstill, but the invaders were getting the worse of it.

When only one foreigner – Dáire's household chieftain – remained, he took to the sea; but a young student of Fionn called Caol followed him and both sank to the bottom of the ocean in deadly combat. Caol's young wife Geilghéis lamented him in verse, and so the battle ended.[85]

There are many echoes here of the Tráigh Rudhraighe source – the role played by Fearghus Fíonbhéil; the nomenclature Conmhael, Druimdherg [Druim Derg], Órarmach and Cró Derg [apparently based on Orlasrach and Muinderg in the other text]; and the Ulster prince who dies fighting for Fionn as the two Connacht princes did. But the battle of Ventry has drawn on other sources also, such as the image of Cúchulainn in the whole episode of Dolar and the Ulster prince; the early mediaeval motif of Suibhne, the man who went mad in battle; and a variety of details from lore of the Tuatha Dé Danann.[86] The pretext for the attempted invasion – the French ladies' love for Fionn – seems to be based on the reason for the Trojan war in classical myth.[87] It is, therefore, clear that the story of the battle of Ventry was coloured from many different sources, and much of this colouring may have been the work of the original author.

Another battle frequently referred to was that of Ollarbha. The tradition of this encounter was old, and we have already mentioned an eighth-century Ulster reference to it (p. 49). In this, Caoilte is made to describe a journey which he and Fionn once made to Moylinny in Co. Antrim:

> We came from Scotland. We met Fothadh Airgthech over here at Ollarbha. We fought a battle there. I made a cast at him, so that it passed through him and went into the ground beyond him and left its iron point in the ground.

In subsequent centuries this encounter with Fothadh Airgthech became developed into a full-scale battle, and so we find in the Colloquy Caoilte describing how three battalions of the Fianna went to the inlet Ollarbha and how only six hundred of them survived the battle. For the first time ever, Fionn began to lose confidence in his men, and he composed a lay mentioning all those nobles who fell in that fearsome struggle:

> Three hundred battles the Fianna troop won, in north and south and west, but they never until now won any battle which had more lamentation![88]

Caoilte tells St Patrick in the Colloquy that Ollarbha was one of the two battles which destroyed the Fianna. The other was the battle of Gowra, a fatal clash after the death of Cormac between the forces of Cairbre Lifeachair and the Fianna. It is therefore a final resolution in lore of the long-repressed rivalry between the interests of Fionn and those of the Uí Néill kingship; and it is significant that the surviving scion of the Morna clan, Oscar mac Garaidh, is put on the side of the Uí Néill in the fighting.

We have references to this battle in twelfth- and thirteenth-century sources,[89] but it does not seem to have been long in existence at that time. The Annals tell us that Cairbre Lifeachair was killed in the battle of Gowra by one Seniach mac Fir Choirb of the Fotharta in the year A.D. 284, but they make no reference to involvement of the Fianna in that battle.[90] It is, therefore, clear that some scholar who had read the Annals conceived the idea that this would be an appropriate context in which to place the Fianna's last great battle, a year after Fionn's reputed death in A.D. 283 (see p. 113).

The new narrative seems to have been invented in the eleventh century, for we have a few verses from that period concerning how Cairbre, seated on a white horse in the battle, cast his spear at Oscar and was in turn slain by Oscar's spear-cast.[91] The oldest surviving full account is late, belonging to about the year 1400, and the reason given for the battle must be equally late. Fionn, we are told with anachronistic taste, had gone on a pilgrimage to Rome accompanied by thrice fifty warriors, and he had left Oisín in command of the troop. Cairbre sent a message to the fort of Almhu, demanding that the Fianna surrender all their hunting rights. They discussed the matter and agreed to give the high-king a refusal; whereupon Cairbre gathered forces from all over the country, as well as the army of Oscar mac Garaidh who had been in exile in Scotland.

The Fianna, with a mere thousand men, were vastly outnumbered, but before the battle they received welcome reinforcements from the same number of Scandinavians who had come to help. But the Scandinavians were wiped out by the forces of Oscar mac Garaidh, who then came face to face with the Fianna champion Oscar mac Oisín.

All the other warriors ceased fighting to watch the terrible combat between these two, and the son of Oisín triumphed and slew his opponent. He then wreaked havoc upon the foe. Cairbre cast a deadly spear at him but, mortally wounded though he was, Oscar beheaded the high-king with a mighty sword-stroke. Finally, he flung himself on Cairbre's crack regiment, the Columns of Tara, before being himself destroyed.

'Until both sea-sand and stars are counted', we are told, 'one third of a third of those whom Oscar, son of Oisín, slew may not be reckoned!'

The day was won, but the Fianna themselves were decimated.[92] This was the battle which, according to the Colloquy, Oisín and Caoilte survived, thus giving the text the framework on which to hang its anthology of lore and legend.

6.

The Hero's Company

The gradual development of tradition meant a gradual change in the portrayal of Fionn's background. In the earliest phase he was a solitary seer-figure, then he became a wise leader of a small fianna band, and finally a leader of a great army. It was therefore inevitable that he should gather a great deal of associated characters to him on his journey through the realm of story. For the redactor's purpose, of course, there must be a limit to the number of actual actors in the drama, and so we find a more or less fixed set of characters revolving around Fionn in the fully fledged narratives of the late Middle Ages.

Fionn's Family

Much stress was placed by Gaelic tradition on kinship in determining the social role of the individual, and so it is not surprising to find that the late mediaeval lore had worked out a complex – though not entirely consistent – pattern of family and relatives for Fionn. We have already discussed his genealogy (pp. 32f), but a few extra details should be mentioned concerning his father Cumhall.

The Boyhood-Deeds text states that the warrior Criomhall was Cumhall's brother. The Colloquy agrees with this, and further tells us that his mother was Meas Muingheal, daughter of king Aenghus of Ulster. There was some fluctuation in such details, however. Cumhall is usually referred to as son of Tréanmhór and grandson of Baoiscne, but the latter is sometimes actually mentioned as his father.[1] And so, instead of Meas Muingheal, a fourteenth-century poem claims that Cumhall's mother was one Báine, daughter of the king of

Connacht, and that she had another son called Feidhlimidh. This poem gives several other details which have obviously crept into the lore since the first Colloquy was written. We are told that Tréanmhór had four sons in all, Criomhall, Cumhall, Conall and Aodh Eangach – the latter two here are borrowings from extra-Fianna sources. Furthermore, Cumhall himself is said to have had three sons – Fionn, Fíothal, and Féinnidh; and two daughters – Suanach who was the mother of Fiachra and Sidhe the mother of Caoilte.

Referring to Fionn's brothers, the poem's author significantly says that 'these are a question for historians', but himself states rather presumptuously that Fíothal was Cumhall's son by Bodhmann and that Féinnidh was his son by a princess of Britain. In fact, these two supposed brothers of Fionn are merely extensions of his own personality. Fíothal is described as a wise and learned man; while Féinnidh's very name represents the second aspect of Fionn's image, that of a fianna warrior.[2]

An earlier tradition of a brother of Fionn is referred to in the Boyhood-Deeds – this is Tulcha, an older son of Cumhall who was in his youth 'an attendant of the king of Scotland'.[3] Surviving references to this Tulcha are few, although he must once have been of some importance. As we have seen (p. 3) his name occurs with that of Fionn in an early genealogical tract and, although he is not there expressly stated to have been a brother of the hero, he is grouped with Fionn and Caoilte as a descendant of Baoiscne.

When we come to consider the wives of Fionn, we are dealing directly with stories rather than with pedigrees. The narrative concerning each wife is more or less a self-contained unit and, although some texts recognise that the hero had various wives at different times, there was no attempt to synchronise these stories. Fionn's wives tend to be mutually exclusive, thereby showing that the lore was circulating in independent and differentiated channels. We have mentioned some of the wives or lovers attributed to him in the earlier lore (p. 107f).

Another woman closely connected with the hero was one Smirnat, whom several twelfth-century sources refer to as his wife. She was daughter of Fothadh Canainne, a fianna figure who was portrayed as hostile to Fionn in much of the early lore.[4] The idea that two warring *féinnidhs* could be reconciled by a marriage arrangement of this kind occurs again in a story which is told in the Colloquy, and here the attempted reconciliation is with the Morna clan.

A girl called Bearrach Bhreac was reared by the parents of Fionn's great rival Goll mac Morna. Fionn asked the girl's father, king Cas Cuailnge of Ulster, for her, and Cas left the decision to Goll. Conditions were arranged, and the marriage took place. She was the most hospitable woman in Ireland and a great patron of poets, and she bore three sons to Fionn – Faolán, Aodh Beag, and Iollann Faobhardhearg. After some time, however, the Morna clan went reaving [*ar foghail ocus ar díbheirg*] against Fionn, and they asked Bearrach to leave her husband and return to them. This she refused to do, and her dwelling by the strand of Doire Tarbhga in Connacht was attacked and burned by her erstwhile guardians. As she left the dwelling to take a boat away with her attendants, Art mac Morna cast his spear and killed her.[5]

Such relationships seem to have had much vogue in mediaeval storytelling, and to have been known to oral as well as literary narrative. An obvious reflection of the Fothadh Canainne connection is a late (fourteenth-century) mention of a wife of Fionn called Luchar, daughter of Mac Nia – reputedly father also of Fothadh. This Luchar is said to have borne two sons to Fionn, called Aodh Beag and Aodh Fada.[6] Again, we have a late reflection of the marriage arrangement between Fionn and the Morna clan, for in the surviving full version of the Diarmaid and Gráinne story we are told that Fionn was a widower for a year – his late wife having been Maighnis, daughter of Garadh mac Morna.[7] Gráinne, daughter of the high-king Cormac, was the most famous of all Fionn's ladies. References from the tenth and the eleventh centuries say that she was married to him for a brief period, but she hated him and loved Diarmaid instead.[8] Later sources describe her only as Fionn's betrothed, but we shall discuss this whole story presently.

For the moment it is sufficient to say that the mediaeval writers used the failed Gráinne marriage as a prelude to

Fionn's more successful marriage to her sister Ailbhe. The latter lady, we are told (p. 107), bore three sons to Fionn – Raighne, Iollann, and Caoince. We have already met with confusion regarding the mothers of Fionn's progeny. Aodh Beag in one case was said to have been born of Luchar and in another of Bearrach. Here we have another of Bearrach's sons, Iollann, described as the son of Ailbhe.

The Colloquy tells a startling story of how Fionn and the Fianna went hunting one day and left their womenfolk at Druim Criadh (now Kildare town) in the care of Garadh mac Morna, who was then an old man. The women demanded that Garadh play chess with them, and when he refused they teased him, saying that all his strength and vigour was gone. Angered by this, Garadh lit a great fire in the palace and walked out, having locked the seven doors. Strangely, we are not told what happened as a result of this, but the tradition must have been that Garadh left the women to burn to death.[9]

The strange and savage act can be explained as a reflex of the fiery foe motif which was associated with Garadh's more famous brother Goll [the one-eyed], who also had the name Aedh [fire]. A late verse-telling of the story (probably fifteenth century) has Fionn's wife Ailbhe playing a leading part in the teasing of Garadh and dying in the blazing palace as a result. Fionn tracked the offender down to a cave, where Garadh was beheaded by his own son (called Aedh) in expiation of his crime. Aedh, however, went mad soon after and drowned himself in a lake.[10]

Fionn is invested with wives from the otherworld also. The Colloquy tells of how he married Sadhbh, the daughter of Bodhbh Derg of Slievenamon, and how he had to leave her to campaign against the Morna clan who were reaving against him. After he was away for a year, he sent a detachment under the command of the two sons of the Munster king to bring Sadhbh to him, but as they returned with her they were waylaid by Goll and his forces and slaughtered to a man. Sadhbh and her female attendants died from the terror of the fight.[11]

A less faithful wife was Scáthach, whom Fionn married in an otherworld dwelling, but he was put to sleep by her magical music and woke up back in the ordinary world (see p. 136). We also read, in the fourteenth-century version of the Colloquy, that Fionn was married to a lady called Scoith-Fhionn daughter of Bran Bhoirne;[12] and a thirteenth-century poem tells of another wife of his called Daolach. She was daughter of Dubh mac Duinn and was drowned while swimming at the High Plain [*Magh Ard*] between the rivers Nanny and Delvin in Co. Meath.[13] Finally, we are told, he married Áine daughter of Morn king of Scotland, who resided at Dún Monaidh. She had always said that Fionn was the only man she wanted, and she proved to be a very hospitable woman to the Fianna.[14] She gave two sons to Fionn, Iollann Faobhardhearg and Aodh Beag – at whose birth she died.

She is thus the third woman who is stated to have been the mother of these two. Indeed, much of the same general pattern of description attaches to the various wives of Fionn – several of them, for instance, are said to have entertained a great host for as long as the guests wished and to have clothed them all from head to foot.

Fionn's eldest son was Oisín, and his mother Blái Derg, as we have suggested (pp. 78ff), seems originally to have been a manifestation of the otherworld daughter of Dearg – a perennial foe of our hero. We have also seen that Oisín was one of the very earliest characters to be associated with Fionn – references to him dating from at least the seventh and eighth centuries. He evolved out of the hunting-lore of fianna bands when it was connected with Fionn, and his portrayal was very much patterned on that of his father. Thus we find him represented as a poet as well as a warrior, with the major stress being put on the former attribute.

By the tenth century or so, Oisín had been given the nickname Guaire Goll, which properly was the name of one of Fionn's servants (see pp. 120f). It is not clear why the name should be applied to Oisín, but it was probably due originally to some scribal error. Around the same time developed the custom of ascribing narrative poems, concerning adventures of the Fianna, to him. The two earliest of these poems which survive are one on the place-lore of Ballyleague (p. 73), and one on the visit to a grotesque otherworld dwelling (pp. 137). Then, from the early twelfth century, we have a poem ascribed to him in which he is portrayed as an old man converted to Christianity and complaining of the loss of his strength and youth.[15]

This illustrates how Oisín's role as narrator of Fianna lore has prepared the ground for the Colloquy, in which he and Caoilte meet St Patrick and describe for him the heroic days of old.

A twelfth-century poem claims that Fionn had six sons and names them as Oisín, Fearghus, Caoince, Iollann, Faobhar, and Raighne.[16] We have met four of these already, as well as some others. All are portrayed as hardy warriors, but no great single achievement of theirs occurs in the mediaeval literature. This is more than compensated for in the case of Oisín's son, Oscar. Known as 'Oscar of the hard blows', he was so renowned as a fighter that it was conventional for writers to have him saving the day for the Fianna whenever all seemed lost. His name came to be used as a common noun, a poetic word for 'champion' [*oscar*], but as we have said it seems to have originated in the same fianna hunting-lore as that of Oisín. Perhaps 'Oscar' was originally no more than an alternate name for Oisín, which in time became personalised as his son.

Oscar does not feature in what survives of the earliest literature, and seems to have come to prominence in the lore during the eleventh century when he was incorporated into the story of the battle of Gowra (p. 150). A thirteenth-century text puts the high opinion of him in succinct terms:

> There will never be after Oscar
> A warrior of so many hardy triumphs,
> Nor in his own time
> Was there a man his match in battles.[17]

There was another grandson of Fionn who had a high profile in late mediaeval narrative. We have mentions of several daughters of Fionn, including Grian, Aoi, Samhaoir, and Lughaidh,[18] and the latter of these gave birth to a famous son who was known as Gaoine or Mac Lughach.

A poem from the twelfth century describes the conception and birth of this great youth. A warrior called Dáire Dearg was welcomed into the Sídh of Bodhbh [the otherworld dwelling of Slievenamon], where he slept with the maiden Lughaidh who was in fosterage with the Tuatha Dé Danann. As a result she gave birth to a baby-boy, who soon after overcame a weasel which tried to steal his food. When he was a year old Lughaidh brought him to Almhu, where he picked out his father from among the warriors. Dáire's wife was overcome by jealousy, but on Fionn's advice she reared the boy for seven years. He then became a member of the Fianna.[19]

This story requires some examination. First of all, Lughaidh is properly a man's rather than a woman's name, and indeed in a text of the period Gaoine is said to have been the son of a great warrior Lughaidh Lághdha.[20] The latter name is in fact a scribal confusion of two famous Munster warriors whom the historians made contemporaneous with Fionn – these were Lughaidh Lágha and Lughaidh Laighde.[21] So we can see how some Munster writer, when inventing a new character for the Fianna band, made him son of a great warrior of that province and called him Mac Lughach [son of Lughaidh].

The basic invention of Mac Lughach seems to have been a simple matter, centering on the international motif of a child recognising his unknown father.[22] The anonimity of the father meant that the term Mac Lughach could not be taken to reflect the name of that parent, and so the notion developed that Lughaidh was the mother. This, of course, meant that another designation had to be found for the father at the denouement. The name Dáire was often associated with Lughaidh in genealogical tracts – Lughaidh Laighde in fact is said to have been son of one Dáire – and so it was a ready to hand substitute. It is obvious also that the Mac Lughach narrative became coloured by that of Fionn's birth – the weasel episode, for instance, is borrowed from the lore of Fionn's youth (see p. 97).

The story of Mac Lughach must have been in existence prior to the writing of the first Colloquy, for the version given in that text shows an extra development in the plot. It is claimed that Dáire Dearg was in fact the maiden Lughaidh's brother, and that he had intercourse with her at a drinking-feast in Temhair Luachra (in Co. Kerry). In that way was Mac Lughach conceived. After the birth, Fionn went to see the child and remarked rather listlessly that he considered it good that it was a son who was born [*'as gaíne leam, óir is mac rucad ann'*]. Those present said that this was a suitable name [*gaíne* or *gaoine* means 'good'], and the child was so called. Fionn gave him to Mongfhind, the great female tutor of young warriors, to rear; and when he was twelve years old he became a member of Fionn's troop. But he also excelled his fellows and treated them so roughly that the three battalions of the Fianna told Fionn to choose between them and Mac Lughach, for they could not tolerate him any further.

Fionn then summoned Mac Lughach, and gave him instructions in poetic form, admonishing him to be co-operative, gentle, quietly-spoken, generous, and prudent. These instructions are patterned on the idealised code of conduct of the Gaelic nobility. For example,

> Give two-thirds of your gentility to women and to floor-servants, to the men of art who make poems, and do not be severe with the common people'.[23]

This version of Mac Lughach's birth and upbringing is a combination of several different elements.

The incest motif was often used in accounts of heroes' births in early and mediaeval Irish literature. The source here seems to be the legend of Pope Gregory the Great, which would have been known to a learned Irish author of the twelfth century. Gregory was said to have been born the offspring of a brother and sister, but the motif in Mac Lughach's case was broadened by material borrowed from the native lore of Cúchulainn – a hero born of father-daughter incest.[24] Thus we have Mac Lughach, like Cúchulainn, excelling his fellows at athletics and rough play.

The verses of advice uttered by Fionn are similar to many such wise counsels known to Irish literature, and were probably suggested here by the maxims of advice reputedly given by Cormac mac Airt to his son Cairbre.[25]

It is clear that writers of Fionn lore regarded his kin-group – known as the Baoiscne clan – as much strengthened by the valour and skills of Fionn's own direct descendants. A twelfth- or thirteenth-century lay has that clan on its own taking over the action in a situation which would normally be regarded as appropriate to the full Fianna troop.

The lay – put in the mouth of Oisín – tells of how Cormac entertained Fionn to a feast at Tara. The king got drunk, insulted Fionn, and challenged him to battle, saying that he would make him pass under the fork of the cauldron. An argument broke out, with Garadh mac Morna taking the side of Cormac, and taunts began to fly hither and thither concerning the battle of Castleknock. But the poet Cithruadh sang some verses for the company, and they ceased to bicker till morning. The Baoiscne clan then departed, and sixteen of them decided to make a foray against Tara. They drove away a thousand head of cattle, and as they passed through Teltown the mustered forces of Cormac fell upon them. Oisín describes what happened then:

> We turned about manfully on the trail, we charged the host of Temhair, we wounded Cormac of the feasts, and we captured Cairbre the fair-skinned!

Cormac had no choice but to offer ransom for his son, but Fionn's son Faolán refused any terms except that Cormac pass under the fork of the cauldron. When Fionn saw Cormac do this, he graciously did the same himself. The members of the Baoiscne clan who took part in this daring raid are named as Fionn, Oisín, Oscar, Fear Logha, Caireall, Aodh Beag, Mac Lughach, Daolghus [i.e. Caoilte], Fearghus, Feardhomhain, Colla, Raighne, Ailbhe, Faobhrachán, Caoince, and Iollann.[26]

The Morna Clan

We have already described how Fionn's archetypal foe was often called Goll and how this name, in the early Middle Ages, gradually developed into a character called Goll son of Morna. This Goll and his relatives were then portrayed as a sept hostile to Fionn. Morna himself is never described in detail, and his only importance is as the father of the hostile family. This family is called *Clann Mhorna* [the children of Morna], and it is in this sense that they are referred to in this book as the Morna clan. They are represented as rivals of Fionn's kin-group, who are called *Clann Bhaoiscne*. There is little evidence for a Morna sept in the genealogies, the only indication being that they were a vassal people in east Connacht.[27]

In the mediaeval Fianna lore they are portrayed as fighting with the Luaighne sept against Cumhall in the battle of Castleknock, and so their name probably belonged to some such martial sub-sept against which Uí Fáilghe had to strive (see p. 45). It is clear that in tradition they took over the function of all those anti-Leinster military forces, such as the Luaighne, the sons of Uirghriu, and the fianna of Fothadh Canainne. The latter influence probably accounts for why the Morna clan are associated with the Connacht area, for Fothadh Canainne was said to have belonged to that province.[28] It suited the purposes of narrative to have Fionn's military rivals condensed into one group, and so the archetypal foe Goll was made to play this role, with the Morna clan as his war-like relatives.

The attempts to synchronise the Fionn tradition with the history of king Cormac mac Airt caused the struggle between the Morna and Baoiscne clans to be transformed into a contest for the chief command of Cormac's forces. And so we are told that Morna once led the Fianna, but after his death Cumhall took over. Cumhall was killed by Goll mac Morna, who in turn had to relinquish the leadership to the young Fionn. But the hostility between the two families never quite subsided and was wont to break out afresh at the slightest provocation. In other words, the dramatic potential of such a feud between two warrior families, each with a great champion, was too much to be ignored by storytellers.

Goll was, from at least the eleventh century, viewed as by no means an ogre, but a worthy opponent of Fionn who did not lack nobility of character. Doubtlessly, this portrayal of him was cultivated by Connacht men, who had come to regard Goll as their own. The Colloquy author had imbibed this perspective sufficiently to have Goll relinquish the Fianna leadership to Fionn. But the rivalry between the two champions was not diminished, and the Colloquy refers to many savage clashes between the Baoiscne and Morna clans, with Goll leading his supporters in reaving expeditions against Fionn.[29] These expeditions, of course, could be taken to belong to the period of the final break between Fionn and Goll, but they are scattered throughout the text without specification and in a manner which suggests that the author was ignoring the long period of peace between them. The conciliation of the two, and the eventual resumption of hostilities, was the subject of a narrative in the twelfth century. It is referred to in the Boyhood-Deeds and is detailed in the *Fotha Catha Cnucha* text:

> Fionn and Goll made peace afterwards, and compensation for his father was given to Fionn by the Morna clan; and they were at peace until a quarrel arose between them at Temhair Luachra over the pig of Slángha and the slaying of Banbh Sionna son of Mael Enaigh.[30]

No further information is available on this clash, but that relations between Fionn and Goll had a tragic ending was well known to tradition.

Goll was a suitable rival for our hero. Several sources describe how brilliant a warrior he was. For instance, a long poem from the twelfth century is put in the mouth of Fionn himself, and it describes the great trail of destruction wrought by Goll and the Morna clan in their final campaign against their Baoiscne opponents. Goll is here said to have been from Gleann Gharaidh, apparently a name for a valley in east Co. Galway. The first victim of the onslaught is said to have been Banbh Sionna and the second Mael Enaigh, so the poem coincides with *Fotha Catha Cnucha* as to the history of the tragic quarrel.[31] Both champions were capable of honourable conduct of the highest order, even in the devastating war between them.

Thus another twelfth-century lay describes an encounter when Goll retired to Connacht intending to hold the fords of the river Shannon. Worn out from the watches, he fell asleep; and Fionn arrived at the river by night and heard the mighty sound of Goll's snoring. Fionn crossed the river alone, and stood over his sleeping foe with drawn sword. Goll awoke and grasped his spear, but Fionn calmly reminded him that 'long since I might have cut off your head' and told him to prepare to fight. At that moment a large body of Goll's forces arrived on the scene, leaving Fionn now in the dire situation. But Goll repaid the debt by escorting him safely back across the river. The armies then joined battle and Goll was forced to retreat. This, the battle of Cronnmhóin, was the turning point of the war.[32]

A different explanation to that of the Slángha pig and Banbh Sionna's death is given for the war in a thirteenth-century source. According to this, at feasts of the Fianna Goll always got 'the champion's portion' [*mír murra*] – that is the best bone of deer with marrow in it. Once while they were feasting at Almhu, however, a warrior from Scotland called Caireall arrived and challenged this privilege of Goll. An argument began, with the usual insulting banter concerning the battle of Castleknock, and this was the beginning of the end of the truce between the Baoiscne and Morna clans which had lasted for over twenty-one years.[33]

This story seems to have borrowed its central motif of the champion's portion at a feast from the other heroic cycle of mediaeval Ireland – that of Cúchulainn and the Ulster warriors.[34] It seems safe to assume that the use of the motif as a pretext for the Fionn/Goll war was an innovation and replaced an older explanation. It may not, in fact, have long preceded the writing of this particular poem, but it suited the context and became very popular in later tradition.

The Colloquy gives the reason for the war as the killing by Goll's brother Garadh of the leader of the Ossory fianna, and it describes the end of the fatal conflict as follows:

> Goll mac Morna retreated west to Carraig Ghoill, and the three battalions of the Fianna besieged him there for a fortnight and a month. And when he was nine nights without food, with his energy and dexterity exhausted, Muc Smaile son of Dubh Dithre went over to the rock and beheaded Goll in full view of the Fianna of Ireland. And he brought the head to Fionn.[35]

It is not clear what exact place was intended by this Carraig Ghoill [Rock of Goll], but there is no doubting the tragic drama of the episode itself, and it became the theme of much verse.

A poem of about the fourteenth century has Goll, driven as far west as he can go, conversing with his wife on the lonely promontory. He is here said to have gone thirty days without food. He begs his wife to leave him, but she refuses, asking where would she go and what other man would be so kind to her.[36] Another poem of the same period has Goll, before his death on the promontory, putting a curse on the family of Baoiscne.[37] The most important of these pro-Goll poems is a very long one, again from the fourteenth century, in which a description of all his heroic deeds is put in his own mouth. Alone on the rock with his faithful wife, Goll says that he has killed no less than thirty hundred warriors during the thirty days of the siege. At the battle of Cronnmhóin he has killed ten hundred, including two of Fionn's sons.

We are given similar hyperbolic accounts of his earlier battles and adventures, from which a full picture emerges of his relations with Fionn. While he was in the service of Conn, Goll tells us, the great Leinster king Cathaoir Mór was killed by him at the battle of Magh Agha [near Teltown in Co. Meath]. This echoes what we have said about the Morna clan as ancient soldiers of the Uí Néill against the Leinstermen. Then, when Cumhall came 'with thrice fifty gallant heroes' to Tara, Conn [said here to have been Cumhall's nephew] promoted him at the expense of Goll. Fighting broke out as a result of this, and Goll had to retire with his supporters to Ulster and from there to Wales. Cumhall with his army followed him there, however, and drove him out. Goll in turn seized the kingdoms of Scandinavia, Scotland, England, France, but was driven out of all these places by the overwhelming power of Cumhall.

Goll was in the city of Bergen when news arrived that Cumhall had quarrelled with the high-king Conn. So he returned to Ireland with his men and killed Cumhall in the battle of Castleknock.

> An eager wounding thrust I drove into the heart of the warrior, so that his heart was riven by me, having empurpled my spears.

For ten years after that he was commander of the Fianna, until Conn gave that position to the young Fionn. Goll was allowed to retain one third of the Fianna troop, and peace prevailed with 'our spirit heightened by banqueting and playing games'. The friendship and alliance lasted until Fionn slew Feadha, son of his own daughter. She was apparently married to Goll, but we are told nothing else of that episode.[38]

Although much of the account given in this poem is uncontrolled late mediaeval expansion – especially the numbers killed in battle and the international stage – in sentiment it accords well with the genuine tradition. For Goll's valour and dignity are nowhere doubted. The Colloquy author felt it appropriate to describe how, when Fionn was missing for a long time from the Fianna, Goll could have been restored to the commander's position, but he refused the honour, saying that he would not take it until Fionn was three years dead, nor would he allow anyone else to do so.[39]

A fifteenth-century Scottish poem in praise of him is aesthetically the most effective of all, with short impressive lists of his qualities.

> High-minded is Goll,
> The man who makes war with Fionn,
> A tall fierce warrior,
> Not timid is his raid.

He is described as handsome, brave, generous, and triumphant.

> Exquisite his form,
> Auspicious his fortune,
> Not stronger is a river
> Than his movement in battle.

And again,

> A friend without guile,
> A fine red mouth,
> His honour and his agility
> And his fame is proclaimed![40]

By late mediaeval times, then, Goll's image had lost all trace of his sinister past. But vestiges of the image of Fionn's fiery and tyrannical foe survived in the portrayal of other members of his clan. The long twelfth-century poem on Goll's final campaign (p. 161) has in it a curious verse:

A hundred queens who spoke no untruth,
Three hundred hounds and three hundred youths,
They burned – great the misery –
In the middle of the house of Almhu.

This appears to be an echo of the story, although taken out of context, of how Goll's elder brother Garadh slaughtered the Fianna women (see p. 154).

The name Garadh in connection with the Morna clan is worthy of note, for not only was Goll's brother so called but also his grandfather, and we have also seen that a place called Gleann Gharaidh was claimed as Goll's native area. The word *garadh* literally means 'cavc',[41] so it is not surprising to find Garadh mac Morna seeking refuge in such a location after he had burned the women. This imagery and name can be taken to derive ultimately from the tradition of Fionn's otherworld contacts who, in their negative aspects, reside in caverns and such underground dwellings.

The hostile character of the Morna clan is expressed in another and equally tangible way, through the personality of Goll's younger brother Conán. This personality shares his name with a certain Conán son of the Liath Luachra, that is son of one of Fionn's great foes in the Boyhood-Deeds and apparently for several centuries before that text was written (see p. 91). That Conán was accordingly portrayed as a natural enemy to Fionn, and a particular story of him is found in several late mediaeval sources.

The Colloquy says that he killed several of Fionn's followers. When Fionn was in west Munster once, resting after a hunt, Conán crept up behind him and seized him. Fionn recognised his captor and asked what did he want. Conán said that he wished to make peace and to enlist in the Fianna, and Fionn had no choice but to agree.[42] Some accounts say that Fionn never forgave him and eventually encompassed his death by sending him to woo the daughter of a man who had vowed to kill the girl's wooer.[43]

It is curious, but significant, that the Colloquy author confuses this Conán with Goll's brother, and it might well be that the Conán Maol of tradition was originally a fusion of Conán son of the Liath Luachra and a character of the Morna clan called Maol.[44] Our first references to Conán Maol are in twelfth-century sources, but already in these he has his usual reputation of being not only an impulsive and foolish man, but also a malicious one and a trouble-maker.

The sinister side of his character is clearly illustrated by an episode in the Colloquy. Conán with two of his men seized three young women who were under Fionn's protection in Almhu. When he brought them to the Morna camp, Goll considered that the captives afforded an opportunity to make peace with Fionn, but Conán insisted on killing them.[45] This murder of women by the Morna clan parallels the story of the conflagration caused by Garadh and so can be related to the destructive acts of Fionn's archetypal foe. The specification of the victims as women probably derives from the fianna context of the early story of Fionn's wife being killed by Cuirreach Life (p. 39). But Conán Maol's personality is the very symbol of destructive impulse, as if he were a psychological embodiment of the fiery foe.

As the Colloquy says, 'he never sought justice from anyone, and he gave his curse to whomsoever did justice to him'. 'Rugged Conán of horrid guise' was notorious for jibes and incitement, and according to the Colloquy it was his cursing which brought disaster to his own clan.[46] A fifteenth-century lay goes so far as to call him 'the destructive man of the Fianna' or 'the man who destroyed the Fianna' [*fear millte na bhFiann*].[47] This word *milleadh* has a special meaning in the term for a magically destructive eye, *súil mhillte*, so it is not surprising that oral tradition attributes to Conán Maol the power of killing his enemies by looking at them through his fingers.[48] There probably is no connection here with Balar's evil eye (see pp. 9f), but the function is the same, and Conán's eye is merely another manifestation of the dangerous forces which Fionn had to contain.

Diarmaid and Gráinne

Not all of Fionn's opponents can be traced back to basic functions, for as his saga developed through the Middle Ages it took on an impetus of its own. This could be expressed through the change and expansion of imagery, and it also meant that dramatic taste could drown out traditional orthodoxy. In the early lore, Fionn was a distinctive figure acting out his part in set environments, but the new impetus resulted in more detailed examination of his personality, seen through mediaeval eyes. Thus Fionn was now being portrayed as having a quite complex psychology – a hero with many great qualities but with some rather ignoble traits of character as well. And, of course, Fionn was aging. The biographical format caused emphasis to be placed on his maturity as well as his youth. So it was possible, and acceptable, to describe him in narrative as a jealous and elderly man.

The story typifying this was that of how Fionn's betrothed, Gráinne, eloped with the fine young warrior, Diarmaid Ó Duibhne. Not ancient myth, but narrative growth, determined the nature of this story, for Diarmaid was a loyal friend, turned foe because of Fionn's own presumption and even envy.

An ancient source for the character of Diarmaid himself has been postulated. He is often called Diarmaid Donn, and has therefore been claimed to represent a leading figure of the Celtic pantheon – Donn, whose function was that of god of the dead. Diarmaid's role as Fionn's opponent might therefore reflect Fionn's contests with the otherworld, and indeed mediaeval texts have Fionn meeting lords of *sí*-dwellings who are called Donn.[49] There is no real evidence, however, that Fionn's relationship with Diarmaid had such an ultimate origin.

The young warrior's name is derived from *dí-fhormait* [meaning, un-envious], and it is far from clear how such an epithet relates to the god Donn. A clue to the real process which brought Diarmaid into the ambit of Fionn is more likely to be found in the other and more usual addition to his name. This is the patronymic ua Duibhne [in modernised form, Ó Duibhne], which is derived from the name of a west Munster sept, the Corcu Duibhne. This suggests that the character Diarmaid originated in a context connected with that area.

We have seen (pp. 39ff) that in a quite early account Fionn was said to have abducted a woman, Badhamair, who symbolised the political interests of west Munster. The same source states that Badhamair had a foster-brother called Dubh ua Duibhne. This text was first written around the year A.D. 800, but what has come down to us is a rewritten version from the eleventh century. Immediately after the name of Dubh ua Duibhne is the phrase 'from whom was Diarmaid son of Dubh son of Duibhne' [*dia raibi Diarmaid mac Duib maic Duibne*]. If this gloss belonged to the original text it would give us a very early date indeed for Diarmaid to feature in the Fianna lore, but it is much more likely to be an interpolation by the eleventh-century redactor.

The character Dubh is of interest, for some sources state that he was killed by Fionn and that his sister was Cochrann, the wife of Fionn's enemy Cuirrech Life.[50] The suggestion is that part of the southern lore which was developing in the eighth and ninth centuries had Dubh ua Duibhne as an opponent of Fionn in the context of abducting women. This would explain the origin of the Fianna character called Diarmaid, a name which has always been popular in the west Munster area of the Corcu Duibhne sept.

The character's actual identity is rather undecided in the first references we have to him. The Colloquy, for instance, calls him *Diarmaid donn*, *Diarmaid ua Duibhne*, and *Diarmaid mac Duinn meic Donnchadha*; while in an eleventh-century source he is called *Diarmait mac Duinn i Duipne*.[51] In these references we have in fact three different appellations associated with the Kerry region – the Corcu Duibhne sept, the name Donn, and a powerful branch of the western Eoghanacht known as the Uí Dhonnchadha. We can take it that the variation reflects confusion in the minds of Leinster writers who were trying to situate a character in a far-away Munster setting. It is not altogether clear that a name Donn was originally intended for Diarmaid, for twice in the Colloquy the word is written as an epithet without an initial capital – *Diarmaid donn*. It could be claimed that it merely signified brown hair, in contrast to his father's designation Dubh [black]. But some sources definitely intend *Donn* as a proper noun, giving this as the actual name of his father.

The cult of the god Donn survived strongly in euhemerised form in the west of Munster,[52] so it is not surprising that vestiges of his name would be attached to a character associated with that area – especially when it could be substituted for a colour name which was already current in the context. Many other characters in the late mediaeval Fionn lore have Donn as an element in their names and, apart from those belonging to otherworld dwellings, it would be difficult to trace these to an ancient god of the dead. All the indications are that Diarmaid is a character who developed exclusively within the lore of Fionn and his Fianna.

Why should such a character be associated with a daughter of the high-king Cormac? The origins for this must lie in the tendency to synchronise Fionn with Cormac which developed from the eighth century onwards. Central to this tendency is the question of the real kingship, whether that was the ceremonial power at Tara or the power of Fionn as Fianna-king. Early Irish tradition symbolised kingship as a woman, who could appear in both ugly and beautiful forms.[53] The name Gráinne originally meant 'ugly', and we can see in its survival to designate a beautiful maiden an example of this dialectical process. Representing sovereignty, the character called Gráinne would thus be a bone of contention between Cormac and Fionn. We have seen, however, how a different type of story was developing in that same period – that of Fionn's wooing of Cormac's daughters (pp. 105ff). The two lines of narrative were sure to converge, and the result was to equate Gráinne, the symbol of power, with a daughter of Cormac. Thus Fionn wooed the king's daughter and this led to contention.

The other stream of narrative connecting Fionn with women was the earlier one of fighting and abduction, which brought the Munster lore of an Ó Duibhne opponent into focus. The muddle had to be resolved in the interests of properly constructed narrative, and a suitable format was borrowed for that purpose. This was a plot, already popular in Irish storytelling and therefore accessible to the Fionn lore. It was a three-cornered plot – that of the young girl betrothed to an aging man while she really loves a particular youth.[54] The importance of the theme of youth versus age in the Fianna cycle guaranteed ease of borrowing, with Fionn now playing the role of middle-age. The fully-developed story of Gráinne's elopement with Diarmaid from Fionn was already in existence in the tenth century, for it is included in a list from that time of tales told by professional tellers. The title is given as 'the Elopement of Gráinne daughter of Cormac with Diarmaid descendant of Duibhne'.[55]

Given its official status in the repertoire of learned men, we can expect that the story was put together by an individual or individuals belonging to that class. The process of composition would have been to join the lore of Fionn's adventures in Munster with the idea of his wooing of Gráinne, and to rationalise the whole by use of the three-cornered plot. Elements were selected for their narrative suitability, and a further element was included to dramatise the tragic ending of the plot. This involved Diarmaid being killed by a fierce boar – a motif which has usually been treated by researchers as a survival from ancient Irish tradition. What we have said concerning Diarmaid's origins, however, renders this improbable. Boar-hunts were in themselves a prominent feature of Fionn lore (see pp. 74f, 128f), so a boar-hunt motif would appeal to the compiler. What he seems to have done is to adapt material for his purpose from one of the Latin texts best known in mediaeval times, the *Metamorphoses* of Ovid. The material was simple and direct, and fitted well into his narrative. This was the account of Adonis, the supremely handsome youth with whom Venus fell in love, but who was killed by a savage boar which she warned him not to hunt.

Unfortunately we have no text for the story of Diarmaid and Gráinne as told by the professional tellers of the tenth century. But in the fifteenth century the romance was put into an expanded form, and this is the version which has come down to us. The main incidents in this latter recension can be summarised as follows:

Fionn rose early one morning in Almhu and sat dejectedly on the green all alone. When he was asked the cause of his depression, he said that he was lonely since the death of his wife Maighnis a year before. One of his men, Diorraing, told him that Gráinne would be a worthy spouse for him. Since he was at hostilities with Cormac, Fionn decided to send Oisín and Diorraing to negotiate the match. Cormac left the decision to Gráinne herself, and she consented, so Fionn went to Tara accompanied by the seven battalions of the Fianna.

A great feast was prepared there to celebrate the betrothal, with Fionn on the right hand of the king. During the feast, Gráinne sent her bondsmaid to Fionn with a drink in a golden goblet. He drank from it and then passed it on to Cormac and his family. All who tasted of it fell asleep from the magical effect of the drink. Then Gráinne approached Oisín and offered him her love. He refused, since she had been promised to Fionn. She made the same proposition to Diarmaid, and he refused also. She then placed *geasa* [magical threats] of destruction on him if he would not take her away, explaining that she had fallen in love with him long before as she saw him defeat her brother Cairbre in a hurling-match at Tara. Oisín, Oscar, Diorraing, and Caoilte all told Diarmaid that he had no choice but to do as she demanded, and he reluctantly agreed to elope with her.

He vaulted on his two spears over the rampart of the fortress, while Gráinne departed through a secret door in her bower. They took the king's chariot and steeds and travelled as far as Athlone on the river Shannon. Leaving the horses there, they swam across the river and went on to a wood called Doire Dá Bhaoth, where Diarmaid made a timber fortress with seven doors.

When Fionn woke up in Tara next morning and found Gráinne gone he was overcome with jealousy. Calling his trackers, the Neamhnann clan, he set off in pursuit and discovered that the fugitives were in Doire Dá Bhaoth. Oisín sent Fionn's hound Bran to warn Diarmaid, and Bran went to him and laid its head on his breast as he slept. Diarmaid refused to act upon the information, however, so Oisín directed Caoilte's servant Fear Goir to shout out a warning. This servant had a prodigiously strong voice, but again Diarmaid ignored the message. Instead, when Fionn with his men arrived at the fortress, he gave three kisses to Gráinne in the sight of all. Fionn said that he would pay for this with his head.

Meanwhile, Aonghus in his otherworld dwelling at Newgrange on the river Boyne learned through his clairvoyance of Diarmaid's plight and travelled to Doire Dá Bhaoth. Diarmaid refused his protection, but allowed him to take Gráinne away to safety under his cloak. Diarmaid then approached each of the seven doors of his fortress and enquired who was there. He refused to depart in safety through the doors guarded by his friends Oisín, Oscar, Caoilte and Conán Maol. At one door he found his enemies, the Neamhnann clann, but would not go through there because of his disdain for them. Finding a door guarded by Fionn himself with four hundred French mercenaries, he vaulted over them with his spears and departed. He then rejoined Gráinne at Limerick, whither Aonghus had brought her as arranged.

The fugitives travelled west as far as the river Laune where Diarmaid caught a fish and they rested for the night. Next day they met a young warrior called Muadhán seeking service. Diarmaid took him into his employ, and Muadhán carried them on his back over the Caragh and Behy rivers. He prepared a refuge for them in a cave overlooking the sea, caught and cooked three fish for them, and stood watch during the night.

Next morning, Diarmaid went to reconnoitre and met with three soldiers from the Channel Islands who had come to Ireland at Fionn's request to hunt Diarmaid. They had a thousand fierce fighters with them and three poisonous armour-clad hounds. Not recognising Diarmaid, they engaged in athletic contests with him for three days running. They could not equal him at riding a barrel downhill, jumping onto a pointed spear, or jumping onto a sword-edge, and they lost many of their men through accidents at these tricks.

Then the fugitives decided to leave their cave and headed for Slieve Logher. When the soldiers from the Channel Isles discovered who their strange opponent had been, they set out in pursuit and unleashed their hounds at Diarmaid. Muadhán took a pup from his belt, and this pup leaped into one hound's gullet and tore its heart out. Diarmaid threw his javelin and killed the second hound. He seized the third by its hind-legs and dashed its head against a rock. He then killed the three soldiers of the Channel Isles with throws of his javelin, and their men fled.

The three travelled back towards Limerick, where Diarmaid killed a massive stag and they had a fine meal. Muadhán left them there, despite their protests, and the elopers went northwards alone. As they travelled, a spurt of water struck

Gráinne's leg and she remarked that this drop was bolder than Diarmaid. It was then that they became lovers, as hitherto Diarmaid had always placed a fishbone between them as they slept as proof to Fionn that he had not betrayed him.

They came to a region controlled by an ogre of the Tuatha Dé Danann called the Searbhán Lochlannach, and he gave them permission to settle there provided they did not interfere with the rich berries on his trees.

Meanwhile, Fionn had heard of the fate of the warriors from the Channel Isles and, as he was taking stock of the situation, two strange warriors approached him. Their fathers had been involved in the killing of Cumhall and had been killed in revenge by Fionn, and they now sought to be reconciled to the Fianna. Fionn promised them that, provided they brought berries to him from the tree which was protected by the Searbhán Lochlannach.

Setting out on this quest, they met Diarmaid, who told them of his arrangement with the Searbhán. When she heard of the berries, however, Gráinne – who was then pregnant – demanded some. Diarmaid therefore went to the Searbhán and killed him in ferocious single combat. He then instructed the two warriors to bury the ogre lest Gráinne might look on his ugliness.

Diarmaid and Gráinne went to live in the ogre's bed at the top of the tree, and the warriors returned to the Fianna with some of the berries. Fionn sniffed these berries and recognised the smell of Diarmaid's skin, so he set out with the seven battalions for the Searbhán's tree, knowing he would find the fugitives there.

In an effort to delay operations, Oisín started to argue with Fionn at the foot of the tree, and Fionn challenged him to a game of chess. Diarmaid repeatedly prompted Oisín by throwing berries at the pieces to move. Finally Diarmaid stood in full view of the Fianna and gave three kisses to Gráinne. Once more Fionn vowed that he would pay for that with his head. But Aonghus again came to Diarmaid's aid, and when Fionn's mercenaries ascended the tree they were slaughtered one by one by that otherworld hero. He then spirited Gráinne away, and Diarmaid vaulted over all the

Fianna troop. The seven battalions followed him, but to no avail, and he rejoined Gráinne at the palace of Aonghus at Newgrange.

After this Aonghus went directly to Fionn and to king Cormac and got terms from them. According to this Diarmaid was forgiven for 'what he did against them while he was in the forest', was allowed to return to his patrimony in Corca Dhuibhne (west Kerry), and was given land to hold from Fionn in Leinster and from Cormac in Connacht. The peace between them held for a long time, and the young couple grew rich and lived in comfortable circumstances. Residing at Ráth Ghráinne in north Connacht, they had four sons and one daughter. Gráinne remarked to her husband one day that they ought to invite the two most celebrated men in Ireland, Cormac and Fionn, to a feast. Diarmaid reluctantly consented, and a year was spent in making the arrangements.

At the end of the year, the couple were sleeping in their rath when Diarmaid heard the baying of a hound three times in the night. Gráinne persuaded him to ignore this, but in the morning he went to investigate. He found Fionn in the wilderness all alone. Diarmaid did not salute his leader, but asked who was engaged in the hunt. Fionn told him that fifty of the Fianna were being slaughtered by the boar of Benbulben and that the rest were in flight.

Diarmaid refused to flee, and was then informed by Fionn that he was under *geasa* [magical prohibitions] since his childhood not to hunt a pig. Diarmaid then understood the danger he was in, and he asked Fionn to leave the hound Bran with him to face the boar, but Fionn refused. When the savage beast charged him, Diarmaid's weapons were of no avail, and he was swept off his feet. He alighted on the boar's back, and after a tremendous struggle he was flung off and his stomach was ripped open before he slew the beast.

When the Fianna arrived on the scene, Diarmaid was already in the pangs of death. He reminded Fionn that ever since the latter had got the salmon of knowledge in the Boyne there was a cure in a drink from his palms. Fionn refused to give the drink, but Diarmaid reminded him of how he saved his life when he was trapped on two occasions. Then Oscar demanded that Fionn bring a drink to Diarmaid.

Fionn went to a well, but twice he allowed the water to slip through his palms. Finally Oscar threatened to kill him if he did not comply with the request, and Fionn brought the drink. But Diarmaid was already dead.

Oscar rose to decapitate Fionn, but his anger was assuaged by Oisín. Fionn then took Diarmaid's dog, intending to keep it, but Oisín took it from him and returned it to Gráinne. When she sent her servants to collect the body, Aonghus was already on the spot with his forces and he took the body with him to his otherworld palace on the Boyne. Then Gráinne called together her children and divided Diarmaid's weapons among them.[56]

A few aspects of this story require comment. Firstly, the means by which Gráinne gets Diarmaid to elope with her are paralleled in the two other well-known stories which are based on the three-cornered plot. In the Ulster Cycle accounts of Deirdre eloping with Naoise the lady also uses *geasa* to persuade her intended lover, while in the Arthurian accounts Tristan is attacted to Isolde by drinking a love-potion.[57] There is some clumsiness in Gráinne's approach, as she uses both *geasa* and a drink.

Oral versions of the story overcome this by substituting a simple and straightforward motif. They claim that Diarmaid had a love-spot [*ball seirce*] on his forehead, and if any woman saw it she would fall helplessly in love with him. He tries to keep it covered, but Gráinne catches a glimpse of it by accident and so the elopement and clash with Fionn are made inevitable. This love-spot motif was part of folk versions of the story all over Ireland and Scotland,[58] and indications are that it was introduced into the narrative in or about the fifteenth century.

The literature often refers to the lustrous countenance which it claims Diarmaid had, and we can take it that this derives from the imagery of Adonis.[59] Diarmaid's lustrous countenance, however, seems to have attracted ideas from the realm of love-magic in living Irish folk-custom, such as markings with special substances, and the love-spot was the result.[60] Literary accounts of Diarmaid studiously avoid this love-spot motif, probably because of the inconsistency involved in a character having such a charm but not wishing to make use of it.

The episode of the boar, as here portrayed, is also worthy of attention. The ferocious animal is said to be from Benbulben ([*Beann Ghulban*], a spectacular razor-shaped mountain in Co. Sligo). This must have been part of the original tenth-century story, for the episode is mentioned in the first Colloquy, but it is not clear why a Munster warrior in the service of Fionn should be associated with a region so far north. It is possible, but hardly probable, that there was a pre-existing tradition of such a great boar, but by far the greater likelihood is that the animal's name reflects the borrowing from the Adonis myth. Ovid describes the fierce boar with a crooked snout which inflicted a mortal bite on Adonis, and the Irish word *gulba* [genitive *gulban*] means a protruding mouth, which fits that imagery well.[61] The boar which killed Diarmaid must have been known by some such descriptive appellation, and the appellation in time came to be explained by reference to the place-name Beann Ghulban.

The oral versions of the story from both Ireland and Scotland again have an alternative here, for they describe Diarmaid killing the boar without himself sustaining a mortal wound. Fionn, however, insisted that Diarmaid measure the huge carcase, and as he leant over its back he slipped and was pierced by a venomous bristle, thus meeting his death.

This motif has a general resemblance to some incidents in other Irish stories.[62] It occurs in a fifteenth-century Scottish poem on Diarmaid's death,[63] and so it must have already crept into the story by that time.

It is difficult to say whether or not the episodes concerning the otherworld lord Aonghus were in the original story, but his assistance to the besieged Diarmaid at least may have been. The source for this is obviously a passage in the Ulster epic *Táin Bó Cuailnge*, which has the young Cúchulainn in dire straits fighting against the men of Ireland and being relieved by the god Lugh.[64] Aonghus also features as a *deus ex machina* in the story of the raid by the Baoiscne clan on Tara (p. 159 above), in which he assists by shepherding the cattle drove while Fionn and his men fight off king Cormac's host.

This is very likely borrowed from Aonghus' aid to Diarmaid, and so the episode in the Diarmaid and Gráinne story appears to predate the thirteenth century at least. Such a context is striking and appropriate, with a deity intervening in support of a brave youth against overwhelming odds. In this case the hero is Diarmaid.

In the earlier lore the archetypal great youth was Fionn himself, but Fionn – as we have said – was aging, and even his great feats of leaping have been taken over in the story by Diarmaid, who belonged to the next generation.

Caoilte

This is the one character who is mentioned alongside Fionn right through the whole tradition. In the Leinster genealogy from the sixth or seventh century (p. 3) Fionn, Tulcha, and Caoilte are referred to as three descendants of Baoiscne. Tulcha was represented in mediaeval lore as Fionn's brother,[65] and Caoilte as Fionn's nephew, but this early reference groups the three together as if they constituted a unit. Tulcha's name is probably a corruption of *tulgha* [sudden javelin], which would signify prowess at fighting.[66] The name Caoilte [old Irish, Caílte] is difficult to interpret, but it seems to be composed of the epithets *cael* [slender, in the sense exact] and *te* [hot, in the sense fierce]. So Caoilte may have been envisaged as a dexterous and keen warrior. It is hard to avoid the conclusion that both Tulcha and Caoilte, companions and clansmen of Fionn, derive from the martial context of the Leinster fianna in their struggle against the Uí Néill.

The figure of Caoilte, as borne out by tradition, is very much that of an able young fiann, for he is a very effective fighter and a great athlete. His speciality from earliest times was running, as evidenced by the texts from both Ulster and Munster which were compiled at the turn of the eighth and ninth centuries.

In the Ulster source (see p. 149), king Mongán in his court at Rathmore in Co. Antrim contradicted his poet Forgoll, who had said that the warrior Fothadh Airgthech was killed in the Duffrey of Leinster. The poet threatened to satirise

Mongán and to destroy the whole territory with the magic of his verse; and Mongán, in an effort to stave off such a calamity, gave the poet the choice of all his goods. Forgoll demanded Mongán's wife within three days. On the evening of the third day the woman was disconsolate, but Mongán told her that help was coming – he could hear feet going through a succession of rivers from the southwest of Ireland northwards, through the Laune, Morning Star, Suir, Barrow, Liffey, Boyne, Dee, and Newry rivers, and finally in the Larne Water near the palace. It was announced that a man was approaching from the south.

The stranger leapt on his spear-shaft across the three ramparts and, coming into the company, he declared that Mongán had been correct in the argument. Fothadh Airgthech had been killed in the battle of Ollarbha near that place. 'It was Caoilte, the foster-child of Fionn [*dalta Find*] who had come to them', and he knew the truth since it was he himself who had killed Fothadh in the battle.[67]

It is not clear from where Caoilte came in that text, but what the author must have had in mind was that he was returning from the otherworld – presumably the House of Donn [*tech Doinn*] off the south-west coast, which was in pre-Christian times believed to be the abode of the dead.[68] What is important here is that he is represented as travelling the whole country by foot in a very short time.

The Munster text from the same period, *Scéla Moshauluim*, merely mentions his name as fighting alongside Fionn and Oisín and says nothing of his running ability. But it does stress his feet, calling him *Caílte camchoss* [Caoilte of the bandy legs], and this seems to be an indirect reference to his fame as a runner.[69] The more appropriate, and no doubt more usual, epithet with his name was *cosluath* [foot-swift]. This is attested by tenth- and eleventh-century texts,[70] and it must have been current for a long time prior to that. His fame as a runner was, in fact, so strong that it is reflected in the early twelfth-century Welsh story *Culhwch ac Olwen*, where we find mention of him under the guise of *Sgilti ysgawndroet* [Sgilti light-foot].[71] That this great prowess of his was often expressed in the context of racing contests is clear from many sources.

The first Colloquy, for instance, has him running two tense races. One has to do with how an ugly hag once came to the Fianna at Croghan in Co. Roscommon, demanding a race with them. Oisín, Diarmaid, and Caoilte ran against her – Caoilte was in the lead going over a ford, and he turned about and struck her head off with his sword. The other story tells of a beautiful young woman called Étaín 'the Fair-Haired' from the *sí*-dwelling of Howth, who came to the Fianna in Munster and challenged any of them to race with her. Caoilte took up the challenge, and they ran from Badhamair in Co. Tipperary to Dublin. Caoilte won, and the Fianna were then entertained with great hospitality in Howth, with Étaín eventually marrying Oscar.

The contrasting images of Caoilte's two competitors here, ugly hag and beautiful maiden, parallel the ideas concerning sovereignty.[72]

We have had occasion to refer to this dual female face of sovereignty in the case of Fionn's wooing of Gráinne. It is as if Caoilte were intimately involved in the way Fionn gained power, and this is what we would expect, given his close connection with Fionn from early times. One is tempted to regard Tulcha and himself as having originally been actual extensions of Fionn, and to suspect that this fianna triad was a conversion of a triplicated divine Fionn. Thus the three Fionns of mythology (pp. 4ff) would have been manifested in the sixth-century martialised context as the three-man warrior group Fionn, Tulcha, and Caoilte, with wisdom, fighting, and athletics, respectively, as their chief qualities.

Even if this formulation is not accurate, there seems to be a strong case for connecting Caoilte with Fionn's power status – this status being symbolised as a tussle with the high-king Cormac over the goddess of sovereignty. Since we have argued that the character Gráinne is an echo of such a tussle, Caoilte would be expected to have some involvement in that sphere, and so indeed he has.

A story written around the year A.D. 1000 tells of how Fionn went to woo Gráinne at Tara [Temhair], but she set an impossible condition:

> The maiden said that she would not accept any present from him except a couple of every wild animal that was

in Ireland to be brought in one drove to the rampart of Temhair. And she vowed that he and she would not unite unless that drove were brought.

'I will go and bring it', said Fionn.

'I shall go', said Caoilte foot-swift. . . .

So Caoilte went and gathered a couple of every wild animal, and brought the straggling drove until they were on the green of Temhair. He went to where Cormac was and told him that his daughter's bridal gift was on the rampart of Temhair.

'Which was hardest for you to bring?' asked Cormac.

'Indeed', said Caoilte, 'I found particular difficulty with the fox.'[73]

This story of the straggling drove [*corr-imirce*] of Caoilte is repeated in several later sources.

A particularly enlightening example comes from the twelfth century, for it entails actual hostility between Fionn and Cormac. This is a poem put in the mouth of Caoilte, in which he states that Fionn was being held in fetters at Tara by Cormac, and describes how he himself waged a campaign of mischief against the high-king to gain his leader's release. He let calves go to their cows, set horses loose, burned mills and kilns, and laid the countryside waste. The king's men could not apprehend him because of 'the swiftness of my feet' [*lúth mo chos*].

He then went to Tara and posed as a candle-bearer for Cormac. The king remarked on what seemed to him 'Caoilte's two eyes' in the servant, but Fionn assured him that he was mistaken. Caoilte then brought moss from the marsh of Seiscenn Uarbheoil (in Co. Wicklow) which had magical properties, and acting as candle-bearer that night he caused the various women to mistake other men for their husbands and to sleep with them. Cormac, who thus had his daughter-in-law as bedfellow, was so exasperated that when morning came he agreed to accept ransom for Fionn. But the ransom was the couple of each animal and bird, as well as 'the fierce wild man'. With great effort Caoilte managed to acquire this ransom, racing the wild man all the way from the hill of Almhu to Crumlin (in Co. Dublin) before he caught him.[74]

The imprisonment of Fionn by Cormac was also part of the story known to the author of the first Colloquy,[75] so we can take it that the struggle between these two was a basic element in it. The third Colloquy text in the fourteenth century has a much expanded telling in prose and verse, which clarifies some aspects of the earlier recensions.

Fionn, we are told, confided a secret to a member of the Fianna called Donn who belonged to the west Munster Eoghanacht. The secret was his intent to bring the Fianna around Tara and to go himself to the high-king's citadel. He was to bring with him seven armed warriors, clad with armour underneath their clothes, and so by treachery to take the kingship from Cormac. Donn betrayed the secret to Cormac, and so when Fionn attempted the ruse he was seized and put in fetters. Having performed his mischief, Caoilte came to Tara, slew the doorkeeper, and took up the torch in his place. He lit the way for Cormac to the privy, and then gave into his hand the moss of Seiscenn Uarbheoil. It was *geis* [a prohibition] for the king to get that moss while in Tara, and Cormac grew suspicious and said that he got the smell of Caoilte's skin from the moss. Then the deal was made concerning the ranson.

A fifteenth-century Scottish version of the poem has several extra stanzas, and says that Caoilte succeeded in keeping his drove overnight at Tara in a mansion with nine open doors![76]

Clearly, then, there was a tradition that Fionn had clashed with Cormac but was saved by Caoilte. Running was the latter's great proclivity, and so this was accommodated to the narrative by making it the means of rescue. That rescue, given the circumstances, was an extremely difficult task, and so some plot was required which would make it possible. The plot was found in a folktale which had a wide circulation around Europe and which the designer of this Caoilte-story in the tenth or eleventh century had heard.

This folktale – known to researchers as 'the Rabbit-herd' – described how a man won a princess in marriage by performing a difficult task set by the king. The task was to herd rabbits, and he succeeded in doing it by use of a magic pipe to call them.[77] The tale was obviously attracted to the

Fionn context by his wooing of Gráinne, and also by the extraordinary ability of his helper Caoilte. This ability meant that Caoilte could outrun each and every type of creature, and so his straggling drove could be made more colourful by replacing the rabbits with a couple of all species of animals. The designer of the story was probably influenced here by the biblical account of Noah's Ark.

We notice how Caoilte's running replaces the magic pipe of the international folktale, and appropriately so, for many texts extend this special ability of his into the realm of magical prowess. The first Colloquy tells us that he sped from the Wave of Clíodhna [Dingle Bay] in the south to the Wave of Rudhraighe [Dundrum Bay] in one single day[78] – an idea which is probably derived from the Ulster text of around the year A.D. 800 (see pp. 177f). The first Colloquy also quotes a poem in praise of the Fianna which includes lines to the following effect:

> The speed of a blackbird between two thickets
> Was a quality of all the Fianna,
> The speed of the wind past the blackbird
> Was that of Caoilte alone.[79]

The involvement of Caoilte and his running in Fionn's relations with Cormac is used as a basis for a new story in a twelfth-century poem.

According to this, Fionn was given a great sword, which had belonged to his forefathers, by his uncle Criomhall. The men of the Fianna expressed surprise that Fionn kept this treasured article for himself, since he was 'one of the five most generous men in the land of Ireland', and Fionn replied that he was willing to give it away. Ailbhe, daughter of Cormac, was his wife at that time, and judgement of the matter was left to her. She decided that all the Fianna must race for the sword. This was done, and Caoilte came to the finish in the lead, closely followed by Fionn himself. Caoilte grabbed the sword, and Fionn took its sheath. Then Fionn demanded a second judgement, claiming that they had reached the finish together. Ailbhe decided in favour of Caoilte, saying that 'to a sword is due its sheath'. King Cormac and his retinue arrived soon after, proposing that peace be restored between himself and Fionn, and inviting Fionn and the Fianna chiefs to a great feast at Tara.[80]

Although the roles have been altered and the characters pressed into a new context in this narrative, the very dislocation itself bears witness to the typical function of Caoilte. In the early mediaeval stories he is companion to Fionn in war and wooing – so close a companion, indeed, that we are led to regard him as the hero's alter-ego. Further support for this view comes from the rather obscure identity of Caoilte himself.

The early Ulster text, as we have seen, makes him a foster-child of Fionn, and later mediaeval sources specify that he was a son of Fionn's sister, whom the Colloquy calls Eithne.[81] The Colloquy is undecided as to his precise genealogy, however, twice calling him 'son of Crundchu son of Rónán' and once simply 'son of Rónán'.[82] Yet the earliest text of the straggling drove story states that his father was one Oisgen son of the Artisan of Músgraighe Dotrut.[83] The name Oisgen [deer-conceived] has strong echoes of the early fianna hunting lore which gives us other character-names like Oisín and Oscar (see p. 77). It is likely, then, that the Crundchu and Rónán genealogy was invented for Caoilte after the eighth century, though for what reason is unclear. The late mediaeval lays have the same indecision as the Colloquy, sometimes calling him 'son of Cronchur [*sic*] son of Rónán', and sometimes 'son of Rónán'.[84] The latter is his accepted patronymic in the post-mediaeval lore, namely Caoilte mac Rónáin.

The marvellous nature of his running ability guaranteed him a clear personality of his own, but the close connection with Fionn was very persistent and had important ramifications in the developing tradition. Not least of these was the role of relaying Fianna history allotted to him in the Colloquy. But his shadowing of Fionn with a special prowess gave rise to another feature of Fianna narrative. This feature was a complex of motifs concerning helpers with extraordinary skills.

Marvellous Helpers

We have met with a reference to Caoilte under the name

'Sgilti light-foot' in Welsh literature of the early twelfth century. Sgilti, we are there told, used to run along the tops of trees and of reeds 'and never did a reed bend, much less break, so light of foot was he'. This description is at one with an athletic test reputedly set for aspirant members of the Fianna (see pp. 104f); and this is obviously a borrowing from Irish lore, with Caoilte being seen as a symbol of Fianna athleticism. The reference to Sgilti occurs in the context of several other characters with extraordinary skills, which suggests that Caoilte was being portrayed in a similar context in Irish lore of the time also. We have seen from the adaptation of the rabbit-herd folktale that Caoilte was seen as performing extremely difficult tasks in the eleventh century, with his stupendous running-skill being the means used.

There are indications that other motifs of a similar nature were attracted to his image in the same period. In the Boyhood-Deeds, for instance, Fionn's companion and helper Fiacail was a fantastically fast runner (p. 94), but this idea is unnecessary to the role which Fiacail plays in Fionn's biography – that of affording protection to the hero in his youth and presenting him with a great spear. In his running, therefore, Fiacail appears to have usurped the imagery of Caoilte in that text. The strange custom attributed to him, wearing balls of lead around his neck to check his speed, gives a clue to the process.

A similar motif, whereby a marvellous runner keeps one leg tied up so as to check his speed, was part of widespread folktales about extraordinary helpers.[85] Given the rabbit-herd borrowing and the fact that running was the special quality of Caoilte in Fianna lore, this idea is very likely to have been connected with him in the first instance. That his imagery could be extended laterally onto other Fianna characters is clear from the echo of his great droving in the first Colloquy, where we have mention of a certain Leargan the Swift, 'who used to bring the does in the afternoon just as each other person brought his own cows'.[86]

The general idea behind Fionn's youth-biography was that some very difficult tasks had to be performed by him. The greatest of the tasks required the use of the great spear with which he killed the fiery foe. Traditionally it was Fiacail who gave him this spear, and so that character had the function of helper. This explains why a motif of another character who gave extraordinary help to Fionn – that is Caoilte with his running – was borrowed to the portrayal of Fiacail in the Boyhood-Deeds.

Being a great hero, the achievement of what to ordinary men would be impossible was an essential part of Fionn stories above and beyond the youth-biography and so, once Caoilte had ensured the adoption of marvellous-helper motifs into Fianna lore, the general suitability of such motifs became apparent. Its potential was fully exploited, and during the following centuries a whole stratum of narrative developed concerning magical assistance which Fionn was represented as getting from strange personalities who visited the Fianna to offer their services. The Colloquy, for instance, tells of how a lake burst forth on Slieve Bloom and was spreading out to cover all of Leinster until Fionn tamed it.

We have already referred to this story (p. 23) and have related it to an early complex of myth. But the important point here is that the Colloquy puts an additional dimension to the telling:

> It was then that Fionn performed the best strong deft exploit that anyone ever did before or after it. That is, [he got] the sucker from the land of India and the magicians from the land of Germany and the female warriors from the lands of the Saxons and Franks, so that they sucked up that wavy chilly lake.[87]

As if the writers recording this new development were personalising the process, the borrowed motifs often occur in the context of foreign warriors seeking service with the Fianna. This identifying of function with source was easy, since the conceit was well established that the fame of Fionn's troop attracted applicants from outside countries. We find, for example, sons of kings of Britain, France, and Greece, and even 'the son of the king of the world' being numbered among the Fianna.[88] A story from the Colloquy shows how adept the author could be at synchronising material.

> 'One day', Caoilte is quoted as saying, 'when we, the three battalions of the Fiann-band, came to this mound we saw three young warriors before us with one hound. And there was no colour in the world which was not on the hound, and it was of wondrous size compared to other hounds.'

The three strangers told Fionn that they were from Norway and sought admission to the Fianna, saying that they were willing to do great deeds. All they asked in return was that they have an encampment apart and that nobody should visit them after dark. They were accepted, and soon proved a great boon to the Fianna. The hound coughed up gold to pay the poets, and once when the troop had no water one of the Norwegians magically filled all the cups with ale.

But one night when the two sons of the Ulster king were on sentry duty for the Fianna they decided to spy on the foreigners:

> They passed through the wall of fire, and when they had done this they laid their arms aside, and they were looking at the three warriors and the hound. The great hound which spent every day hunting and chasing was then no bigger than a lapdog of a queen or noble lady. One of these warriors had a keen naked sword in his hand watching the hound, and another warrior had a bright silver goblet at the hound's mouth. And every type of ale which each of them requested the hound would emit from its mouth into the goblet. Then one of the warriors said to the hound:
>
> 'Yes, indeed, o noble and true one, o man's son, notice the betrayal which has been done by the prince, by Fionn, against you!'
>
> Then accordingly the hound shook its tail, so that a hostile magical wind came from it, so that their [the Ulster princes'] shields fell from their shoulders and their spears from their hands and their swords from their sides and went into the wall of fire before them. And those warriors killed the two sons of the Ulster king, and the hound turned after the men were killed and blew its breath over their bodies, so that they were turned into bits and ashes. And neither blood nor flesh nor bone of them was found on that spot.

Later in the Colloquy we are told that the Fianna planned to kill the three strangers, but Fionn would not allow this on account of their qualities. One of them could heal all diseases, another could provide anything requested of him, and the third could put anybody to sleep with his flute. It is described how they defended the Fianna from three ravaging warriors of the Tuatha Dé Danann, but the existing Colloquy text tells no more of their adventures except that they were called Dubh, Ágh, and Ilar.[89]

A poem which was probably composed a little earlier than the Colloquy gives much the same account of the three Norwegians, but has certain other details which we can take to belong to the original plot. Here it is stated that their names were Sela, Dorait, and Domhnán, and their wonderful hound is called Fáilinis. After the death of the Ulster prince Dubhán – here only one of their two victims is mentioned – Fionn demanded compensation, and they offered the hound. Before it was handed over, however, they killed it and took its skin with them to Scandinavia. Whereupon Fionn organised a great Fianna force comprising Irishmen, Welshmen, Picts, and Scots, and went after the three. A great battle was fought in Scandinavia, in which the Fianna were victorious, and they took the skin of the hound back with them to Ireland. The poem states that this was the same hound which the sons of Tuireann had once brought to Lugh.[90] Thus we are told what the direct source of the motif was.

An eleventh-century entry on Lugh in the *Lebor Gabála* refers to how the three sons of Tuirill [*sic*] slew the father of Lugh when he was in the form of a lapdog. In compensation Lugh demanded that they bring several wonderful things to him, among which was –

> The whelp of the royal smith of Norway, which is a hound by night and a sheep by day, and every water put in its skin becomes wine.[91]

It is clear that, when this Lugh story was borrowed into the Fianna context, the idea of difficult tasks set for the three brothers was transformed into three brothers who were marvellous task-performers. The Norwegian home of the wondrous hound was retained and applied also to the three marvellous brothers, so that it became their hound.

Although the Greek myth of Jason and the Argonauts is in the background to the Lugh story, it is clear that – apart from the motif of the golden fleece – the Greek source has been used quite sparingly. There were marvellous helpers in the Jason myth, but they do not come through the Lugh story, and the Fianna story doubtlessly got the idea of such helpers from existing Fionn lore. This lore must have had a taste for variety, as evidenced by the use of such diverse narrative marvels as the gold-producing dog, the fiery breath of the same dog, the strange wind and wall of fire, and the magical abilities of the three brothers.

Here the borrowed material has been deftly handled, giving the three strangers magical capabilities suitable to the story-line in preference to the more physical ones – like marvellous speed, sight, hearing, climbing – which feature in standard folktales of extraordinary helpers. The version told in the first Colloquy lacks an ending, but this may be due to the fact that no complete manuscript of that work survives. Other narratives of magical strangers can be more cumbersome, such as a story found in the fourteenth- to fifteenth-century *Feis Tighe Chonáin*, which has the marvellous helpers in combination with several disparate elements.

We are told that after the pregnant Tuirne [i.e. Uirne] had been turned into a bitch (see p. 124), she was sent to the house of Fearghus Finnliath, king of Dublin, and become a great favourite with him. At the same time as the bitch had two pups – one male and one female – the wife of Fearghus gave birth to a son. But a giant [*fomhóir*] used to come from the sea and take away every child which that woman used to bear, and in this way she had already lost seven babies.

Fionn happened to be hunting that very day, and he was approached by eleven youths who told him that they had searched the world for a worthy master. They were, respectively, the best answerer of questions in the world, kindler of fires, server at table, divider of wealth, listener, strong man, swift runner, shooter, climber, and tracker. Fionn took them into his employ and asked the answerer [*Freagartach*] what were the worst deeds to be done in Ireland that night. He was told that a giant would come and take the new-born child in Dublin.

So Fionn, with his new-found retainers, headed for Dublin and undertook to watch over the baby. In the house of Fearghus, Fionn's kindler lit a great fire for the company, his divider carved the meat, and his server gave out the drink, so that all the household had a fine meal and fell asleep.

Fionn asked the listener and the strong man to stand guard, and after a while the listener reported that he heard the din and tumult of the giant crossing the sea and coming through Howth. Soon the giant stretched his 'hard hand, long, sinuous, and powerful' through the top of the house. The strong man seized the arm and pulled it clean off the giant's body, but – as Fionn and his men gazed in astonishment at the monstrous limb – the giant snatched the baby away with his other hand. When Fearghus' wife heard what had happened she upbraided Fionn for his inability to defend a mere child and, overcome with shame, the hero called his tracker and they followed the giant's trail to Howth. Then he called the answerer and asked him to get a boat for them. Immediately they saw a fine curragh coming towards them on the sea.

They went on board and came to an island where they found a fortress surrounded by staked heads. The lord of the place was called Aodh Ruadh, and he had a daughter who was a great runner. Any man who came seeking her hand had to race against her, and if defeated he lost his head. Fionn asked Aodh Ruadh for his daughter, and instructed the runner – called 'Swift as the Wind' [*Comhluath re Gaoith*] – to compete for him. They went out onto the green for the race, but the girl put a sleeping charm on Fionn's runner.

Seeing this, Fionn called on his shooter to awaken the runner, which he did by sending a spear-throw glancing off his head. The runner then started off after the girl and won the race. They spent six weeks there feasting, and then shame came on Fionn again for prolonging his task and they resumed the track of the giant.

Coming to a great stone peak in the sea, and finding the

track ending there, they decided that the giant must be there. So Fionn sent his climber up the cliff, and the climber returned and said he had seen the giant sleeping, with the baby beside him and six youths playing with two pups. Fionn then told him to take the tracker on his back and climb up again; and in this way they stole not only the baby and youths and pups, but all the giant's valuables as well. They headed out to sea, but were soon followed by the awakened and enraged giant, who caught up with them at Howth. The male pup rushed at the giant and tore his entrails out with its paw, whereupon Fionn cut the giant's head off with one swipe of his sword. They were welcomed back by Fearghus and his wife, delighted to have their baby and six other sons restored to them. The eleven helpers then left Fionn, and he returned to where his own Fianna warriors were, bringing the two pups with him and naming the male one Bran and the female Sceolaing.[92]

This complicated story has been studied by various scholars, and from these studies a definite pattern for its development has emerged. There was a story current in either Ireland or Wales, or in both, which described how a baby was stolen by a giant hand coming through the roof, and this story has expropriated to itself the popular Celtic motif of congenital animals. This combination is attested in the twelfth-century Welsh story *Pwyll.*[93]

In Ireland, the independent lore of Uirne's transformation into a hound became connected with the composite story, because the pups' birth was seen to accord with the idea of congenital animals. In this way Fionn became the hero who rescued the baby from the giant. But this was a feat near-impossible to perform and was therefore an ideal context for the introduction of his marvellous helpers.

The accounts adapted to dramatise the plot were two international folktales. One of these is known to researchers by the title 'the Helpers' and involves several extraordinary characters who assist a man in difficult tasks. These helpers include a strong man, a great shooter, a great hearer, a great runner, and so forth. One of the tasks is to defeat a princess in a race for her hand.[94] The other folktale is known to researchers as 'the Four Skilful Brothers', and has the four rescuing a princess who has been stolen away to a rock in the sea. Their respective feats include tracing the princess' whereabouts, stealing her from her dragon guard, shooting the dragon, and sewing a boat together.[95]

When the elements of these two folktales were superimposed onto the other material to make this Fionn story is a matter for conjecture, but that may not have long preceded the writing of the *Feis Tighe Chonáin* text.

So it is clear that stories involving marvellous helpers were quite popular in late mediaeval Ireland, and were adaptable enough to repeatedly intrude into Fianna narrative and to become naturalised there. The fifteenth-century version of the Diarmaid and Gráinne romance bears incidental witness to such intrusion, in the case of Caoilte's servant Fear Goir whose every shout was so wondrously loud that it could be heard over an area of three baronies [*trí tríocha céad*].[96]

A manuscript of the Colloquy from the same time refers to several characters with extraordinary abilities in Fionn's troop. These include one Allae Baschenn who was 'the man of hearing' of the Fianna –

> No bird would stir from ford or waterfall or river or estuary without him noticing it, for he would hear it by night or by day.

Also one Dabhur 'the Blind Poet' who 'never threw an inaccurate cast by day or night', and the three Bailbh Bhodhra [deaf mutes] who could do anything which they put their hand to.[97]

We shall meet more such extraordinary characters assisting Fionn in his adventures in the later literature and folklore.

7.

Lays and Romances

Despite the efforts of its author, the Colloquy did not accommodate all aspects of the Fianna lore as current at the time. The several twelfth-century narrative poems, containing extra-Colloquy material, which we have mentioned and discussed, bear witness to this. The custom of composing and preserving such narrative poems on the Fianna originated in the eleventh century, and it is clear that they were the work of learned men.[1] These men were poets, whose function was to make verse suitable for recitation.

Poetry in the early period was preoccupied with questions of knowledge – both physical and mystical – rather than with narrative entertainment, but this was changing. Some, at least, of eleventh- and twelfth-century poets began to take an interest in Fianna stories – a process which is reflected in the increasing tendency to attribute verse of a narrative type to the characters Fionn, Oisín, and Caoilte. These mediaeval poets were well aware of how their fellow-composers and reciters, the professional storytellers, were encountering a growing demand for Fianna-lore. In this type of atmosphere, verse joined prose as a vehicle for developing and transmitting the tradition.

The multiplicity of texts in both mediums during the following five hundred years shows how great the hunger was for new adventures concerning Fionn and his company. The basic personalities and the imagery within the lore were so strongly established that motifs and plots could be borrowed from any available sources and yet the lore could retain enough of its integrity to continue its appeal for the tradition-loving Gaelic public. In time, this renewed creative impulse settled into a number of particular narrative moulds.

The Affairs of the Fianna

The picture of the Fianna troop, of Fionn's dealings with its principal personalities, and of his relations with the high-king Cormac, was clearly delineated and a matter of common knowledge in the twelfth century. In effect, it constituted a society of the imagination, a paradigm in which human qualities and passions could be made to play out their functions and create adventure. And so we have many stories growing out of this fertile context.

One of the most basic of all Fianna activities, at all times, was hunting, and no mediaeval audience wanted this theme neglected. We have seen (chapter 5) how accounts of Fianna hunts were dramatised in twelfth- to fourteenth-century sources, but neither would the actual arrangements for hunting be ignored by the mediaeval mind pondering the fanciful Fianna society. Thus we have, in the first Colloquy text, a description of how 'the three battalions' of the Fianna plundered an area in the present Co. Donegal in revenge for one of their members.

This man, Garbh Doire, had been killed by the people of that area after he had carried out a great hunt there; and in retaliation the Fianna killed the three local kings together with many of their followers, except a party who 'escaped into the islands'.[2]

The third Colloquy describes further complications of the hunt, but this time the scene is in Co. Mayo. Lughaidh Lámhdhearg son of Forga, king of Umhall [the Owles] in that county, would not allow Fionn's men to hunt in his territory.

Once, when the Fianna heard that Lughaidh had gone on a visit to Munster, they hunted there. Unknown to Fionn during these proceedings, Oscar went with three hundred men to abduct Lughaidh's wife from his fortress in Erris. Lughaidh, it transpired, had not left his area at all, but was himself hunting in the Owles. He and his two companions heard the screams of his wife and her serving lady, and they attacked and slaughtered Oscar's band. When only Oscar himself remained Lughaidh fought a single combat with him. Oscar was overcome and tied up, and was only ransomed by Fionn and Cormac at the cost of certifying Lughaidh as the sole possessor of hunting rights in the province of Connacht. In that combat Oscar lost a testicle, the worst injury he ever suffered.[3]

There is much in this account which recalls the primitive lore of fianna life which we have discussed in chapter 2, and obviously the author of the third Colloquy was drawing on some older stratum of tradition than was otherwise current in the fourteenth century. The author states that Connacht was forbidden hunting territory to the Fianna since the time of the high-king Conn and Conall of Croghan, and thus a political rivalry between Connacht and the Leinster fianna is postulated. The stratum of tradition in question seems therefore to predate the assimilation of Connacht hostility into the figure of Goll mac Morna (p. 160). Once this latter process was completed the realm of Connacht tended to be internalised within the context of Fionn's men, as is clear from a late lay (about fifteenth century) which is much influenced by nomenclature from mediaeval literature.

According to this, Cormac held a great banquet at Tara, and in the course of the feasting an argument began between Goll and Lughaidh Lágha. Goll was praising the qualities of Conn, and Lughaidh was boasting of his father Eoghan – the great Munster king and rival of Conn. Fisticuffs broke out between the two warriors, and soon they had recourse to knives. Hundreds of their followers were killed in the tumult which followed, but the celebrated Munster hero Mac Con acted as mediator and got both sides to accept a solution – Fionn's judgement for Lughaidh and Conán's judgement for Goll. Conán Maol declared that he wished to decapitate every living Munsterman as vengeance for the blow which had been struck on Goll, but this was naturally not accepted. Mac Con himself then ruled that Goll should return to Croghan in Connacht and Lughaidh to Munster. Goll was more than two months recuperating from his wounds in Formoyle, and Lughaidh was for a whole year being healed in Aherlow.[4]

The writer of the lay was using as source the fourteenth century text *Cath Maighe Léna* which had Goll fighting on the side of Conn against the Munstermen aided by Fionn.[5] This exemplifies a factor which guaranteed stability within traditional Fianna lore, that factor being respect for precedence and adherence to the character portrayals as found in the sources used. Here, accordingly, we find the old breakdown of political forces – that of Goll with the Uí Néill opposing Fionn's Leinstermen with their Munster allies.

As well as following the pattern of old alignments, some lays also show remarkable innovation. Thus, one from the fourteenth century tells a new story of a daughter of Diarmaid and Gráinne, called Éachtach. On hearing of her father's death through the scheming of Fionn, we are told that Éachtach called her brothers together and waged a guerrilla campaign against the Fianna leader. She challenged Fionn to a duel, in which she shattered his shield with a blow of her sword and had him at her mercy had not a young Fianna warrior called Lodhorn gone to his rescue and killed her. Fionn spent three and a half years recovering from his wounds.[6]

The innovation here is striking in two ways – the invented personality of Diarmaid's daughter and the unprecedented image of Fionn's weakness and cowardice. But even the innovation is dependent on a time-honoured theme – that of an aggrieved person who resorts to reaving [*díbherg*] to get satisfaction for an injustice. Earlier sources outside of this cycle represent alienated women in that role as well as alienated men.[7]

Family tensions could be envisaged as approaching nearer to Fionn's person than such an angry young step-daughter. A fifteenth-century lay, which takes a distinctly dynastic view of the Fianna leadership, has a serious quarrel developing between Fionn and his usually very loyal son Oisín. It is almost as if the growing profile of Oisín within the lore was beginning to rival the prestige of the hero himself.

Oisín, we are told, asked Fionn for command of half of the Fianna. He was refused and was told that even after his father's death he would not inherit the leadership. Hearing this, Oisín and Oscar grew rebellious, and Oscar clashed with Caireall, who took Fionn's part. Fionn and Goll separated them, and Fionn then relented and granted Oisín his wishes.[8]

The most plausible rivalry, of course, and that which continued to have most dramatic appeal, was between Fionn's

Baoiscne clan and the Morna clan of Goll. We have discussed in chapter 6 several prose and verse accounts of serious ruptures between the two families. Much of the data from these twelfth- to fourteenth-century accounts are utilised in a prose text, which has the title *Bruidhean Bheag na hAlmhan* [the Little Contention at Allen] and which can be summarised as follows:

Fionn held a great feast at Almhain for all the Fianna. He himself sat among his own clan, while Goll sat among his. Fearghus Finnbhéil, the poet, began to recite and was awarded various treasures by Fionn, Oscar, Oisín, and Mac Lughach. Then Fearghus went to the Morna clan and recited poems to them of their ancestors' deeds. Goll called his female messenger and asked her had she collected the Scandinavian tribute for him. She produced these treasures, and Goll gave generously of them to Fearghus and to all the other poets and men of art who were present. Fionn angrily protested, saying that Goll had no right to exact tribute from Scandinavia, as that was his own prerogative.

Realising that Fionn was envious, Goll explained that he had had to leave Ireland long ago when Fionn's father Cumhall, together with the high-king Conn, had declared war on him. He had gone to Wales and conquered it, but Cumhall had driven him from there and from other countries also. Finally he had conquered Scandinavia and, since Cumhall did not follow him there, he had exacted tribute from its inhabitants. Later, when he was called by Conn to the battle of Castleknock, he had killed Cumhall in that battle.

When Fionn himself had visited Scandinavia, the king's wife had fallen in love with him and as a result Fionn with fifteen of his men had been held captive underground for a year with the intention of putting them to death. Goll, however, had arrived, had slain the Scandinavian king, and had set Fionn and his men free. That was the second time he had exacted the Scandinavian tribute, and he had since held that country in stewardship for Fionn.

'You have admitted that you came from the city of Bergen to the battle of Cnucha and that you killed my father there!' answered Fionn fiercely.

Goll declared that although he had indeed killed Fionn's father, Cumhall had been responsible for his own death. He further stated that he would do the same to Fionn if given cause. Tempers becoming frayed, Conán Maol came to blows with Caireall, who was of Fionn's clan. The other warriors joined in, and soon the whole palace was resounding to the noise of a fearsome conflict between the Baoiscne and Morna adherents.

The poet Fearghus Finnbhéil stood up and began to recite, and as a result the warriors desisted and gave their arms to the poets. Fionn, however, vowed that he would not make peace with the Morna clan until the king of Ireland and his judges would decide the issue between them. The poets therefore arranged that a fortnight from that day king Cormac mac Airt would pass judgement on the lawn of Tara.

Then the dead and wounded were counted. Fionn had lost twelve hundred men and women, while Goll had lost eleven men and fifty women – the women having died from terror as they observed the fighting.

When they assembled at Tara, Fearghus Finnbhéil explained to the judges that it was Fionn who wronged Goll and that Caireall had struck Conán with his fist on the forehead, thus starting the fight. He explained that Goll had protected his own followers with his shield, saving them from heavier casualties.

One judge, Flaithrí, ruled that honour-price should be paid to the Morna clan since they were attacked first. Cormac objected, however, saying that a warrior owes loyalty to his lord. Flaithrí said that loyalty no longer holds after bloodshed. Then another judge, Fítheal, made a ruling which was accepted by all.

According to it, the Baoiscne clan were excused from paying compensation on account of the great losses they had sustained, and the Morna clan were similarly excused because it was they who were first attacked.[9]

This text was written sometime around the year 1500, as indicated by the language and style and confirmed by the occurrence of certain motifs. The account of Goll's conquests overseas is borrowed directly from a fourteenth-century lay (see p. 163), while the fisticuffs at the feast is likely to come from the lay mentioned above which describes Goll's altercation with Lughaidh Lágha.

The plot of how the Scandinavian queen falls in love with Fionn and his being rescued by Goll is borrowed from the third Colloquy, which has a long poem describing how Fionn and a few of his followers once enlisted as mercenaries in Scandinavia. Things turned sour for them when their employer, the king, discovered that his wife was in love with Fionn. As a result of this, they were imprisoned and were to be put to death immediately, but Fionn secured a reprieve by saying that they should be allowed to do the year's service for which they had been paid.

Meanwhile Goll travelled from Ireland to rescue them, and he fought a fierce duel for three days with the Scandinavian king, but to no avail. The queen inveigled the secret of his invulnerability from her husband – that he could only be wounded with his own sword. She secretly took that sword from its scabbard and replaced it with Goll's, so that on the morrow the king found himself faced by his own sword in the hand of Goll and was accordingly killed. Fionn and his companions were then released from prison and, having plundered the country, they returned in triumph to Ireland.[10]

This story is interesting for the use it makes of floating motifs, such as that of the treacherous wife [as with the biblical Delilah][11] and the covert exchange of an ordinary sword for a magical one – a motif found also in Germanic romance of the time.[12] There probably was no deliberate borrowing involved here, but rather spontaneous use of what were well-known narrative devices.

The rivalry between Fionn's party and that of Goll, seething under the surface and liable at any moment to erupt, is the subject again of a fifteenth-century lay which is preserved in a Scottish manuscript. Here we are told of how Fionn once held a great feast, and a stranger arrived and invited Fionn to follow him. Conán Maol threatened to behead the stranger, which earned for him a severe reprimand from Fionn. Stung by this, Conán grew provocative, and fighting soon broke out between the Baoiscne and Morna clans at the feast. A son of Fionn and a son of Goll (neither of whom is named) were killed in the tumult before Fearghus the poet managed to restore peace. A magic mist then descended on the valley, and the strange visitor was nowhere to be seen.[13]

This plot of a magical visitor provoking internecine strife is found in another lay of the same period, which is obviously related to the foregoing. Fionn and the Fianna, we are told, were hunting at Benbulben (Co. Sligo) when they saw a warrior approaching with a sword through his head. The stranger claimed that Manannán had put the sword in him during a combat and that he was under injunctions [*geasa*] to search the world for somebody who could withdraw it. Conán tried to do so, but fell limp to the ground. Then the Morna clan went to attack the stranger, but the Baoiscne clan intercepted them and havoc ensued until Goll restored the peace. The stranger announced that he was in fact Manannán and that he had come out of his hatred to cause strife among the Fianna. He then drew the sword from his own head and Conán was resuscitated. Conán tried to attack Manannán, but Fionn protected him with his shield. Manannán then swished his sword, mesmerising the Fianna, before he departed.[14]

The idea of a supernatural figure coming in disguise to the Fianna on either a hostile or an amicable visit seems to be derived from native sources, such as a ninth-century text in the Ulster cycle, *Fled Bricrend*.[15]

A narrative which reflects less learned lore of the Middle Ages is employed in a fourteenth-century poem. We have discussed above the part of this poem which has Fionn being rescued by Goll in Scandinavia. The untypical action of Fionn in leaving Ireland to become a mercenary abroad is explained as an attempt by him to trace the lost women of the Fianna. And the manner in which the women went missing shows all the marks of a borrowing from folklore, with the requirements of plot drowning out all psychological subtlety.

One day, we are told, the Fianna were playing chess at Drom Crot [in the Galtee Mountains, Co. Tipperary], and they began to squabble over the game. Fionn rose to make peace between them, and scarcely had the row subsided when a tall handsome warrior came on the scene, accompanied by a beautiful woman. He challenged the fourteen Fianna chiefs to play chess, with his woman and their wives as stakes. He won every game, but the Fianna wished to go back on their word, and he would not have been allowed to depart with the women but for Oisín's protection.

A hare rose up before the Fianna, and the stranger disappeared with the women as if swallowed by the sea. It was following on this that Fionn went to Scandinavia and enlisted as a mercenary, in the hope of finding out something of the whereabouts of the women. When they returned to Ireland after their adventure, the Fianna group met Mac Reithe, one of their men, who told them that the women were in the Brugh [Newgrange] and that the otherworld lord Aonghus had had them there all the while. It was Aonghus who had come in disguise to play chess with them, and he explained that he had done this in order to discourage quarrelling among them. Furthermore, the genial Aonghus was pleased to compensate them for the ruse with much gold.[16]

Here the magical stranger is a good friend, and the idea of the helpful Aonghus must be basic to this kind of Fianna narrative. We have met with Aonghus intervening on the side of the Fianna in a text from around the year 1200, and the theme became something of a favourite (see p. 176), so it is logical to presume that stories of this kind lie behind the plot which has such mysterious figures coming to the troop. As these visitors become more frequent in the post-fourteenth century lore, however, it is clear that the native theme came under the influence of similar materials from Arthurian romance. One story, which has been the subject of much scholarly interest, can best be discussed in that context.

It is told in a lay written around the beginning of the fifteenth century, and concerns how a woman wearing nothing but a cloak came to Almhain once when Fionn was drinking with his companions Diarmaid, Mac Reithe, Oisín, Oscar, and Conán Maol, and their wives. The drink having gone to their heads, the women were boasting of their purity, but the stranger revealed that her cloak could test the virtue of any woman on whom it was put. If the woman were pure it would cover her completely.

Conán demanded that the cloak be put on his wife, but it rumpled up on her side, and in a fit of anger Conán speared his wife to death. Diarmaid, Oscar, and Oisín likewise tried it on their ladies, but it covered none of them properly. Even Fionn's wife, called Maighean, failed the test. Then Mac Reithe's wife put on the garment, and it spread out all over her body until it covered her completely, with the exception of her little toe. She explained that the cloak would have reached the ground but for a kiss which she had once secretly given to Diarmaid.

Then the stranger left, stating triumphantly that she had material for gossip concerning them and revealing that she was the daughter of the Dearg and had once slept with Fionn. Fionn angrily cursed her and told her to depart and never again come near his company.[17]

Although some scholars have argued the opposite, it is most plausible to regard the plot of this story as a borrowing from Arthurian tradition, which has twelfth- to fifteenth-century versions of it in several western European languages.[18] When the plot was adopted into Fianna lore it was made to fit comfortably there, such as in the matters of Conán's impulsiveness and Diarmaid's attractiveness to women. But one old theme was seen as particularly amenable to the plot. This was the ancient animosity of the otherworld daughter of Dearg towards Fionn and the affair that she once had with him (see p. 80) – a dramatic theme which could rationalise the plot as being the doings of a jealous jilted mistress.

So it is again clear that in stories of Fionn – in common with all Gaelic tradition – the otherworld can be either friendly or hostile in a quite arbitrary pattern. When entertainment became the principal function of Fianna lore the logic of relations with the otherworld became totally confused, so that divine figures who were properly sympathisers with the Fianna could be cast in mischievous roles without any compunction on the part of the writers. Thus we have seen Fionn's old associate Manannán described in a fifteenth-century text as trying to wreak havoc on the troop.

Even such a staunch supporter as Aonghus might be denigrated, as instanced by a lay composed not long after that. This tells of how he hosted a feast in Newgrange, at which he boasted that the life which he led was superior to that of hunters. Fionn disagreed, and the feast ended on a sour note. A year later, Aonghus out of his acrimony put his own son in the shape of a great pig to torment the Fianna when they were hunting in the Galtee Mountains. But things took a wrong turn when the fine hound Bran killed the pig, and the Fianna – incensed at the loss of many of their men in the chase – decided that the quarry should be burnt. This was accordingly done and, deprived thus of any chance of resuscitating his son, Aonghus was livid with anger and cursed Bran. The bad feeling continued until Fionn sent his own Raighne into fosterage with Aonghus, and the latter sent another son of his to Fionn.[19]

The Fianna Trapped

Nowhere is the transition from early myth to entertaining narrative more obvious than in the case of the *bruidhean*-stories, which have the Fianna being trapped in sinister abodes. The word *bruidhean* [modernised spelling *bruíon*] meant a mansion, but in mediaeval Irish lore it usually denotes a hostile and macabre underworld, with the word *sídh* being increasingly used in the sense of distinctly bright and friendly otherworld dwellings.[20]

We have discussed in chapter 5 the relationship between these two faces of the spirit realm, and have related both back to Fionn as an ancient symbol of seer-craft. The fear of the unknown, together with the dramatic potential of viewing the otherworld as a destructive force, guaranteed that there would be accounts bringing Fionn into conflict with that realm. Such accounts increased in popularity through the Middle Ages, assisted by Christian propaganda against the idea of a pagan otherworld, and in post-mediaeval times they came close to dominating the whole tradition.

In this way, the structure of Fianna narrative underwent a marked change, but the new emphasis accorded well enough with other ideas to ensure that the basic character of the lore was not greatly altered. It was, in fact, a singular instance of integral imagery passing 'from ritual to romance'.

In several of the *bruidhean*-stories there is a lingering sense that behind the actual adventure which is being described lie ideas concerning quest-visits to the realm of darkness. There may even be scattered images from ancient accounts of Fionn, such as in two stories which are found together in verse form in the third Colloquy.

Put in the mouth of Caoilte, the verses tell of a female hostelier called Deamhnach who lived at Toireamh [in the parish of Manulla, Co. Mayo] and who had thirty great milking cows. Every herdsman she sent with the cows used to disappear, and when nine of the Fianna visited her house one evening they found her weeping for her lost servants and for nine of the cows which had also failed to return.

Caoilte went to investigate and, coming to the Erris estuary he saw a white-haired [*foilt-fhionn*] maiden on a hill. This maiden put him to sleep with harp-strains and then brought him to a mysterious island, where he was flung 'into a black dark cave' [*i n-uaimh nduibh ndorchu*]. The maiden's name was Dá Bhiolla, and she had seventy warriors fettered in the cave. When the sea rose it poured in on them, and when it sank they fell onto sharp rocks. Three days Caoilte was a captive there, until Oisín grew anxious and set out from Deamhnach's house in search of his comrade.

He arrived at the mysterious dwelling [here called a *síodhán*] where Dá Bhiolla put him also to sleep with music. But the Fianna converged on that place from all sides and forced her to release the prisoners and the stolen cattle.[21]

The second story does not involve a sinister dwelling, but features a character who clearly belongs to the realm of the dead.

Once, when Fionn, Oisín, and Caoilte were in a wood at Feeguile [in Co. Offaly] a headless spectre appeared and spoke fiercely to them, demanding one of their heads. Fionn promised him any other thing he wished, and the stranger said that the only other head he would accept was that which he had been continuously seeking. At that, Oisín and Caoilte struck with their swords at the oak-tree, and a huge head fell from its branches. The stranger thanked Fionn, as this was his own head which had been hidden by magic from him ever since he had been decapitated by three foes at Howth.[22]

These two stories – with their lonely location, fair-haired figures, and severed heads – are redolent of early seer lore regarding Fionn.

We have discussed (pp. 137f) an eleventh-century story of Fionn being trapped in a macabre dwelling inhabited by several monstrous beings, including a headless man. That adventures of this kind were being invented and elaborated at this time is evidenced by an account which is given briefly in a thirteenth-century lay. The author of the lay seems to be referring to a pre-existing story, of which he is giving the mere outline.[23] A prose-text of some centuries later tells the same story, and the source for this latter work is either the lay (to which it closely conforms) or a lost original. It is called *Bruidhean Chéise Corainn* [the Mansion of Keshcorran, in Co. Sligo] and can be summarised as follows:

During a great hunt Fionn, accompanied by Conán Maol, set up his camp on top of the hill of Keshcorran. The lord of the otherworld mansion in that hill, Conarán of the Tuatha Dé Danann, ordered his three ugly daughters to wreak vengeance on the Fianna for hunting there. Going to the door of their cave, these three placed three great irons around three briar-trunks and began to twist them withershins.

When they saw the witches, the complexions of Fionn and Conán grew wan and turned red, and white, and then black, before the two warriors collapsed to the ground. The witches tied them up and brought them into the mansion. When Oisín, Oscar and Mac Lughach came to the hill, they were similarly captured, as in turn were four whole battalions of the Fianna.

The witches went out to reconnoitre before beheading their captives, and they saw coming towards them a fine warrior. This was Goll mac Morna. They attacked him, and with one great stroke of his sword he killed two of them – Camóg and Cuilleann. The third witch, Iarnach, gripped him from behind, and a titanic wrestling contest ensued. Eventually Goll laid her low and bound her with the straps of his shield. She begged quarter, swearing to release the Fianna, and he set her free.

Goll then went to the cave where the captives were being held, and they were released at his word. But, before they left the cave, they found its entrance blocked by the horrific Iarnach, who now demanded single combat. Oisín, Oscar, Mac Lughach, Diarmaid, Caoilte, and the rest refused; and Fionn said that he himself would fight her. Then Goll restrained him, saying that the loyal friend is discovered in hard circumstances. Goll himself took the field, and after a fierce encounter he killed her with a cast of his javelin. He then plundered and burned the otherworld mansion and, in appreciation of what he had done, Fionn gave Goll his own daughter Caon in marriage that very day.[24]

Two of the witch figures in this story can be traced to pre-existing material. Camóg, daughter of Conarán, is described in an early eleventh-century poem as a witch who was blind in one eye and who could knock down a yew tree by tying a magic thread around it.[25] This is obviously what suggested the strange magical practice of the hags in *Bruidhean Chéise Corainn*. Cuilleann seems to have been indigenous to Fianna tradition, as her death at the hands of the Fianna is given in an earlier story as the reason why the phantoms trapped Fionn at Iubharghlenn (p. 138). The phantoms claimed that she had been their sister, but do not mention either Camóg or Iarnach, from which we can gather that this triad of Keshcorran sisters were not yet part of Fianna lore in the eleventh century. The most horrendous of the three, Iarnach [literally, the iron one] has her name from the iron rings which they use in their magic,[26] and she does not occur outside of the Keshcorran story. In fact, the general idea of a hostile trio of witches seems to have been suggested to the shapers of the Fianna tradition by similar figures in texts of the Ulster cycle, such as *Brislech Mór Maige Muirthemne* and *Togail Bruidne Da Derga*.[27]

The possibility of a *bruidhean* being not altogether an evil place was not lost sight of, however, as is clear from a lay composed around the year 1400 which rationalises the name of Fionn's sword (see p. 121). This borrows the placename

Keshcorran, but little else, from the previous story; and it retains the ancient idea within the Fionn lore of gifts being received from the otherworld.

One day, we are told, the Fianna were in the vicinity of Slieve Logher (in Co. Kerry) when a strange black-faced warrior approached, announcing that he was Lon mac Líomhtha, a master-smith, and had come from Bergen. He placed injunctions of *troigh mhná troghain* [the heavy step of a pregnant woman] on them to follow him to his smithy. He ran like the wind, but Daolghus caught up with him as they entered the cave of Keshcorran, with Fionn close behind. There was a 'grim gathering' within. Lon began work in the forge there, and Daolghus growing hot the surly smiths enquired who was 'the slender warm man' [*an fear cáilte*]. Fionn said that this should be Daolghus' name henceforth, i.e. Caoilte. Lon then ordered that the guests be given fine beds, and he made weapons for them. The marvellous sword made for Fionn was therefore called Mac an Luin [the son of Lon]. Next morning they woke up back again on Slieve Logher, but they still had the seven swords and nine spears which had been forged for them.[28]

This is another example of the dream-visit plot, as above, in the case of the Iubharghlenn phantoms. But here the influence of reputed Fianna warring against the Norsemen has intervened, so that it is not clear whether or not Keshcorran is understood as a Norse stronghold. This confusion points to a very interesting functional development in the late mediaeval lore, that is that the concept of the otherworld is in practice extended to cover faraway regions. The basic idea in question is the realm of the unknown, and we shall meet with many more examples of phantastic and grotesque figures inhabiting foreign parts just as they do the mysterious fortresses under the earth.

As if to overtly exemplify the confluence of otherworld with external world, we have a late [perhaps sixteenth-century] lay which joins the story of how Goll saved Fionn in Scandinavia with the account of Lon mac Líomhtha. In this, the whole seven battalions of the Fianna are bound by magic in Scandinavia, and their captor – called Mac an Dáin [son of Art] – intends to behead them. But Goll arrives on the scene, slays hundreds of the foe, demolishes the prison, and releases Fionn and his men. Goll re-arms them all and conducts them home in safety.[29]

Much of the development in Fianna narrative is a kind of chain-reaction by which the plot of one text suggests another. Thus, based on the above account of Lon, we have a lay written soon afterwards which has Fionn again on Slieve Logher when he was approached by a tall warrior in a red suit and carrying a golden bird-crib. This warrior invited Fionn and his three score companions to a feast and led them to Inbhear dhá Shál [perhaps Arklow in Co. Wicklow]. As soon as they entered his stronghold there, he went out and closed a rough iron door on them. For seven days and nights they were imprisoned and hungry in that earthen fortress. Then Fionn made a crib in imitation of the one he had seen with the stranger, and they caught enough birds to feed themselves. Finally their host came to them, expecting to find them dead, but they to a man rose up and seized him. Fionn's companions wished to put their tormentor to death, but the leader would not allow it and he conducted him safely from among them. This, we are told, was 'the best clemency ever done' by Fionn.

The strange visitor in this lay is called 'mac Troghain', which reflects the conventional formula for putting an injunction [*troigh mhná troghain*] in the lay of Lon. The selection of the word *troghan* as name for the stranger here shows how loose and arbitrary the borrowing of details could be.[30]

The otherworld proper is the hostile environment in one long prose-tale, which was composed around the year 1500. This is entitled *Bruidhean Eochaidh Bhig Dheirg* [the Mansion of little red Eochaidh]. The name of the hostile entertainer in this case is significant, as it echoes aspects of Fionn's archetypal foe. The element Dearg [older form Derg] we can take to be adjectival, as meaning 'red', but it also coincides with the name of an ancient otherworld foe of Fionn (see chapters 1 and 2). Secondly, the designation Eochaidh recalls a king of that name in a very old Irish story. This was Eochaidh *Aonsúile* [the one-eyed],[31] and although this character was famed for his generosity his imagery on the surface could be taken loosely by a late author as coinciding with that of Fionn's one-eyed opponent. The text of *Bruidhean Eochaidh Bhig Dheirg* is here summarised:

Fionn used to find a deer to hunt on the hill of Galway every seven years. One Halloween he and the seven battalions went hunting there. He asked Conán Maol to quarter them, but the latter refused. Caoilte also refused, so great was the multitude to be catered for, but Gal Gaoithe accepted. This character had the ability to count every man and hound of the Fianna at a single glance. Fourteen men had gone with Conán to play chess behind a hillock, and when Gal Gaoithe discovered that he had omitted them he asked to be beheaded for his mistake. Conán chided him, saying that he was called Gal Gaoithe (puff of wind] because he was wont to be demented by fear in battle and that no such lunatic should be beheaded. Gal Gaoithe thereupon grew very angry and left the Fianna.

Soon a strange warrior arrived and offered to quarter the whole troop from then until the following May. Conán persuaded the stranger that it was enough to bring the fifteen with him and that the rest of the Fianna could find lodgings for themselves. The stranger then gave them an apple each, and he said that he had seven whole orchards of such sweet apples at his dwelling. He then set off, running at the speed of a swallow or a doe, and with the fifteen Fianna warriors following him, until they reached his mansion. The stranger told them to enter and said that he would go to prepare food for them.

The warriors did not know where they were; but one of them, Diarmaid, was suspicious and sent Conán out to see if there was a large standing-stone in the doorpost. Conán saw that there was, and then Diarmaid told them that he and Fionn had once spent the night on that spot and that Fionn had dreamt that a mansion would be built there – a mansion which would be the most dangerous trap of all for the Fianna. Their host, Diarmaid now realised, was Eochaidh Beag Dearg of the Tuatha Dé Danann, and that trap had been in preparation for them for seven and a half years.

Meanwhile, Fionn and the rest of the Fianna had got

lodgings from a generous hostelier. Before settling in, he washed his hands and put his thumb under his tooth of knowledge to check if all his men were safe. Discovering the position the fifteen were in, he slipped away from his lodgings and headed for Eochaidh's mansion. His son Aodh Beag saw him depart and followed him. They joined the captives, and soon Eochaidh came in and announced the arrival of twice three hundred men and a further three hundred female warriors of the Tuatha Dé. Anxious at the presence of this hostile company, Fionn set Conán Maol to watch the door of the mansion for the night.

Soon a monstrously ugly warrior came in and demanded the seat of the best man of the Fianna. Fionn said that Conán was the best. The ugly man began to wrestle with Conán, who threw him and cut his head off. Then a hag from among the female warriors tackled Conán, overcame him, and tied him up. Conán called on Diarmaid to help him, and the latter aimed his spear at the hag but was stopped by Fionn, who would not allow interference in a duel. The hag then said that she had once been courted by Conán while she was in Fionn's service. Conán, however, managed to untie his bonds and was about to decapitate her when she offered to withdraw her three hundred female warriors if he spared her life. Fionn instructed Conán to accept her offer, and she departed with her force.

Soon after they had another visitor, a huge warrior with a fire-breathing black hound, who challenged Fionn to a dog-fight. The hound killed several of the Fianna dogs, including those belonging to Conán, Oisín, and Diarmaid. Finally Bran engaged the ferocious beast, but could not kill it as one of Bran's paws was covered with a silver shoe. Diarmaid held the two hounds apart while Conán removed the shoe, and Bran tore its opponent open with its claw. Conán then beheaded the hound's owner.

Another strange warrior arrived, carrying a trough of water and challenging the best man of the Fianna to wash his hands and feet in it. Conán put his little toe into the water and it was burned to a cinder. Overcome with rage, Conán flung the owner himself into the trough so that he was consumed, and then sprinkled the water on the Tuatha Dé who were present, with devastating effect.

Next arrival was a warrior with a boar on his shoulders. He threw it on the floor, saying that this was Eochaidh's fare for them and that they would have to cook it themselves. Conán attempted to do so but was scalded, and he forced the warrior who had brought it to do the cooking. He then refused any of the pork to the Tuatha Dé, and in the resulting fracas beheaded one of them.

A horrid churl came, with one eye in the centre of his head and a huge chain in his hand. Again asking for the best man of the Fianna he engaged Conán in a tug-of-war with the chain. Each had his head in a link of the chain as they pulled back to back. The churl won, and he was about to decapitate Conán when the latter called to Diarmaid for help. Again Fionn restrained Diarmaid, but the latter threw his apple and blinded the churl. Conán seized his opportunity and tied up his opponent. The churl revealed that he and his twenty-nine sons had been trained in hell and engaged by Eochaidh to kill the Fianna. He was allowed by Fionn to depart, on condition that he withdrew his sons from Eochaidh's service. Conán then asked Diarmaid to bring him a drink, and when Diarmaid hesitated he reminded him of how his brother Goll had relieved Diarmaid's thirst at the battle of Ventry.

Diarmaid went out and, accompanied by Bran, he slew a large number of the Tuatha Dé who were surrounding the mansion. He spared the life of one enemy, who directed him to the Well of the Bright Stream. This well was guarded by a beautiful lady warrior, who was in love with Diarmaid and therefore promised to help him. She gave him food and drink for Conán, as well as clay from the Island of Victory which would protect its possessor from magical harm.

When Diarmaid returned, Conán ate and drank his fill and then went outside the mansion with Bran to slaughter the foes. He was joined by Diarmaid, and Eochaidh implored Fionn to strike up the special hum, the *dord fiann*, to recall them.

They were not long returned when a huge warrior with a club entered. He also wrestled with Conán, who beheaded him. Exasperated by all these failures, the Tuatha Dé made an all-out attack on the seventeen Fianna warriors, who formed a phalanx and successfully fought them off. A truce was arranged on condition that Fionn and the Tuatha Dé leader, Aodh, would fight a single combat on the morrow. Another horrendous hag appeared in the doorway then and blew a terrible note with a trumpet into Conán's ear. He killed her with one thrust, and in his delirium lashed out left and right at the Tuatha Dé. Diarmaid again joined him, and they were restrained with great difficulty by Fionn.

The battle was joined next morning on the green outside the mansion. The seventeen Fianna warriors wreaked havoc on their foes, but they were hopelessly outnumbered and all seemed lost when Fionn perceived the whole Fianna troop coming to their relief. The Tuatha Dé fighters were slaughtered to a man. The seven battalions of the Fianna had been assembled by Fionn's own mother Muirn, who had a charm by virtue of which she could travel all Ireland in twenty-four hours.[32]

This story illustrates well the desire for comprehensiveness which characterises the Fianna cycle at its best.

Many motifs and images which had become domiciled in the cycle are utilised by the author and put to good dramatic effect. Among these motifs are Fionn's seer-craft, Conán's mischief and savagery in the fight, and Diarmaid's attractiveness to women. Motifs derived from the marvellous-helper theme are used in a rather oblique but effective way, such as the amazing counting ability of Gal Gaoithe, the magical travelling ability of Muirn, and the running speed of Eochaidh. Images and details from the lore which occur are the Halloween situation, the continuous beheading, the one-eyed foe, the name Aodh for an important enemy, the *dord fiann*, and the cooking of a pig; while Bran's fight with the black hound is taken from a slightly earlier lay on that subject (see p. 290)

Material from outside the Fianna lore is also used by the author. The dementia of Gal Gaoithe is taken from the mediaeval story of Suibhne's madness [*Buile Shuibhne*],[33] the wizards trained in hell from the Ulster cycle story *Brislech Mór Maige Muirthemne*,[34] the wondrous apples from a source like the early mediaeval text *Echtra Conla*,[35] and the idea of special protective clay is probably borrowed from folk belief.[36] But, as well as this, some more novel themes surface in the story, such as Diarmaid's close friendship with Conán and the comical way in which the latter is plagued and tormented by hags. These themes were destined to become very popular, and they recur in several later texts, as we shall see.

Defending the Country

A very well-known prose story has foreign invaders in the place of spiritual foes, and therefore represents a climax of the development which has been discussed above, i.e. the confluence of otherworld beings and Norse invaders. This text is entitled *Bruidhean Chaorthainn* [The Quicken Mansion], and the array of foreign foes – including the 'King of the World' – mentioned in it shows that its author has drawn on the Battle of Ventry (pp. 146ff). The evidence suggests a date of composition of the text in the second quarter of the sixteenth century. It is one of the best-written of all the Fianna tales, with a flowing style, deft use of conversation, and several striking passages, but the plot is poor and the episodes rather disjointed. This is a synopsis of the action:

The king of Scandinavia, Colgán 'the Hard-Armed', held a great assembly in Bergen, and announced that he intended to make good his title 'King of the Islands' by subduing Ireland. He organised a great force and put to sea, landing in Ulster and laying waste the countryside.

When news of this reached Tara, king Cormac mac Airt alerted Fionn at Almhain. Fionn called together the seven battalions of the Fianna and marched to face the invaders. In a fierce battle, Oscar beheaded Colgán and the Norse host was routed. Colgán's two elder sons were also killed, and his youngest son Míodhach was taken prisoner. Fionn gave his protection to Míodhach, brought him to Almhain, and proclaimed him king of Scandinavia. Míodhach, for his part, pledged tribute to Fionn and remained with him.

One day Goll mac Morna remarked to Fionn that it was dangerous to bestow so much trust on Míodhach, and at Oisín's prompting Fionn decided to give territory to him in another part of Ireland. Míodhach chose two baronies, one on each side of the river Shannon in Munster, where he had access to a good port. There the Norse prince lived for fifteen years, and he grew very rich. He secretly brought a large force of Norsemen in through the mouth of the Shannon, and plotted revenge on Fionn for his father's death.

It happened once that Fionn was hunting in Munster, and he rested at Knockfierna [a hill in Co. Limerick]. A strange young nobleman approached and put riddles to him in poetic form. Fionn answered each riddle correctly, and then asked the stranger who he was. Conán Maol interrupted, remarking to Fionn that he should know his enemies better than his friends and that this was Míodhach son of Colgán. Míodhach told Fionn that he had long intended to invite him to a feast but had been too humble to do so, but that he was now insisting that Fionn and the Fianna come to him for a great banquet. He had two mansions prepared, one on land and the other on an island, and the guests might have their choice of the locations. Fionn agreed to go, and Míodhach took his leave for the moment.

Having arranged that Oisín, Diarmaid, Caoilte, and some others were to collect the rest of the Fianna nobles, Fionn set out with Goll, Conán Maol, and seven others. When they reached the mansion on land they entered and wondered at the splendour and comfort of the place. Fionn, however, was surprised that Míodhach did not join them; and they soon noticed that the place was magically losing its grandeur and becoming a cold and foul dwelling. The seven fine doors had disappeared, and in their place was a narrow miserable door facing north. Fionn said there was a prohibition [*geas*] on him against being in a mansion with only one door, and he ordered his men to cut their way out. But they then found that they were magically stuck to the ground.

Goll asked Fionn to put his thumb under his tooth of knowledge, and when he did so he discovered that the Norse prince was planning treachery. He heaved a great sigh, saying that Míodhach had a huge host with him in the island mansion, including the King of the World (called Sinsear na gCath [ancestor of battles]), and the three kings of Inis Tuile [Thule Island]. The latter three were evil wizards who had designed the trap, and nothing could release the Fianna from the ground but the blood of these three. Realising that they were soon to be beheaded, the captured warriors began a desolate cry, but Fionn told them to stop keening like women. They then pressed their lips together and struck up their special hum, the *dord fiann*.

Meanwhile, Oisín had grown anxious at not having any news from Fionn, and had sent Fiachna son of Fionn and Inse son of Suibhne Seilge to investigate. These two heard the *dord fiann*, and Fionn spoke to them from inside the mansion and told them of his predicament. He wished that Inse, who was his foster-child, should go to safety, but Inse insisted on staying. Leaving Inse to guard that spot, Fiachna then set out for the island-mansion.

A Greek earl with a hundred knights soon came to behead the captives, but they were intercepted by Inse, who killed the hundred and was himself slain by the earl. The earl decided to return to display Inse's head to the King of the World, but on his way he met Fiachna and mistook him for one of the King's men.

'I do not belong to his household', said Fiachna, 'and neither do you any longer!'

Fiachna slew the earl in combat, and brought Inse's head back to its body before burying it with honour. Having told Fionn what had happened, he himself stood guard in Inse's place.

Soon another Greek earl arrived with four hundred knights, and these were all killed by a rampant Fiachna. When Míodhach heard of this, he devised a plan to bring the best of food to the quicken mansion and to eat it there, in order to drive the gluttonous Conán insane. Coming with five hundred knights, he chanced upon Fiachna and a fierce fight ensued.

Oisín was wondering why it took the two warriors so long to return, and Diarmaid decided to go to investigate, accompanied by Fathadh Canainn. They arrived as Fiachna was contending with Míodhach's force.

'Save the son of the Ríghfhéinnidh', said Fathadh, 'or Fionn will say that you willingly let him be killed!' Diarmaid then cast his javelin at Míodhach.

'That is the javelin of Diarmaid Ó Duibhne which has been thrust into me', said Míodhach, and before he died he decapitated Fiachna.

Diarmaid then cut Míodhach's head off for Fionn in compensation for his son. He then went to tell the captive Fionn what had happened, and stood guard over the mansion. Conán demanded that Diarmaid bring a drink to him, and Fathadh suggested that the food and drink brought by Míodhach would suffice. But Diarmaid said that Conán would chide him for bringing the food of dead men, and he reluctantly set out for the island-mansion to procure what Conán wanted.

Diarmaid went straight into the banqueting-hall on the island, slew a servant and seized his full goblet, and then kicked the King of the World in the chest and seized his food. Returning to the quicken mansion, he found Fathadh asleep there. The cantankerous Conán told him to throw the food through the door to him, and to pour the drink through a hole in the roof. This he did, but soon the three kings of Thule arrived with a thousand knights. Diarmaid fell to blows with them, and Fathadh was awakened by the tumult and joined in. The entire hostile force was slain, with Diarmaid himself killing the three wizards. Fionn then told Diarmaid to rub the blood of the wizards onto the door. The door opened immediately, and then Diarmaid rubbed the blood on all the captive Fianna, and they were released from the floor. All except Conán, for whom no blood remained. So Diarmaid and Fathadh had to pull him off the floor, leaving the skin of his heels, buttocks, shoulder-blades, and poll behind him. So he was called Conán 'the Bald' (*Maol*).

The son of the King of the World, called Borb, now came to the quicken mansion with a thousand warriors to behead Fionn. They were engaged by Diarmaid and Fathadh, and during the fighting Oisín and the rest of the Fianna arrived at the scene. They joined in the battle, and Goll beheaded Borb. Hearing report of this on the island, the King of the World flung all his forces into the attack. There was horrific slaughter, but 'it was like tying knots in sand to go into combat with the Fianna of Ireland at that time', and the invaders were completely overthrown. Oscar beheaded the

King of the World himself, and only a few of the foreign host managed to reach their ships through headlong flight.[37]

The author of this story shows that he was well acquainted with the literature of his time. As well as *Cath Fionntrágha* [the battle of Ventry text], the episode of Diarmaid bringing food and drink to Conán reflects a scene from *Bruidhean Eochaidh Bhig Dheirg*. But, whereas the latter text seems to have been written in Connacht, *Bruidhean Chaorthainn*'s topography indicates that its author was from either Co. Clare or Co. Limerick. He apparently also knew the Keshcorran story, for his three wizards fit the same pattern as the witches of *Bruidhean Chéise Corainn*. The episode which has Diarmaid enter the enemies' banquet, kick the feasting king, and forcibly take food and drink, is based on a motif which was popular in European romance, but the immediate source here may be an Irish tale from outside the Fianna cycle, *Eachtra Chonaill Ghulban*, which was composed about the year 1530.[38]

The novel explanation given for Conán's nickname is of particular interest and indicates that the author had direct access to classical sources, for it is based on an account given by Apollodorus of the Athenian hero Theseus. According to this, Theseus visited Hades and his host – feigning hospitality – beguiled him into sitting in a magic chair, to which he stuck. He remained there for four years, until Heracles pulled him free, but he left a great part of his buttocks behind him.[39]

The similarity of context between the prison-mansion of Fianna lore and the Greek Hades caused the author of *Bruidhean Chaorthainn* to notice how suitable such a motif would be to provide a comical interlude as well as to explain Conán's nickname.

As we have seen in chapter 5, the memory of the Norse wars had already imposed itself onto Fianna lore by the end of the eleventh century. As the taste for dramatic adventure increased, and as the cycle became stabilised around a number of clear-cut characters, invading Scandinavian forces became increasingly more suitable as background props to the action. They could be introduced at will to help construct new narrative patterns.

We have a good example of the function of these invading forces in a thirteenth-century lay, according to which the Fianna were hunting one day at Bregia [in Co. Meath]. A little deer escaped from them into the huge corn-field owned by Caoilte's wife, and Fionn directed his men to reap the corn and in this way to discover the deer. Three thousand of the Fianna were reaping, having all laid their swords aside except Fionn, Oisín, and Oscar. While they were thus engaged, Dolar king of Scandinavia arrived on the scene with seven fully-armed battalions. The Fianna rose up unarmed and came to grips with the foe as best they could, while Caoilte raced to Tara in order to collect their weapons. He returned, before anybody had fallen, 'like the blast of a keen wind' and carrying a great load which consisted of a thousand swords and shields. The Fianna, thus armed, won the day.[40]

That story is clearly a eulogy of Caoilte, with the stress on his special ability and his importance to the Fianna troop. Similar dire situations could be the backdrop to more down-to-earth portrayals of the characters, and by the fifteenth century this latter type of account had become commonplace.

For instance, one lay of that time tells that when Fionn was once preparing for a hunt at Slieve Gullion (in Co. Armagh) a large dark warrior approached. Conán mocked Fionn, saying that he was afraid of the stranger, and the two men almost came to blows, but Conán apologised. The stranger said he was Dubh mac Díorfaidh and that he wanted Ireland to submit to him. Oscar undertook to fight him, but Caoilte remarked that Oscar's father was no fighter, and a fierce argument resulted. Oisín attacked Caoilte, who fled from him all the way to Thurles (in Co. Tipperary) and back again to Slieve Gullion, but Oisín caught him and put him in fetters. Fionn awarded compensation from Caoilte to Oisín and reconciled the two. He then said that the Fianna should not oppose Dubh.

Incensed by this, Oscar insulted Fionn, saying that 'your counsel has ruined the Fianna-troop', and mocked him by saying that he himself would never 'eat the marrow of my hands' as Fionn did by chewing his fingers. Fionn, however, kept his patience and, inspired by Oscar's courage, he lost his fear of the stranger. Oscar then led the Fianna against Dubh.

The stranger slew many warriors, including Fionn's son Raighne, but Oscar engaged and killed him. His body was brought by the Fianna to the great cave on Slieve Gullion and hurled into it. Oscar was a year recuperating from his wounds.[41]

The enemy host led by a great single warrior was a very popular theme. There are several lays from the fifteenth century based on this simple pattern of limited dramatic potential. The tension is usually built up by having the stranger defeat several redoubtable fighters before finally being defeated by an invincible Fianna champion. The lay of Dearg mac Droichil is a case in point.

Dearg, a marvellously handsome prince, came to Howth from the Land of Fair Men in the east. Raighne and Caol were guarding Howth; but they had fallen asleep, and when they awoke they saw the stranger, who told them that he was demanding the high-kingship of Ireland. Caol fought him, but was overcome and bound. Similarly with Raighne. He released them on condition that they not oppose him again, and then he proceeded to Tara. There he made his demand, and killed three hundred of Cormac's men in one day.

Cormac sent word to Fionn, and Fionn came and greeted Dearg but refused to submit to him. Following on this, Dearg overcame three hundred men of the Fianna, including Conán son of the Liath Luachra. Faolán also engaged the stranger, but was overcome and bound. Fionn then asked Goll to take the field, and Goll – laying aside memories of their feud – agreed. 'The men of Ireland all fell silent on hearing the blows of the fight', which lasted for three days until Goll slew the stranger. Goll was a year recuperating.

If Dearg had been allowed to sleep, we are told, he would have conquered all, but what this means is not explained.[42] It is likely that some stanzas have been lost, for a sixteenth-century account in English states that Fionn kept Dearg awake for three nights running by telling him stories. 'till he was so amazed and weary for lack of sleep that he had not half his strength, by reason whereof he was slain'.[43]

Once the invasion-plot became common it was necessary, in order to hold an audience's attention, to introduce a good amount of personality colouring. An obvious artistic success is a lay which has the Fianna at Dunbo (in Co. Derry), protecting the harbour on the orders of Cairbre Lifeachair, when a huge man with a club sailed in and demanded combat.

Fionn went to his tent disguised as a poet, accompanied by Ferghus Fíonbhéil, and also Cnú Dearóil the dwarf-harper, and the latter's wife Bláthnait. They were received hospitably by the huge man, who told them that his name was Laighne Mór and that he was the son of the Fomhóire king in the east. He came to Ireland demanding tribute. The visitor persuaded him to swear that he would never ask tribute from a poet, and then revealed himself as Fionn. Laighne kept his word and hosted the Fianna to a fine ale-feast there. Hence the place was called *Port an Rígh-Óil* [the Port of the Kingly Feast].[44]

Much depended, of course, on the degree of respect which each particular author had for the Fianna tradition, and this included an assessment of the figure of Fionn himself. He could be admired as a fearless warrior, valued for his wit and smartness, or belittled for his vengefulness and spite. One lay takes as dim a view as possible, attributing cowardice to him while extolling Goll. There was a definite train of thought since late mediaeval times which wished to make the latter the real hero of the cycle and which exaggerated the general high opinion of Goll as Fionn's magnanimous rival. It is plausible to suggest that this was a special input into the lore from sources in Connacht – the province with which Goll was associated.

The present lay belongs to the fifteenth century and describes how two thousand Scandinavian vessels came ashore in Ireland and commenced to burn the countryside. The hostile fleet was commanded by Maghnus Mór [Magnus the great], and the Fianna out of fright advised Fionn to leave the country to the invader. When Goll saw Fionn prepare to embark and depart the country, he was enraged and went to fight Maghnus. In a horrific duel, he overcome and decapitated the invader.[45]

The denigration could extend to other characters besides Fionn, depending on the whim of the author. One writer of a lay in the same period, aware of the theme of Caoilte's alienation from the high-king Cormac in the story of the straggling drove (pp. 179ff), decided to create a rift between Caoilte and Fionn himself.

So, we are told, Fionn once forgot to invite some of the Fianna to a feast in Almhain. Among those overlooked were Caoilte and Aille, and the two, in a pique, left Ireland and joined the service of the Scandinavian king. The king was called Airghreann, and his wife fell in love with Aille and lay with him in the king's own bed. As a result, Caoilte and Aille had to flee, and they returned to Almhain. But Airghreann followed them with a great army and encamped near Fionn's residence. Fionn offered compensation to Airghreann, but the latter slew Aille and then insisted on battle. Goll led a raid on Airghreann's camp, and after eight days of fighting Airghreann and all his men were slain.[46]

The qualities of the Fianna were much lauded in the Colloquy and related texts. For instance, when St Patrick asked Caoilte in the Colloquy what sustained the Fianna, he was given the answer:

> Truth in our hearts
> And strength in our arms
> And deed according to our word.[47]

But the author of the sixteenth-century prose-text *Eachtra Iollainn Iolchrothaigh* took a very sarcastic view of such platitudes and was determined to present Fionn and his men as selfish opportunists. This is a summary:

After Cormac had spent thirty years of excellent rule over Ireland he held a great fair at Tara. During the fair a fine warrior, Iollann Iolchrothach son of the Spanish king, approached and announced that he had come seeking the head of the king of Ireland, in order to avenge the deaths of his two brothers. Cormac said that Fionn was in effect the real king, and he directed him on to Almhain.

Arriving there, Iollann demanded single combat. Diarmaid refused to take the field, saying that he had little cause to fight for Fionn. Oisín refused, saying that none of the Fianna could compete with the stranger. Oisín's son, Fear Lúigheadh, refused, saying that Fionn acted treacherously towards him. He had wooed a Connacht princess who demanded that he bring the head of a great warrior from Inse Starainn [perhaps the Tyrrhenian Islands] to her. When he set out with two hundred men to achieve this, Fionn had recalled half of them in the hope that Mac Lúigheadh would be killed and that he himself would have the woman. Oscar also refused to fight Iollann, since he had not yet recovered from a great overseas quest a year before. So Fionn himself had to face Iollann.

The two were fighting for some time when Fionn's shield shrieked, as it always did when he was in danger. The rest of the Fianna came to save him, and Iollann turned his fury on them until he came face to face with Oscar. As Fionn was carried away to Almhain to have his wounds treated, Oscar and Iollann fought savagely all day. When night came, Iollann sought respite, and they feasted in Fionn's residence. Oscar asked Fionn to keep Iollann awake in conversation till morning, so that he would be tired and weak on the next day.

So Fionn went to Iollann's room and kept him awake, assuring him that Oscar also was awake and carousing with the Fianna. Iollann began to relate his adventures in full, and as he finished the morning had arrived and Oscar was banging his shield ready for combat. Then Iollann understood that he had been tricked, and in the ensuing contest he was slain by Oscar.[48]

This story is obviously influenced by contemporaneous lays both in plot and perspective, and it is the culmination of the anti-Fionn strain which had quite a prominence for a while but which did not survive in the tradition. The motif of how the fierce warrior is deprived of sleep is borrowed from the lay of Dearg mac Droichil, but here it is used in such a way as to make Fionn guilty of blatant cowardice and treachery. Fionn's double-dealing in the Diarmaid and Gráinne story — which is indirectly referred to here — was surely a contributory factor, but the real reason for this antipathy towards the hero is pro-Goll feeling. In refusing to fight for him, Diarmaid is quoted as saying to Fionn:

> There is nobody of the Fianna of Ireland who has less obligation to go and fight on your behalf than me, and Goll mac Morna is another such man!

We notice that not only Fionn, but other leading members of the Baoiscne clan, are belittled in the story, which – to judge from the history of its manuscripts – seems to have been composed in Connacht. This was the province with which Goll was associated, and the impetus to extoll his merits seems to have come from there (see p. 160).

Rescuing Ladies

Though much of their culture is warlike and ruthless, the Fianna by the late mediaeval period were being portrayed as having sensitivity in some contexts. A favourite such context is rendering assistance and protection to ladies. The initial impulse for this came from the Old Irish love stories, several of which had beautiful women – usually from the otherworld – coming to offer their love to human heroes.[49] Beautiful women from this world also are portrayed in early sources as falling in love 'by repute' with heroes whom they had never seen.[50] So we are not surprised to find such themes entering the Fianna lore in the first Colloquy.

One story in that text describes how Irish poets sang the praises of the Fianna in the court of the Scottish prince Mál mac Aoil in Ross, and how Mál's wife Aoife fell in love with Mac Lughach through hearing of him. At the first opportunity she set out for Ireland in a ship with nine lady attendants. The Fianna were at that time engaged in a great hunt across Leinster, and Fionn himself was at Howth when the ship arrived. Aoife was brought to where Mac Lughach was hunting at Slieve Bloom, and the couple were married. A year and a month later, Mál came from Scotland with an army to regain Aoife, and in a battle in the plain of Leinster he was defeated and killed by Mac Lughach.[51]

Also in the Colloquy, we find a twist to the same theme which became very popular in later Fianna lore – a woman fleeing from an unwanted spouse whom she had been forced to marry.

A very tall woman, we are told, came to Fionn as he hunted with the three battalions of the Fianna at Slemish [in Co. Kerry]. She explained that she was Béibhionn daughter of Tréan, king of the Island of Maidens, who had forcibly married her to a prince from the Island of Men. She had come to seek Fionn's protection. He entrusted her to the care of Goll, and soon her husband, called Aedh Álainn, arrived.

He was even taller than herself, and he lost no time in putting his intent into effect. He drove his spear through her, killing her immediately, and then made off. Followed by the Fianna, he was tackled in the water at Tralee by Caoilte, and a great wave came, giving him the opportunity to board a ship there and make good his escape.[52]

The unusual size of the strange couple here, as well as the exotic names of their native places, gives them an aura of wonder akin to that of the marvels met with in the Old Irish texts concerning mystical sea-voyages.[53] It is clear that such visitors to the Fianna are closely related to the otherworld and that the phantastic nature of the foreign parts from which they come have the same function – the realm of the unknown. The general plot allowed for parallels to be drawn with similar situations regarding damsels in distress who visited the royal court in Arthurian romance of the thirteenth and fourteenth centuries. But there was enough in native tradition to dramatise the plot with a minimum of borrowing from outside. This is well illustrated by the very popular sixteenth-century lay called *Cath Chnoic an Áir* [the Battle of Knockanaar, in Co. Kerry].

This tells of how the Fianna were hunting at Knockanaar, when they saw a lady 'more beautiful than the sun' approaching. She told Fionn that her name was Niamh Nuachrothach, daughter of the king of Greece, and explained that her father had married her to a monstrous warrior. This warrior was called Tailc mac Tréin, had the ears, head, and tail of a cat, and was a horrific fighter. He had devastated Greece twice over in order to force the match with her, and she had fled throughout the whole world from this unbearable husband. Fionn promised to protect her, saying that there was no warrior alive but would find his better among the Fianna.

Soon after, Tailc 'the King of the Cat-Heads' arrived, and immediately demanded battle for his wife. No less than ten hundred men of the Fianna, who opposed him, were slaughtered by the stranger, and then the disheartened Fionn asked Oscar to take the field. For five whole days and nights without a break the two were locked in deadly combat, but in the end Oscar prevailed and slew his opponent. The Fianna raised three great cries on seeing this – one cry of lament for their fallen comrades, and two of celebration for Tailc's death. Seeing the extent of the carnage, Niamh fell dead from shame, and her death was a greater cause of woe than anything else to the Fianna. They named the place Cnoc an Áir [the Hill of the Slaughter].[54]

It seems clear that the author of this lay had read the foregoing story from the Colloquy and that he had got the plot from that source. The animal physiognomy of Tailc has antecedents in earlier Fionn lore. The Battle of Ventry story had a group of invaders called 'dog-heads' [*coinchinn*];[55] and a lay from sometime around the year 1300, which was influenced by that story, had Fionn facing and defeating an invasion force of similar beings at Dún Gaire [possibly in Co. Wicklow],[56] So this sixteenth-century account of Tailc is fully within native tradition. The same can hardly be said of a prose-text from the same period, *Tóraigheacht Shaidhbhe* [the Pursuit of Sadhbh], the plot of which closely resembles the *roman d'aventure* in French and English literature. Oscar going on a fantastic foreign quest to rescue a lady – as he does in this text – might almost be taken for a Gaelic version of Bevis of Hampton[57] or Huon of Bordeaux,[58] but the author is careful to set his narrative in a conventionally Fianna context and gives it as Irish a flavour as possible by using personal and place names from the native history and lore. He is also careful to avoid mediaeval Christian anachronisms in what was known to all Irish audiences as the pagan culture of the ancient Fianna. This is a summary:

One night Fionn held a great feast at Teamhair Luachra [near Slieve Logher in Co. Kerry], and next day he and his company set out to hunt. They left their womenfolk behind them, and Fionn's wife Maighnis, daughter of Garadh mac Morna, suggested that they go swimming. One young lady, Sadbhh daughter of Eoghan son of Oilill Ólom, refused to go. She was wife to Glas mac Aoinchearda Béarra, and the couple were both foster-children of Fionn. Sadhbh loved the Fianna so much that she would go nowhere without them, but when chided by Maighnis she agreed reluctantly to join the rest of the women. They tried several rivers in the area, but found only one to their satisfaction – an estuary at Slieve Logher. All plunged in there, but Sadhbh did not undress and stayed on land.

Soon a ship came in from the sea, and before the women could put their clothes on a big strong warrior came ashore and asked them who they were. They told him all about Cormac, Fionn, Goll, and the affairs of the Fianna. Hearing of his power, the stranger remarked that Fionn should be king of Ireland. He then revealed that his own name was Ciotach, high-king of Drólainn Mhór, a region in the eastern world. He said that he had nothing but disdain for Fionn's power and that he had a son, called Dorn [fist] who far excelled Fionn's son Oisín. He chose Sadhbh, saying that she would be a suitable wife for his son, but before he left Maighnis put him under prohibitions [*geasa*] not to allow any man to sleep with the girl for a year's duration.

When Fionn returned from the hunt and learned what had happened, he wondered whether he should set out immediately or wait for the fair of Teltown – at which he had to give an account for the Fianna's activities each year in the presence of the high-king. Goll told him to keep his appointment and that he would bring a thousand warriors on the quest for Sadhbh. So Goll put to sea in Fionn's ship (which was called the *Breac-Bhuadhach*, [speckled victorious one]), accompanied by Oisín, Fathadh Canainn, Diarmaid, Caoilte, Mac Lughach, Conán Maol, and the rest – including Sadhbh's husband Glas. Coming to a beautiful island, they discovered that it was ruled by a king named Toircheall, who had once spent seven years with Fionn. Toircheall invited them all to his palace, and they were there enjoying themselves for a fortnight. Glas grew uneasy, and they resumed their journey towards Drólainn Mhór, arriving at the island of another friendly king, Gormshúileach [blue-eyed], and after another fortnight there Glas again urged them to proceed on their quest. Siogra, son of Gormshúileach, went with them.

Finally they reached their destination, and found that

Ciotach was away collecting tribute, but his son Dorn was there. Siogra and one of Oisín's men called Mac Rí Ó Liatháin slipped into the enemy palace by night, stabbed Dorn with his lance, and took Sadhbh with them to her husband. The son of the Scandinavian king, who was among the foe, went and took Sadhbh back from the Fianna in the same manner, stabbing Glas with his lance. Then Goll went and took her back again, but the Scandinavian took her once more, and the wounded Dorn ordered her to be put into a locked building with women attendants. But Diarmaid went and took Sadhbh and the women with him to the ship.

Next day the enemy attacked, and in the thick of the fighting Glas slew Dorn, Diarmaid slew the Scandinavian prince, while Goll went through the foe three times dealing destruction. Siogra engaged the son of the Greek king, but was struck down by a javelin hurled by Mac Lughach. Conán Maol chided Mac Lughach for killing their ally, but Mac Lughach explained that he had heard Siogra say that the Greek prince would defeat the Fianna warriors and that Siogra himself could then boast that he could overcome the man who defeated the Fianna. At that Siogra revived, resumed combat with the Greek, and beheaded him. Inspired by this Oisín and his men swept the foe before them and burned their city. They then embarked for Ireland in triumph.

When Ciotach returned to his kingdom he found utter desolation and was told that Oisín and his men had done that. He set sail for Ireland immediately, arriving at Howth, and ran all the way to Tara. There he began to incite the high-king Cormac against Fionn, and sought his offices to arrange single combat with the Fianna. Siogra took the field, but was beheaded in a terrific duel. Following this, Ciotach defeated several of the Baoiscne clan – including Oisín – in wrestling contests, and tied them all up. Oscar was at that time only sixteen years of age, but despite Fionn's attempts to restrain him he was determined to oppose his father's humiliator. For three whole days Oscar fought Ciotach on the green of Tara. At length young Oscar drove his javelin through the foreigner and cut his head off. The victorious youth then went and realeased Oisín and the rest from their bonds.[59]

The Adventures Overseas

We have seen that, from the thirteenth century onwards, Goll mac Morna was claimed to have conquered several foreign countries but to have been dislodged from them all by Cumhall (p. 163). Such involvement of the Fianna on international battlefields is a derivation from the Norse theme, but it was given special impetus by reports of the Crusades, which were in full swing at the time. Thus it is not surprising to find the country of the Saracens taking the place of Scandinavia in a straggling poem of that thirteenth century.

According to this, Fionn held a great feast for Cormac at Sídh Truim [a rath between Tara and Teltown]. Two strange visitors arrived – a wight [*gruagach*] playing beautiful music accompanied by a huge man carrying a massive cauldron. Fionn offered whatever gift the wight might desire, and enough gold to fill the cauldron was sought. Luckily, Fionn had by him a shipload of gold, and he gave this. The big man said that he was Fear Dochair [man of harm] from Syria, and that the wight was his son and the best warrior in the world. Oscar wagered that he would overcome the wight. Hearing this, Fionn blushed deeply at the insult given by Oscar to a guest, but Oscar persisted and Fionn had to provide an escort for the two to conduct them safely home. The wight told Oscar that if he followed him to Syria he could have single combat.

The eight Fianna escorts – who included Mac Lughach, Caoilte, and Caireall – were feasted in Syria, but a boasting contest broke out and the eight Fianna had to fight their way back to their ship and return in a hurry to Ireland. Then Oscar set sail for Syria with a mere twenty-seven men. On their way they conquered Scotland, England, France, Spain, Germany, Greece, and India. Reaching Syria, they fought a great battle there which lasted for fifteen days, and Oscar slew the wight in a duel. On their way home they conquered the Hesperides, Italy, Scandinavia, and Wales. Tribute was thereafter sent each year from all these places to Oscar.[60]

The word used several times to describe the Saracen champion in the text is *gruagach*. This basically means a hairy fellow, but its secondary meaning of 'wight' or even 'wizard' is more often the sense in which it is employed in storytelling.[61] In the case of a mysterious visitor from foreign parts, it has strong connotations of magical powers or abilities, and here again we find the shared function of the otherworld and of the outside world. In a lay from around the year 1500, a *gruagach* turns out to be the otherworld lord Aonghus, a good friend of the Fianna, and the hostile character is called a churl [*aitheach*].

We are told that a quarrel arose one day at Benbulben between Conán Maol and Mac Lughach. The Baoiscne and Morna clans joined opposite sides, and a clash was imminent, but a huge churl approached playing music on an iron harp. The music magically caused all the Fianna to fall down as if dying. He announced himself as Sdirén from the cold regions, and when he departed he took away all the weapons of the incapacitated Fianna. After a month they recovered, and peace was made between the Baoiscne and Morna clans.

They set out together for the cold regions, where they encountered a band of monstrous churls (one of whom had one eye in his forehead). They killed several of these, and when the battle was going against the Fianna a single well-dressed wight arrived, playing harp-music which confused and scattered the foe. He then healed the Fianna's wounds.

The newcomer was none other than Aonghus, and when the Fianna returned to Ireland they visited his residence at Newgrange. He gave them great entertainment there, and restored to them their weapons, which he had recovered. He further promised to rescue them in every strait.[62]

In effect, the visiting otherworld figure can be in either attractive or horrid guise. By far the most interesting of this type of Fianna story is a long prose text composed in the sixteenth century, called *Tóraigheacht an Ghiolla Dheacair* [The Pursuit of the Difficult Servant]. It is obviously a Munster text, and can be summarised as follows:

One day, while undertaking their first hunt of the summer, Fionn and his principal warriors were on the hill of Knockainey [in Co. Limerick]. They saw coming to visit them a great big ugly man leading a bony recalcitrant horse. The stranger asked to be allowed to serve Fionn for a year, as he had heard of the leader's fame in his travels throughout the world. His name, he said, was 'the Difficult Servant', which he was called because of his truculent and difficult disposition.

Fionn engaged him immediately, and the Servant loosed his horse among those of the Fianna. But the ill-tempered nag savaged the other horses, finally attacking Conán Maol's horse which was kept in a separate pasture. Conán bridled the savage beast and, egged on by Fearghus Fíonbhéil, he mounted it, but it refused to move. Fearghus said that the horse was accustomed to a heavier rider than Conán, and fourteen more of the Fianna sat up behind Conán. Still the beast would not move.

Seeing what had happened, the Servant said that the fame of the Fianna was unfounded, and despite Fionn's protestations he left the hill and headed off towards the south-west. The horse immediately followed him, with the warriors still on its back.

As they left, Conán began to revile the Fianna and placed them under injunctions [*geasa*] to follow and release himself and the other fourteen. Travelling at great speed, the Servant and his horse plunged into the sea off the Dingle peninsula with their cargo. A fast runner of the Fianna, called Liagán, caught up with the nag as it entered the sea, but was pulled helplessly after it, clinging with his two hands to its mane all the while.

Fionn and the Fianna, meanwhile, travelled towards Howth – a harbour with the magical property of always having a boat fitted out for use. On the way they met the two sons of the king of India, who had come to Ireland having heard the good repute of Fionn. Each of these two had a magical ability – Fearadhach could make any number of ships with three blows of his axe on his sling, while Foltleabhair was so good a tracker that he could follow wild duck by land and sea to its nest. Fionn accepted them, and they all returned to Dingle Bay, where Fearadhach made fine ships for them, and they set sail.

They came to a great cliff, which Diarmaid scaled. On top he found himself in a strange and beautiful country and, when he stopped at a well to drink, he was approached by a warrior in full armour who challenged him to fight. The contest lasted for four days, with the strange warrior disappearing down the well each night. At the conclusion of the fourth day Diarmaid seized his opponent as he was entering the well, and both fell in. They arrived at an underground country, where Diarmaid was set upon by a whole troop of soldiers. He slaughtered a great number of them, and the rest fled before him.

Wearied by his exertions Diarmaid fell asleep, but he was soon awoken by another stranger, who brought him to a fine palace where he was regaled and entertained. This stranger explained that he was in Tír fó Thuinn [the Land under Wave], that his own name was Ridire an Ghaiscidh [the knight of the feat], and that he had once spent a year in Fionn's company. He further explained that the warrior who had fought against Diarmaid was his brother, who had usurped the kingdom, and he now sought Diarmaid's assistance to regain the throne. This was promised, and in the ensuing battle Diarmaid wrought havoc on the enemy and killed the usurper.

Diarmaid then told the grateful Ridire an Ghaiscidh the cause of his quest, and was informed that the Difficult Servant must be none other than Abharthach mac Ildathaigh, who resided in Tír Tairngire [Land of Prophecy] and was the most powerful magician in the world. Accompanied by the Ridire and his men, Diarmaid then set out for where he had left Fionn.

Meanwhile, Fionn and his men had grown anxious for Diarmaid's safety, and the Indian princes had made a ladder of their ship-ropes, scaled the great cliff, and dragged the rest up. Meeting the king of Syria, they joined him in a campaign against the Greek king – called King of the World – who had invaded his country. In this campaign, Oscar and Goll fought prodigiously, and Fionn killed the Greek king's son, who was a celebrated warrior, in single combat.

The Greek king had a beautiful daughter, called Taise Thaoibhgheal, who fell in love with Fionn and escaped from her father's camp to be with him. One of her father's henchmen, however, put Fionn and his men to sleep by shaking a magical branch, and took Taise back to the Greek camp. Then the king of Greece with his army sailed home to their own country. Fionn was broken-hearted, but before he decided on what to do Diarmaid arrived on the scene with Ridire an Ghaiscidh and his men. On Diarmaid's advice, Fionn sent Goll, Oscar, and Fearghus to abduct Taise, and these three members of the Fianna brought the girl from Athens amid great slaughter.

Guided by the tracker Foltleabhair, Fionn's party finally reached Tír Tairngire. Fionn himself wished to destroy that country, but Diarmaid recommended negotiations with Abharthach. This was done, and peace was arranged. Abharthach promised Fionn whatever compensation he desired, but Fionn forgave him all. Conán, however, insisted that the fourteen finest women who lived in Tír Tairngire be made to ride on the horse's back all the way from there to Knockainey, and that they be accompanied by Abharthach accoutred as formerly. Moreover, Abharthach's wife was to be tied to the horse's tail.

Thus Fionn and his men returned to Ireland, but as soon as they reached Knockainey and looked around for their fellow-travellers, they found that the Difficult Servant and his crew had disappeared they knew not where.[63]

The huge cliff which has to be scaled in this romance comes from the story of the children stolen by a giant (pp. 189f). It is thus a derivative of the extraordinary helpers' motif – a motif of which the author shows himself to be aware by having the two Indian princes perform marvellous tasks for Fionn. But elements of more antiquity from native lore also occur. Diarmaid going into Tír fó Thuinn through a well, for instance, reflects accounts in early Irish literature of entry into the otherworld. The place name Tír Tairngire was also a common designation for the otherworld in the early period.[64] So the question arises, are the strange magical nag and its owner really an echo of some kind of ancient Irish psychopomp? This has been argued by some scholars,[65] but there is no evidence of such sophisticated otherworld adventures in the early Fionn lore.

What we have seen of that lore in chapters 1-3 makes it clear that the otherworld visits were concerned with Fionn as an individual and were part of seer-rituals rather than of eschatology. The well of entry and the place name Tír Tairngire, it seems obvious, were selected from the corpus of available marvellous data by an author who was thinking in terms of adventure rather than of philosophy. The likelihood is that the magical horse was also a creation of the author, using some motifs of phantastic horses known to him from oral tradition.[66]

That humorous descriptions of horses similar to that of the Difficult Servant were current in mediaeval storytelling is suggested by a twelfth-century Welsh triad. This refers to three horses who carried several people on their backs on great journeys. One of them carried seven and a half persons from Penllech in north Wales to Penllech in Anglesey – the 'half' being a man 'who swam with his two hands to the horse's crupper'.[67] This parallels the account of how Liagán clung to the mane of the Difficult Servant's horse, and would appear to have been a popular jest which circulated in folklore. The nag in this Irish romance is a comical creature, but ideas of fairy-horses and spirit-horses of various kinds helped to make it an ideal vehicle for the now favourite Fianna plot of kidnappings and phantastic journeys to foreign parts.

8.

Literature and Lore

We have referred often to oral lore and its importance within the Fianna tradition. The material examined in the initial chapters represents the ultimate origins and the early phases of the tradition, and much of what was discussed there lies further back than the literature and was accordingly formed and developed by oral culture. This does not necessarily mean that the narratives originated with the general folk. We have argued that important facets of the material were sprung from the ideology of seers, educators, and even propagandists. The narratives proved to have a strong appeal in popular story-telling, however, and the cultural scope of the twelfth-century texts – especially the Colloquy – makes it clear that tales of Fionn and his Fianna were alive and thriving among the ordinary people of many localities at that time.

In the case of Fionn's youth biography, we have seen that important insights into some of the stories can be gained by studying versions of them collected from the folklore of recent centuries. We have also seen that, at all stages, there have been instances of motifs and plots from extraneous lore influencing particular Fianna narratives. Although post-twelfth-century lays and romances were for the most part conscious literary creations, their authors were far from operating in isolation from popular ideas – indeed the reason for their composition was to satisfy popular demand. The convergence of folk interest with special purpose, therefore, and the interplay between oral and literary culture, have played a vital part in the whole tradition of Fionn and his Fianna.

The relationships between different media of transmission could be many and varied, and it is necessary to examine each story in its own context as well as against the general framework of the cycle. A number of stories have been analysed in that manner in preceding chapters, but there are some products of the tradition for which there is sufficient evidence to allow special study of permutations within the media of transmission.

The Allegorical Adventure

It is in the nature of things that some stories would not have been committed to writing, and that some of those written down would not survive due to the loss of manuscripts. It is probably the latter cause which leaves us with no early version of a story which has been collected from the folklore of Irish-speaking districts throughout Ireland.

These oral versions tell of how Fionn and some companions went astray in a fog while out hunting and arrived at a strange house. There they found an old man, a beautiful young woman, and a ram. Food was set on the table before them, but the ram butted the table and upset the food before they could partake of it. Each man of the Fianna group tried to tie the ram to the wall, but in vain. Then the old man did so without difficulty. The Fianna ate their fill, and then went to bed.

During the night, Fionn tried to enter the young woman's bed but was rejected with the words:

'You had me once, and you will never have me again!'

Fionn was amazed at all of this, and before he left next morning he sought an explanation from the old man. The latter explained that the ram was life, he himself age, and the girl was youth.[1]

The similarity between this and an early thirteenth-century Icelandic text, which tells of a visit made by the god Thor to Útgard,[2] has often been commented on, for several of the same motifs occur in both stories. Because the account in the Icelandic text is enmeshed with different narratives, and because the Irish story has an independent and coherent plot, it appears that an Irish recension was the basic one. This becomes all the more plausible when we realise that the allegorical genre had some currency in mediaeval Irish literature. Close examination of the Fianna tradition, indeed, makes an origin for the story in the context of Fionn and his men quite probable.

The twelfth-century Colloquy gives characteristics as names to various characters – a practice which by its nature tends towards allegory.[3] Furthermore, some of these names – such as Luath [swift] and Eolus [knowledge] correspond to concepts which were found in the only literary version which we have of the ram-allegory. This is in the fifteenth-century anthology *Feis Tighe Chonáin*, and it states that the strange house [at Cahernarry in Co. Limerick] belonged to an otherworld man called Cuanna.

The Fianna group comprises Fionn, Oisín, Caoilte, Mac Lughach, and Diarmaid; and the dwelling contains the host Cuanna himself, a giant, a beautiful woman, an aged grey-haired twelve-eyed man, an old woman with a cloak like ashes, and a ram. This animal here has a black head, white belly, blue horns, and green feet – an exotic colouring system apparently based on that of Fionn's hound Bran (see p. 132). When the meal is prepared, the ram speaks and claims that the division of the pork is unfair. It snatches the portion awarded to Fionn's men and itself devours it, while they struggle unavailingly to prevent him. Then an aged man by the fireside chides them for their uselessness and throws the ram out. An old woman, who is present, gets up and throws her cloak over the Fianna, transforming them into withered old men. When she removes the cloak they are returned to their normal form.

The host Cuanna then explains that the giant personifies sloth, the ram humanity, and the aged man who overcame it is the world. The elderly woman is old age, and the young woman is intellect [*meanma*] – she can travel faster in the flick of an eye than an ordinary person could in forty years. Cuanna then explains that he had wished to teach Fionn not to attach too much importance to this life. The Fianna group are entertained hospitably in the house, but when they awake in the morning they find themselves on the summit of the hill of Cahernarry [*Carn Fhearadhaigh*].[4]

The style of this literary version is verbose, and the allegorical figures are somewhat cluttered, yet in some regards it reflects a more original form of the story than do the modern folk versions. The contrasting figures of an old and a young woman, for instance, parallel similar characters in allegories from mediaeval Irish and Continental literature. The young woman standing for intellect is also typical of mediaeval representation, and it is significant that she has a parallel in the Icelandic story, where one of Thor's men has to race against a character called Hugi [literally, thought]. The same idea is found in the early twelfth-century Welsh text, *Culhwch ac Olwen*, where a great runner is described as being 'swifter than thought'.[5]

This text was influenced by Irish Fianna lore (see p. 178), and it is therefore likely that the idea has been borrowed from that source. It seems to have first come to prominence in the Fionn context on the basis of a passage in the tenth-century text on the wooing of Ailbhe (p. 106). This involves Fionn putting a series of rhetorical questions to the maiden, all of which she immediately answers. Among these are the following questions and answers:

> 'What is swifter than wind?'
> 'Intellect [*meanma*]'.
>
> 'What is sharper than a sword?'
> 'Understanding [*ciall*]'.
>
> 'What is lighter than a feather?'
> 'The mind [*ciall*] of a woman between two men'.[6]

The notion that great Fianna runners, such as Caoilte, could travel faster than the wind is connected with the theme of marvellous helpers. Since that theme, as we saw (pp. 183ff), developed through the tenth and eleventh centuries based on Caoilte's great running ability, there was ample opportunity for the speedy thought motif to combine with the image of a marvellous runner in that period. And, since an abstract concept like the intellect was grammatically and allegorically feminine, the stress tended to go onto the conventional portrayal of a fickle female mind.

Yet another prominent motif in mediaeval Fianna lore had Caoilte racing against an otherworld woman. There are two examples of this in the twelfth-century Colloquy and one in *Feis Tighe Chonáin.*[7] This comes from the common epical theme of a warrior winning a contest against an Amazon opponent,[8] but it was attracted to the Fianna context because of the fanciful comparison of Caoilte's running ability with the speed of a woman's thought.

In the Icelandic text the male runner Hugi [thought] seems to have taken the place of a female character Roskva [swiftness] who figures in the background; and this makes it all the more likely that the whole Irish complex of female/intellect/racing lies behind this part of the Thor allegory. The probable date of borrowing – given the history of contact between Irish and Norse as well as this analysis – was in or about the eleventh century. A difficulty is presented by the fact that there is no ram in the Icelandic text. The nearest corresponding figure is a large cat, which Thor is challenged to lift off the ground, but all he can do is to lift one paw.

Some Irish oral versions of the allegory have a cat personifying death in place of the old man,[9] and this rather unsuitable arrangement seems to result from some dislocation in the plot. The dislocation could well have been caused by the intrusion of the ram into the story at some stage preceding the house of Cuanna version, with an original cat being replaced by the newcomer. In the house of Cuanna the ram in fact behaves more like a cat when it snatches the pork and eats it in its own lair. Great and dangerous cats occur in various Irish stories since mediaeval times, usually as a variant type of monster. It might perhaps be apposite to mention that Fionn himself is said in a fourteenth-century lay to have slain such a savage cat in Dublin [*Áth Cliath*].[10] A monstrous cat would be an appropriate creature for the Fianna to meet in an otherworld dwelling, and this proposition gains some further support from an episode in an eleventh-century recension of the Ulster cycle tale *Fled Bricrenn.*

Here Cúchulainn and two other warriors, Laoghaire Buadhach and Conall Cearnach, are being tested to ascertain which is the greatest. As they are dining at the Connacht court, three magical cats are released from the cave of

Croghan nearby and these beasts go to eat the food. Laoghaire and Conall leave their meal to two of the cats and flee to the rafters of the house, but Cúchulainn strikes his cat with a sword. The blow glances off the beast, but it nevertheless cowers back and does not dare to approach either hero or food all night long.[11]

This account is not allegorical, but may reflect some of the source-material which the composer of the allegory had to hand.

We have already suggested that Fionn and his men were actors in that original composition. That suggestion is supported by several mediaeval narratives which have kindred material in them. In chapter 5 references have been made to accounts from the eleventh and twelfth centuries in which the Fianna enter otherworld dwellings and explanations are given to them of what occurs in these places.

Staying overnight in one such dwelling, Fionn, Oisín, and Caoilte meet sinister beings including a giant, an old woman, and a one-eyed man (p. 138). Accompanied by the same two comrades, as well as Diarmaid, Oscar, and Mac Lughach, Fionn shelters from bad weather in another dwelling, where a beautiful maiden brings them food and drink, and they stay there for a long period (pp. 135f).

These accounts are not allegories, but the mysterious atmosphere in them would suit such a narrative mode, and the otherworld setting is ideal for allegory. It is therefore more than plausible that some scholar in eleventh-century Ireland, influenced by the general literary passion for allegory in Western Europe at the time, would regard Fianna lore as providing a suitable framework for composing such a story.

This lost original described how Fionn and some of his men spent a night in an otherworld dwelling, in which they met several personifications of ideas, and before leaving they had the meanings of these explained to them. The personifications included a fleet-footed lady representing intellect, an obstreporous beast (probably a cat) representing base appetites, and an elderly man representing age.

The earliest surviving version [the house of Cuanna] has several other allegorical explanations in the story, and these seem to be either in full or in part later additions. This version has a somewhat confused and disjointed plot, which results from the weight of interpretations, but some of the imagery which it contains above and beyond the oral versions seems to have belonged to the original. We can see this by comparing it to another and quite distinct allegory, which is found in a fourteenth-century text concerning the high-king Cormac.

According to it, Cormac's daughter and son, Ailbhe and Cairbre, and his wife Eithne are taken away into Tír Tairngire [the Prophesied Land], and the king visits that place to search for them. Among the things he sees there is a well flowing into five streams which have seers drinking from them. There are nine hazel-trees surrounding the well, and five salmon are eating the nuts which fall from these trees. He finds a handsome couple in a palace there, and a servant enters carrying a pig which he puts into a cauldron. The pig is boiled in three stages by three true stories told by the strangers. The lord of the palace reveals that he is Manannán, and he returns Cormac's family to him. He has brought Cormac there in order to show him how true poets do not waste their time seeking worldly riches but instead continually consume the drink of wisdom. The whole experience was a dream-adventure, and Cormac awakes next morning on the green lawn of Tara.[12]

This is a curious story, as it uses materials from the Boyne valley cult of knowledge – materials which are more properly related to Fionn himself than to Cormac (see chapter 3). It may well have been an early form of the Fionn allegory which gave the fourteenth-century author the idea of turning Cormac's otherworld visit into an allegory.

The house of Cuanna text can be taken to preserve some of the original details of Fionn's visit to the strange dwelling. He and his men, we are told, saw a churl carrying a pig and a beautiful lady accompanying him, and they followed this couple through the magical mist to the house. They saw two springs, from each of which Fionn takes a drink. One drink was sweet and the other bitter – the former, it turns out, was falsehood and the latter truth. Inside the house, the churl cooked the pig in a cauldron for them, but there is no mention of the magical effect of telling true stories.

The strange lady and cooking pig belonged to Fionn tradition – we have met them in eighth- to ninth-century texts (pp. 53ff). The sweet and bitter drinks may well come from some Latin source, as do the figures of seers drinking from streams in the Cormac story,[13] but the important thing is that a complex of seer-imagery intimately associated with Fionn had a high profile in mediaeval Irish allegory.

Unlike the house of Cuanna version, the Fionn allegory maintained a strict and well-constructed plot in oral tradition down through the centuries. But that is not to say that it did not undergo change and development. Folk versions from different parts of the country agree with each other in this, thereby showing that some extra elements got attached to the narrative not long before the house of Cuanna version was penned in the fifteenth century. Folklore decided that the five Fianna characters involved were Fionn, Diarmaid, Oisín, Oscar, and Conán Maol; and, before they left the house, made them each get a gift from the beautiful lady, who was made to represent youth rather than intellect. This lady told them that they could have whichever gift they chose.

Drawing on the already well-established idea that Diarmaid had a love-spot on his forehead (see p. 175), he was made to ask for that spot so that women would be attracted to him. Oisín was made to ask for 'the grace of God', thus rationalising how he lived on to meet St Patrick as in the Colloquy tradition. Oscar asked for an unbreakable thong for his flail, an idea which grew up within that same Christianised lore and which we shall discuss presently. Conán asked for the power to kill hundreds [*marú na gcéadta*], which gift he received, but unknown to himself (see p. 166). Finally, Fionn's strange request was to be relieved of an odour of clay which clung to him. This, we are told, was the result of an act of necrophilia which he once committed with a dead woman. Naturally, the odour was a source of great embarrassment to him on this account, and he was glad to be rid of it.

We have seen how a sense of phantasy regarding sexual matters had steadily grown in Fianna lore through the Middle Ages, and how the synchronising of various stories caused

Fionn himself to be regarded as a womaniser *par excellence* (pp. 152ff). Thus the author of *Feis Tighe Chonáin* considered it appropriate to describe a rather impolite haste on Fionn's part to sleep with women he encountered in otherworld palaces.[14] This type of portrayal would have contributed to the notion of his involvement in necrophilia. In the twelfth-century Colloquy it is stated that 'there was a prohibition on Fionn to see a corpse, unless it had been killed by weapons',[15] but this seems to mean simply that, since he was a great warrior, death was appropriate to his character only in the context of battle.

Such a notion, however, would lend itself to other interpretations and invite extraneous motifs. It found one such motif in necrophilia, a type of contact with the dead which was most prohibited and which fitted in with the increasingly phantastic sexual imagery of the lore. This development seems to have taken place in or about the fourteenth century. Perhaps it derives from a legend of Charlemagne's bewitched love of his dead wife.[16] It is clear that the motif had become attached to Fionn by the time *Feis Tighe Chonáin* was written, for in that text he is pointedly asked:

'Why is there the stench of a corpse from your offspring and the coldness of bronze in your skin?'

Unfortunately Fionn's answer to the question is not given, but elsewhere the author has him listing among the wonders of the Fianna,

> A woman whom I myself have, and she is dead every night and alive every day, and I hold no woman I ever had in greater affection than her.[17]

This sounds suspiciously like an account of a fairy mistress whom Charlemagne had – a mistress who was wont to become alive when the Emperor visited her but to be dead when he departed.[18]

Oisín and the Saint

The tradition that Caoilte and Oisín survived to meet St Patrick must have originated with clerical sources. An early eleventh-century account of cemeteries claims that three great worthies of pagan Ireland – the Ulster cycle king Conchubhar mac Neasa, the jurist Móraind, and the high-king Cormac mac Airt – were believers in Christ before the coming of the saint.[19] This demonstrates how the Church was trying to reconcile respect for great pagan heroes of old with devout practice of Christianity. Since Patrick was regarded as the full and proper originator of the faith in Ireland, however, there was an inconsistency, even an unorthodoxy, about making old heroes Christian by good works alone or by special revelation. So some other device was required to solve the problem – a device which would somehow bridge the time-gap between the ancient great ones and the coming of the saint.

The solution was found in a Christian legend concerning Pope Gregory the Great, which told of how that Pope was once walking through the forum of the ancient pagan Emperor Trajan in Rome. Marvelling at a charitable deed done by Trajan, he thought it appropriate to 'a Christian rather than a pagan'; and so Gregory prayed earnestly for the soul of the dead Emperor and miraculously secured baptism for him.[20]

The influence of this story is already evident in an eighth-century Latin biography of Patrick. This has the saint coming to a huge grave and striking it with his crozier. The buried giant was resuscitated for a short time, and he explained that he was called Cas and had been slain by the *fiann*-band of Mac Con a hundred years before. Patrick baptised him, and he was placed once more in the grave.[21]

This story was repeated in the ninth-century biography of Patrick in Irish,[22] and since none of Fionn's Fianna are mentioned there we may presume that the idea of Caoilte or Oisín meeting the saint had not yet developed. Nor had the desire to reconcile the ancient Irish heroes with Patrician lore developed sufficiently at that time to substitute one of these famous characters for the giant. But this was soon to happen.

An eleventh-century text tells of how Patrick was once travelling with the high-king Laoghaire towards Newgrange when Cúchulainn in his chariot appeared. The ancient hero beseeched Patrick to bring him into heaven with the other believers and instructed Laoghaire to become a Christian. He also relayed in verse-form several of his great adventures in life, and the saint gained heaven for him.[23] There is a twelfth-century text, a short poem put in Oisín's mouth, which claims that eight men of the Fianna believed in Christ before Patrick's coming, and refers to several other warriors – not Fianna members – who took the faith.[24]

It is clear from this that the idea of ancient pagans turning to Christianity in pre-Patrician times was very popular in eleventh- and twelfth-century Irish culture. It is clear also that in the Fianna context Oisín had become the mouthpiece for the idea. This has to do with the portrayal of Oisín as an old poet, a survivor of the battle of Gowra, who recites narrative verse – a portrayal which had currency at that period (see pp. 155f). One early twelfth-century poem ascribed to Oisín has him lamenting his lost youth and thanking the Creator for his conversion, which he describes as 'solace with great joy'.[25] Another poem of the same time has Caoilte after the coming of Patrick lamenting his lost fleetness of foot and his fighting prowess.

'I and Oisín son of Fionn', he says, 'our blows were dealt in unison, our deeds were great, our boasts were small!'[26]

So it was not the Colloquy author who invented the idea of surviving members of Fionn's band meeting Patrick. But it was he who, writing around the year 1175, gave a definite and elaborate structure to the idea. According to this, the saint was travelling Ireland on his work of conversion when he encountered the Fianna survivors. After the destruction of the troop, Oisín and Caoilte – portrayed as by then two old men – had separated from each other. Oisín went into the *sí*-dwelling of Ocht Cleitigh [near Newgrange], where his mother Blái daughter of Derg resided. Caoilte with nine warriors went towards the rath of Druim Derg [now Drumcliff in Co. Sligo], where Patrick was praying with his flock.

> The clerics saw these coming, and terror and fear seized them before the big men, with their big hounds with them, for they were not people of the same period or the same time as themselves.

Patrick went and sprinkled holy water on Caoilte and his

companions, driving a legion of devils away from over their heads, and then the long friendship of Caoilte and Patrick began. The old hero was baptised, and they travelled west together, Caoilte rendering much assistance to the saint and relating stories of Fionn and his Fianna to him.

The fact that both Caoilte and Oisín are spokesmen in the Colloquy causes some duplication of function and difficulty of plot. In Connacht, the author makes Caoilte leave Patrick's company to go and search for any other members of the Fianna who may survive. While he is in Cinél Chonaill [Co. Donegal] he receives a message from Patrick and Oisín, who have met under the auspices of the high-king Diarmaid mac Cearbhaill. Caoilte therefore goes to Ushnagh [in Co. Westmeath], where he and Oisín rejoin each other's company and have a long conversation in the hearing of all, relaying much information on the lost heroic epoch of Fionn and his troop. Caoilte returns then to Ulster, telling more adventures to the noble assemblage there, and he later meets Patrick with a large company of clerics near Armagh. The travelling and story-telling resumes, as they go together through Connacht, Leinster, and Munster. Finally, they return to the high-king's court for the festival of Tara, where Caoilte and Patrick meet Oisín once more and the two old Fianna warriors resume their engrossing conversation

Patrick's guardian angel, we are told, encouraged the saint to take an interest in this lore and have all that the old men said written down, so it is not surprising that the Colloquy author felt free to include over sixty heroic and onomastic stories, along with several descriptions of the Fianna's life and customs and much other incidental detail.[27]

The second or 'Little' Colloquy, from the thirteenth century, gives a new and quite different plot arrangement. Here we are told that the two old warriors, with their followers, were at Sliabh gCrot [the Galtee Mountains in Co. Tipperary] when Caoilte's servant reported that he had seen a strange group of three hundred clerics. Oisín assumes that the leader of that group must be the 'Adze-head' [i.e. Patrick] long ago prophesied by Fionn. Caoilte with his followers decides to flee to the wilderness to avoid the ecclesiastics, while Oisín goes to kill them but instead is baptised. Patrick later chances upon Caoilte sleeping in a forest and proposes conversion to him, whereupon he and his men are filled with God's grace. Having been baptised by the saint, Caoilte gives accounts of several Fianna adventures.[28]

The third Colloquy text is an ingenious attempt at reconciling the two earlier ones and including some other material seen as apposite. Perhaps relying on the Little Colloquy, or perhaps influenced by other sources, this text makes Oisín the first to meet Patrick. It also makes him the principal spokesman for the Fianna and transfers several accounts given by Caoilte in the first Colloquy into his mouth.[29]

A striking aspect of the first Colloquy, scrupulously followed by the other two recensions, is the humility shown in the presence of Patrick by the two old warriors. They repeatedly defer to him, and in token of submission place their heads in his breast.[30] A less committed author would make some kind of critical comparison between the heroic and saintly lifestyles, but this writer is fully on the clerical side and he allows no arguments – even initially – to the Fianna spokesmen. The warriors may be the better entertainers, but the issues of real importance are baptism and salvation, and therefore all the odds are stacked in Patrick's favour. Once Caoilte, Oisín, and their men become Christians heaven is assured them, but the question had to arise – what of the dead Fianna heroes? And so Caoilte intercedes with Patrick to achieve the seemingly impossible, that is to have the departed pagan heroes released from hell.

This, of course, involves the same miracle which was accomplished by Pope Gregory for Trajan, and we might expect Patrick also to succeed. He has Fionn and some others released, but only as a very special boon to his genial old companions.[31] Elsewhere in the Colloquy we are told that Fionn himself gained heaven by prophesying the coming of Saint Ciarán,[32] but this is a variant tradition on a par with the retrospective Christianising of Cormac mac Airt and others, and in this case a propaganda point of extra significance to the early Irish church (see pp. 37f).

The Colloquy's portrayal of Patrick conversing with Oisín and Caoilte and converting them became very popular in the succeeding literature. A short poem from the fourteenth century refers to how 'Patrick of the smooth hand baptised them at the end of their age – he called Oisín "Art" and Caoilte "Conn"'. The use of names of other great ancient heroes as baptismal christenings for the two is not found in earlier sources, and we can regard it as an idiosyncracy of this poet. The references made to the deaths of the two, however, deserve more attention. Regarding the demise of Caoilte, we are told that he was drowned at Tara in his old age. Whether this was part of the original Colloquy we do not know, since no surviving manuscript has the end of that text. The reference to the death of the other hero is even more enigmatic: 'The prince's son fell by the cast of the cleric – Oisín, though he was stout and solid, did not rise after the cast.'[33] Whether or not the cleric in question was Patrick we are not told, but it is probably correct to assume that the episode in question was accidental.

It is tempting to relate such a 'cast' to a motif which featured in the later lore all over Ireland – that is that in baptising Oisín Patrick unwittingly stuck his crozier through the old man's foot. When the ceremony was over, the saint noticed blood on the ground and enquired of Oisín why he had not told him. Oisín replied that he thought it was part of the ceremony and had therefore gladly endured the pain.[34]

This episode first appears in ninth-century biographies of Patrick, but the patient victim in these cases is the Munster king Aenghus. The motif seems to have been borrowed originally from Continental hagiography.[35] When it crossed from Aenghus to Oisín is difficult to say, but the lines from the fourteenth-century poem quoted above might refer to the saint casting his crozier aside and accidentally pinning the foot of the aged Oisín to the ground. It is unlikely that the episode featured in the Oisín context much earlier than that, however.

Texts of a later date than the Colloquy do not accept the total submission of Caoilte and Oisín to Patrick. In fact, as the centuries wore on, poets were inclined to picture the conversations between them as being more strained. In a thirteenth-century poem, Oisín complains to Patrick of his present life 'attending to hours and matins' and 'without largess, without making raids, without the acclaim of grateful poets'. He goes further and says:

'Dearer to me were the chant [*orgán*] of the Fianna, and the sound of the chase on every upland, and Caoilte's cry which was pleasant, than heaven and your joys, o Adze-head.'

Patrick kindly admonishes him to repent for his smiting in battles, but Oisín replies that if Mac Lughach and Caoilte lived they would not be in a church taking dictation from Patrick.

The references here to Caoilte are of interest, as they show that the author of this poem was not properly conversant with the plot of the Colloquy. Tamed at last, Oisín concludes by saying:

'I beseech the High-king of heaven, who is in the angelic city, since my fierce glory has departed, not to forget me for the great feast!'[36]

The same ideas are found in a poem of the fifteenth century, and this author appears to have read the foregoing text. He inflates Oisín's obstinacy, having him call Patrick 'a miserable cleric' who is 'bleating and whimpering' and threaten to strike the saint on the head with his own bell. If the Fianna were alive, Oisín says, they would kill all the clerics; and if Caoilte were to hear the bell ringing he would have broken it. Oisín does admit, at the end of the poem, that he has become a Christian believer, though he again laments the loss of his Fianna comrades and of his fine poets.[37]

Patrick's patience, as we might expect, was running out. By the sixteenth century we have him speaking in a cantankerous, even vindictive, way and condemning all that the nostalgic old warrior has to say. In a lay of that time the conversation is all tension and hostility. When Oisín criticises the clerical music, Patrick retorts that 'you are decrepid, stupid, and grey'; and when Oisín recalls the beautiful sounds of birds and the cries of nature, the sound of the hunt and the harp-strings of Cnú Dearóil, he is rudely told that all these things are now gone forever. Incensed at this, Oisín launches into a long eulogy of Fionn. The Fianna leader was the most generous ever bestower of gold, he fought battles in many foreign countries and nine score battles in Ireland, and his sway extended from 'the river in which Christ was baptised [i.e. the Jordan]' to 'the house of

Donn [off the Kerry coast]. 'Never in my time have I heard of one as good as him!' Oisín begs of Patrick to pray earnestly so as to gain access into heaven for Fionn and the Fianna.

Angered by Oisín's flippancy, Patrick says that he will not do that, and when the old man insinuates that if Patrick had himself known Fionn he would have ignored God, the enraged saint declares that Fionn is in hell for his deeds. Oisín refuses to believe this and again stresses Fionn's generosity, but Patrick insists that he is imprisoned in hell and suffering torments there. Undaunted by this, Oisín makes a proud vaunt:

'If the Morna clan were inside there, or the Baoiscne clan, those strong men would bring Fionn out, or else take possession of the house!'

The saint says that not all of the five provinces of Ireland or the seven battalions of the Fianna could do that, but Oisín protests that it would be unjust of God to consign to 'cold hell' a man who had been so generous with gold and food to both rich and poor – a man whose only joys had been to listen to scholars and poets, to give gifts, and to follow the hunt. But it was precisely because of such godless pastimes that he was damned, says Patrick, again admonishing Oisín to concentrate on his own approaching death.[38]

This poem is the ultimate in personality-clash between the warrior and the saint, and it shows how much the situation had changed from the mutual friendship and affection of the Colloquy. The question of Fionn's situation in the afterlife was, as we have seen, a preoccupation at least since the Colloquy was written. The clear resolution in that text, which had Patrick gaining heaven for Fionn, did not drown out the dramatic value of speculation. And so a poem of around the year 1400 represents a conversation between Oisín and the ghost of Fionn.

The great Fianna leader still has his handsome looks as of yore, but his appearance is distorted by the torments of hell. He tells Oisín of how after his death the Morna clan – despite the old feud – came to defend him against the devils. Goll and Conán Maol joined forces with Oscar and Mac Lughach and tried to escort him from the infernal regions. But it was only through the mercy of God that, after sixty years in 'cold hell', he was allowed out from that place for one night, and so he has come to speak to Oisín.

He advises Oisín to become a Christian, and though there is no mention of the possible release of himself and the Fianna from torments it is clear that the poem belongs to that general tradition. Fionn tells Oisín to go to where Cúchulainn is buried, thus showing that the author knew of the eleventh-century text referred to above, which had that ancient hero freed from hell.[39] Oral lore found its own resolution to the problem.

Drawing on the original Colloquy mention of how Patrick had Fionn freed from damnation, and in train with the boasts of Oisín in the lays that hell could not hold such magnificent fighters, the folk developed an account of a daring escape from that horrendous prison. Of all the stories which told of Fionn and his men breaking out of macabre underworld dwellings, this was surely the most amazing. No other straits were ever so dire, and no greater effort ever required. The story was told in folklore all over Ireland of how the Fianna fought their way out – though usually with the support of Patrick's prayers – and how their retreat was covered at the most critical stage by their supreme champion in the hour of need, 'Oscar of the blows'. As Fionn and his men emerged to freedom, Oscar stood at the gate of hell and kept the ferocious demons at bay by wielding his mighty flail.[40]

The image of this strange weapon seems to be derived from the Battle of Ventry text, which has Oscar defeating a flail-wielding warrior.[41] Once Oscar had come to be associated with the use of a flail in battle, a general tale-pattern was attracted which developed the image and suited the context of battle against fearsome foes. This pattern was that of an international folktale, known to researchers by the title 'Strong John', which was circulating in Irish folklore. This told of how an enormously strong man broke a flail while threshing, made another from roof-beams, and went to hell and overcame the devils there.[42]

Since the Colloquy tradition had the ancient Fianna heroes as stupendously strong men, all of these motifs fitted well into the general picture and were well suited to the idea of how they – and particularly their champion Oscar – could defeat the infernal foes. Perhaps, since their battle-victory was functionally taking the place of Patrick's miracle, the terms of the Church's mandate 'the gates of hell shall not prevail against you' had its application switched to this context also. At any rate, on account of its crucial importance in the folk story, the flail had to be an extraordinary and unbreakable one. And so Oscar was provisioned with a flail which had an unbreakable thong in it. The fact that this latter idea occurs in the allegory as a gift which Oscar received from the lady shows that the escape from hell predated the surviving folk versions of that allegory.

We have concluded that the prototype of these versions could not long predate the house of Cuanna text, but given an analysis of it and of its distribution it could hardly be later than the seventeenth century. The folk narrative of the great escape from hell must therefore have originated some time before that. Taking it to postdate the full Battle of Ventry text and the poem of Fionn's one-night parole from hell, this would be in the fifteenth or sixteenth centuries, coinciding with the poems which show a sharpened debate between the warrior values of Oisín and the religious ones of Patrick.

Oisín and the Lost Epoch

The actual competition between the perspectives of Oisín and Patrick continued to fascinate the popular mind, as is clear from lays, and rewritings of lays, in the seventeenth and eighteenth centuries. Some stanzas from these lays are of a quite controversial nature. For example, Oisín chides the saint for his excessive orthodoxy by saying:

> Great would be the shame for God not to take the shackles of pain from Fionn, for if God himself were in bonds the chief would fight for him!

Another stanza, which became widely known in oral tradition, has Oisín compare the strength of the Fianna champion to that of Patrick's champion:

> If my son Oscar and God were in hand-to-hand combat on yonder hill, if I saw Oscar laid low I would believe that God was a strong man![43]

There is no doubt that in this late literature the life-styles are being compared, but we should not ignore the essentially humorous nature of the speeches. The audience is expected to simultaneously admire the might of Oisín's comrades, and to laugh at his naive obstinacy in the face of spiritual truth.

Oisín, through his criticism of the saint, is himself being made to look somewhat stupid. Several of his arguments, however, display a slightly impious awareness of genuine Christian values which Patrick lacks, and it is clear that part of the joke is on the petty puritanism of clerics – represented by the saint. The humour can even extend as far as pranks and buffoonery in the late lays. For instance, Oisín complains of being practically starved by a stingy Patrick, while the saint tries to win him over by pretending that the bread given to him by the housekeeper has come from God and that a blow from a cleric has been given by God.[44] Furthermore, Munster folklore rationalises the escape from hell by having Oisín trick the saint. Having obtained a guarantee that Fionn would be freed, the wily old warrior declares that all the Fianna are fair [*fionn*] to him – '*is Fionn liom iad go léir*!'[45]

The general tendency to make Oisín critical of clerical life is reflected in a folk story which was known throughout Ireland and also in Scotland. According to this, Oisín argued with the housekeeper of Patrick over the type of food he was given to eat. He said that in the time of the Fianna he had seen a blackbird's leg which was larger than the joint of meat she was cooking, a rowan-berry larger than her butter, and an ivy-leaf larger than her cake. She refused to believe this; so to settle the question Oisín went out into the forest and returned with three such items – survivals from his lost epoch.[46]

This has certain resemblances to an episode in the Colloquy, which tells of how the high-king Diarmaid mac Cerbhaill, when he was at Ushnagh with Oisín, asked for water. Oisín took a pail and went to a forgotten well, which had not been frequented since the days of the Fianna. There he caught eight salmon, put eight stalks of watercress and of brooklime over them, and brought the lot in the pail to the king. All present were amazed, because each stalk was as thick as the king's knee.[47]

Indications are that the idea that the Fianna were enormously big men owed its popularity to the influence of the Colloquy (see pp. 303f below), and so this folk story must have been invented on the basis of the Colloquy passage. Versions of the story usually embody a special adventure:

Patrick, we are told, had a bitch in pup, and Oisín told his servant to watch the animal and to note which pup was first born. The servant, due to some distraction, failed to do this, whereupon Oisín directed him to fasten a sheepskin against a wall and to throw the pups one by one at it. Only one pup clung to the skin, and this one Oisín took aside and kept by him. Before long he set out with the servant and the pup to the forest, where they found a trumpet. Oisín bade his servant blow the trumpet and soon a huge blackbird came flying towards them. The pup was loosed against the bird and it killed it. The young hound became demented from its triumph, and Oisín – though failing of sight – accurately threw a metal ball into its gullet. Then he told the servant to seize it by the hind-legs and dash its head against a rock. Oisín cut a quarter from the dead bird and, procuring also a huge rowan-berry and ivy-leaf, he returned to Patrick's housekeeper to win the argument.

This in-tale is in both Irish and Scottish versions, so it is likely to have been part of the story from the beginning. The manner in which the pup is killed closely parallels how Cúchulainn killed a great hound in the Ulster cycle, and so it is clear that the composer of the story, as well as being acquainted with some version of the Colloquy, also knew a version of the Ulster epic *Táin Bó Cuailnge*. This latter was in all probability the fifteenth-century recension of the *Táin*, which became very popular in later manuscripts.[48] It seems, therefore, that the story of Oisín's argument with the housekeeper, although surviving only in oral sources, originated with some literate person in the sixteenth or seventeenth century.

One celebrated story grew up within the context of Oisín's encounter with Patrick. The earliest surviving version of it is in a lay written by a Co. Clare poet. Micheál Coimín, about the year 1750. In the lay, Patrick asks Oisín how he happened to outlive the Fianna. In answer, the old warrior describes how, after the battle of Gowra, Fionn and the remaining Fianna were hunting at Loch Léin in Co. Kerry when a beautiful lady riding a white steed approached. She spoke to Fionn, saying that she was Niamh of the Golden Hair, daughter of the king of *Tír na nÓg* [the Land of the Young], and that she had fallen in love with Oisín. The feeling was mutual, and Oisín sat on the steed and went away with her. The steed raced over the sea as on firm ground, and eventually they reached the beautiful land where people remained forever young. They were married there, and had two sons and a daughter, and three hundred years passed without being noticed. But at length Oisín grew lonesome for Fionn and his company and expressed a desire to go to visit them. Niamh warned him not to set foot on the soil of Ireland, but instead to remain mounted on the steed.

He set out and, on reaching Ireland, he met a large group of people and spoke of Fionn to them. Noting his huge size, these people guessed who he was for they had read of Fionn in the old books and of how Oisín had gone away with a beautiful lady to Tír na nÓg. Realising that all his friends were dead, Oisín rode on in dejection to Almhain, where he found only weeds and nettles. He then proceeded to Glenasmole [either in Co. Dublin or Co. Kerry] which the Fianna used to frequent, and met a large assemblage of men there stumbling under the weight of a large block of marble. They sought his help, and Oisín leaned over in the saddle and raised the weight for them, but the saddle-girth snapped with the strain and he landed on the ground on his two feet. The steed took fright at this and raced away, leaving Oisín transformed into a decrepid old man.[49]

Micheál Coimín did not invent this story, as it is a version of an old and widespread international folktale which describes how a man goes to the land of the immortals, where he magically remains young, but ages suddenly when he returns to his native land. Several echoes of the folktale are in fact found in mediaeval Irish literature, but these do not involve Oisín or the Fianna.[50] That some version had come to be associated with Oisín before Coimín wrote his lay emerges from what we find in folklore.

Many of the tellings collected in this century from Irish folklore have the decorative details of Coimín's lay, i.e. the lady's name Niamh, the white steed, and the broken saddle girth.[51] These details result from readings of the lay, which was popular in manuscripts through the nineteenth century and was first published in 1859. There are other folklore versions, from various parts of Ireland and also from Scotland, which do not have these decorative details. They have Oisín leaving Ireland with a beautiful but unnamed woman and going to the Land of Youth [usually called *Tír na hÓige*]. Returning after three hundred years on a horse [of unspecified colour] he sees a group of men trying to lift a large weight. The weight consists of some usual items of rural life, such as a load of turf, of fish, of stones, or of logs. Oisín jumps down off his horse to assist them, and then becomes old.[52]

These oral versions we can accept as representing the general form of the folk story which Coimín had heard and which he decided to write up into a lay. When this folk account of Oisín itself originated is difficult to say. There is no hint of it in any of the Colloquy manuscripts, even though Oisín is there as elsewhere given a special connection with the otherworld through the tradition of the daughter of Derg, his deer-mother. The Colloquy has him parting with Caoilte and going to spend a while in the *sí*-dwelling of Ocht Cleitigh (near Newgrange) where she was. That text has Niamh as a favourite name for beautiful ladies, one of whom in fact elopes with Oisín. She is daughter of a Munster king and she dies of shame when her father's men, in their search for her, come upon her bathing.[53] She is not an otherworld lady, however, nor does she come from the Land of Youth, so the likelihood is that Coimín merely borrowed her name from the Colloquy and bestowed it on the other lady of Oisín, of whom the folk story told.

We recall that in the allegorical story the gift given to Oisín by the lady Youth is 'the grace of God'. This lady could be the proto-figure which attracted to Oisín the unrelated folktale of going with a beautiful lady to the Land of Youth. But it is more likely that the Land of Youth was already associated with Oisín and that this helped to strengthen the youth-symbolism of the lady in the allegory. Either way, Oisín's three-hundred-year sojourn in the timeless other-world and his sad return to Ireland can hardly have been part of Fianna lore until post-mediaeval times. We must presume that the mediaeval writers ignored it as an explanation for Oisín's survival for the simple reason that they did not know it.

More Adventures and Further Questions

There are a number of stories which have a confused history within the context of oral/literary relationships. This has to do with the strengthening and weakening of particular motifs within the oral stream, and with the development and recession of the roles attributed to particular characters.

Perhaps the best example is furnished by the lore concerning a young warrior called Feardhomhain. This character is mentioned in various eleventh- to twelfth-century sources, and the Colloquy makes him one of the nine leading members of the Fianna. He is several times identified as the son of Bodhbh Derg – a scion of the Tuatha Dé Danann – and must therefore have his origins in the otherworld realm.[54] Elsewhere in the Colloquy, however, we find Feardhomhain described as son of Imoman of Cúige Ghailian [i.e. Leinster], which accords with the Leinster origin of Fionn's Fianna.[55] In fact, there is a reference to him in a stanza of a mediaeval poem, which may be based on a source compiled as early as the eighth century. This stanza mentions also a certain *Lecht Máil* [the Gravestone of Mál], a landmark which recurs in the Colloquy under the designation *Tulach an Mháil* [the Mound of Mál] in the plain of Leinster. It must have featured in the early lore of that province, but its meaning has been lost by the time of the Colloquy, for that text tells a newly-invented story which claims that Mál was a Scottish prince (p. 222).[56]

The character of Feardhomhain probably reflects the genesis of Fianna tradition as we know it, with echoes of the Boyne valley cult (namely, son of Bodhbh Derg] being encapsuled into Leinster warrior lore [namely, son of Imoman of the Gailiain]. There are other identifications given for Feardhomhain in twelfth- to fourteenth-century texts – one describes him as fiann-chief of Uí Chinsealaigh [in Co. Wexford], another as son of Niamh and grandson of one of king Cormac's champions, yet another as son of a first-cousin of Fionn called Lughaidh.[57] It is obvious that memory of him had become confused and his name was being used in differing narrative contexts. The Colloquy refers twice to a story of his death which was in some way connected with that of a certain Conán. We are cryptically told that Finnine, daughter of Bodhbh, was slain by her own husband Conán, and that he and Feardhomhain slew each other.[58] An eleventh-century source identifies Feardhomhain with one Aedh Rinn son of Rónán,[59] and a story from that time describes how this same Aedh Rinn was killed by Conán son of the Liath Luachra.

According to it Fionn advised Conán to go to woo Eargna, daughter of Aedh, full knowing that Aedh vowed to kill any such suitor. Conán managed to abduct the maiden, but Fionn later taunted Aedh with the fact and in this way he caused the two men to fight a duel in which they were both killed.[60]

This is clearly a variant of the story of Finnine – confused with the plot of the grandfather myth – and we may presume that there was a tradition that Feardhomhain had been killed in combat with his sister's husband, over his sister, as a result of Fionn's treachery. Little is known either of another story referred to in the Colloquy, which concerned Feardhomhain and a ferocious water-monster from Loch Lurgan (a lake to the west of the bog of Allen in Co. Offaly).[61] A twelfth- or thirteenth-century hagiographical text in Latin describes how Feardhomhain slew the monster by cutting it in half with his sword.[62]

Incidental references to characters called Feardhomhain in Fianna lays down through the centuries show that the name had become a floating element in Fianna tradition. Curiously, one well-developed story concerning Feardhomhain was very popular in the folklore of Co. Donegal, but apparently was not known further afield. It told of how Fionn wished to bring about the death of this young warrior and, knowing that he was a brave youth, he advised him to avoid a fierce pig which inhabited a certain glen. Feardhomhain, as expected by Fionn, went to the glen with his three dogs. Each dog was killed in turn by the pig, and then Feardhomhain and the pig both fell in combat with each other. The young hero's sister, called Finngheal, went to aid him, but she was drowned in Lough Finn in her haste.[63]

The background to this folk story is puzzling, since it reflects aspects which we have found in the mediaeval lore of the character called Feardhomhain – Fionn's treacherous advice, and the deaths of Feardhomhain and his sister. The conclusion must be that an echo of this mediaeval lore survived through the centuries in Donegal – the likely reason being a perceived association between the lady's name and the local landmark Lough Finn [*Loch Fhinne*]. The Colloquy, as we have seen, mentions the killing of a monster in Loch Lurgan by Feardhomhain, and it further tells us that a sister of Fionn was drowned while observing that monster.[64] All the indications, therefore, are that the ur-type of the Donegal folk story sprang from a confused rendering of the ancient lore of Feardhomhain, perhaps based on some late mediaeval literary source which is now lost. The folk story, as we have it, borrows the portrayal of Feardhomhain's death from the story of Diarmaid's death (p. 174). This latter was the best-known account of Fionn's treachery by taking advantage of a young rival's bravery, and so a ferocious pig, rather than a lake-monster, was made Feardhomhain's opponent in the suicidal combat.

Another Fianna story which presents problems is concerned with a young hero called Céadach. This name occurs in the Colloquy, but it refers to a completely different character; and the first real reference we have to our Céadach is in a thirteenth-century poem lamenting a litany of Fianna heroes, where he is called 'Céadach the joyful'.[65] All indications are that he developed comparatively late as a character, and he was usually regarded as the son of a foreign king who gained admission to Fionn's troop. Sources from the fourteenth to the seventeenth centuries call him variously 'son of the Scandinavian king', 'son of the Saracen king', and 'son of the Thule king'.[66] These descriptions place him firmly within the post-twelfth century Fianna lore which presupposes a wide international stage. His role in the literature is thus a very minor one, and his personality is general and rather unspecific – a factor which makes the great popularity of one unique story of him in folklore quite surprising. This had an involved plot, and was known to storytellers throughout Ireland and Gaelic Scotland.

It tells of how Céadach, the son of a foreign king, was a member of Fionn's troop, and a beautiful maiden chose him rather than his friend Lon Dubh as suitor. Lon Dubh sought as recompense the right to strike one undefended blow on Céadach. Meanwhile, Fionn was embarking on an overseas adventure, and he took Céadach with him. The young warrior fought many combats on Fionn's behalf and through his valour the expedition proved a great success. On the return-voyage Lon Dubh struck the undefended blow, and in the resultant struggle both young men were killed. Fionn had arranged with Céadach's sweetheart that he would hoist a black sail if the young hero were dead, but he now raised a white sail instead. When she was given the dead body she was disconsolate, but, noticing two birds revive a third, she copied their actions and brought Céadach back to life again.[67]

All versions of this story are from oral tradition in the last two centuries, but its wide provenance throughout the Gaelic world points to a much older origin. The only possible explanation is that it derives from a literary story which is now lost, but which was hardly composed before the sixteenth century.

A well-written story from around the year 1600 presents no such problems. Its title is *Eachtra Bhodaigh an Chóta Lachtna* [The Adventure of the Grey-Cloaked Churl], and its author seems to have been from either Clare or Limerick. He got the basic idea for his romance from a passage in the third Colloquy, which has a strange warrior called 'Dubhthaidh of the speckled cloak' spending a year in the Fianna. When Fionn brashly boasted that Oisín was the fastest runner in the world, Dubhthaidh challenged the Fianna to a race and then outran both men and hounds.[68] This plot had a potential for surprise and humour, and so it could be combined with the theme of an otherworld visitor coming in disguise to the Fianna. The Adventure of the Grey-Cloaked Churl can be summarised as follows:

One day Fionn held an assembly of his seven battalions at Howth, and they saw a ship approaching on the sea. A fine handsome warrior came ashore, and announced himself as Caol an Iarainn [slender fellow of the iron], son of the king of Thessaly. He had subdued every country which he visited, and now intended to do the same in Ireland. In order to show his superiority, he first challenged the best man among them to a race. Fionn said that his best runner, Caoilte mac Rónáin, was absent, and asked the stranger to bide his time until he could be found. Caol agreed, and Fionn set out for Tara seeking Caoilte.

As he passed through a wood, he met a huge and horridly ugly churl with a grey cloak. They fell into conversation, and Fionn explained to the churl what had happened. The churl said that if Caoilte was their only hope then Ireland was lost, for he would not defeat the stranger.

'If so', said Fionn, 'I do not know what I can do!'

The churl offered to run the race himself, but Fionn was very sceptical as he had seen how slowly the churl moved. In desperation, however, he accepted the offer, and they went to Howth together.

The course for the race was arranged as one hundred and twenty Irish miles, from Slieve Logher to Howth. So Caol and the churl set out together. When they reached the starting-point, the churl suggested that they build a hut in a wood there for the night and find something to eat. Caol refused to help, so the churl built the hut of timber, and caught a pig and cooked it. He then ran at the speed of a swallow or of a doe to the house of the Baron of Inchiquin [in Co. Clare] thirty Irish miles away to collect a table, chairs, wine and bread, and spent the night in his hut feasting and sleeping. Caol slept apart on the hillside, and when morning came he set off running.

The churl slept on and ate a late breakfast. He then folded the pigs' bones in the tail of his cloak and ran like the wind. Soon he overtook his opponent and, when he had drawn well ahead of him, he stopped to eat berries from the bushes on the roadside.

When Caol reached that place, he told the churl that he had seen a piece of his cloak on a tree twenty miles back and another piece a further ten miles behind that. The churl immediately returned to collect the pieces, while Caol continued to race forward. Finding the pieces, the churl sat down and sewed them back onto his cloak, then resumed the race and soon overtook Caol again.

He surged ahead at the speed of the wind in March and came to the slope of a high hill within five miles of Howth. Here he stopped to eat a large feed of blackberries from the bushes, and sewed his cloak together in the form of a sack, and filled it with more berries. He ran on then like a hare, with the 'sack' on his shoulder.

Fionn had placed a warrior as look-out on a hillside, and when this warrior saw a figure approaching in the distance he thought it was Caol with the churl dead on his shoulder. The Fianna were crestfallen on hearing this, but Fionn offered a suit of armour to whoever would bring better news.

One of the company went out and saw the churl coming up towards the crowd. All the Fianna were overjoyed, but the churl complained of hunger and emptied his sack to eat. Soon Caol arrived and, in his pique, drew his sword to wreak havoc on the Fianna. The churl threw a handful of meal and berries at him, however, and knocked his head off with the force. Picking up the head then, the churl slammed it onto the shoulders back to front, and tied up the revivified Caol, whom he made swear to pay tribute from Thessaly each year to the Fianna. After this he released Caol, took him to his ship, and sent him out to sea. The churl returned to the Fianna, and,

> The wind and sun lit up his face and head, and Fionn and the Fiann-troop realised that it was Manannán mac Lir, the phantom from Ráth Chruachan, who was there, and who had come to save them from the very dire situation they were in at that time.

He was honoured by the Fianna and kept feasting for a month and a day.[69]

This text exemplifies a tendency away from respect for tradition in favour of the burlesque demands of humour. Caoilte was conventionally the great runner of the Fianna, but here his skill is denigrated in the interests of the incongruity which provides the story with its drama. The loosening of traditional bonds shows clearly also in another text composed in the Clare-Limerick area in the early seventeenth century. This is called *Eachtra Lomnochtáin an tSléibhe Riffe* [the Adventure of the Stark-Naked Fellow of Riff Mountain]. The character's name here, Lomnochtán, is borrowed arbitrarily from the traditional stock of humorous designations, and he does not in fact appear stark naked in the text. Otherwise, commonplace plot-devices are used, such as a strange visitor to the Fianna and an overseas adventure. The author also shows acquaintance with the texts of Eochaidh's Mansion and the Quicken Mansion (see pp. 208ff).

Fionn dreamed that a sea-monster would swallow the whole city of Limerick, so he hurried there and set nine warriors to guard the place, including Goll, Oscar, and Diarmaid. Soon a ship approached, with only one person on board. This was a monstrous warrior, who announced that he had been a friend of Goll's father and that they had campaigned together in the eastern world. Goll's father had left him in charge of a great treasure on an eastern island, and he had now come to bring Goll to receive that treasure. He said that he and his wife had been turned into a horrid shape by a poisonous drink served to them by one of their own people. Diarmaid was suspicious, but at Conán's urging the nine warriors went on board the ship. The stranger told them that his name was Lomnochtán and that he came from the Riff Mountain in Africa.

They set sail and eventually reached the island in question. Conán refused to leave the food-filled ship, and ate and drank to such excess that he fell into a deep slumber and remained while the rest went ashore. In the stranger's fortress they were given a drink, as a result of which their strength ebbed away from them, and then Lomnochtán revealed that he had brought them there to avenge the death of his father and relatives at the hands of the Fianna. He would kill them at once, except that the king of the island had ordered that they be publicly tortured and decapitated. He also revealed that it was intended to entice more of the Fianna to their death in similar manner.

When Lomnochtán went to inform the king of the island of their capture, the king's daughter came to them to offer her help, for she had fallen in love with Diarmaid. She informed them that the monstrous Lomnochtán could only be killed through a birthmark underneath his right ear. Conán had meanwhile been awoken by the barking of Bran and Sceolaing, and he came to the fortress. He was told by Diarmaid to return to Ireland and warn the Fianna, but he refused and went to attack Lomnochtán instead. Bran bit the monster under the ear, and Conán flung a spear at the wound and killed him. Lomnochtán's wife then attacked Conán, and in a terrible fracas she tore the flesh off his head with her claws. Sceolaing then leaped into the hag's gullet and tore her heart out.

Returning to the Fianna captives, Conán threatened to kill the helpful princess, but he was restrained by Diarmaid who reminded him of how he rescued him at the Quicken Mansion. The princess, who was called Bláthmhar Sciamhach [flowerlike and beautiful], went to where her father was and got a magical drink there to restore the Fianna warriors to health. When they had recovered, Diarmaid killed a sheep and put its skin on Conán's head in place of his severed scalp. Then Diarmaid and Conán set off together to attack the foe, and scattered them. The king was captured, and he swore allegiance to the Fianna and gave his daughter Bláthmhar to Diarmaid in marriage.[70]

It is interesting to note the new twist given to the motif of how Conán became bald. The vicious attack on him by the hag is far more hilarious than the episode in Eochaidh's Mansion which was its source, and the confusion of this with the baldness from the Quicken Mansion is a deliberate appeal by the author to farcical taste. In fact, he seems in this to be reacting to dramatic inflation in oral Fianna lore, for the motif was in great demand there. The substitution of a sheepskin for Conán's missing skin and hair is found widely in folklore, which further adds the detail that the Fianna used to shear him each year and thus were never short of fine woollen socks![71]

Late Romances

By the end of the seventeenth century literary men felt free to describe any type of adventure in the Fianna context, entertainment of the readers being the sole consideration. The overseas adventure, of course, was a stock-piece of entertaining narrative, and by this time it had gone far beyond the point of interest to the range of tedium and even triteness. An example of this is the east Ulster text *Tóraigheacht Taise Taoibhghile* [the Pursuit of Taise the bright-sided]. It is extremely long – almost the length of a novel – but can be synopsised as follows:

Fionn, whose power was almost as great as that of the high-king Cormac, held a great hunt at Howth. He and his men saw a boat approaching, from which a beautiful lady came ashore, curtsied to Fionn, and told him that she had searched the world for him. For she loved him, and now she placed injunctions [*geasa*] on him to follow her and take her from her own city with no more than eighteen warriors. She refused to tell where the city was, and then departed. Oisín told Fionn to put his thumb under his tooth of knowledge, and he did this, having first bathed his face and hands.

His face reddened, whitened, blackened, and the appearance of death came on him. He had discovered that the lady was called Taise Thaoibhgheal, wife of the king of Thule Island, and that she was very accomplished at magic. Two poets had argued at her court as to whether her husband Cuilleann 'the Hard-Armed' or Fionn was the better; and it was to decide this question that she had enjoined on Fionn to follow her. Fionn also discovered that many hazards lay before him on the journey to Thule, and that Cuilleann could only be killed by a spear and sword which were in the possession of the Norwegian king, who was a great smith.

As Fionn was selecting men for the expedition, a stranger arrived at Almhain offering his services. He was Labhraidh Lámhfhada, a great leech of the Tuatha Dé Danann, who could magically heal wounds. They were also joined by another Tuatha Dé scion, Aonghus of Newgrange, who promised to deliver Fionn from whatever danger might beset him. Fionn's select group, which included both of these and the best-known Fianna characters, set sail from Howth in Fionn's ship, called the *Breacbharc*.

Arriving in Norway, they defeated the king's forces in a great battle, with Goll killing the king himself. Fionn gave control of Norway to the dead king's brother, called Míodhach, who had been wrongfully displaced, and himself got the special sword and spear. They travelled on then, but Conán Maol caused trouble on board the ship by insulting Aonghus. Goll reprimanded Conán, but Oscar took Conán's part. The bitter quarrel which ensued between the two great warriors, Goll and Oscar, was contained only by the efforts of the Fianna poet, Fearghus Fíonbhéil.

They arrived at the land of Antuaith [Bad Country] and had to fight many engagements against hostile forces there, but eventually they slew the king in battle and placed his more amicable son Iollann Órarmach on the throne. Next they went to 'the Land of the Dark Men', and on their way were joined by a wondrously handsome warrior. Aonghus recognised the newcomer as his teacher Manannán, who then took them into his boat – the only boat which, he disclosed, could bring them to their destination. Manannán left them in that land, and soon a churlish wizard and a hag began to assail them; but they were protected by Labhraidh and Aonghus, who surrounded the group with a wall of fire. Fionn killed the wizard with a spear-cast, and Diarmaid killed the hag with a sling-shot. Next they were attacked by nine poisonous hounds, which were killed one by one by the Fianna warriors. A savage lion also attacked them, and this was slain by Oisín. Finally, the whole muster of warriors from that country made an onslaught on them, and after three days of ferocious fighting Fionn and his men prevailed. The king of the Dark Men was a very powerful magician and for this reason had never been defeated in combat, but the whole Fianna group joined together and speared him to death.

Having taken much treasure from that land, they returned to their own ship and continued on their journey. They had to cross a sea which was un-navigable due to a great forest growing through it, and a mountain which flamed with fire, but Aonghus put the *fé fia* [a cloak belonging to Manannán] around the group and this brought them through all obstacles until they reached Thule. More conflicts awaited them there, including magical churls, a knight with a great chain, and poisonous hounds, but these were all overcome. Smaller combats inevitably led to all-out warfare between Cuilleann's forces and Fionn's group. Taise went with thrice fifty fair-haired women to the Fianna camp, bringing food, refreshments, and advice.

Meanwhile Fionn's poet, Fearghus, passed to and fro between the camps, being royally entertained by Cuilleann on account of his profession, and bringing intelligence information to Fionn. Cuilleann sent a hag to the Fianna, who played harp-music for them and put them to sleep with the intention of beheading them, but Caoilte stayed awake by driving his spear through his feet and fastening them to the ground. He therefore was able to kill the hag before she achieved her purpose, and he further slew a hundred warriors sent on a night-attack by Cuilleann.

The Fianna group, due to the continuous fighting, were so incapacitated with wounds that only Mac Lughach could stand guard on the ford leading to their camp. He slew hundreds, but had to retire due to his wounds. He was replaced by Oscar, who by his great prowess continued to wreak havoc on the assailants.[72]

The solitary manuscript for this story is defective, but we can be sure that the ending involved a great victory for the Fianna, and perhaps several other motifs adopted at random from the Fianna store. The *bruidhean*-type plot of entrapment in the underworld had also become subordinated to free phantasy, and the authors added plots at will and included all and every kind of motif which would add colour to the narrative. Two lays composed in Munster around the end of the eighteenth century are good illustrations of this. One has the title *Seilg Sléibhe Fuaid*, which means the Hunt of Deadman's Hill in Co. Armagh – this place name 'Sliabh Fuaid' being a conventional one in the topography of Fianna literature.

The lay tells of how Fionn, with his two hounds Bran and Sceolaing and a Fianna comrade called Dáire, went astray while hunting a deer. They met a beautiful lady, who told them that her name was Glanlua and that her husband had gone missing while hunting in that area. They soon heard strange music, which weakened them and caused them to collapse. When they awoke they found themselves near a golden fortress, which was surrounded by the sea. A warrior and a woman swam over to them and brought them to the fortress. The warrior told them that his name was Draíontóir [magician] and that he was seeking vengeance for the slaying of particular warriors by the Fianna. The woman with him was his sister Áille, wife of one of the dead warriors.

Fionn, Dáire, and Glanlua were bound by magic, but on Áille's request Glanlua was released. Draíontóir's intention was to lure all of the Fianna to their destruction, so he made Dáire play music. When they heard this, the Fianna champions came and were captured and bound. Finally Draíontóir came to behead them all. Conán Maol jumped up in terror, leaving the skin of his buttocks stuck to the seat, so that Draíontóir had to magically apply a furry skin to him in its place. Conán then begged the magician to spare him, and Draíontóir took him to his secret chamber and gave him a magical phial to carry.

Returning to execute the captives, Conán pretended to have forgotten the phial, and when Draíontóir angrily departed to collect it Conán used it to free the Fianna. Áille dropped dead from shock, and Oscar killed Draíontóir. Then Fionn and his men feasted mightily in the fortress, before falling asleep. They awoke on the morrow to find no trace of the fortress.[73]

The other late *bruidhean*-lay is called *Seilg Ghleanna an Smóil* [The Chase of Glenasmole]. Here again we find the bricolage of Fianna tradition being re-arranged to form a rather off-the-cuff unit. Fionn and his men were hunting one morning in Glenasmole [another conventional placename, here probably referring to a place in Co. Kerry]. A doe with one white and one black side rose up before them, and the hounds went out of sight chasing it. Fionn put his thumb under his tooth of knowledge and discovered that only one of the hounds would return. Soon a beautiful blonde woman came on the scene and invited the Fianna to a feast which the daughter of the Greek king had prepared for them at Inch (in Co. Kerry). When they went there, however, they found that it was a trap.

The Greek princess was a frightfully ugly woman with a half-black and half-white cloak. She had been the doe, and she now demanded that Fionn marry her. Bran was the only hound which had survived the chase. She beheaded all her Fianna guests except the leaders, whom she weakened with magic music and bound. Fionn craftily said that he would marry her but for possible objections from Goll, who had been a friend of his first wife.

She accordingly went to Howth where Goll was, and was locked in combat with him for three days. Meanwhile, Diarmaid proposed marriage to a lady who was guarding him and the other Fianna leaders. She fell in love with him and released them, whereupon they hurried to Howth. Oscar replaced the tiring Goll in the combat, and he slew the hag. As she died she explained that she had been a beautiful maiden but that her father had magically transformed her on account of a prophecy that if she had a son he would kill her father. She had thus been seeking a warrior who would give her a world-conquering son and by that act restore her to her former self.[74]

The use of the latter motif in this case is curious, since it parallels what we have found to be a strong theme in early Fionn stories (see chapter 1). It is very unlikely that the writer of this text would have been aware of the motif's early association with Fionn, however, so his source appears to have been rather the Lugh myth, which was current in folklore. Writers did not hesitate to borrow copiously from oral stories, even from ones having no connection with Fianna tradition. An Ulster writer of around the year 1700 retells the battle of Knockanaar (pp. 223f) in prose-form, and then stitches wondrous plots and imagery from various sources into his narrative. Immediately after the lady Niamh dropped dead in the Knockanaar lay, the author of this text tells us, a horrid hag arrived on the scene and announced that she was the mother of the slain cat-headed warrior Tailc:

She put injunctions on Oscar to follow her to her home and give compensation there for her son's death. As soon as Oscar was healed of his wounds he set out, accompanied by Goll, Diarmaid, and others. They sailed from Howth to Greece, where Oscar overcame and tied up the greatest warrior in that country. He was received by the king, who explained that he had been forced to give his daughter to the monstrous Tailc. Oscar told him what had happened in Ireland and produced the body of Niamh, which he had brought with him. When placed in the stream of the Nine Maidens [i.e. the Muses], Niamh came back to life again. The Fianna group were publicly welcomed to the city of Athens, and Oscar was married to Niamh. A ship was sent to Ireland, with Caoilte and a hundred Greek warriors on board, to bring the bodies of those Fianna who had been killed by Tailc to be resuscitated also.

Meanwhile Goll suggested that the rest of the group set out for the land of Tailc's mother. The Greek king assembled his best magicians to assist them, and one particularly powerful female wizard conjured the hag into their presence so that Oscar could identify her. The hag's name, Oscar was told, was Carthann Chas Dubh, and she lived on an island accompanied by two giants. The female wizard further said that only three warriors – Goll, Oscar, and Diarmaid – should go to the island, and that she would send an otter to direct their course, and she told them how to kill the giants.

Reaching the island, Goll tackled and overcame one of these, but the giant turned himself into a salmon. Remembering the advice he had been given, Goll threw a pea at where the giant was, and the pea turned into an otter which ate the salmon. Similarly, Oscar's opponent turned himself into a deer and was killed by a hound which came from Oscar's pea. The hag became a dove, but Diarmaid's pea became a hawk and killed her.

When Caoilte returned to Greece with the dead Fianna

warriors these were all restored to life, and there was great rejoicing when Oscar, Goll, and Diarmaid arrived to find their comrades alive once more. The stream had failed to revive four of the dead, but on the female wizard's instructions the salmon, deer, and dove were cooked in one vessel and a touch of their meat brought the four back to life. The Fianna group then returned in triumph to Ireland, with Oscar accompanied by his bride Niamh.[75]

The thirst for new motifs, from whatever source, was in full swing by the eighteenth century. Some Limerick author, who was acquainted with a translation of the Arabian Nights into English,[76] wrote a continuation of *Eachtra Lomnochtáin* sometime around 1740. Borrowing the giant story and its imagery from the third voyage of Sinbad the Sailor, he tacked it onto elements of longer pedigree in Irish lore, such as the dripping candle motif and fights with hags, to give a comical series of adventures to Conán:

When Bláthmhar, daughter of the king of the island which had been conquered by nine fianna warriors, was given in marriage to Diarmaid, her brother Maoghnas and her wooer Macaomh Mór objected and attacked the Fianna group. In a great battle, the Fianna defeated and killed them. Conán then insisted on going to attack the king's household, despite the agreement which had been reached with the king, and he engaged the Black Knight there in single combat. The Black Knight seized him and tied him under a dripping candle.

There were four reputedly invincible warriors in the royal service, and the four younger Fianna warriors went to fight these but were tied up along with Conán. Finally, the other four Fianna – Oscar, Goll, Garbh, and Diarmaid – took the field, and after a ferocious combat they prevailed and tied up the four warriors. When he heard what had happened, a triumphant craze seized Conán and he tore his bonds asunder and killed all his guards.

After several other adventures, including Oscar's marriage to a Scandinavian princess, the nine Fianna were ready to return to Ireland, but Conán Maol was kidnapped by a giant who sent him to cut firewood. The giant's mother whipped him unmercifully as he worked, but Diarmaid came and slew both hag and giant. Conán was overcome by shame at his adventures with hags, and he refused to return to Ireland with them until his companions swore not to refer to such matters. As they docked at Limerick, however, Fionn remarked to him that he had not returned without treasure,

'For that is a nice cap on you!'

The Fianna troop burst out laughing at that, and Conán left them in anger and never returned to them. He demanded single combat from a nobleman who lived seven Irish miles south of Limerick, slew him, and took over his land and his wife. The fortress in that place was afterwards called Ráth Chonáin, and he was buried there when he died.[77]

The place being referred to here is Rathcannon in Co. Limerick, but the proper Irish for it is Ráth Cheanainn,[78] which has no connection with Conán. The writer, however, engaged in this pseudo-archaising in order to give an air of authenticity to his creation. In fact, the north Munster region was a focal point for the composition of new Fianna texts in this period. We have another substantial story which was written in the last quarter of the eighteenth century by a Clareman who had read both the allegory concerning Cormac mac Airt (p. 239) and the allegory of the house of Cuanna (pp. 234ff) and had noticed the parallels between the two. He was also acquainted with the oral recension of the house of Cuanna episode. He therefore used the roasting pig motif as found in both texts; took the troublesome animal and the wooing motifs from the Fianna allegory; and took the motifs of Manannán as host, the dream setting, and miscellaneous marvels from the Cormac allegory. Placing all of these within the time-honoured theme of a deity in disguise, he gave a comic atmosphere to the events. This is a synopsis:

Fionn held an assembly of the Fianna on Slieve Callan (in Co. Clare), and they saw approaching an ugly little man. He told them that his name was Maol Ó Manannáin, and he invited the seven standing battalions and the thirty reserve battalions of the Fianna to dine in his fortress, which was near at hand. But first he challenged one of them to race him.

Diarmaid took up the challenge. Maol set off like the wind, crossing the river Shannon into west Munster and from there to Leinster. Worn out by fatigue, Diarmaid fell asleep, and when he awoke he found Maol waiting for him. They set out north as far as Donegal and raced down through Connacht. Diarmaid lost sight of Maol as they came to the Burren (in Co. Clare), and when he reached Slieve Callan he found no sign of the Fianna. He went into a house there and saw Maol lying on the floor humming to himself. Maol told Diarmaid to blow his bugle, and at that the whole Fianna troop came and the house increased in size to fit them all in.

The house soon grew terribly cold; and Conán, Faolán, and Caoilte in turn tried to displace Maol's son from the fireside, but each had his ankles broken by the monstrous boy. Maol himself with a word healed their injuries, and then Conán demanded something to eat. He was told to bring in three boars from the sty. He was knocked down by one of the pigs, however, and they raced out of the sty. Conán followed them for a while, but had to give up and return to the house. Diarmaid then went to the sty and found the pigs there again, but they escaped from him also. Caoilte then tried, and he kept pace with the pigs all the way to Co. Cork, but eventually he too had to admit failure. Then Maol's son went out and brought a pig into the house without difficulty. Conán, Diarmaid, and Goll each tried to kill the pig with a sledge-hammer, but to no avail. Again Maol's son succeeded with ease and prepared the pig for cooking.

A beautiful fair-haired lady entered the room through a miserable little door. She told Fionn that she was a daughter of the king of Thule Island which lay near the Equator (!). Her name was Eithne, and she had refused to marry a prince of Syria. As a result a great battle had been fought between Thule and Syria, in which Eithne's side triumphed, but her brother died from his wounds.

One day, she had been swept away by a great wind as she lamented at his grave, and in this manner brought to Maol's fortress. She described how she had married Maol and had given birth to a son. Maol suspected that the child was not his, but she insisted that it was. At that part of her account, those present noticed that a third of the pig was cooked, and Maol rejoiced that his wife had been telling the truth. In similar manner she described the births of two further sons, and the two other thirds of the pig were cooked. They then sat up to table expecting a great feast, but Maol blew his breath at the pig and it jumped up alive and ran away.

Conán complained that his host was a demon, but the lady told him to have patience and he would get his fill to eat. She laid a cloth on the table, and it was immediately full of exquisite food and drink. They feasted, and went to sleep with the cloth over them. They had fallen in love with the lady and, during the night, Fionn tried to cut his way with a knife through the little door which led to her quarters. Diarmaid did likewise, and both remained cutting – unknown to each other – all night long, but to no avail.

Dawn came, and they found themselves on the plain of Tara. A fine tree there had been almost cut down by Fionn and Diarmaid, and the rest of the Fianna were lying naked on the plain. Fionn then realised that their host Maol Ó Manannáin had in reality been Donn, who had an otherworld residence at the Doughs [i.e. the sandhills near Dunbeg on the Clare coast]. Diarmaid spoke angrily of Donn, but Fionn answered:

'We will not interfere with him, for he is a good friend!'[79]

This author had a good knowledge of literature and lore, for in addition to the sources we have already mentioned he borrowed the changing nature of the otherworld dwelling from the Quicken Mansion story and the imagery of Donn from local folk belief.[80] In his use of earlier Fianna materials and his development of a new context, he shows that even at this late stage the old methods of composition of Fianna narratives could still be undertaken with success. The greater demand at the end of the eighteenth century, however, was for complete novelty, as is again evidenced by a lay composed somewhere in south Ulster.

This tells of how the Fianna were hunting at Kesh (in Co. Armagh) when Diarmaid and Conán Maol dropped behind. A little man came to them and invited them to a meal in his fortress. His name was Cab an Dosáin [mouth of the tuft]. After the meal, Conán demanded a woman for the night, and he was put sleeping in a chamber where a beautiful lady was. When he went to her bed, however, he imagined that he was being sucked into a bog. Hearing his shouts, the hosts and the rest of the household came and found him sitting in a cauldron. After they left, Conán tried again to approach the woman, but he imagined he was fleeing up a tree from savage cats. Hearing his shouts again, the others came and found him sitting on a candlestick with a kitten licking his mouth. When they left once more, he again approached the woman, but she made him reverse sexual roles. He then imagined he was giving birth to a baby, and called on Diarmaid to act as midwife. Fionn had meanwhile been searching for the two warriors and, 'since he had some magic himself', he and Goll managed to have them released from their weird surroundings.[81]

This *narratio lubrica* draws on a plot which was common in humorous Irish prose literature of the time – the magically frustrated love-adventure – but the man who imagines he is giving birth is a motif from ordinary folklore.[82] Manuscripts of the foregoing story were common in Munster, and a further humorous lay concerning Conán was composed in the southern province which seems to owe something to it.

The Fianna were hunting when they met a beautiful fair-haired lady who invited them to her fortress. Conán Maol advised them to accept, but when they reached the fortress they were stuck by magic to the floor. Conán roared so loudly that his voice was heard throughout Ireland, calling on the only man who could save them, Gabha na gCeard [the smith of the trades].

This smith came and struck Conán on the hands with his mallet, so that Conán went wild with pain and tore himself free, leaving much of his skin behind him. The lady then offered Conán a goblet and, despite the pleas of Fionn and the Fianna, he began to drink. The goblet stuck to his mouth, and the lady told him he could set the magic aside by placing one hand on his shoulder and the other on the base of the goblet. He did so, and both hands stuck. The lady also bound Gabha na gCeard, but she released them all on condition that they fight the first man who came to see her.

Soon a great black-faced warrior arrived. He was engaged

by Oscar, who beheaded him, and further supporters of his who came were overcome and slain also by the Fianna.[83]

The possibilities for composing further Fianna stories were now unlimited; but the conventions had grown stale, with too much stress on descriptions of action and little heed paid to the personal or social traits of Fionn and his company. It is clear that Conán alone was seen as capable of character development in these late centuries of the literature. But he had become debased to a farcical buffoon, and if the heroic atmosphere of the cycle was to be re-established the writers had to invent new characters while avoiding anachronism. Such a task was, of course, an impossible one, even if Fionn's marvellous helpers were themselves to come to life and attempt to aid the writers, for the world of the Fianna was by now absolutely archaic and divorced from any type of contemporary reality. Only on a psychological level could the gap be bridged, and traditional literature coming to the end of its tether had little concern for psychology. Perhaps the best illustration of the crisis in Fianna literature is provided by a novel-length prose text composed in Co. Limerick around 1770.

Here we have a new warrior introduced, Dearg son of Fionn and his wife Ailbhe, who at the age of seven was already a great fighter and runner. Fearing for his safety, Fionn had him confined while the Fianna went to hunt a ferocious boar which had killed thousands. But Dearg escaped and tackled the boar at Knockainey. Leaping onto its back, he stabbed it continually all the way to where the three rivers meet near Waterford and killed it there.

There are echoes of Cúchulainn here, as well as of the Fianna heroes Diarmaid and Oscar. The rest of the story is similarly based on earlier Irish heroic and romance tradition, with a somewhat vapid feast of motifs such as the hero's battle-frenzy, his great hurling ability, his killing of giant-warriors, and his marvellous adventures overseas.[84]

9.

The Oral Tradition

Several accounts and versions of stories from late folk sources have been cited and discussed, but the lore of Fionn and the Fianna was so rich and varied in oral tradition that it is necessary to deal with it in more detail. Throughout the Gaelic world old stories combined with new ideas to keep the cycle alive and of interest in the mouths and minds of people who had little opportunity and perhaps less inclination to consult written sources. Yet the literature was usually in the background, and it was always relevant.

From mediaeval times, despite the difficulties, a thriving manuscript tradition was maintained, and literate men were accustomed to read aloud both tales and lays to eager listeners. We have references from Ireland, Scotland, and the Isle of Man which suggest that Fianna literature was very popular in such readings from at least the seventeenth century.[1] The narratives heard in this way mingled in the folk mind with older stories and with imagery which had been in circulation since the Middle Ages and earlier. So the corpus of lore concerning Fionn and the Fianna which has been collected from unlettered story-tellers during the last two hundred years is the result of this process of revitalising old tradition.

Fionn's Life in Folklore

The earliest and also the best-known story which has survived in oral tradition is the Boyhood-Deeds of Fionn. We have discussed this in chapters 3 and 4 and have concluded that, although its genesis was as far back as the ninth century, it did not gain folk currency outside of Leinster until a few hundred years later. The transmission of the story is striking, for – since it was established in popular lore – it seems to have thrived and spread for over five centuries without any help from literature.

We have also argued that some of the motifs which are found in oral versions, though lacking in the only full literary text (that of the twelfth century), did in fact belong to the story in mediaeval times. These include the danger from his maternal grandfather to Fionn, the hiding of him as a baby in a tree-trunk, his flight through the forests with the nurse on his shoulders, and the killing by him of the one-eyed seer after tasting the salmon of knowledge. But, as one might expect, some details have been added through parallels being drawn with, and through confusion with, other stories known to the folk. Thus in the adventure between Fionn and the old seer, folklore tellings[2] presume that the encounter took place, not on the Boyne, but at the falls of Assaroe [*Eas Ruadh*]. This is due to an identification of the salmon of the Boyne with the salmon of Assaroe (in Co. Donegal), which was celebrated as a surviving antediluvian creature possessing a great knowledge of history.

The confusion had apparently occurred before the story of Fionn's youth spread to Scotland, for Assaroe is the stated venue in that country as well as in Ireland. Munster versions have a peculiar late development in this nomenclature, calling Fionn's foe the *Gruagach Leathchaoch Rua* [red-haired half-blind wizard/warrior]. The epithets arise from a mishearing by some southerner of the salmon's designation *Bradán Easa Rua*. *Leathchaoch* was taken as a tolerable phonemic substitute for *Easa*, especially since it describes the traditional one-eyed image of the character; and since only *Rua* remained to be explained he was taken to be red-haired.

Scottish versions have Fionn directly attacking and slaying the hostile warrior-seer when he realises, through tasting the salmon, that this was the man who killed his father Cumhall. This, we have argued, reflects the original form of the story (p. 60). In Irish folklore, however, the account has been developed into a new form by the influence of the Greek myth of Polyphemus. This is no doubt due to the image of a one-eyed foe common to both stories. And so Fionn is said to have blinded the one-eyed seer, now portrayed as a giant, by ramming the cooking-spit into his eye. The giant fumbled about, trying to catch hold of his tormentor, and he called out to his ring – which he had earlier placed on Fionn's finger – to tell where it was. The ring answered, but Fionn cleverly cut off his own finger and threw it away, thus deceiving the seer. Seizing his opportunity, Fionn attacked the misguided seer with a hatchet and beheaded him.

There can be little doubt but that the influence came directly from classical literature, for the blinded Polyphemus is there said to have sent his ram after the hero Odysseus with the words,

'If only you could sympathise and get the power of speech to say where he is skulking from my rage!'[3]

The speaking ring on Fionn's finger was probably suggested by the motif of the thumb of knowledge, and the killing of the foe with a hatchet while he was off his guard is a reflex from the manner in which Fionn's nurse tricked and killed the man who made a hollow for them in a tree-trunk (pp. 98ff); It is difficult to put a date to the influence of Polyphemus, but the sixteenth or seventeenth century seems likely.

In both Ireland and Scotland there is a tendency to assimilate Fionn's tyrant grandfather, from whom he has to be spirited away as a baby, to the biblical king Herod. We are often told that the grandfather ordered the slaughter of all baby-boys so as to ensure Fionn's annihilation and so avoid the prophecy that he would be displaced by his grandson. The borrowing of this motif is likely to have occurred independently in different versions of the story, for people would have been well acquainted with the New Testament account of Herod and could hardly have failed to notice the parallel. Several other incidental additions are found in various folk versions, mostly due to a confusion of the imagery, nomenclature, and motifs within the lore itself.

In Scotland, for instance, Fionn's nurse is often called Luas Lurgan [speed of ankles] an account of her great running. This is an echo from the name of Leargan Luath, a great male runner of the Fianna in the mediaeval literature. Again, in one Scottish version, after tasting the salmon Fionn asks his newly-discovered foe to describe the death of his father Cumhall, and is told that 'he roared like a calf and broke wind like a gelding when my spear went through his back'. This recalls the vindictive talk of Garadh mac Morna to Fionn (p. 144), but the phraseology derives from *Cath Chrionna*, a non-Fianna tale in traditional manuscripts.[4]

Some details from the twelfth-century Boyhood-Deeds, which are not preserved by Irish folklore, appear in a somewhat altered setting in Scottish oral versions. The spear made by the Munster smith whose daughter Fionn loved appears in these as a sword made for him by an Ulster smith with whom Fionn's mother resided. The sword was to be tempered in the blood of the first living being which entered the smithy after its manufacture, and accordingly Fionn's mother put a little dog through the door. This sword was called *Mac a' Luin*, a factor which shows that the influence of the Lay of Keshcorran (p. 206) has intervened. Alternately, both Irish and Scottish versions tell that Fionn recovered the sword of Cumhall by slaying his father's killer in the salmon episode.

This is a confused rendering of the crane-bag episode in the Boyhood-Deeds and in the lays, according to which Fionn regained that treasure of Cumhall by slaying the Liath Luachra (p. 90f). The Boyhood-Deeds account also relates how the young Fionn found the remnants of his father's Fianna hiding away in the wilderness in Connacht, but since that text lacks an ending we do not know how the author squared this with the Colloquy story of how Fionn inherited his father's position as head of the Fianna at Tara. There seem, in fact, to have been variant mediaeval strands of tradition – the Boyhood-Deeds author taking a martial perspective, and other texts (such as the Almhu poem and the Colloquy) taking a mythological one.

Scottish lore accords with the martial perspective, telling of how Fionn found the remnants of his father's force hiding in caves by the sea-shore, all overgrown with hair and beard so that Fionn had to shave them with his sword. Realising who he was, the downhearted warriors raised a loud cheer, declaring that 'the prophecy has come true!' Fionn brought with him a magical bag containing apples and pins, which his mother had given him. None of the Fianna could lift this bag, but Fionn could carry it on his little finger.[5] This is of course the crane-bag, in a much altered but still distinguishable form.

The folklore of Ireland has better preserved the episode of how Fionn saved Tara from the burner at Halloween. The location of Tara and the time of Halloween are rarely specified, and in many versions the action of the hostile being is to knock down a fortress rather than to burn it. The fortress was newly-built for the umpteenth time by the exasperated Fianna, the hostile being having repeatedly destroyed their work. The identity of this being varies. It may be a hag, a spirit, a fierce bull, or even a grandparent of Fionn who does this in order to give him the opportunity of proving himself to the Fianna. The one constant factor is that Fionn always triumphs over it, either killing it or driving it off, and then is declared leader of the Fianna.[6]

In Scotland, there is little regarding this 'mythological' way for Fionn to gain social power, and what traces there are we find subordinated to the 'martial' perspective. One Scottish example illustrates this well by simplifying the fire-motif and relating it directly to Fionn's contest for the treasure-bag. None of the Morna clan, we are told, could lift that bag, and Goll broke three of his ribs in the effort. Then Fionn took it on the point of a twig. The palace (called in fact, *Teamhair* [Tara]) then took fire, whereupon Fionn took three pins out of the bag and placed a pin at each end of the palace and one in the centre. The fire was thereby magically extinguished.[7]

Concerning the death of Fionn very little has survived in the folk memory, but what does can be taken to come from literary sources of one kind or other. We have discussed in chapter 4 the mediaeval ideas of how he died, and later literary accounts follow the same pattern. The third Colloquy, for instance, states that 'Fionn was drowned by his leap in old age, which was a leap of foolishness';[8] and the description in *Feis Tighe Chonáin* of how he was put under injunctions on pain of death by a woman to jump over a rock and back each year (pp. 116f) is a by-product of the same idea. A related story in *Feis Tighe Chonáin* has him jumping over a chasm in order to win a woman's love (p. 116), and this has proved to be very popular in Irish folklore. Versions of it – sometimes localised but apparently all derived from the literary text – have been collected from counties as far apart as Donegal, Sligo, Mayo, Galway, Clare, Kerry, Cork, Waterford, and Kilkenny.[9] The prominence of this story has probably erased the account of Fionn's drowning in latter centuries by assimilating it and removing the tragic element.

This process is exemplified by a nineteenth-century report from Waterford, which tells of how Fionn was wont to give a mighty leap forwards and backwards every May morning across the glen of the river Dalgan near Dungarvan. As he came to the glen to jump it on one occasion he met a red-haired woman, which was an ill omen, and as a result he fell into the glen on his backward leap and was killed.[10]

The Annals of the Kingdom of Ireland [*Annála Ríoghachta Éireann*], compiled in the early seventeenth century, give the more 'historical' account of Fionn's death adhered to by several early sources. In the year A.D. 283, these Annals tell us, 'Fionn grandson of Baoiscne fell by Aichlech son of Duibhriu, and by the sons of Uirghriu of the Luaighne of Temhair, at Áth Bréa on the Bóinn', and then the old quatrain concerning that event is quoted (see p. 108). The second line of the quatrain originally read *gan niach guin* and meant 'without a hero's wound', but this is an obscure phrase and the Annalist has altered it to *go ndiach guin* and he glosses it to mean 'by the fishing-gaffs he was wounded'.[11] A manuscript from the year 1765 elaborates this further by saying that Fionn was 'without anger or malice' in the Rath of Bregia by the Boyne when he was slain by Aichlech with gaffs and then beheaded.[12] Both sources state that he was avenged by Caoilte.

An account collected from the folklore of Perthshire in the late eighteenth century shows that oral tradition was in general accord with these literary portrayals. This states that Fionn went to court a lady of the Cuilgeadan clan in Glen Dochart, and he was challenged to make a great leap onto an island on Loch Iubhair. He succeeded, but when challenged to leap backwards he fell and was beheaded by a Cuilgeadan warrior called Taileuchd. The slayer was put to death by the twisting of his arms and legs, and Fionn was buried at Killin near the end of Loch Tay.

This is a good example of name-attraction, for Killin was, mistakenly, taken to be *Cill Fhinn* [the Cemetery of Fionn] and therefore was referred to our hero.[13]

Fionn and His World

Folk tradition has no definite sense of chronology, and so the fitting of different characters and adventures into the over-all framework, which sometimes disrupted the texts of literary writers, presents no problem here. The oral story-tellers knew many different narratives concerning Fionn, and they valued and relayed these as individual items worthy of memorisation and entertaining to audiences. Fionn had become so much a figure of story, even of free imagination, that the troublesome business of setting him in an ordinary existential context was irrelevant. Drama was what made him attractive – drama internalised in his personality and externalised in his adventures. The same can be said, in varying degrees, of the other characters in the cycle.

One subject which had an obvious fascination for the folk mind was Fionn's relations with women. We have discussed in chapter 3 the ancient lore concerning the conception and youth of Oisín and have pointed out that it retained its popularity in oral lore down through the ages. The folk generally held that Fionn's wife – usually unnamed – was turned into a deer by a rival or foe and that in this form she gave birth to the hero's son, Oisín, as a human baby. Fionn was hunting some years later and his hounds were enticed by this enchanted deer to a lonely spot where he found his son.

Whereas in Ireland the plot itself was regarded as being sufficiently dramatic, Scottish story-tellers saw the potential for development and added more detail. When Oisín was born in the wilderness, they said, his deer-mother began to lick a corner of his brow and the deer's hair [*colg an fhéidh*] grew there. She then stopped licking him, so as to ensure that he would grow up a man rather than a deer. A folk etymology was used to support this, namely, *Oisein* which means 'corner'.[14]

The imagery here is reminiscent of Diarmaid's celebrated love-spot on his forehead. We have argued (p. 175) that this marking on Diarmaid derives from the lore of love-magic, and this magic often involved attempts at transferring the strength of emotion involved in maternal animal love into the context of human sexual love.[15] It is therefore reasonable to assume that speculation regarding Diarmaid's magical attractiveness lies at the basis of this episode of Oisín being licked by his deer-mother.

A further motif in the same vein was current in Scottish lore. This had the young Oisín going hunting with the Fianna and being separated from them by a magic mist. In a lonely glen he met a hind who spoke to him and said that she was his mother. She brought him into an otherworld dwelling within a hill, where she regained human form and feasted him. Before he left he made a song – his first ever composition – warning her to be careful of the hunting-hounds of the Fianna. It is significant that the Colloquy also has Oisín visiting his mother in a *sí*-dwelling (p. 254), from which we can infer that she was not in deer-form. The Scottish lore states that she was in the form of a hind abroad and of a woman in the *sí*-dwelling, and it calls the enchantment put on her *fáth fíth*.[16] This is a corruption of *féth fiadha* [art of semblance] – variant forms *fé fiadh* and *fé fia* – which occurs repeatedly in the early literature as a cloak of invisibility which the Tuatha Dé Danann used to conceal themselves.

There are several instances of the motif in Fianna literature, but the reason for its occurrence here is that the word *fiadh*, as well as having the meaning of 'semblance' also designates a deer.[17] The encounter between the adolescent Oisín and his otherworld mother seems to belong to the early idea of Blái Derg, Fionn's mistress in cervine shape, and so the use of *féth fiadha* in the context could be very old.

Another account of the birth and upbringing of a son of Fionn does not appear to be so ancient. One version of this, from Kerry, tells of how a strange woman came to the Fianna from overseas and challenged Fionn to a game of chess. She won and demanded as prize that he marry her. He had no choice but to comply, and she became pregnant by him. She left Fionn before she gave birth, however, and Fionn drove his sword into a tree-stump and said:

'Call your son Faolán and never send him to me until he is able to draw the sword from this stump!'

She took the stump with her, and Faolán was born soon after. As he grew he was taunted by a playmate with not knowing who his father was, so he went to his mother and said:

'Who is my father? I will never stop nor stay till I find him!'

On being told his background, he drew the sword without delay and set out for Ireland. Reaching there, he saw the Fianna champions on the strand competing at throwing a heavy sledge-hammer. He knew Fionn from his mother's description and went to him.

'If you are a son of mine', said the Fianna leader, 'you are able to hurl this sledge!'

Diarmaid, who was present, protested that it was unfair to ask a mere boy to throw such a weight, but Faolán hurled it seven paces beyond the best man of them. Then Fionn accepted the youth, 'and his heart grew big at having such a son'.[18]

This is a version of an international story in epic, which has a warrior-father meeting his unknown son.[19] We have seen (pp. 49f) that the motif was used in the Fionn/Oisín context as early as the eighth century, but the account of the contest with the mother suggests that the source here is the mediaeval story of Cúchulainn and his son Conlaí, in which Cúchulainn first overcomes the lady in combat.[20]

This folklore story seems to have been confined to Munster, where recensions which differ widely in detail have been collected. One Clare telling calls the young hero Neart son of Fionn, but the usual format concerns Oscar son of Oisín.[21] The drawing of the sword in the above version obviously is an echo from Arthurian romance, but the Oscar versions follow the more standard plot with Oisín giving a sword to his lady and telling her to give that to her son as a token of recognition. Oscar's feat with the Fianna may be lifting a tree, winning a ball-game or some other such contest, always with the purpose of showing his worth.

All tellings contain accounts of miscellaneous quests and triumphs of the young warrior, but these are rather spontaneous additions to the narrative. A lengthy tradition of this Munster story of a son rediscovered by either Fionn or Oisín cannot be postulated. What actually happened is clear – a modernised text of the Cúchulainn/Conlaí story was common in sixteenth- to eighteenth-century manuscripts and, as a result, has been collected from the late Irish and Scottish folklore of many areas.[22] In Munster, this story was converted into the Fianna context – probably towards the end of the eighteenth century – but it never achieved a really stable form.

In some versions Oscar, on his arrival, has an altercation with Goll mac Morna, whose right to the marrow of the bones at a feast he disputes. This is adapted from a widespread Fianna tale, according to which Goll was allowed this privilege on account of his surpassing strength. The earliest version of this which we have is in a thirteenth-century lay.

According to it, Fionn held a great feast at Almhain and a young warrior called Caireall mac Conbhróin arrived during it. 'Every bone of a deer in which there was marrow was always given to Goll', but Caireall demanded this 'champion's portion' [*mír murra*]. Goll refused and, as the argument progressed, Fionn took the side of Caireall who was his kinsman, and when the old sore of the battle of Castleknock was reopened, the inevitable rift occured between Fionn and Goll which led to the tragic death of the latter (see p. 162).

The story has obviously been forced into Fianna chronology here, and there is every indication that in itself it was a borrowing into the cycle. Squabbles over a joint of meat called the 'champion's portion' [*curadh-mhír*] were a feature of the Ulster cycle, where they reflect ancient Celtic warrior conventions.[23] Several lays were composed in Scotland, basing their theme on that of the thirteenth century, and in these we are told that Goll slew Caireall in single combat as a result of the dispute.[24] But in the folk tradition there was a tendency in both Ireland and Scotland to substitute the better-known Oscar, champion of the Baoiscne clan, for Caireall; and Oscar settles the matter by defeating Goll in either a tug-of-war or a bout of wrestling.[25]

The reading of manuscripts is relevant also to the lore of Fionn's dealings with Cormac mac Airt and the wooing of that king's daughters. Although the versified account of Caoilte's straggling drove as found in the late mediaeval lay (p. 181) has not been collected from Scottish folklore, copies of that lay did have some influence on Irish story-telling, as is clear from various scraps of material from it which have been collected.[26] Regarding the question and answer session between Fionn and Ailbhe when he was wooing her (p. 236), a modernised and somewhat simplified version of this was current in manuscripts from the seventeenth century onwards. As a result, it has been collected almost word for word from nineteenth-century Scottish story-tellers in Barra and Argyll.[27] One fragment is widespread – the question 'what is swifter than the wind' with its answer 'the mind of a woman between two men'; but this was probably in existence independent of any written source. That the late manuscripts exerted an influence on Irish oral lore appears from a fragment collected in the Dingle Peninsula in Kerry. This refers to 'magical questions which Fionn put to his wife' and then gives a riddle not found in the manuscripts but which has been forced into service in this context.[28]

By far the most popular of Fionn's wooings was that concerning Gráinne. We have already argued that oral versions of the Diarmaid and Gráinne story contain some material which shows independent folk development (pp. 175f).

Definite oral recensions were circulating as early as the surviving prose-text, and this antiquity is probably reflected by the strong tendency throughout the Gaelic world to localise incidents from the pursuit of the young lovers by Fionn and his men.[29] It should be mentioned here that Scottish tradition had two extra vehicles for transmitting the story. One was a lay describing Diarmaid's death which was composed in the fifteenth century and attained wide popularity in folklore.[30] The other was the claim by the Campbells of Argyll to be related to Diarmaid, based on the occurrence in their genealogical tracts of a character called

Duibhne – which was the name also of Diarmaid's grandfather.[31]

Such a use of Fianna lore to bolster family history is almost unique, the only other known instance being that of the Dál gCais [O'Brien] sept some centuries earlier in Ireland, who claimed to have had an ancestor Cormac Cas who married a daughter of Fionn called Samhaoir.[32] The Campbells and O'Briens were ascendant septs with obscure backgrounds, and their use of the lore in their genealogies is in reality another admission that Fionn's Fianna were ahistorical.

The literature names many characters as belonging to the Fianna, but in practice – and this even more so in the folklore – only a limited number of individuals are important to the narrative. Oral tellers have found the marvellous helpers' theme very suitable for their purpose and, apart from the famous members of Fionn's company, such characters are usually the only other members of his retinue to play a part in the action. New individuals of this marvellous type are created in off-the-cuff manner to suit various adventures. Thus we have a Lúbán Léimfhada [supple fellow of the long leap] in a Cork story, while a Donegal tale has a certain Ioscadán Lom [bare-calved fellow] as a great runner.[33]

Regarding Fionn's accoutrements also, imagination combines with hints from the literature to ascribe a wondrous nature to them. Kerry lore tells us that he had a trumpet called the *Barra Bua* [bar of triumph], a blast from which 'could be heard at the four corners of the world' and which he used to call his men together and warn them of danger. An Argyll account calls this implement the *Gurra Fiodha* [wooden crier] and states that 'its sound would pass through the seven edges of the world'. Other accounts from the same area refer to Fionn's mallet [*Ord Fhinn*] which could be heard throughout all Ireland, and to his shield the screech of which had a similar range. A Kerry story refers to a knife which he had as a gift from the daughter of the king of the Underseas Land – 'if Fionn ate three meals without using it he would die.' This is an echo of the prohibitions theme, so popular in the literature. The same story tells us that 'Fionn had a mantle from the eastern world, and when spread it grew till it covered the Fianna entirely – not a man of them ever waked when it was over him'.

This motif comes from the late literary text of the Invitation of Maol Ó Manannáin (pp. 270ff), in which the otherworld lady had 'a mantle she had received from the son of the Scandinavian king, and all the Fianna together lay under it and all of them were dry and satisfied'. A Donegal source is apparently under the influence of the literary story of the three Norse princes (p. 186) when it attributes a wondrous purse to Fionn, one which 'when he shook it seven fills of gold would fall out of it each time'.[34]

A Mayo storyteller stated that, after Fionn lost Gráinne to Diarmaid, he was destined never to marry again until he slept for three days and nights in the skin of a certain fox which resided in the north. This fox emerged from its lair only once in every seven years and coursed around Ireland at great speed before returning to it again.

A pygmy-sized magical helper called Grabaire [grabber] came to Fionn and chased this fox. Just as it re-entered its lair, he caught it by the tail. He killed and skinned it, and Fionn was put sleeping in its skin for the required period, after which he got a woman without difficulty.[35] This story is a distant echo of Caoilte's straggling drove to Tara in order to win Gráinne, daughter of King Cormac, for Fionn (p. 180). The image of Fionn covered by the fox-pelt probably derives from the passage in *Feis Tighe Chonáin* which has him wooing and winning a lady while dressed in skins (p. 116).

Some oral portrayals can be quite at odds with tradition. One Kerry storyteller, for instance, felt free to say that 'Fionn made a law that if any of his men were not at home by ten o'clock at night he would have to remain out until morning,' and he did this because 'they used to be womanising and all that sort of thing'.[36] This is an extreme example of the regimental perspective, which had always been overshadowed by the independence of the *fianna* ethos. It also attributes a rather puritanical attitude to Fionn which is not consistent with his traditional personality. The clock-timing, of course, is an anachronism, though not as blatantly so as with a Sutherland storyteller, who had Fionn being summoned to an overseas quest by a telegram![37]

Adventures in Folklore

Many of the romances and lays which we have discussed in previous chapters passed into oral tradition through being read out. Apart from the story of Diarmaid and Gráinne, the most popular of the romances was that of the Quicken Mansion [*Bruidhean Chaorthainn*]. Folk tellings of this have been collected from different parts of Ireland and western Scotland in the past two centuries,[38] most of them following closely the original plot. Fionn's ungrateful enemy Míodhach, however, in some versions from both countries has his image influenced by the magical helper image. So he performs impossible tasks for Fionn, but only in order to more effectively entice him and the Fianna into the trap. When they are stuck to the ground in the sinister mansion, Fionn summons assistance in the original text by having his men strike up the hum called the *dord Fiann*, but oral tellings visualise this as a blow on Fionn's whistle or trumpet. The only other noticeable departure from the original is the addition in Irish tellings of the sheepskin graft to Conán's back. Regarding the sticking motif itself, this had such dramatic value that it became a floating convention in narratives of Fionn and his men, and it was used by story-tellers quite spontaneously in any story where it could raise the tempo (see pp. 262ff).

Of almost equal popularity was the story of the entrapment of Fionn and his men in the Mansion of Eochaidh [*Bruidhean Eochaidh*].[39] The plot in this text is more rambling, and so it is not surprising that there is a greater tendency to fold up the narrative and to omit events in a random fashion. The combat between Conán and the hag, and the combat between Bran and the fierce black hound, were well remembered by the story-tellers, but the episodes of differing hostile visitors to the trapped Fianna guests were less stable.

In the literary text the main Fianna force comes to the relief of their comrades as a result of being alerted by Fionn's mother, but the oral tellings tend to give the warning-function to a blow of Fionn's whistle or the shrieking of his shield. This mansion of Eochaidh was usually called 'the House of the Yellow Field' [*Tigh a' Bhlàir Bhuidhe*] in Scotland, where the story was especially popular.

The other great entrapment story of the manuscripts, *Bruidhean Chéise Corainn*, has been collected in but a few parts of Ireland, though elements from it have influenced other folk stories. Only in west Cork have fairly full tellings of it been recorded, and these seem to be separated from the manuscripts by no more than a few generations.[40]

The Battle of Ventry [*Cath Fionntrágha*] is a text which, with its high drama of an invasion by the King of the World, one would expect to exert a heavy influence on folk fancy. But versions of the story have, in fact, been collected only from Galway and Kerry, and all of these derive from late manuscripts of the fifteenth-century text.[41] The story was naturally in great demand in the Dingle Peninsula, where Ventry itself is situated, and folk tellings of it there gave rise to an extra derivative, that is that Fionn defeated an invasion force in that place, but the invaders were revived each night by a balsam-carrying hag. Only by staying up at night and discovering and killing that hag did young Oscar manage to bring matters to a conclusion.[42] This is an example of the motif of 'the Everlasting Fight' which was a trait of the mediaeval romance of western Europe and which was borrowed into the sixteenth-century non-Fianna text *Eachtra Chonaill Ghulban*.[43] From that text it spread in Irish folklore and was attracted to the Ventry context by the rambling description of a year-long battle in *Cath Fionntrágha.*

Another literary romance which has been collected several times in oral form in both Galway and Kerry is the Pursuit of Sadhbh [*Tóraigheacht Shaidhbhe*]. Since the plot of this is direct and logical these oral versions remain fairly true to the original.[44] The same can be said of the small number of tellings of the Iollann Iolchrothach story which have been recorded, all of which are very close to the manuscripts.[45] Neither the romance of the Difficult Servant nor that of the Grey-Cloaked Churl (pp. 228ff, 259ff), have featured much in oral tradition, despite their interesting plots and dramatic action. The probable reason for this is that they did not give a sufficiently central role to Fionn and his men.

The most popular lay was the seventeenth-century Hunt

of Slieve Gullion, which has Fionn's hair being turned grey when he dives into a lake to recover a ring for whom he thinks is an innocent lady. This story was known in folklore throughout Ireland.[46] The lay itself is based on much earlier tradition (see pp. 23, 80), but all surviving oral versions of the story seem to derive from it rather than from some older prototype. Other lays which have been popular in both Ireland and Scotland for a few centuries and have been copiously recorded in folklore are the Battle of the Sheaves, the Lay of the Black Hound, the Lay of Magnus, and the Lay of Dearg mac Droichil.[47]

A further lay, on a son of that Dearg called Conn, was composed in the north of Ireland in the seventeenth century. It described how Conn came to seek vengeance for his father's death and slew a great number of the Fianna, but was eventually slain in combat by Goll. This soon passed into folklore, and for some reason spread with unusual rapidity in Scotland.[48] Also current in Scotland and the north of Ireland were the lays concerning how Goll and his men had to leave Tara after fisticuffs broke out between the Morna and Baoiscne clans,[49] and how Garadh mac Morna burned the women of the Fianna. Scottish versions of the latter situate the episode at a certain House of Fearmalach [*Brugh Fearmalaich*] near Dunscaith in the Isle of Skye, and add a striking detail.

When Garadh was condemned to death, they say, he was allowed to select the mode of execution. He chose beheading and that he be allowed to rest his neck on Fionn's thigh. Seven hides and seven bundles of twigs were placed on Fionn's thigh to protect him, but Garadh's cunning plan worked. When his head was cut off by a blow of Fionn's sword 'Mac a' Luin', wielded by Oscar, the Fianna leader was severely wounded also. With arteries cut in his knee, Fionn was near to death and had to depart for Rome to find a cure. Hence the Scottish saying that 'the end of the Fianna was Fionn's going to Rome' [*deireadh na Feinne turus Fhinn dhol do'n Roimh*], for it was in Fionn's absence that the new high-king, Cairbre son of Cormac, provoked the Fianna into the final tragic battle of Gowra.[50]

Thus did Scottish folklore provide its own logical countdown to the final disaster, by connecting the story of Garadh's atrocity with the lay from about 1400 (p. 150) which had Fionn away on a pilgrimage when that battle took place. In Donegal versions of the lay Garadh's place as burner is taken by his brother Goll, and Goll's fatal clash with Fionn is thus directly precipitated. These Donegal versions, of course, identify the rock, Carraig Ghoill, on which Goll was slain with the islet of that name off Rosgill.[51]

Of the other lays, the most notable survivors in oral tradition were those concerning Fionn's imprisonment in Scandinavia (current in different parts of Ireland and Gaelic Scotland); that concerning how Caoilte got his name in the smithy at Keshcorran (Scotland, north of Ireland, Isle of Man); the Chase of Lough Derg (Ulster and Munster); and the Chase of Glenasmole (Connacht and Munster).[52] The chanting of Fianna lays has not died out in the west of Scotland even in our own time, and the various collections of lays made in the nineteenth century testify to the strength and variety which this aspect of Fianna lore enjoyed in that country.

Among the lays which were current in Scotland, but apparently were unknown in Ireland, was one which described how the Fianna in a sea-battle slew a fierce hag called the 'Muilgheartach', who came from Norway to take from Fionn a magical cup which he had. This was known as the *Corn Buadhach* [victorious cup] because it ensured triumph in battle to whosoever drank from it.[53]

As well as all those traditional stories, any amount of new story-patterns could be formed by combining different elements of the romances and the lays, as well as motifs from outside the Fianna lore, such as quests for particular items and fights with horrific creatures. New plots consisting of such pot-pourris, however, had little or no stability and were rarely transmitted beyond an individual story-teller. One general framework – unparalleled in the literature – which gained general currency, should be mentioned.

According to this Fionn plays a chess or card game with a hag. She wins and therefore has the right to impose injunctions [*geasa*] on him. She orders him to undertake various difficult tasks, which he carries out only with the assistance of comrades like Diarmaid and Goll, or alternately through the agency of his marvellous helpers. The details of the adventures vary according to the narrators' knowledge and choice of motifs, but usually they include a ferocious fight at 'the house of mercenaries' [*teach na n-amhas*]. After victory in this, Fionn returns home and he or one of his comrades kills the hag in combat.[54]

Folk Characterisation

The strong emphasis which was placed on the leading characters allowed for a varied, but fundamentally consistent, series of adventures to be developed concerning the Fianna. Oral narrative by its very nature answers directly to the question of transmission, and it can thus be expected to illustrate what are the aspects of these personalities which guarantee their appeal. We have noticed again and again that distinctive roles were assigned to the half-dozen or so leading members of the group by post-mediaeval literature. It is significant that folklore is at one with the literature in this, except that it gives clearer and more marked outline to these roles by making the characterisation wholly subservient to them. How true fresh portrayals could be to the whole pulse of the cycle is shown by the many coincidental returns to old imagery and even to old ideas.

An instance of this is the continuing tension between Fionn and the high-king Cormac, which from political motives in ancient times became a question of family squabbles in the mediaeval literature, and returned to the context of a power-struggle – though with a different slant – in later sources. The Battle of Ventry text, for example, has Cormac awaiting the opportunity to offset what he saw as in practice Fionn's control of the country. Texts of the sixteenth and seventeenth centuries give details. Fionn, they tell us, had large expanses of land in every region, almost exclusive hunting and fishing rights, the right to quarter his men on the country from November to May, a hound from each household, and even the first choice of the hand of every maiden for one of his troop.[55]

The folklore of the cycle goes even further, regarding Fionn the Fianna-king [*rí na Féinne*] as the person of paramount importance in his time and rarely mentioning Cormac at all. More than anything else, the cycle from start to finish stresses the great ability possessed by Fionn of gaining knowledge from his thumb. This was always a central image, always an essential narrative device. The formula in Irish folklore for how he used this ability was as follows:

> Fionn put his thumb under his tooth of knowledge, and he chewed it from the skin to the flesh, from the flesh to the bone, from the bone to the marrow, and from the marrow to the juice, and then he understood.

Scottish lore is less emphatic and is usually content with describing how he used to place a finger under his tooth of knowledge and chew it to a joint.

According to both literary and oral accounts, the Fianna were wont to ask their leader to discover some information of importance to them by using this ability of his, and not unexpectedly there was a tendency to rationalise it into a personality trait. Thus one Hebridean story-teller stated that 'Fionn was a patient worthy man, and they used always to take his counsel'.[56]

As we have seen again and again, it was endemic to the cycle to envisage the social life of the Fianna on the axis of personal attributes. But folklore goes furthest in this regard, and does not hesitate to make narratives from ideas which are mentioned but not exemplified in the literature. Thus, on the theme of Fionn's great generosity, a Mayo story-teller probes into the hero's personal attitudes and reactions:

> Nobody ever came to Fionn's door that he let away hungry or thirsty. He would divide his last bit with the poor.
>
> One day a beggar came to his door when the only bit he had was in his mouth. He couldn't with manners take it out of his mouth, and he was sorry and ashamed to have to refuse.
>
> So the greatest shame that Fionn felt was to have a bite of food in his mouth without being able to divide it.[57]

Munster and other Connacht variants of the saying have Fionn's greatest embarassment as 'something in his mouth and nothing in his hand!'[58]

The strength of Goll was celebrated throughout the Gaelic world, but particularly in the province of Connacht which claimed him. A Roscommon story-teller declared that 'great Goll was the strongest of all the Fianna', while a common Galway expression in referring to an unduly heavy task was 'even Goll mac Morna could not do it!'[59] Further afield too he gave rise to fascination. In Islay it was said that 'Goll was the strongest man that was in the Fiann-band, and he could eat seven stags at his dinner'.[60] A rather curious Donegal source relates a heroic youth-biography of him, somewhat on the lines of that of Fionn.

It tells of how three days after his birth Goll began to cry, and a wise old man revealed that seven women would be required to provide him with milk. After a year he tore the nipples of these nursemaids and had to be weaned. The wise old man then recommended that he be put in a cage and fed only meat. At the age of three he broke out of the cage and slew several youths at a hurling-match.

Hearing of this prodigious youth, Cumhall sent to Connacht for him, but the boy Goll killed the messenger. Then he went to France and subdued that country. Cumhall caught up with him in Spain, and they arranged to fight a great battle at home in Ireland. In this battle Goll had inferior forces, and when the fighting was joined Cumhall knocked out one of his eyes, but Goll drove his sword through Cumhall's helmet and cut him in halves.[61]

It is clear that one of the lays on the Battle of Castleknock (p. 144) is in the background, for the narrator remarks that Goll was 'telling this story to the son of Cumhall'. He further states that Goll told Fionn that he was conceived on that very day, 'for your father never saw a woman walking the dew of the morning but he wished to satisfy his heart with her!' Both Irish and Scottish sources stress this craze for women which supposedly affected Cumhall. 'Any woman on whom he set his eye had no way of escaping him' is the way a Mayo story-teller put it.[62] This is a stereotyping in folklore of the function which Cumhall fulfilled in the mediaeval tradition – that of the kidnapper of Muirne and thereby the begetter of Fionn against the wishes of her father.

'Fionn for knowledge, Goll for strength, Conán for prowess!' was a popular saying in Connacht regarding the material of Fianna narrative.[63]

The 'prowess' [*bua*] attributed to Conán Maol was his ability to kill hundreds by looking through his fingers at them (p. 240). Of all the Fianna characters, the portrayal of Conán underwent most change in the literature, and this change was brought further by oral lore. In the mediaeval texts he was a satiric and ruthless man, but the later romances have him as an ill-tempered buffoon. His baldness might have originally had implications that he was some kind of satirist (see pp. 87f), and not necessarily implied ugliness. His portrayal as either repulsive or dignified would thus depend on the attitude and purpose of the various mediaeval writers, and in fact as late as the fifteenth century we have him described in a Scottish poem as 'the noble blue-eyed man'.[64] But the romances and later lays give a totally different picture, describing him as a loutish fellow with bald pate and narrow legs.[65] Based on the food-episodes in the Quicken Mansion story and succeeding texts, he is portrayed as having a voracious appetite, so much so that an ordinary expression to denote great hunger is *goile Chonáin* [the appetite of Conán]. Again based on the descriptions in romance texts of rough treatment endured by him at the hands of hags and giant warriors, a severe beating was in Connacht called a *liúradh Chonáin* [beating of Conán].[66]

Known in the literature as 'Conán of the Curses' and 'the badly-spoken man of the Fiann-band', in folklore he is one who never spoke well and always spoke ill of others.[67] He was notoriously contentious and provocative. An Argyll account says of him that 'he never saw a man frown but he thought it his duty to strike him, nor saw a door open that he did not enter'.[68]

Since he was generally envisaged by the folk as a weak and awkward fellow, he provided contrast and comic relief within the Fianna *vis-à-vis* the deeds of the great champions. A Galway rhyme translates thus: 'Water falling into a lake is no heavier than Conán Maol throwing stones', and it was said that in combat even a woman could overcome him.[69] A curious tradition – obviously derived from the Samson account in the Bible – was current in Scotland concerning him, according to which he was absolutely weak because of his baldness. If his hair but grew, he would be enormously strong and would have been able to oppose single-handed a hundred men. The Fianna wisely kept him cropped [*maol*] for 'he was so cross that if the hair grew he would kill them all'.[70]

The cropping of his hair is clearly a substitution for his older image of baldness, and these Scottish accounts have developed on the basis of lore which survives in different parts of Ireland – the notion, already referred to, that Conán had destructive power in his glance if a certain ritual were followed, but the Fianna feared for their own safety and kept this a secret from him.

In the imagined debate between St Patrick and Oisín concerning the crisis of the Fianna in hell, Conán's impatience was naturally a focus of interest. Thus Scottish lore has him remarking bitterly concerning the devils, 'If I am in bad straits they are no better off!' His image in romance of tussling with hags was also projected onto the infernal context – as another Scottish expression has it: 'Blow for blow and scratch for scratch, as Conán said to the demons!'[71] A source from faraway south Kerry pictures things differently. Conán, according to it, took the place of the classical Charon and acted as ferryman on the flaming river to hell until he and the rest of the Fianna gained their freedom.[72]

We have already dealt with Oscar's great fighting skill, Diarmaid's handsome looks and 'love-spot', and Oisín's magical longevity, all of which themes were so suited to folk imagination and dramatic narrative as to be accepted as basic tenets of the Fianna cycle. A few words more need to be said, however, on one of the most persistently popular images in the whole tradition. That is, Caoilte as a stupendously fast runner. Scottish lore uses an optical illusion to express his speed. When running at full stretch he appeared as three individuals. One description puts this graphically:

> When Caoilte was at full speed, you might see three heads on him. His two shoulders would be rising aloft, as though

> they were two heads, and his head would be crouching down – he would be going, as it seems, half bent!

Some, however, maintained that the appearance of three was caused by the height to which he lifted his feet while running.[73] Attention, inevitably, was directed to his legs.

An Argyll account has it that when hunting the Fianna used to bind his knees so that, when he was forced to walk with this awkward gait, they could keep pace with him.[74] The early mediaeval literature, as we have seen, called him 'Caoilte foot-swift' (p. 178), and a description from the folklore of Roscommon in Ireland reverts to the same type of imagery. Calling him 'Caoilte of the Long Legs' it states that he had 'the wild blood of the magical hares in him' and that he travelled like lightning.[75]

A story collected from west Galway shows the debris of ancient narratives being reassembled into a new unit in a way which is typical of Fianna tradition:

> There was a king in Ireland long ago, and he wished to have the sand from each shore brought to him every morning – from north, south, east, and west. He would know by examining the sand if any foe had landed in the country during the night. Three men applied for the job as his messenger.
>
> 'How long would it take you to collect the sands?' said the king to the first man.
>
> 'While the leaf is falling from a tree!' said the man.
>
> 'Oh, you would not be fast enough', said the king.
>
> The second man said he would collect the sands as fast as a cat slipping between two houses.
>
> 'Not fast enough', said the king. The third man was Caoilte. 'How long would it take you?' the king asked.
>
> 'As long as it takes a woman to change her mind!' said Caoilte.
>
> 'Did you set out yet?' asked the king.
>
> 'I returned just now!' said Caoilte.[76]

There are many echoes here from the mediaeval literature. The defence of Irish strands is from the Battle of Ventry, the king's ability to detect the smell of a person from a substance is from the poem of Caoilte's reaving (p. 181), Caoilte's performing of a seemingly impossible task for the king is from the poem of the straggling drove (pp. 179ff), picturesque images of Caoilte's speed, similar to those above, are found in the Colloquy (p. 182), and the speed of woman's thought is from Fionn's riddle-contest with Ailbhe.

These are some of the elements which belong to, as it were, the metastructure of Fianna tradition. With this storyteller they are joined together within the framework of a plot which was common in humorous anecdotes outside of the Fianna cycle.[77] In such ways did Fianna lore keep its basic aspects, ever hungry for new formulae to give them life.

The Wondrous Realm

The continuing popularity of the lore, despite its antique setting, might seem something of a puzzle, even when the very conservative nature of Gaelic tradition is borne in mind. How could warriors whose lives and actions belonged totally to the ancient world be of such great interest to a folk living in recent centuries?

We have several times referred to the entertaining nature of the narratives and to how the leading personalities were dramatised, and these must have been major contributing factors to the survival of the Fianna in song and story. But there was another factor of importance. The tendency to historicise Fionn in early Leinster tradition was aborted but left behind it in mediaeval lore a cultural reflex which suggested that Fionn had in some way really existed. As the lore spread so too did this attitude towards the Fianna hero and his troop, and the natural association of real fianna bands with aspects of the landscape was developed in the new and specific context.

So this semi-historical or pseudo-historical cycle, rich in symbolism, took on the fanciful function of myth. Yet the cycle never became a full myth, for in post-mediaeval times there was no immediate cultural referential, and the popular imagination was cultivated rather than restrained by the scope of the imagery. The many conflicting portrayals of Fionn's troop, which nevertheless always remained the same identifiable Fianna, demonstrates this. And late folklore, as the penultimate expression of the whole tradition, provides specimens of the various tendencies in their full fruition. The folk attitude to the Fianna is that their realm was full of fanciful things, and thus fascinating to the mind, precisely because they belonged to the ancient world. Their lives and their actions were not hedged about by the ordinary rules of this world because they were primal. Living outside, and therefore before, the cruel experience of genuine history, their life style was free and governed only by the interplay of personality.

Given this state of affairs, there would naturally be a strong inclination to view the primal world as an ideal one. This in folklore applied to the very climate itself. We have seen (p. 141) that there was an old idea that Fionn and his men divided the year into two halves – one for hunting and the other for feats of arms. A different emphasis is found in the common folk saw: 'A foggy winter, a frosty spring, a variable summer, and a sunny autumn is what the Fianna desired'. This refers to an agricultural rather than an heroic life style and shows the folk inserting their own perspective into the lore. A Donegal folk-verse has Oisín telling St Patrick that the wind used to blow from the east in the spring, from the south in summer, from the west in autumn, and from the north in winter. The first of these winds dried the ground for the Fianna, the second made the crops grow, the third made the crops ripe, and they cared not what the fourth did. This, of course, is the most suitable climate for a peasant society.[78]

Other details from the folklore of the Fianna reflect the social values of its transmitters. For example, the ideal of self-sufficiency is encapsuled in the Irish dictum: 'The greatest shame that ever came on Fionn, a glass in his hand but nothing to put in it!' The ideal of co-operation is expressed in a Scottish phrase to the effect that 'Fionn never abandoned a friend who stood at his right hand!' Magnanimity is encouraged by another Scottish phrase which has it that 'Fionn never fought a battle without offering terms'; but conversely the ideal of success in worldly affairs is expressed rather bluntly in the Ulster quatrain:

> Four things to which Fionn gave his hatred –
> A lean hound and a slow steed,
> A leader of a country without shrewdness,
> And a man's wife who bears no children!'[79]

Whatever points of contact which could be deciphered between Fionn's world and that of the ordinary countryman were treasured and amplified in folklore. The literature and the inherited stories, for instance, placed great emphasis on the hounds of the Fianna. Thus Fionn was believed to have been a man with a fine eye for dogs. A Scottish maxim tells of how he selected a hound:

> An eye like a sloe, an ear like a leaf, a chest like a horse, a hock like a sickle, and the pith-joint a good distance from the head.[80]

Southwards in Cork, a story-teller attributed twelve hounds to Fionn and gave their names as 'Morning, Dawn, Leash, Tracker, Panter, Greedy, Servant, Caller, Big Fellow, Flayer, Fanged Fellow, and Bran which never failed'.[81] Other Cork sources are even more imaginative, furnishing us with the names of a dozen cats which Fionn is claimed to have had: 'Slender Cat, Old Cat, Fierce Cat, Excellent Cat, Fat Cat, Morbid Cat, Striped Cat, Black Cat, Grey Cat, Wild Cat, Yearling Kitten, and Malingerer.'[82] The Fianna leader, in such accounts, is well on the way to being a mythic patron of domestic animals, even if there is a strong tinge of humour.

It seems that Fionn could be made to play a primal role in ordinary human affairs also. Another Cork source gives a weary objection to over-work as 'Fionn told me to sit down!', while a Kerry source cautions against chill by saying 'Fionn used not to go out on an autumn night'. According to a widespread Irish expression, 'due to frost at the beginning of night Fionn sold his shoes'. This frost was taken to portend rain, which militated against farm-work and meant that shoes would not be required for its duration. A Scottish quatrain attributes further weather-wisdom to him, saying that a red sky at evening would cause him to rise early next morning, but a red sky at morning would cause him to sleep on.[83] There were even ideas that Fionn left his mark on the physical environment. For instance, it was said in Munster that Fionn, reduced once by extreme penury to beachcombing for food, put a curse on limpets, and that this is why they are black ever since.[84]

The Fianna troop was also a fertile subject for fancy. As we have seen from literary examples in chapter 4, there were numerous ways in which the organisation of the troop was envisaged. The stereotyped phrase *seacht gcatha na Féinne* from the literature meant that oral sources throughout the Gaelic world envisaged the troop as consisting of seven battalions. But there was room for much elaboration on this, and folklore was more than capable of absorbing ideas. The association of Fionn's men with enumeration attracted a widespread international puzzle to the context. This, known in Latin as *Ludus Sancti Petri*, posed the question 'how can fifteen black and fifteen white counters be arranged in a circle so that all the black ones can be thrown out by counting out every ninth counter around the circle?'

The puzzle, in various parts of Europe, belongs to an anecdotal context with the different colours personalised as different population groups – usually as Christians and unbelievers.[85] There is a four-stanza poem, entitled *Goid Fhinn agus Dubháin* [the Thieving of Fionn and Dubhán], which attributes the achievement of this to our hero. The poem is found in manuscripts from the eighteenth century onwards and was also part of common Gaelic folklore in Ireland and western Scotland. It is obvious that the personalised counter 'fair-haired' [*Fionn*] and 'dark-haired' [*Dubhán*] gave rise to the association of the puzzle with the Fianna context. Most folk recensions follow the standard international pattern, situating the two companies on board a ship which runs into difficulties and has to shed half its crew. However, a more apt Fianna setting has developed in Ulster and in parts of Scotland, according to which Fionn with fifteen of his men pays a visit to the house of Dubhán, who also has fifteen men. A quarrel arises and Fionn gets permission from Dubhán to expel every ninth man from the house. In this way he gets rid of all of Dubhán's men, and his own company have the feast to themselves.

The stanzas in the manuscript text, which was probably

composed in the sixteenth century and on which the folk versions are based, go as follows in translation:

> Four fair-haired Fiann-warriors first –
> though great be the joy of their adventures –
> and five men from the fortress along with them
> of the true counsellors of Dubhán!
>
> Two from the son of generous Cumhall,
> and a man from smooth-countenanced Dubhán,
> three from Fionn – though hard the judgement –
> and a man from proud Dubhán!
>
> Fionn sat in the white mansion,
> with two dark men on his right hand,
> with their two other Fiann-warriors
> of the household of Fionn of Almhain!
>
> Two from the fortress with dear Dubhán,
> and a man from Fionn against them,
> two from the dark warrior whose hand was not weak,
> two from Fionn, and a man from Dubhán![86]

Inspired by this very difficult mathematical puzzle, Connacht lore has developed counting-games based on supposed enumerating systems of the Fianna troop itself. One Galway source says of their stronghold at Crumlin that there were twelve houses there, with twelve fires in each house, and a hundred and four Fianna at each hearth. This amounts to 14,976 men in all. Another version is similar, but puts a hundred and one at each hearth.

These numbers are incredible enough, but they do not compete in extravagance with another Galway riddle. According to this 'Fionn had a hundred and one houses, with a hundred and one fires in each house, and a hundred and one men at each hearth' – that is, 1,030,301 warriors, surely a little too much for an Iron Age chief – even a fantastic one like Fionn. Another type of counting-game was popular with children in both Galway and Mayo, according to which Fionn was said to have had twelve sons, and by a trick each son was represented by one of the ten fingers.[87]

A different kind of mathematical speculation is involved in

an account from South Uist which describes how the Fianna-group was first set up. The king of Ireland, we are told, was tormented by Norse depredations and he sought advice from his counsellor. The counsellor urged a long-time strategy as follows:

> Marry the hundred biggest men and women in Ireland to each other, marry the second race to each other again, and let the third generation go to face the Norse!

This was done, and the third generation was the Fianna, with Cumhall as their leader.[88]

Incongruous and non-traditional as this account may be, it nevertheless stresses one idea which has played a prominent part in the cycle for a long time. This is that the Fianna had colossal strength. The idea is at least as old as the Colloquy, which has Caoilte and Oisín lifting great rocks and making superhuman spear casts.[89] The Colloquy in fact repeatedly states that the ancient heroes, Fianna and others, were of enormous size – the average envisaged having been about five times that of contemporary humans. Thus, when they first encountered Oisín and Caoilte, St Patrick and his followers are said to have been 'seized with dread and fear' before the big men, because – it is significantly stated – 'they were not of the same period and time as themselves'.[90]

The author of the Colloquy shared the prevalent antiquarian opinion that ancient peoples were very large in stature.[91] The immediate source which caused him to knit that opinion into his text appears to have been Patrician biography. A seventh-century Latin account of Patrick has the saint resuscitating a dead giant in order to baptise him, and this incident recurs in a late ninth-century account in Irish. Those present, we are told, were amazed at the massive size of the giant's grave.[92] This situation of awe is found several times in the Colloquy, which has huge mounds in different parts of the country being explained by Oisín and Caoilte as the graves of dead Fianna heroes and heroines.[93] And the inflation of Fianna dimensions suited another and more logical purpose, for it helped to explain the time lapse between the ancient days of heroism and the new days of religion. If the physical size could be maximised, the life-span of the heroes could be maximised accordingly.

So Oisín and Caoilte could be envisaged as bridging the great gap of five ordinary lifetimes between the third century (the period assigned by the chronologists to the Fianna) and the coming of Patrick in the fifth century. Fionn himself, the Colloquy claims, lived to an age of two hundred and thirty years,[94] and a little juggling with the dates was therefore sufficient to surmise that he had barely missed the saint.

These curious references in the Colloquy to the huge dimensions of the Fianna have echoes in later sources. For instance, some sixteenth-century Scottish writers in English make reference to them as giants. Hector Boece says that Fionn 'was of an enormous size, and a great hunter', while David Lyndsay describes a huge jawbone which he takes to have once belonged to one of Fionn's men. Comic lines attributed to William Dunbar have Goll wading through the ocean with the moon unable to rise above his knee.[95] The Irish historian Seathrún Céitinn, writing in the seventeenth century, found it necessary to rebut the notion that Fionn was a giant.

'It is plain', says Céitinn, 'that he was not of abnormal size as compared with his contemporaries.'[96]

In other words, there were certain tendencies to regard Fionn and his company as very big in size, but not outlandishly so and not to the extent that this coloured their dealings with fellow humans. Even the pseudo-learned idea in the Colloquy does not affect the general narratives in that text. The envisaging of the Fianna as big men, therefore, was limited to the context of antiquarian speculation and was irrelevant outside of that. Both literature and folklore, in fact, often portray the Fianna as dwarfed by huge opponents.

We have discussed the late mediaeval story which has Fionn, through the agency of his marvellous helpers, defeat and slay a giant and win back the babies and pups which the latter has stolen (pp. 188ff). This story was so widespread and popular throughout the Gaelic world that it encouraged many other contests between Fionn and giants. In these a fierce giant is overcome by Fionn, usually through smartness or trickery. The third Colloquy has a story of how our hero talked a huge spectre out of his aggressive intentions (see pp. 203f), and the number of incidental references from the fifteenth and sixteenth centuries indicates that lore of such contests was already current by then.[97]

One of the most popular tales in the folklore of Ireland concerns how a visiting giant in aggressive mood was bluffed by Fionn into departing without the single combat he sought. Fionn saw the giant approaching his house, and he jumped into the cradle in the kitchen. When the hero's wife explained to the giant that he was not at home, the visitor said that he would wait and started to play with the 'baby'. But the occupant of the cradle bit the visitor's finger off, and the agonised giant was informed by Fionn's wife that 'the children of the Fianna are born with teeth!' Fearing that the baby's father would be a horrific fighter, the giant beat a hasty retreat.[98]

This tale has a plot-structure which is borrowed from ordinary international lore of how ogres are overcome by quick human wit, and to judge by its provenance throughout the Gaelic world – there are variants from Scotland and the Isle of Man[99] – it must be part of Fionn lore for a few centuries. Additional motifs sometimes connected with it are how Fionn's wife broke the giant's teeth by giving him a cake to eat in which she had secreted the griddle, and telling him that the Fianna passed their time by flinging a huge boulder single-handed to and fro over the house without allowing it to touch the ground. The first of these is obviously an elaboration of the ruse that Fianna infants had teeth – thus the cakes eaten by the Fianna would be extremely hard! The second borrows its imagery from Fionn's great leaping over obstacles with a weight on his palms (p. 109, p. 116). The giant, of course, has the boulder fall on top of him as he races around the house to catch it, and nearly gets killed!

Leaving trickery aside, Fionn and his men could also compete with giants on their own terms. The point here is not that the Fianna champions were large in size, but that they – like the Greek Heracles – had colossal strength. A blessing from ordinary Mayo speech expresses the import of the lore when it wishes 'that every bone of your body be as strong as the bones of the Fianna!'[100] There are miscellaneous manifestations of this notion, the most usual being a contest between Fionn and a giant in which they each seize a horn of a bull which the giant was trying to steal. The unfortunate bull was torn asunder between them![101] On a similar note, an international folktale concerning a strong man is adapted to the personality of Oisín, so that he is said to have pulled up trees and used them to flail more corn in one day than any ordinary man could in twelve months.[102] In Wicklow it was said that Fionn made a cleft in a mountain near Glendalough with his sword, while a Kerry story has Diarmaid making a glen by digging up seven shovelfuls of earth.[103]

Exaggeration was always allowed some rein in Fianna lore, and since mediaeval times it has been made an integral part of the tradition. The Welsh poet Iolo Goch was jibing at it in the fourteenth century when, among the incongruous wonders of storytelling he referred to a great gust of wind carrying away the wife of Fionn mac Cumhaill [*dirvawr lynges i ddwyn gwraic Ffin vab Koel i drais*].[104] The tendency towards exaggeration was greatly fuelled by the stress on the marvellous helpers' theme, but other mechanisms were at work also. One was the age-old association of the Fianna with the landscape.

As early as the Colloquy we have reference to *Suidhe Finn* [Fionn's seat] as a name for an elevated spot, the idea being that the hero sat there while observing and directing the hunt. The place meant in the Colloquy was a hill-top west of Lough Arrow in Co. Sligo, but the designation spread rapidly – or perhaps had already spread – so that we find it applied to elevated spots in widely disparate areas. Usually anglicised as 'Seefin', it occurs in all four Irish provinces. In Munster, we have it on Slievenamon in Tipperary, in the Comeragh Mountains of Waterford, in the Nagle's Mountains in Cork, in the Ballyhoura mountains and on a hill near Pallasgreen in Limerick, as well as a mountain peak near Glenbeigh in Kerry. In Connacht, hill-tops have that name in the parishes of Athenry and Killogilleen in Galway, Crossboyne in Mayo, and the above-mentioned Sligo instance in Kilfree. In Ulster it is the name of hill-tops in the parishes of Knockbride in Cavan and Maghera in Derry; while Leinster has five locations which claim the designation. One, mentioned in the literature, was a hill-top near Newgrange in Meath, others are in north Co. Wicklow, at Fore in Westmeath and Birr in Offaly, and a fourth – quite appropriately, is the cairn on top of the hill of Allen [Fionn's own Almhain] in Kildare. Scotland, too, has several examples – including peaks called *Cathair Suidhe Finn* on the Isle of Skye and the Isle of Arran, and *Suidheachan Fhinn* in the Ross parish of Lochbroom.[105]

The fact that Fionn and his men were imagined in the context of such eminences combined with the antiquarian view of them as huge men, and so a humorous extravaganza was prompted. This became very strong in the later lore. An account from Argyll has St Patrick himself castigate Oisín for exaggeration. According to it, the saint used to put Oisín's descriptions of the Fianna into writing. When, however, he heard about the bone of a huge deer, in the marrow-hole of which the bone of an ordinary large deer could turn, he thought that all of the old warrior's stories were mere invention 'and in his indignation he threw the writings into the fire'.[106]

It was easy for the exaggeration to develop into farce in the mouths of story-tellers already too familiar with the plots and eager to give distinctive and stylised renderings. So the proportions of characters and events could be inflated, and the portrayals of Fionn and the Fianna could often be tinged with unreality and humour. A Galway story-teller, for instance, rhetorically described the mode of travel of the Fianna as follows:

> They covered acres, roods, and odd perches with a step; they put a hill and twenty behind them with a leap and a valley and ten with a skip![107]

And so the general trend of the later lore facilitated gross dimensions in the narrative.

The old strand of antiquarianism was taken up and developed so that large cairns, especially on high ground, in different parts of the Gaelic world were claimed by folklore to be graves of Fionn, Oisín, and Oscar. Alternately, making use of the similarity in imagery between the grave and a bed, such sites were often said to have been beds of the heroes.[108] The Colloquy itself describes the Fianna as raising three standing stones in order to place the bed of a sick man on them, and it also refers to a gravestone as 'the bed of Diarmaid'.[109]

Dolmens or cromlechs, that is prehistoric burial sites consisting of a large flat rock resting on two or more others, are found throughout Ireland and also in Scotland. The popular designation of such a structure is 'the Bed of Diarmaid and Gráinne', the fancy being that the young lovers slept on top of them in order to hide from Fionn or have a vantage point from which to fight off the foe if surprised.[110] The implication of associating huge landmarks in stone with the Fianna is that they were able to construct them due to their enormous strength.

It is not surprising, therefore, to find that folklore extended this imagery to various rock formations and imagined them as being used as items of furniture by these old heroes. For instance, large rocks on lofty eminences might be their tables. One picturesque version of this concerns a stone called 'Fionn's Table' [*Bord Fhinn*] on the above-mentioned peak of Seefin in the Comeragh Mountains of Waterford. Leeks growing around this stone were said to have been dropped by Fionn while eating. A ring of rounded flags – about nine yards in diameter – on top of Ballycarrigeen Hill near Baltinglass in Wicklow are called 'Fionn's Griddle Stones'. Fionn and his wife were said to have baked their bread on a large griddle placed on these stones. Near Killarney in Kerry Fionn made a rest for a punch bowl in a mountain by stamping his foot in the rock. In Scotland many rocky and rugged sites have been pointed out as once being occupied by houses belonging to the hero or his men.

There are many 'forts of the Fianna. [*caistealan na Féinne*] in Glen Lyon in Perthshire, but perhaps the most striking is the Fianna house-site [*làrach tigh nam Fiann*], eighty yards in diameter, on the island of Lismore. The big stones on which their cauldron rested are on the Isle of Skye near Scoirinish, while Fionn's oven is in Glen Dochart in Perth. An utterly farcical tradition from Cavan in Ireland states that Fionn lived in a house on top of Murmod hill near

Virginia, and to get water he used to stretch his ladle across two fields to a well which still bears his name.[111] In the same area, an alignment of five standing stones on a hill near Cavan town is known as 'Fionn's Fingers'.[112]

This identification of Fionn's very body with the landscape is the extreme in aetiological speculation. Much more in line with the ancient tradition is the frequent association of lonely caves with the Fianna in Scotland and to a lesser degree in Ireland.[113] There could well be a direct connection here with the mysterious caves which recur right through the mediaeval texts and – as we have argued – have their ultimate roots in Fionn's knowledge ritual. At any rate, the idea of the Fianna being trapped in otherworld dwellings, so popular in the romances, helped to attract a legend which began to spread throughout Europe at the end of the Middle Ages.

This concerned great political heroes who, after their death, were said to be sleeping with their armies in hidden caverns, bound by magic and unable to return to succour their people until certain conditions were fulfilled.[114] In Britain this legend was told particularly of King Arthur, and it seems obvious that some such version from southern Scotland was borrowed by the Highlanders, who replaced Arthur with Fionn. Thus Fionn is said to sleep with his men in a hidden cavern in, among other places, Tomnahiurich in Inverness, Glenorchy in Argyll, and Creag a' Ghobha on the Isle of Skye. The form of this legend of Fionn corresponds to later versions concerning Arthur – a man stumbles on the cave entrance, he half-wakens the sleepers by blowing a horn or making some clang, and he is scolded by Fionn for not making enough noise to rouse them fully.[115]

It is hardly feasible to regard the legend as being attached to Fionn earlier than, say, the sixteenth century. In Ireland, versions of the legend follow the usual international norm of having the sleeping hero a political figure from history. These versions originated in the fifteenth or sixteenth century with the Fitzgeralds of Desmond, and were told of heroes of that family and afterwards of the O'Neills and O'Donnells. One solitary telling from Leitrim naming the leader of the enchanted army as Fionn is definitely improvising his name because of the image of a great army of old.[116]

A common, but quite late, idea is that Fionn and his men were capable of hurling great boulders over large distances. Many rocks, such as 'Fionn's quoits' in the Comeragh Mountains, are said to have reached their present position by this means. Some are more spectacular than others. For example, a huge rock is pointed out on a mountain beside Carlingford Lough, in Louth, and Fionn is said to have thrown it there from a distance of three miles across the water when fighting against a Scottish giant. A similar fight resulted in Fionn scooping up a sod of earth in Ulster, thus giving rise to Lough Neagh. His cast, however, fell short, and the sod fell into the Irish Sea and became the Isle of Man! In Leinster also he helped to shape the landscape, flinging all the way from Glendalough in Wicklow as far as Dublin Bay a rock which became the island of Ireland's Eye.[117]

These late farcical stories are far removed from the integral tradition. Probably no older than recent centuries, they are based on the motif of boulder-throwing from ordinary giant-lore. But it is significant that even such a far-fetched motif could be made to relate back to the original context, in this case the geographical cradle of the cycle in central Leinster. For the folklore of that area claims that Fionn, when on the run from his foes in his youth, hurled a rock from the top of Slieve Bloom down to beside the Brosna river at Carrigalassa. There are no other rocks thereabouts, the distance of the throw having been about twelve miles across the landscape.[118] It is almost as if the basic strands of Fionn tradition were insisting on hauling the lore into line.

It is this repetitive quality which gives the cycle its unique blend of permanence and dynamism. An Argyll saying typifies it with its ready inflation of an abstract notion into concrete drama: 'If the Fianna were twenty-four hours without anyone mentioning them they would rise again!'[119]

10.

Conclusion

The Influence of Fionn

To traditional Gaelic poets and scholars, the lore of Fionn was a great resource on which they could draw for terms of reference in their work. Political and social leaders were lauded by comparing their prowess, generosity, and wisdom to the great Fianna chief whose name was a by-word for drama and colour and who had prophesied many things of import. But the lore of Fionn was not by any means perceived as a unified corpus. The fact that different levels of pseudo-history, literary ornamentation, and folk fancy existed within it was well-known to those with discerning minds, and particularly to the learned.

In 1633 the priest-historian Seathrún Céitinn argued against those who denied the historicity of Fionn, citing three things which he regarded as proof:

> We hear it from mouth to mouth that Fionn and the Fiann-troop existed, and there are numerous documents testifying to it, and furthermore antique remains are named after them.

In other words, Céitinn found the combined oral and literary accounts so compelling that he believed that their basic authenticity must be accepted. He did not hesitate, however, to reject the more romantic and phantastic of the stories, listing as 'poetical legends' written 'for amusement' such tales as the Battle of Ventry, the Quicken Mansion, and the Pursuit of the Difficult Servant. These were relatively recent texts in Céitinn's time, and we can see that for him antiquity meant authority. He found nothing untoward in viewing

Fionn as a leader of soldiers under the high-king Cormac mac Airt and accepted in good faith the general descriptions of the Fianna given in mediaeval texts.[1] In this he was in agreement with the general perspective on Fionn in which, as is usual with traditional thought, credulity increased in ratio to length of time.

Céitinn was generally dismissive of what English writers had to say concerning Irish history and culture, but it is interesting to note that such a writer two generations before him held similar views on this question. Richard Stanihurst in 1577 had stated:

> The Irish historians hammer manie fables in this forge of Finn mac Coile and his champions, as the French historie dooth of king Arthur and the knights of the round table, but doubtlesse the place seemeth to beare the shew of an ancient and famous monument.[2]

From around the same time, the anonymous author of the Book of Howth gave accurate descriptions in English of several stories of the Fianna, such as the burning of the women by Garadh mac Morna, the Battle of Gowra, the defeat of Dearg mac Droichil, the Battle of Ventry, and the conversation between Oisín and Patrick.[3] So it is clear that scholars of that time were evaluating the inherited literature as source material and that English as well as Irish writers were intent on being as accurate as possible in this area of their deliberations.

The Book of Howth also gives a version of the story of Fionn's adventures in Scandinavia (see p. 198), which account caused Meredith Hammer at the end of the sixteenth century to expound the theory that Fionn and his men were originally Danes and had come to Ireland as mercenaries. This theory, which was to resurface in scholarly circles three hundred years later, has no foundation. It is understandable why it should have vogue, however, given the proliferation of Norse invaders and invasions in late mediaeval texts which portray Fionn and his men as defenders of Ireland. This development itself was based on real memories of Norse attacks on the Gaelic world in the Middle Ages, and we have seen that the Fianna lore mirrors certain mutual influences of the two cultures, but the Irish cult of Fionn long predated Norse contact. Hanmer gives an unparalleled account of the hero's demise, namely, 'and the end of Fin Mac Coill was that he dyed a beggar and in great miserie'.[4] This is clearly erroneous, Fionn being confused with some other character of whom the writer had heard in Ireland.

Hanmer was no doubt at a disadvantage in a strange culture with a strange language. The same can be said of his contemporary William Camden who referred to 'the gyants Fin-Mac-Huyle, Osshin-Mac-Owim' and reported that the Irish people 'say through illusion that they often see them'.[5] The latter statement is unclear, but it seems to entail a notion that the Fianna lived on as some kind of spirits. This must be another misunderstanding. The only motif from the Fianna tradition which resembles it is that of the sleeping army (see p. 309), which we have argued was derived in Scotland from Arthurian lore and hardly existed at all in the Fianna context in Ireland.

Despite some inaccuracies, it is clear that these writers were not trying to expropriate the figure of Fionn or to place him in an untypical setting. The same cannot be said of the most famous writer on Fionn, the Scotsman James Macpherson who between 1760 and 1765 published texts which he claimed were translations of ancient Fianna tales. Fionn he called 'Fingal' – an incorrect designation which had been used in the fourteenth century by another Scottish writer in English, John Barbour.[6] Macpherson himself invented anglicised forms of other names, such as 'Ossian' for Oisín, 'Gaul' for Goll, and 'Co-Alt' for Caoilte; and introduced some characters and names not previously found in the tradition. He also combined several plots from genuine Fianna ballads in a hotch-potch manner, invented new narratives, and confused material from the Ulster cycle with the Fianna lore.

None of these transgressions affected the fortunes of Macpherson's flowery prose texts, which were translated into several other languages and had a sensational impact on the *belles lettres* and sophisticated tastes of his time. In England his admirers included Byron and Coleridge; in America Thomas Jefferson and James Fenimore Cooper; in Germany Klopstock, Herder, and even Goethe; in France

Rousseau and Saint-Simon; and a variety of writers as far afield as Scandinavia, Spain, and Russia. His work had a noted impact on music also, giving inspiration to composers such as Schubert, Mendelssohn, and Brahms. Even the political world succumbed to his influence. Napoleon was a devoted reader of the poems of Fingal and Ossian, and regarded them as embodying true heroic lifestyles which he himself attempted to emulate.[7] But Macpherson had his detractors too, some Irishmen and Scotsmen who knew how far removed from real Fianna lore his writings were.

He was particularly opposed by Samuel Johnson, the most influential figure on the English literary scene at the time. Johnson himself knew little or nothing of Gaelic tradition, but the bitter controversy with him damaged Macpherson's standing and cast serious doubts on his work. The suspicions were confirmed by the publication in 1805, nine years after his death, of a report of exhaustive investigations into the matter by the Highland Society of Scotland. Yet his influence lingered on, both among those who admired his literary style and some antiquarians who were reluctant to accept that they had been duped.

Apart from characters and plots, Macpherson's most striking divergence from the authentic tradition is in the sphere of feeling. Present-day critics can readily identify the atmosphere and imagery in Macpherson's work as belonging to the Romantic school of eighteenth-century literature rather than to ancient epic. Consciously wild and animated scenery alternates with brooding melancholy in a way which traditional Gaelic writers and story-tellers would find alien and unwarranted, and the wandering style would not long be tolerated in the proper realm of Fionn. But Macpherson had a rudimentary knowledge of Gaelic and was acquainted with a good number of the Fianna ballads, so it is not surprising that aspects of the genuine lore come through.[8] Ossian is represented as recounting the adventures of Fingal and his company, and the all-pervading gloom is an over-grown development from the actual sadness which the aged Oisín often expresses in the Gaelic sources.

Much has been said and written on these questions, but the real importance of Macpherson lies in a different direction, for – however inconsistent with Fianna tradition his work generally is – credit cannot be denied him for bringing Fionn [albeit a barely recognisable Fionn] into the mainstream of European culture for the first and only time in the long saga of this hero of the Gaelic world. The 'Ossianic' poems, and the attempts to refute them, were instrumental in bringing into being what we now know as Celtic studies. Macpherson's other achievement is less marked, but viewed from within the Fianna tradition equally significant – he transformed the figure of Fionn into a vehicle for conscious literary expression. The figure of Fingal personified the taste of eighteenth-century literati, being a hero overwhelmed by the massiveness of space and time but none the less noble and high-minded for that. Though lacking the very human and down-to-earth characteristics of the true Fionn, he was colourful in the special way that an idealised figure of Romantic literature can be.

While interest in the Fianna was being stimulated in Scotland by the Macpherson issue, the images of Fionn and his company were undergoing some different, and quite dissimilar, developments in Ireland. Translations of some Fianna literature from the seventeenth to the nineteenth centuries, such as those of Roderic O'Flaherty (into Latin), and Dermod O'Connor, Charlotte Brooke, and Theophilius O'Flanagan (into English) were faithful to their originals. They reinforced accounts which were current in manuscripts and oral lore and, by recalling a heroic age of yore, had a natural appeal in a time of badly buffeted national pride. A clear indication of this is how the revolutionary movement, the Irish Republican Brotherhood, adopted the name 'Fenians' in the year 1858. The man responsible for the naming was John O'Mahony, one of the movement's leaders who had translated Céitinn's history of Ireland into English.

'Fenian' was a neologism for Fiann, and had been in use since the antiquarian Sylvester O'Halloran had given the false etymology 'Fenius' for Fionn in 1772.[9] Another of O'Halloran's readers was Standish James O'Grady, who in 1892 published a novel entitled *Fionn and His Companions.* This was the first in a long series of adaptations of Fianna lore as reading material for the young, of which by far the most impressive and influential was the account given by Lady Gregory in her *Gods and Fighting Men* in 1904. In this, the author searched literary and folk anthologies and attempted to reconcile the various, and often contradictory, descriptions of Fionn and his company.

Another perspective had developed, however, according to which Fionn was a comical, even farcical, figure. We have discussed in chapter 9 how motifs concerning giants had, since the late Middle Ages, gradually come to influence the narratives and how, because comedy was inherent in such motifs, one type of portrayal of Fionn had him as a quick-witted trickster. We have also seen how continuous oral transmission had led to a degree of humorous exaggeration in the indigenous Gaelic tradition itself. So it can be said that great familiarity with the lore gave it a homely atmosphere and caused it to accommodate comic relief. Seizing on this trait, some writers in Ireland treated of the Fianna lore in a flippant, and sometimes caustic, manner.

In the nineteenth century, Caesar Otway, William Carleton, and Samuel Lover retold some of the humorous stories in such a way as to make Fionn himself sound ridiculous.[10] Since such tellings were widely read they had strong influence on popular taste in an Ireland which was quickly losing its native language and with it any appreciation of the complexity of Fionn. A combination of factors, therefore, caused our hero to be regarded in a farcical light, but it is important to stress that this is almost exclusive to the English language. In living Irish and Scottish Gaelic folklore Fionn remains essentially a character of adventure, and the indigenous humorous elements in no way detract from the high drama.

Some twentieth-century Irish writers have taken strong cognisance of the farcical tendency, the two most striking instances being James Joyce and Flann O'Brien. A good deal of discussion has taken place concerning the many allusions to Fionn in Joyce's exuberant and deliberately abstruse novel *Finnegans Wake*, and the hero's name is a fanciful element in the very title itself. Joyce inclined towards the theory that the tradition of Fionn had Norse origins,[11] and thus regarded him as an ideal symbol of the culture of Dublin city, with its mixed Norse-Gaelic background.

In the novel, there is much punning on the name Fionn, entailing many similar-sounding words in Irish, English, and other languages, and the purpose of the hero's repeated intrusions into the narrative seems to be to illustrate a backdrop within the consciousness of the burlesque contemporary Dubliner Tim Finnegan [Finn-again]. The absurdity which Joyce was aiming at had a strong mock-heroic sense, and to this end he used a variety of stylistic devices. For instance, he revelled in topographical allusions, and we have seen that emphasis on toponymics was a marked trait of Fianna lore. Thus Joyce, parodying Fionn's personifying function as well as the motif of the sleeping hero waiting to return, could have him as a giant interred under the sweep of Dublin city with his head at Howth and his feet at Castleknock.

Not only the geographical plane, but the historical also, is exploited. The wordplay on the names of Fionn's relations ['Cool', 'Tulka', 'Saar', 'Ocean', 'Oscar'] covers three generations and thus evokes the idea of heritage; while a riddle which entails a massive range of characters from human history is reduced to the simple answer 'Finn MacCool'. Joyce is jibing at the Fianna tradition itself as well as at tautology in the Dublin rhetoric of his time, but his very choice of Fionn pays tribute to the richness of imagery which attaches to the hero and makes him a suitable medium.

The contrast between past and present, and their ultimate convergence, is also the theme of O'Brien's use of Fionn in his novel *At Swim-Two-Birds* published in 1939, In this case also the title has connections with the hero, for a mediaeval text associates an adventure of Fionn with a place of that name [in Irish, *Snámh dá Éan* or *Druim Den* – p. 118]. O'Brien has Fionn as a lodger in a seedy Dublin hotel, who relates the great adventures of old to a group of lazy and impish students. This identification of the hero is absurd, and several aspects of Gaelic epic are caricatured through the person and conversation of O'Brien's Fionn. These include hyperbolic description of heroes and their deeds, mystical accounts of poets and seers, and the colourful nature poetry which was a much admired aspect of Fianna lore. Fionn is described with absolute farce as follows:

> Though not mentally robust, he was a man of superb physique and development. Each of his thighs was as thick as a horse's belly, narrowing to a calf as thick as the belly of a foal. Three fifties of fosterlings could engage with a handball against the wideness of his backside, which was large enough to halt the march of men through a mountain-pass.

This atavistic Fionn gradually fades out from the narrative, but we are left with the feeling that the author had a genuine fascination with Fianna lore.

O'Brien's real name was Brian Ó Nualláin, and he was also well-known as a writer in Irish and had a minute knowledge of Gaelic tradition. Though continually tilting at literary convention, he betrays a grudging respect for the multiformity of the old hero as opposed to the drabness and cynicism of modern society.

A time-honoured tradition of contradictory world-views existed within the lore itself, of course, in terms of the debate between Oisín and St Patrick. This caught the attention of latter-day creative writers almost as much as it attracted their counterparts of earlier ages. One of the first poems published by W. B. Yeats, entitled 'The Wanderings of Oisín', uses the setting to advance the author's opinions on art withstanding the rigours of time. Yeats was well aware of the reputations of both Oisín and Fionn as poets, and he has them embodying mystic wisdom as opposed to the regimentation and disguised worldliness which he attributes to Patrick.

An even stronger anti-clericalism is expressed in a novel called *The Return of the Hero* by Darrell Figgis which was published in 1923. Here Oisín, badgered by Patrick's censorious attitudes, puts an elaborate case for a spirituality which respects rather than penalises human nature. Fionn, the old pagan hero, is described as 'childlike and wise, happy and grave, simple and fearless in his welcome of all simple and fearless things, proud and wild and unashamed'. There is a depth and seriousness in this which differs from the humorous banter of the debate in traditional sources.

More in keeping with these latter is a neatly written poem

in Scottish Gaelic by Deorsa Caimbeal Hay in his collection *Fuaran Sleibh* (1947), with Oisín protesting against current sabbatarianism and teetotalling – for which Patrick is made the spokesman.

The section of Fianna tradition which has proved of most interest to creative writers in this century is far removed from either humour or ideology, but is nevertheless ideal raw material for psychological probing. This is the romance of Diarmaid and Gráinne, and how these two young lovers were pursued by the aging and jealous Fionn. This story has been the subject of many poems and plays, but only a few of them can be referred to here. Perhaps the most engrossing is the long poem in seven parts by Austin Clarke, first published in 1917.

Clarke, one of the leading Irish poets in the English language, often used material from older Gaelic literature and had a fine gift for reproducing the spirit of these sources in his work. When he wrote this poem he was a mere twenty-one years old, which makes it all the more surprising that he begins at a point when the lovers were married and in middle age and reconciled to Fionn. But the effect of this is to give full range to the psychological tussle which unfolds between the three central characters on the occasion of the tragic boar-hunt, and Clarke feels free to include the thoughts and conversations of several background characters not found in the pre-existing plot. Another innovation is the rich use made of colours to suggest the contending mentalities. Gráinne, for instance, is 'the golden, the beautiful', while Fionn is 'the druid-dark' [a rather untypical epithet for him], and Diarmaid's hunt of the boar is an entry into 'the forest's jaws when yonder sun is red'.

The movement of the poem is through reminiscences and premonitions, and there is no direct description of Diarmaid's death. In fact, it is hardly a narrative poem at all in that it presupposes a knowledge of the plot – which is given in a prose-preamble – but Clarke's interest is in the contrasts rather than the action. Particularly important is the contrast between youth and old age, a theme which recurs often in the general body of Clarke's poetry and which he had no doubt noticed as a general trait in Fianna lore. The general portrayal of the characters is typical of Clarke's archetypal framework. Gráinne is the voluptuous woman who forced Diarmaid to elope with her through the threat of 'ancient bonds'. Diarmaid is full of warrior-strength and honesty and cannot avoid his fate, while Fionn is the soured remains of a great man whose mind 'groped' after the fine physique of his lost youth.

A further treatment of the story is instanced by a three-act play in Irish from the year 1935 by the celebrated actor Micheál Mac Liammóir. This author uses motifs from the folk versions – including Diarmaid's love-spot – within the standard literary structure, but he follows Clarke in introducing some minor characters of his own invention who comment on the events and provide relief on stage from the main protagonists. A tendency towards melodrama and exotic language threatens the over-all movement but, as one might expect, Mac Liammóir intended the actors to carry the weight of presentation. He himself acted the part of Diarmaid in the first stage-production.

Great emphasis is placed on an artistic vision of freedom which the lovers have, and on the tension between this and Diarmaid's friendship and real affection for Fionn. There are some fine touches, such as the barely-disguised animosity of Fionn which penetrates through his insincere words of friendship, and the description of the boar which comes as a savage embodiment of fate out of the darkness and the unknown. A frightened plebeian who has seen the beast is made to remark:

> When I saw it first, standing between me and the sky without moving but putting its eyes through the moon which was rising out of the fog, I thought that a dark flame was circling around its head and a cloud of green smoke was rising up from the ground where it stood.

The dark side of the mind is rejected by John Redwood Anderson in his very long poem from the year 1950 entitled *The Pursuit of Diarmuid and Graunia*. The poem is in six parts, and in plot it follows closely that of the standard literary version from the fifteenth century, which Anderson knew in translation. Again, this poet concentrates on the psychology behind the events, but he is sympathetic to all three protagonists and presents Fionn's actions as the result of loneliness and desertion rather than malice.

The style, in free verse, is direct, sparing, and evocative, and we are treated to many fine vignettes as we move from episode to episode. One significant aspect of the poem is its tendency to give animation to natural elements – such as the weather and the landscape – as witnesses to the pre-destined events. This is, of course, a departure from the sources, but it recalls some features of Macpherson's work and shows that the latter's techniques could yield better results in more scrupulous hands.

Scrupulosity is hardly the word to describe a quite original version of the Diarmaid and Gráinne theme in another long poem, this by the prolific Eugene Watters in 1964. Watters, like O'Brien, was a creative writer in Irish as well as in English, and thus would have been particularly close to the lore in its distinctive form. Yet his handling of the material is probably the most externalised and intrepid of all.

Like Joyce and O'Brien, he takes Fionn out of the realm of past myth and forces him into that of present fiction. The poem is put in the mouth of Dermot [Diarmaid] who elopes to Donegal with a Dublin shop-girl called Grace [an anglicised version of Gráinne]. Fionn is again the aging man, but he is almost depersonalised and represents the agony of Ireland's past from which the young lovers try to escape into freedom. *The Weekend of Dermot and Grace* is a quite profound and philosophical poem but, even more so than in Clarke and Mac Liammóir, Fionn is rather a haunting presence than a fully fledged character.

No other individual Fianna story has attracted much interest among creative writers in the twentieth century. Lore from the cycle has generally been used only as background material, stray metaphors hinting at a crystallised world which can be made to shed light on some aspects of contemporary reality. The reason why it is thus chosen has generally been the same as ensured its survival down through the ages – the many and varied sets of contrasts contained within it which make it equally suitable for oral transmission and for artistic analysis. But the sense of contrast goes deeper than the level of motifs and images, reaching into the very function of the lore itself. Of all the cycles in Gaelic heroic tradition its sentiment is closest to popular taste, yet its world is totally at variance with the experienced reality of history. This contrast is essential, for the Fianna lore offered escape from the misery and drudgery endured by an oppressed people – an escape into a colourful world of the imagination where courage, generosity, and the virtues and passions of human nature had their proper focus. While the cycle contradicts the existing world it also typifies the human sentiments which exist within that world.

Watters in his poem has expressed this as 'the year half-blinded and the strenuous limbs between the two profundities'. The contemporary poet Eavan Boland touches a similar vein in a composition of hers which has the elopement of Diarmaid and Gráinne symbolise the whole complex of human relationships:

Listen. This is the noise of myth. It makes
the same sound as shadow. Can you hear it?
Daylight greys in the preceptories.
Her head begins to shine
pivoting the planets of a harsh nativity.
They were never mine. This is mine.
This sequence of evicted possibilities.
Displaced facts. Tricks of light. Reflections.
Invention. Legend. Myth. What you will.
The shifts and fluencies are infinite.

Fionn has never been in history, has been only by necessity in books, has cut a fine figure through words, and has always had his true realm in the mind, individualised, but also the common property of people for long enough to be remembered. The present writer has made his own humble contribution in lines of a poem which translate:

From this hill over across the expanse,
by a clump of trees, by land, by a stream,
the contoured face of Fionn mac Cumhaill of the hounds,
and the deer racing softly through the morning. . . .

Between a view so free
and my step of fatigue. . . .

Notes

CHAPTER 1 (pp. 3–26)

1. The sources are enumerated in Meyer (1910), xvi-xxxi; and Murphy (1953) lv-lxx, 441.
2. O'Brien, 22. See also Meyer (1910), xvii-xviii; Murphy (1953), lv.
3. O'Brien, 99. See also Murphy (1953), lv.
4. See T. F. O'Rahilly (1946), 159; Wagner (1970), 23.
5. RIA Dictionary, s.v. *finn*.
6. Foster; Nagy (1985), 236. See note 15 below.
7. Murphy (1953), lxxviii-lxxix.
8. Loc. cit.
9. Loc. cit.; MacCana (1970), 48-9.
10. Holder *3*, 349; Thevenot, 110-12.
11. Holder *3*, 342-3; Murphy (1953), lxxxii-lxxxiii; Schmidt, 295-6.
12. Holder *3*, 328-50. *Vindobōna*, ibid., 344-5.
13. See Dillon and Chadwick, 28-9.
14. Holder *1*, 477.
15. Pokorny, 1125-6.
16. Loc. cit. For example Latin *vid-*, Germanic *find-*. See also Wagner (1970), 23.
17. Pettazzoni, 194-219; Anne Ross, 107-12.
18. T. F. O'Rahilly (1946), 308-17.
19. See de Vries (1961), 158-63.
20. See Williams and Ní Mhuirgheasa, 19-49; Ó hÓgáin (1982), *passim*.
21. Pettazzoni, 197-9.
22. Toponymics in Holder *2*, 308-46. *Lughnasadh* festival minutely examined in Máire Mac Neill. List of Irish texts concerning Lugh in Gray, 126-7. List of Welsh texts concerning Lleu in Gruffydd (1928), 55-60.
23. For indications of the cult on the Continent, see Máire MacNeill, 1, 385-91, 418-19. Lugh's arrival in narrative, Gray, 38-42, 91.
24. RIA Dictionary, s.v. *trogan*. See also Powell, 119-20.
25. For *lux* see Murphy (1953), 207. For **lugio*, see Wagner (1970), 22-5.
26. The texts on the battle of Moytura in Gray, 24-72; MacAlister, 116-20; Ó Cuív, 19-57. See also Gray, 7-11; Ó Cuív, 4-9. For the Devas/Asuras and the Aesir/Vanir parallels, see Dumézil.

27. See Murphy (1953), l-liv.
28. Stokes (1900), 47-50. The name 'Aillén' seems to mean simply 'spirit', T. F. O'Rahilly (1946), 300.
29. Ibid., 58-74, 310-317. The substitution of a sling seems to be due to the influence of the David and Goliath story in the Bible.
30. Gwynn (1924), 282. Goll is also mentioned in the earliest surviving text, Gray, 56. For Balor being one-eyed in folklore, see Murphy (1953), lxxi-lxxiii.
31. For *Samhain*, see Rees and Rees, 83-94, 146-72; Le Roux; Guyonvarc'h. As if to exemplify the confusion in the myths of the two festivals, the earliest surviving text has the battle of Moytura being fought at *Samhain* rather than at *Lughnasadh*, Gray, 44.
32. Discussions in Gruffydd (1928), 366-75; Hartland, 1-13; Krappe, 1-43; Rank, 12-44; Saintyves.
33. Gwynn (1906), 72-6.
34. *Revue Celtique 2*, 86-92. See also chapter 4, note 2.
35. See T. F. O'Rahilly (1946), 319-20.
36. Bieler, 102.
37. Máire MacNeill, 433-51 *et passim.*
38. Bieler, 110.
39. See T. F. O'Rahilly (1946), 122.
40. Gray, 66-8.
41. T. F. O'Rahilly (1946), 59-60.
42. O'Daly, 88.
43. References in Murphy (1953), 357. For early occurrences of the name Dáire Dearg in contexts close to that of Fionn's fiery foe, see O'Brien, 99; Murphy (1953), lxiii; Gwynn (1906), 64; see chapter 2, pp. 46-8.
44. Foster; Carey.
45. Such a direct acquaintance with the Irish *Fionn* could have been the genesis of the tendency in mediaeval Welsh lore (Carey, 16-17) to ascribe prophecies to an obscure character called Lludd (<Nudd).
46. Carey, 1-4; T. F. O'Rahilly (1946), 527.
47. Carey, 9.
48. The story is quoted and discussed in chapter 3.
49. *Revue Celtique 5*, 202.
50. T. F. O'Rahilly (1946), 318-19. A character called 'Old Fionn' (*Gwyn hen* and *Henwen*) occurs in mediaeval Welsh literature, Williams, 44; Anne Ross, 398; T. F. O'Rahilly (1946), 278. Also, perhaps, apposite is a certain 'Fionn son of Fintan' in Irish, ibid., 275. The epithet *find* is applied to opponents of Fionn in several cases, see Meyer (1910), xxii.
51. *Ériu 4*, 128-64; *Anecdota 1*, 24-39.
52. Realm of dead in shamanism, Eliade (1964), *passim*. For rituals of Irish poets, see Ó hÓgáin (1982), 80-127, 168-280; Ellis (1943), 109-10; and note 20 above.

53. *Revue Celtique 26*, 18.
54. See T. F. O'Rahilly (1946), 320; Carey, 5-7.
55. Ibid., 322-3; RIA Dictionary, s.v. *boand*. The earliest attested form of the river's name is in Ptolemy's geography – 'Buvinda'. This dates from the second century A.D. and may reflect quite earlier sources. It would represent a primitive Irish **bóu-vind*. See T. F. O'Rahilly (1946), 3; Holder *1*, 646-7.
56. Knott, 6; Gwynn (1913), 286. Further references in Ó hÓgáin (1982), 273-9, 442.
57. Ériu 12, 142; Best, Bergin, and O'Brien, 818.
58. For references, see Ó hÓgáin (1982), 258-64, 440-41.
59. Gray, 24.
60. Best, Bergin, and O'Brien, 1373. See Murphy (1953), lxxix.
61. See T.F. O'Rahilly (1946), 516-17. The historical aspect of O'Rahilly's theory differs from the interpretation advanced here.
62. *Ériu 12*, 142-6.
63. Perhaps the acount of how Mac ind Óc took Newgrange from Nuadhu is a confused echo of Fionn's triumph over his ancestor. The Noende and Umhall reference is in O'Brien, 285. For a further connection of this complex with Fionn, see T. F. O'Rahilly (1946), 276.
64. Gwynn (1906), 74.
65. *Irische Texte 3*, 188-90.
66. *Zeitschrift 20*, 196-7.
67. See, for instance, the name Mongfhinn for a character who, although divorced from Fionn's personality, belongs to the same context, chapter 3, notes 67-68.
68. Meyer (1895), 42-3.
69. Ibid., 48.
70. See Jung and Kerenyi, 25-69; Nilsson (1927), 533-83.
71. Jung and Kerenyi, 46-51, 66-8; Ellis (1964), 104-6.
72. References in chapter 4, note 19.
73. *Revue Celtique 6*, 177-8. See also Nagy (1985), 111, 270.
74. *Revue Celtique 5*, 199-200. See chapter 4, note 9.
75. Gwynn (1906), 74; Stokes (1900), 47. Variant traditions in Meyer (1910), 46; *Revue Celtique 2*, 90; *5*, 201.
76. Stokes (1900), 123.
77. For references see Cross (1952), Motifs A920-939.
78. Joynt, 34-40.
79. Meyer (1910), 14-16.
80. Cited from Mac Cana (1972), 136-7.
81. Meyer (1895), 25-7.
82. The shape-shifting of the Norse god of wisdom provides an interesting parallel, see Turville-Petre, 35-41, 56-61. The imagined taking of shapes of various animals is a common feature of shamanism, see Eliade (1964), 574.
83. Meyer (1912), 87-8.
84. *Revue Celtique 25*, 348.

85. See RIA Dictionary.
86. References and discussion in chapter 2, notes 43-44.
87. See Ions, 71; Budge, 466-95.

CHAPTER 2 (pp. 27–51)

1. *Zeitschrift 1*, 472.
2. See Herity and Eogan, 57-79; Smyth (1982), 34; MacAlister, 106-36; Rees and Rees, 146-72.
3. See Rees and Rees, 147-56, 171; Binchy (1958), 127-38; Carney (1955), 334-5; Baudiš, 101-7.
4. For the lore of these, see Best and Bergin, 127-32.
5. Gwynn (1903), 46. The author of the poem associated the mound with Find File of Knockaulin (p. 48), but this character-specification is surely an accretion.
6. See Byrne, 54-5.
7. Ibid., 70-82, 130-34; Mac Niocaill (1972), 9-21.
8. For Labhraidh, see Dillon (1946), 4-10. For Nuadhu in Leinster Genealogies, see O'Brien, 1-24, 99.
9. Ibid., 23-4; Smyth (1982), 34.
10. Meyer (1914), 9-14.
11. Byrne, 138; Smyth (1982), 20, 51.
12. Ibid., 68-9; T. F. O'Rahilly (1946), 19; Dillon (1962), 150-68. See also Byrne, 138-42.
13. Mac Niocaill (1972), 17-18. For the Uí Fáilghe generally, see Smyth (1974), 121-43, 503-23.
14. *Revue Celtique 13*, 42-50. See chapter 4, note 31; and chapter 5, note 11.
15. Meyer (1885), 76; T. F. O'Rahilly (1946), 19; Eoin MacNeill, liii-lv; Stokes (1900), see the locating of Druim Críad on pp. 20, 38.
16. Ibid., 181.
17. See Hogan, 437.
18. O'Brien, 22, 99; Meyer (1885), 76; Eoin MacNeill, lii.
19. Rhys, 179; Sjoestedt, 27; Wagner (1977), 10-11.
20. Murphy (1953), lxxvii-lxxix.
21. Vendryes, 1-23. Note also the name 'Finnigu daughter of Umhall' in a mediaeval text, Best, Bergin, and O'Brien, 855.
22. RIA Dictionary, s.v. *Fíngen*.
23. Gwynn (1924), 272.
24. O'Brien, 22.
25. RIA Dictionary, s.v. *amall*; Dwelly, s.v. *amhall*.
26. O'Brien, 99.
27. See RIA Dictionary, *trén, mór, baíscne, so-alt, eltan*.
28. Ibid., s.v. *fían, fíanlach*.
29. *Irische Texte 3*, 378-80.
30. Meyer (1910), v-vii.
31. Meyer (1909), 8; *Revue Celtique 26*, 46.
32. O'Donovan (1865), *1*, 206; Binchy (1978), 395, 1322, 1699.
33. Best and Bergin, 294.

34. *Zeitschrift 3*, 453; *Celtica 8*, 72.
35. For a full discussion, see Sharpe. Also McCone, 28-9.
36. For studies, see Weiser; Höfler; Nilsson (1952); Wikander; and other works referred to in Nagy (1985), 232; and Lincoln, 122.
37. Stokes and Strachan, 293.
38. Meyer (1909), 46.
39. RIA Dictionary, s.v. *óc*.
40. Ibid., *óclach*.
41. Sharpe, 86-90.
42. Carney (1967), 2, 97-8.
43. Henry, 109-10.
44. Stokes (1900), 148. Reference to this also, ibid., 52.
45. The prophesied Leinster saints are Ciarán, Moling, Maodhóg, and Caoimhghein, Stokes (1900), 52, 69, 75-6, 183-4; Plummer (1922), *1*, 125, 131, 158, 192; *Revue Celtique 13*, 10-11. The prophecy of the Munster saint Findchua (Stokes (1880), clxxii) may have been suggested by the similarity of his name to that of Fionn (i.e. Find).
46. Murphy (1953), lxii-lxiii. Use of suitable native lore was officially encouraged by Church policy in the sixth to seventh centuries, see Bréhier and Aigrain, 287.
47. O'Brien, 99.
48. T. F. O'Rahilly (1946), 6, 10-11, 34; O'Brien, 656; *Revue Celtique 14*, 241-9; Meyer 4-6.
49. Meyer (1910), 4; *Zeitschrift 20*, 401.
50. See notes 48, 67, 68; also Maura Power, 43.
51. *Revue Celtique 14*, 242-3; Hull (1941), 323-4.
52. Smyth (1982), 16-17, 74-5.
53. T. F. O'Rahilly (1946), 11.
54. Byrne, 195-6, 206.
55. For Leinster/Munster political relations, see Byrne, 168-9, 194. Ecclesiastical connections, ibid., 169-71. As well as Fionn, the adoption into east Munster of Nuadhu is evidenced by the alias Mugh Nuadhat for the Eoghanacht ancestor Eoghan Taídhlech (*Zeitschrift 8*, 312-13), and also by that deity's association with Slievenamon, see chapter 3, note 45.
56. Meyer (1910), xv.
57. Bieler, 154. See also Meyer (1912), 75.
58. T. F. O'Rahilly (1946), 49-50, 78-80, 201-2; O'Daly, 9-11, 38-101; *Ériu 11*, 49.
59. Ibid., 84; Meyer (1910), xx-xxi.
60. O'Daly, 88.
61. Loc. cit.
62. Meyer (1912), 87-8. Another version, in the Law Tracts, has Fionn holding the woman's baby in his arms when Lomhna gives the inscribed rod to him, *Ériu 11*, 48-9, 58-61.
63. See Meyer (1910), xii-xiii; T. F. O'Rahilly (1946), 391-4, 556; Smyth (1982), 177.

64. Stokes (1862), 34-5 (= O'Donovan and Stokes, 129-31).
65. See chapter 3, note 31.
66. Meyer (1912), 87.
67. No known text of this story survives, but see Mac Cana (1980), 48, 58; Meyer (1892), 210; *Revue Celtique 14*, 248; *Celtica 5*, 73.
68. *Revue Celtique 16*, 43; Meyer (1910), 4-17; *Zeitschrift 20*, 400-404.
69. *Revue Celtique 25*, 344-9. See also *Ériu 11*, 152-3.
70. Thompson (1955-1958), Motif K2111.
71. See Mac Cana (1970), 42-8; Anne Ross, 421-3, 517; Thevenot, 144-52.
72. RIA Dictionary, s.v. *daighre*.
73. O'Daly, 82.
74. Meyer (1895), 48.
75. Meyer (1912), 24-7.
76. For references and discussions, see Aarne and Thompson, Type 873; Potter, 6-96; de Vries (1953). An Old Irish version features the hero Cúchulainn and his son Conlaí, van Hamel, 9-15.
77. *Revue Celtique 5*, 198, 200.

CHAPTER 3 (pp. 52-80)

1. RIA Dictionary, s.v. *fis*.
2. Pokorny, 1125-6; Wagner (1970), 22-3.
3. *Revue Celtique 25*, 344-6.
4. Gwynn (1906), 64. See Nagy (1985), 277.
5. Meyer (1910), 46; Eoin MacNeill, 33; Joynt, 5.
6. Meyer (1910), xxiii.
7. *Revue Celtique 14*, 245-6; Hull (1941), 329-33.
8. *Revue Celtique 5*, 201.
9. For references, see chapter 1, note 46.
10. *Zeitschrift 8*, 120.
11. For references and discussion, see T. F. O'Rahilly (1946), 322-3.
12. Gwynn (1913), 26.
13. *Revue Celtique 5*, 202. The pool in the Boyne is called *lind find Féic na Fían* in a tenth-century poem, Gwynn (1906), 10, 92. This can be translated 'the wisdom pool of Fiacc of the Fianna' or perhaps even 'the pool of keen-witted Fionn (*Find féig*) of the Fianna'.
14. *Anecdota 1*, 26-8; Evans 246.
15. Aarne and Thompson, Type 673.
16. Bugge, 219-26. For discussion and two slightly later recensions, see Scott, 193-201. See also Lie.
17. Scott, 204-10; Ellis (1942), 216-36; and Lang, 83-9.
18. Golther. See also Scott, 201-4.
19. RIA Dictionary, s.v. *dorchacht*. See also Ó hÓgáin (1982), 111-13.
20. RIA Dictionary, s.v. *iarmbérla*. Meyer (1912), 64.
21. See Watkins.
22. Meyer (1912), 64. See T. F. O'Rahilly (1946), 336-40.

23. RIA Dictionary, s.v. *imbas*. See also Ford, 73-4.
24. Dillon (1953), 9; Knott, 4. See also Ó hÓgáin, (1982), 271-3.
25. O'Donovan (1865), 42. See also Ó hÓgáin (1982), 20-22.
26. For references and discussion, see Chadwick, 103-25.
27. Stokes and Strachan, *2*, 249.
28. See RIA Dictionary.
29. *Zeitschrift 1*, 464-5.
30. Chadwick, 120-26.
31. References by Polybius, Livy, and particularly Diodorus and Strabo, see Jackson (1964), 35-7; Tierney, 32.
32. Meyer (1910), 8; *Zeitschrift* 20, 401
33. Von Sydow, 23-5.
34. Ó Riain, 26-8.
35. See Adhalsteinsson, 103-23.
36. Best, Bergin, and O'Brien, 49.
37. T. F. O'Rahilly (1946), 281-3, 514-15.
38. Ibid., 282.
39. Williams (1930), 44-7. See also Mac Cana (1958), 91-5.
40. RIA Dictionary, s.v. *sidh*; Ó Cathasaigh.
41. See, for example, the in-depth discussion of this in Norse sources in Ellis (1943), 100-111.
42. Williams (1930), 9.
43. *Revue Celtique 26*, 18.
44. *Ériu 12*, 142; T. F. O'Rahilly (1946), 320; Gwynn (1906), 10.
45. *Irische Texte 3*, 326; *Zeitschrift 13*, 195-250.
46. See Chadwick and Chadwick, *1*, 648-9.
47. See RIA Dictionary for examples.
48. *Ériu 13*, 38.
49. RIA Dictionary, s.v. *boand*; T. F. O'Rahilly (1946), 3; Ó hÓgáin (1982), 258-63. See chapter 1, notes 55-58.
50. *Zeitschrift 27*, 33-4.
51. Stokes (1900), 192. Other references to her: ibid., 189, 199-202; Meid, 1. See T. F. O'Rahilly (1946), 305. For other ladies from the otherworld with the same designation, see Stokes (1900), 350; *Ériu 12*, 180; RIA Dictionary, s.v. *bé*. See also Ó hÓgáin (1982), 196.
52. *Revue Celtique 25*, 344.
53. See Hogan, 611.
54. See RIA Dictionary.
55. Knott, 6.
56. Meyer (1885), 74-5.
57. See T. F. O'Rahilly (1946), 334-6.
58. Meyer (1885), 75.
59. Ní Shéaghdha (1945), 109.
60. Murphy (1962), 156-9, 233-4.
61. Meyer (1903), 16-22.
62. Murphy (1962), 160, 235-6; *Revue Celtique 20*, 258.
63. *Zeitschrift 13*, 270-280. For a contemporaneous riddle-dialogue

of courtship between Cúchulainn and Emer, see van Hamel, 26-32. An eighth-century account of a riddle-contest between Irish seer-poets, in *Revue Celtique 26*, 14-32. See also Ó hÓgáin (1982), 19-22. For riddle-contests between seers in other ancient cultures, see Gonda (1950), 57-61; Gonda (1963), 13-18; Huizinga, 105-18.

64. Texts in Gwynn (1913), 96-9; Gwynn (1924), 324; Best, Bergin, and O'Brien, 978-88; Stokes (1880), clxxii; Stokes (1900), 75-6, 110; Plummer (1922), *1*, 192-3; *Irish Texts 4*, 43-4; Joynt, 38-41. See also the verses ascribed to Fionn within texts: Meyer (1906), 30; *Revue Celtique 5*, 203.
65. Eoin MacNeill, 24-5.
66. *Irische Texte 3*, 66.
67. O'Grady, 332.
68. *Revue Celtique 15*, 447; Stokes (1900), 16.
69. See Binchy (1958), 113, 127-38.
70. *Lia Fáil 1*, 84; Eoin MacNeill, 49.
71. *Revue Celtique 5*, 202.
72. Gwynn (1924), 36-42, 382-4.
73. Meyer (1910), xxiv; Mac Cana (1980), 152, 155.
74. Meyer (1906), 4.
75. Ibid., 30.
76. *Lia Fáil 1*, 104-6.
77. Ó Ríordáin, 43-5, 100; O'Kelly, 135-46.
78. Meyer (1912), 46.
79. Stokes (1900), 21, 43-4, 74. For other references see RIA Dictionary, s.v. *fulacht*.
80. Céitinn, 328.
81. Meyer (1912), 46. For other references, see RIA Dictionary.
82. *Zeitschrift 13*, 262; Stokes (1900), 22, 25, 183; Joynt, 20-21; Murphy (1933), 178, 204-6; Mac Piarais (1908), 17; Ní Shéaghdha and Ní Mhuirgheasa, 82-3.
83. Céitinn, 328.
84. See Weisweiler, 39.
85. See Meyer (1910), xviii; RIA Dictionary, s.v. *oisén*.
86. Best, Bergin, and O'Brien, 729.
87. For references, see Murphy (1953), xxi; *Béaloideas 2*, 259; *3*, 146; J. F. Campbell (1872), 198-200.
88. Ibid., 198.
89. British Museum MS. Egerton 161, pp. 209-10 (=ff. 102-3).
90. Gwynn (1906), 66-70. The motif of a woman being turned into the shape of a doe occurs in a Fianna text of the twelfth century, Stokes (1900), 139. Somewhat looser parallels in Fianna texts of the same period, Eoin MacNeill, 21, 31.
91. See Cross (1918-1919), 158-62; Stokes (1900), 68-9, 135-6, 208; Joynt, 44. See also chapter 4, note 41; chapter 5, notes 6, 7; chapter 9, note 10.

CHAPTER 4 (pp. 81–113)

1. Gwynn (1906), 72-6.
2. *Revue Celtique 5*, 197-204. See Nagy (1985), 209-18, 302-4.
3. *Revue Celtique 2*, 86-92. See note 5 below.
4. Dillon (1962), 150-75. See also Byrne, 138-9.
5. For dating, see Murphy (1953), lx.
6. It lacks an ending in the sole surviving manuscript.
7. For the location, see Price, 146, 160-161; but also Hogan, 597. See further chapter 5, note 40; and chapter 6, note 76.
8. See Gougaud, 201-5; Nagy (1981), 8-14.
9. This plain (*Magh Life*) is the Curragh of Kildare, which has no lake. Perhaps swimming in the river Liffey itself is intended. The portrayal of this area as hostile terrain echoes the earlier foe of Fionn, Cuirrech Life, a personification of the area's rival interests within Leinster, see chapter 2, pp. 39-40.
10. Cecile O'Rahilly (1976), 13-19.
11. An account of this crane-bag (*corr-bholg*) is in Eoin MacNeill, 21-22. See also Meyer (1910), 50; and T. F. O'Rahilly (1946), 72-4.
12. References in Murphy (1953), 377.
13. See Ó hÓgáin (1982), 273-80.
14. For similar ideas, see Thompson (1953-1955), Motifs under F681.
15. Meyer (1910), xxiii.
16. Ibid., 46-50.
17. Eoin MacNeill, 33-4. See also Murphy (1953), 31-4.
18. For references see chapter 9, note 2.
19. *Béaloideas 1*, 406; Ó Duilearga and Ó hÓgáin, 13; Breathnach, 276.
20. Meyer (1912), 11.
21. Hogan, 324.
22. Cecile O'Rahilly (1976), 124.
23. Hull (1941), 324.
24. Stokes (1900), 47, 49.
25. Ibid., 50.
26. Meyer (1910), 44.
27. *Revue Celtique 7*, 292; Gwynn (1913), 130, 250. See also Stokes (1900), 146.
28. *Irische Texte 3*, 199.
29. *Zeitschrift 1*, 472.
30. O'Grady (1892), 92-3.
31. Best, Bergin, and O'Brien, 1275-87.
32. *Revue Celtique 20*, 154-6, 264; Ní Shéaghdha (1967), 130-36.
33. *Zeitschrift 13*, 254-82. The reference to 'the stream of Sadhbh' [*srut Sodbae*] is puzzling. Perhaps it is a corruption of *sreth so-adbthae* [a series of good dwellings], and, if so, could refer to Fionn's visits to otherworld places. For the riddle-contest, see also chapter 3, note 63.

34. *Zeitschrift 12*, 274-5; *18*, 422-4.
35. Meyer (1910), xxix.
36. There was a broadly parallel development in the mediaeval lore of Charlemagne on the Continent, see Paris, 385-99.
37. Meyer (1910), xxi.
38. Gwynn (1906), 12; Best, Bergin, and O'Brien, 131.
39. *Revue Celtique 23*, 310; *Zeitschrift 1*, 465; O'Donovan (1848), 120.
40. Stokes (1887), 536.
41. *Zeitschrift 1*, 464.
42. Best, Bergin, and O'Brien, 729.
43. Meyer (1885), 73-5.
44. Stokes (1900), 50.
45. *Zeitschrift 1*, 462.
46. Meyer (1910), 92-8.
47. *Revue Celtique 17*, 21.
48. For contrasting views, see Meyer (1910), xxviii-xxix; and Mac Cana (1980), 105-7, 158.
49. Best, Bergin, and O'Brien, 587.

CHAPTER 5 (pp. 114–150)

1. The first version edited by Stokes (1900). The second (known as the Little Colloquy) edited in part by Dubhglas de hÍde in *Lia Fáil 1*, 80-106. The third version edited, with sources listed, by Ní Shéaghdha, vols 1, 2 (1942), vol. 3 (1945).
2. See editions and comments by Eoin MacNeill, Murphy (1933 and 1953), Neil Ross, Ó Siochfhradha (1941). See also versions collected from oral traditions from the eighteenth century onwards in J. F. Campbell (1872) and Cameron. Further references in chapters 7-9.
3. Joynt. See also Bruford, 261.
4. Stokes (1900), 47.
5. Jackson (1938), 39, 58.
6. Joynt, 5-6.
7. Ibid., 43-4.
8. The lay is in the second (or Little) Colloquy, RIA 23 H 6:194a. It is repeated in Murphy (1933), 100-112, and partially in Ní Shéaghdha *2* (1942), 57-9.
9. Gwynn (1913), 242-53.
10. Ibid., 96-9.
11. Ibid., 128-33. The place Cnámhros was associated with Fionn, probably because of the mediaeval Leinster tradition that he had won a battle there, see chapter 4, p. 105.
12. For references see Murphy (1953), 377; Nagy (1985), 335.
13. Stokes (1900), 4, 211.
14. Neil Ross, 190-192.
15. Stokes (1900), 116.
16. Ibid., 178-80.

17. Ibid., 38. See also a fourteenth-century reference to an impetuous act by Fionn – the blinding of Caireall's father Dianghus – which he regretted ever after, in Murphy (1933), 110.
18. Stokes (1900), 62.
19. Eoin MacNeill, 34-8.
20. For the *corr-bholg* see reference in chapter 4, note 11. For the Biorgha, with which Fionn slew his archetypal foe (chapter 1), see Meyer (1910), xxiii; *Revue Celtique 5*, 202-4; Stokes (1900), 47-50. For identification of it with the crane-bag, see T. F. O'Rahilly (1946), 72-4.
21. Joynt 3, 11 (Mac an Luinn), 53 (shield). For how Fionn got Mac an Luinn, re-interpreted as 'Mac an Luin', see chapter 7, p. 206.
22. The motif of the shrieking shield occurs in the Ulster cycle, see Best, Bergin, and O'Brien, 394. The giving of names and personalities to weapons is common in mediaeval epics in European languages.
23. Neill Ross, 194-6 (house), 88 (banner).
24. Eoin MacNeill, 25-7. For Fearghus, see Ó Cadhlaigh, 500.
25. Meyer (1903), 18-22.
26. Stokes (1900), 18-20.
27. RIA Dictionary, s.v. *cú*, *conán*. For the name Conán among the Fianna, see Stokes (1900), 352; Murphy (1953), 353; Ní Shéaghdha (1945), 202. Humans in dog shape, Stokes (1900), 215-16. For warriors compared to hounds in various civilisations, see Gerstein; Eliade (1972), 1-20.
28. Murphy (1953), 103-4.
29. Stokes (1900), 97.
30. Ibid., 62-3.
31. Ibid., 5-9.
32. See Ní Shéaghdha (1967), x-xii.
33. Murphy (1933), 184-92.
34. Stokes (1900), 127; Eoin Mac Neill, 81.
35. Stokes (1900), 183.
36. Ibid., 181.
37. Joynt, 1-2.
38. Meyer (1910), 52, 64.
39. Murphy (1933), 217-20.
40. Evans, 243-54. Ysgeir Oervel mentioned on pp. 235, 250.
41. Lot, 217. See also Loomis, 191-2; and Murphy (1953), 199-200.
42. This 'fair' is mentioned in a series of metaphors for occult knowledge in an Irish text of around the year A.D. 800, *Revue Celtique 26*, 6. The Cormac's Glossary reference to the fair of *Orc Tréith* is in Meyer (1912), 86-7. See also RIA Dictionary, s.v. *tríath*.
43. Ibid., s.v. *treithirne*. MacAlister, 122.
44. See T. F. O'Rahilly (1946), 318-19.
45. Eoin MacNeill, 38-45
46. Ibid., 30-32.
47. Stokes (1900), 68-9.

48. See Ó hÓgáin (1983).
49. Neil Ross, 194.
50. Eoin MacNeill, 75-80.
51. Murphy (1933), 234-8.
52. See Nagy (1985), 273.
53. J. G. Campbell, 219-24. In an eighteenth-century Munster literary text Bran and Sceolaing help to kill a giant and a hag in similar manner, Ó hAimhirgin and Mac Néill, 17-18.
54. For ravens and the name Bran, see Anne Ross, 318-30, 366-8. The association of the Britonic Nodons (ibid., 230-33; T. F. O'Rahilly, (1946), 527), with hounds and hunting, is hardly relevant in this context, see chapter 1, pp. 16-18. The same can be said of Arthur and the Welsh Gwynn (Murphy, (1953), 198-201), but the latter may have borrowed a small amount of the imagery from Fionn – because of the identicality of name – in the tenth or eleventh century.
55. Murphy (1933), 198-202.
56. Many references in Murphy (1953), 123; and Christiansen, 179. Other version in *Claidheamh* 20/6/1908, 6.
57. Eoin MacNeill, 85.
58. Murphy (1933), 154-66. Other political prophecies ascribed to Fionn in O'Curry, 622-4; O'Donovan, 1797. See chapter 3, notes 59-66, 70.
59. Joynt, 40-41.
60. Ibid., 14-20.
61. Ibid., 34-40.
62. Stokes (1900), 189, 350 (*Bé-bind*); T. F. O'Rahilly (1946), 305, 320. *Find* is the Old Irish form of Fionn's name.
63. Stokes (1900), 136-47.
64. Ibid., 155-7.
65. Eoin MacNeill, 38-45. A slightly later version in Ní Shéaghdha (1945), 20-42. For the dream-visit to fairyland, see Thompson (1955-1958), Motif F370. The story in note 60 above is also put in the context of a dream.
66. Joynt, 1-57.
67. *Revue Celtique 7*, 290-305; *13*, 3-12; Eoin MacNeill, 28-30. Also in Ní Shéaghdha (1942), *1*, 169-81.
68. Stokes (1900), 21 etc. (three battalions), 160 (full complement).
69. Ibid., 161.
70. Ibid., 93. See also ibid., 67-8.
71. Ní Shéaghdha (1945), 184-5.
72. Joynt, 8, 11, 38.
73. Céitinn, 326-32.
74. Stokes (1900), 163.
75. Joynt, 8.
76. Ibid., 14.
77. *Zeitschrift 1*, 472.
78. Eoin MacNeill, 36-8.

79. Ibid., 4.
80. Neil Ross, 184-8.
81. Stokes (1900), 88-90. See Christiansen, 84-5.
82. Binchy (1952), 36-9.
83. For red and slaughter, see Cecile O'Rahilly (1976), 2; Knott, 9. For the juxtaposition white/red, see Ó hÓgáin (1983), 88-92; Bruford, 120.
84. Stokes (1900), 21-5, 136; Eoin MacNeill, 37; Murphy (1933), 86, 124. See also Cecile O'Rahilly (1962), x-xiv.
85. Ibid., 1-47.
86. Ibid., xiv-xviii, 76-7. For Suibhne, see O'Keeffe.
87. Graves *2*, 273-4. See also Cecile O'Rahilly (1962), xvi-xvii.
88. Stokes (1900), 31-2.
89. Ibid., 1, 31, 222; MacNeill 37, 48, 81; Murphy (1933), 108.
90. *Revue Celtique 17*, 23; O'Donovan (1848), 120.
91. *Irische Texte 1*, 158.
92. Murphy (1933), 32-56. Later accounts in verse in Neil Ross, 148-50; Ó Siochfhradha (1941), 200-212. Rome is not specifically mentioned as the pilgrims' venue in Murphy, but it is in Ó Siochfhradha (1941), 200.

CHAPTER 6 (pp. 151-191)

1. *Revue Celtique* 5, 201; Stokes (1900), 71-2, 158; Murphy (1953), 356-7. See also Meyer (1910), xxi; Anne Ross, 120.
2. Murphy (1933), 100-107.
3. *Revue Celtique 5*, 198, 200.
4. Meyer (1885), 74; Meyer (1910), xxix; Stokes (1900), 102. For Fionn's enmity with Fothadh Canainne, see chapter 2 and Stokes (1900), 96.
5. Stokes (1900), 60-62.
6. Murphy (1933), 104.
7. Ní Shéaghdha (1967), 1.
8. *Zeitschrift 1*, 458-9; *13*, 254; *Revue Celtique 20*, 264.
9. Stokes (1900), 38-41.
10. *Ériu 1*, 13-37. The English writer of the Book of Howth around the year 1580 knew the story in this form, Brewer and Bullen, 7-8.
11. Stokes (1900), 78-81.
12. Ní Shéaghdha (1945), 96.
13. Murphy (1933), 20-29.
14. Stokes (1900), 86-8.
15. *Revue Celtique 6*, 186.
16. Eoin MacNeill, 25.
17. Ibid., 74.
18. Stokes (1900), 29, 178-80; Murphy (1933), 108; and notes 19 and 23 below.
19. Murphy (1933), 66-78.
20. Ibid., 24. See also Murphy (1953), 206.

21. For them, see O'Daly, 11-12.
22. Thompson (1955-1958), Motif H481.
23. Stokes (1900), 16-18.
24. Aarne and Thompson, Type 933; Baum, 590-602; Plummer (1910) *1*, cxxxv; Mac Eoin, 198-201; van Hamel, 3-8.
25. Meyer (1909).
26. Eoin MacNeill, 4-6; Murphy (1933), 344-60.
27. Eoin MacNeill, xxxi.
28. Meyer (1910), 4; *Zeitschrift 20*, 401.
29. Stokes (1900), 60-62, 73-80, 132, 183, 186-7, 204-5, 206, 219-20. See also *Zeitschrift 8*, 105.
30. *Revue Celtique 5*, 198, *2*, 90-92. For other mentions of Banbh Sionna, who was a member of the Fianna, see Stokes (1900), 57; Murphy (1953), 345.
31. Best, Bergin, and O'Brien, 978-88.
32. Eoin MacNeill, 7-10. See also ibid., 10-14.
33. Ibid., 60-61.
34. For the Ulster cycle motif, see chapter 9, note 23.
35. Stokes (1900), 56.
36. Eoin MacNeill, 23-4.
37. Ibid., 22-3.
38. Ibid., 86-92. This contradicts the source of note 30 above.
39. Stokes (1900), 144-5.
40. Neil Ross, 60-68.
41. For this Morna clan genealogy, see Eoin MacNeill, 17. See *garad* in RIA Dictionary.
42. Stokes (1900), 101-2.
43. Gwynn (1924), 362-6; Eoin MacNeill, 1-3; Stokes (1900), 101-2; *Revue Celtique 13*, 7-10; Ní Shéaghdha (1967), 56-64. See also Murphy (1953), 3-6.
44. Stokes (1900), 52, 113. See also Ní Shéaghdha (1967), 24. An eleventh-century text has Fionn at a feast which is hosted by one Mael Mac Iachtadon mac Morna, Stokes (1880), clxxii. See also chapter 9, p. 296.
45. Ibid., 203-5.
46. Ibid., 186; Eoin MacNeill, 57.
47. Murphy (1933), 258.
48. For *milleadh*, see RIA Dictionary under *milliud*, *milltech*, *súil*. For folklore of Conán's destructive eye, see Power, 271-2; Murphy (1953), xx; *Béaloideas 7*, 123; IFC 44:237-8, 78:10-11, 191:203, 1186:404-8. See also chapter 9, notes 63 and 70.
49. See Stokes (1900), 354.
50. Meyer (1910), xxiv; Mac Niocaill, 49.
51. Stokes (1900), 7, 43, 86, 100; T. F. O'Rahilly (1927), 267; Ní Shéaghdha (1967), 130.
52. Müller-Lisowski, 147-53 *et passim*. See also Stokes (1900), 19; and Murphy (1953), 360.
53. See Mac Cana (1970), 94-5.

54. Schoepperle, 391-470.
55. Meyer (1910), xxiv. See also Mac Cana (1980), 46, 57, 86.
56. Ní Shéaghdha (1967), 1-104.
57. Hull, 46; Schoepperle, 21-4, 401-10.
58. References in Bruford, 108, 265. Also de hÍde, 125; and IFC 1170:277.
59. Eoin MacNeill, 45; Ní Shéaghdha (1967), 8; Ní Mhuirgheasa (1941), 13, 41; Mac Piarais (1908), 2; Ó Siochfhradha (1941), 142 etc. See discussion in Ó hÓgáin (1987).
60. For love-magic in Irish lore, see Cross, Motifs D1355, D1900; Ó Cátháin (1980), 87-91; Ó hÓgáin (1985), 267-72. See the twelfth-century account of love-charms sent to Fionn, discussed in chapter 5, p. 118.
61. RIA Dictionary, s.v. *gulba.*
62. See O'Daly, 60, 117; Bruford, 107, 113.
63. Neil Ross, 70-76.
64. Cecile O'Rahilly (1976), 64-7.
65. *Revue Celtique 5*, 198, 200.
66. RIA Dictionary, s.v. *tul, ga.*
67. Meyer (1895), 45-8.
68. See T. F. O'Rahilly (1946), 125-6, 198, 481-4; and note 42 above. 'From the House of Donn to the Strand of Dundrum' [*ó Thigh Duinn co Tráigh Rudhraighe*] was a proverbial expression for the extent of Ireland, see O'Keeffe, 68.
69. O'Daly, 82, 141.
70. Meyer (1910), xxiii; *Zeitschrift 1*, 459.
71. Evans, 232.
72. Stokes (1900), 112-13, 155-7.
73. *Zeitschrift 1*, 458-9.
74. Eoin MacNeill, 19-21.
75. Stokes (1900), 103, 136, 205.
76. Ní Shéaghdha (1945), 67-83. Scottish version in Neil Ross, 40-58.
77. Aarne and Thompson, Type 570.
78. Stokes (1900), 205.
79. Ibid., 115.
80. Murphy (1933), 124-40.
81. Stokes (1900), 189; Eoin MacNeill, 6.
82. Stokes (1900), 1, 3, 182.
83. *Zeitschrift 1*, 459.
84. See Murphy (1953), 348.
85. Thompson (1955-1958), Motif F681.1. The motif occurs in the folktale Types 513 and 514 in Aarne and Thompson.
86. Stokes (1900), 182.
87. Ibid., 123.
88. Ibid., 6, 106, 108, 124, 152, 211.
89. Ibid., 149-51, 154, 168-73. See also *Lia Fáil 1*, 107.
90. Stern, 7-19; *Zeitschrift 3*, 433. The author of the third Colloquy

knew both this poem and the first Colloquy account and he combined them, Ní Shéaghdha (1942) *2*, 16-27. See also Christiansen, 78-83.

91. MacAlister, 134-6.
92. Joynt, 21-34.
93. See Gruffydd (1953), 58-67; Jackson (1961), 88-95, 98-99.
94. Aarne and Thompson, Types 513-514.
95. Ibid., Type 653.
96. Ní Shéaghdha (1967), 20.
97. Stokes (1900), 328-9.

CHAPTER 7 (pp. 192—232)

1. See the gradual development of such texts in the lists of Meyer, xxv-xxx; and Murphy (1953), lx-lxi.
2. Stokes (1900), 58.
3. Ní Shéaghdha (1945), 54-62.
4. Ó Siochfhradha (1941), 146-50.
5. Jackson (1938).
6. Eoin MacNeill, 45-7.
7. See Nagy (1985), 46-50, 246-7.
8. Murphy (1933), 288-96.
9. Ní Mhuirgheasa (1941), 16-39.
10. Ní Shéaghdha (1945), 100-109.
11. The Samson story in Judges: 16 of the Old Testament.
12. Mudrak, 94-5; Thompson (1955-1958), Motif K97.2.
13. Neil Ross, 96-100.
14. Murphy (1933), 240-46.
15. Henderson.
16. Ní Shéaghdha (1945), 91-110.
17. Murphy (1953), 330-34; Neil Ross, 30-34.
18. See Murphy (1953), 155; Cross (1918-1919), 153-6.
19. Ó Siochfhradha (1941), 113-17.
20. See the occurrences listed in RIA Directory, *bruiden*, *síd*, *síth*.
21. Ní Shéaghdha (1942) *2*, 47-51.
22. Ibid., 52-3.
23. Eoin MacNeill, 91-2.
24. Ní Mhuirgheasa (1941), 3-15.
25. *Zeitschrift 5*, 22.
26. The rings, and twisting of them around briar-trunks, was probably part of folklore of the time. For similar ideas, see Thompson (1955-1958), Motifs D801, D1791.
27. Van Hamel, 72-4; Knott, 12-13, 16-17.
28. Murphy (1933), 2-14.
29. Ó Siochfhradha (1941), 149-50.
30. Murphy (1933), 60-64.
31. *Revue Celtique 8*, 48. See T. F. O'Rahilly (1946), 59.
32. Ní Mhuirgheasa (1941), 40-91.
33. O'Keeffe, 7-8.

34. Van Hamel, 72-4.
35. Best and Bergin, 302-3.
36. See Ó Súilleabháin (1942), 268, 395.
37. Mac Piarais (1908). See also Bruford, 251-2.
38. Edited in IFC 1121:59.
39. Frazer, 152-3. See Murphy (1953), xxx-xxxi.
40. Eoin MacNeill, 56-7.
41. Murphy (1933), 248-78.
42. Ibid., 298-316.
43. Brewer and Bullen, 10-11.
44. Murphy (1933), 222-32.
45. Ibid., 318-28.
46. Ibid., 362-8.
47. Stokes (1900), 4.
48. Ó Gallchobhair, 49-68. See Bruford, 262-3.
49. Cross (1952), Motifs F301-F304.
50. Ibid., Motif T11.
51. Stokes (1900), 126-9.
52. Ibid., 163-7.
53. Dillon (1948), 101-31.
54. Ó Siochfhradha (1941), 28-31.
55. Cecile Ó'Rahilly (1962), 13. See Murphy (1953), 91.
56. Murphy (1933), 20-28.
57. English text edited by Kölbing. Fourteenth-century Irish version in Robinson, 17, 173-98.
58. French text edited by Pernoud and Suard. English by Lee.
59. Ó Gallchobhair, 17-46. See Bruford, 266.
60. Eoin MacNeill, 61-73.
61. RIA Dictionary, s.v. *grúagach.*
62. Murphy (1933), 374-98.
63. Ó Siochfhradha (1938); O'Grady, 257-75.
64. RIA Dictionary, s.v. *tairngire.*
65. See Murphy (1953), xxxii-xxxiii and (1971), 52.
66. See Thompson (1955-1958), and Cross (1952), Motif B181.
67. Bromwich, 44, 110-12.

CHAPTER 8 (pp. 233–274)

1. Rosemary Power, 222-38, 261-94. Extra version in Dunne, 344-5.
2. Jónsson, 69-76. See Rosemary Power, 238-57.
3. Stokes (1900), 169-70 etc.
4. Joynt, 14-20.
5. Evans, 234.
6. *Zeitschrift 13*, 270-72.
7. Stokes (1900), 112-13, 155; Joynt, 52-3.
8. See van Hamel, 52-7; Mudrak, 153-6.
9. See Rosemary Power, 253.
10. Ibid., 254. Fionn kills savage cat, Eoin MacNeill, 79.
11. Best and Bergin, 265.

12. *Irische Texte 3*, 183-229.
13. The author of this story seems to have known the twelfth-century Continental allegory *Fons Philosophiae*, by Godfrey of St Victor, see Patch, 89.
14. Joynt, 42-3, 47. See also Murphy (1953), 153-4.
15. Stokes (1900), 150.
16. See Paris, 378-85; Moe, 175-9, 319-21.
17. The question put to Fionn, Joynt, 34, 60. The reference to bronze [*umha*] may have originally read *uamha* [cave or grave], see Ó hÓgáin (1988), 240. Fionn's strange woman, Joynt, 14.
18. Paris, 384-5. The motif was known in Fionn lore as early as the twelfth century, see Stokes (1900), 150, where a live warrior is dead every third night.
19. Best and Bergin, 127.
20. Colgrave, 126-8.
21. Bieler, 154.
22. Mulchrone, 76-7.
23. Best and Bergin, 278-87.
24. *Zeitschrift 5*, 180.
25. *Revue Celtique 6*, 186.
26. *Ériu 1*, 72.
27. Stokes (1900).
28. *Lia Fáil 1*, 79-107.
29. Ní Shéaghdha, *1-3* (1942-1945).
30. e.g. Stokes (1900), 64, 122, 216; Ní Shéaghdha (1942) *1*, 154 and *2*, 114.
31. Ibid., 117.
32. Ibid., 52.
33. Murphy (1933), 174. Another text gives Senchán and MacCoinde as baptismal names for the two, Maura Power, 44.
34. Many versions in IFC Catalogue.
35. Aenghus and Patrick, Stokes (1857), 159, 196, 468-70; Mulchrone, 118. The background for this would appear to be ecclesiastical lore of the conversion and baptism of great kings, see Tessier, 129-67. For a similar story in a twelfth-century Moslem source, see Shah, 70.
36. Eoin MacNeill, 74-5.
37. Murphy (1933), 178-82.
38. Ibid., 204-14.
39. Ibid., 168-72.
40. Sources and discussions in Christiansen, 17-19; Murphy (1953), 56, 116. Also, in *Claidheamh*, 17/9/1904, 5; *Irisleabhar 2*, 371; IFC 485:154-5; Ó hÓgáin (1980), 37.
41. Cecile O'Rahilly (1962), 31-2. Flails are mentioned as weapons used by the Fianna in Ní Shéaghdha (1942) *2*, 40.
42. Aarne and Thompson, Type 650A.
43. Ó Siochfhradha (1941), 85
44. Ibid., 227-40.
45. *An Lóchrann* 11/1920, 5; Ua Murchadha, 11-13; IFC 88:243.

46. Lists of versions in *Béaloideas 2*, 68, 260; Murphy (1953), xx; IFC Catalogue. Scottish versions in J. F. Campbell (1872), 38-9; J. G. Campbell, 82-4.
47. Stokes (1900), 66-7.
48. Cecile O'Rahilly (1961), 30-31. For manuscripts, see ibid., vii-x.
49. O'Looney. Also in Ó Siochfhradha (1941), 213-26.
50. Aarne and Thompson, Type 470*. For references to heroes brought away to the otherworld in mediaeval Irish literature, see Murphy (1953), xxii-xxiii, 439-40, and Dillon (1948), 101-31. See also Ó hÓgáin (1987), 234.
51. Many versions in IFC Catalogue. See also Ó Súilleabháin and Christiansen, under Type 470*.
52. See Curtin (1890), 327-42; IFC 27:116-22, 33:17-18, 71:170-72, 191:207-12, 438:117-35.
53. Oisín and his mother, Stokes (1900), 2. Ladies called Niamh, ibid., 29-30, 84-5, 208-9.
54. Ibid., 7, 26, 78, 86, 113; MacAlister, 188.
55. Stokes (1900), 123. See Dobbs, 166-7.
56. Dobbs, 166; Stokes (1900), 126-9.
57. Eoin MacNeill, 12, 13, 25; *Ériu 11*, 44.
58. Stokes (1900), 52, 113.
59. Gwynn (1924), 362-6.
60. For references to the several mediaeval versions, see chapter 6, note 43.
61. Stokes (1900), 123-4. See Dobbs, 167.
62. Plummer (1910), *2*, 250.
63. Murphy (1953), 181; Ó Catháin (1985), 69-70, 85-6; several versions in IFC MSS.
64. Stokes (1900), 123.
65. Eoin MacNeill, 48.
66. Bruford, 123; Murphy (1953), 177.
67. For discussion and references, see Bruford, 123-7, 258-9.
68. Ní Shéaghdha (1942), *2*, 54-5.
69. Mac Piarais (1906). See also Bruford, 252-3.
70. Ó hAimhirgin and Mac Néill, 3-30. See Bruford, 262.
71. *Béaloideas 6*, 20, 106.
72. Ní Mhuirgheasa (1954).
73. Ó Siochfhradha (1941), 93-110.
74. Ibid., 137-45.
75. Ní Mhuirgheasa and Ó Ceithearnaigh, 241-99. Motifs are borrowed from Types 302, 325 in Aarne and Thompson.
76. The first English rendering of the Arabian Nights, called the 'Grub Street version', appeared in 1706-1708, being a translation from the French of Antoine Galland.
77. Ó hAimhirgin and Mac Néill, 30-96.
78. See Mac Spealáin, 205.
79. *Lia Fáil 3*, 91-113.
80. Mac Piarais (1908), 13-14. For Donn in Clare lore, see Müller-Lisowski, 168-79.

81. RIA 23 Q 18:85m-89. Discussion and list of references in Seosamh Watson, 67-9.
82. Frustrated love, Seosamh Watson, 60-74. Imagined birth, Thompson (1955-1958), Motif J2321; Aarne and Thompson, Type 1739.
83. Ó Briain, 163-75.
84. RIA 24 B 14:151-271. See Bruford, 50-51, 259.

CHAPTER 9 (pp. 275–310)

1. Bruford, 55-68; Thomson, 246-7; Cubbon, xi, 1-2.
2. Ó Súilleabháin and Christiansen, Type 673; Ó Duilearga, 198-202, 427; Ó Duilearga and Ó hÓgáin, 12-24; Breathnach, 275-85; Gruffydd (1928), 119-27; J. G. Campbell, 16-27; J. F. Campbell (1872), 35-8.
3. From Homer's Odyssey, Book IX.
4. J. G. Campbell, 20; O'Grady, 325; Flower, 401.
5. Ibid., 22-3.
6. Murphy (1953), l-lii; and Irish references in note 2 above.
7. J. G. Campbell, 22.
8. Ní Shéaghdha (1945), 181
9. IFC MSS (see Card Catalogue).
10. O'Kearney (1855), 131.
11. O'Donovan (1848), 118-20.
12. TCD H 1 7:14b.
13. J. F. Campbell (1872), 195. For *Cill Fhinn*, see Glennie, 104; Waddell, 85-7.
14. J. F. Campbell (1872), 198; J. G. Campbell, 78-80; Carmichael, 22-5.
15. Lewis and Short, s.v. *amor*, *hippomanes*.
16. Carmichael, 22-5; J. F. Campbell (1872), 198-200.
17. RIA Dictionary, s.v. *féth*, *fiadh*. In Fianna literature, see Stokes (1900), 143, 402; Joynt, 51, 53, 56; *Lia Fáil 3*, 87-8.
18. Curtin (1894), 484-8.
19. Aarne and Thompson, Type 873; de Vries (1953).
20. Van Hamel, 11-15.
21. IFC 3:484-504, 24:424-9, 27:503-18, 37:221-44, 51:189-98, 86:202-60, 96:59-64, 259:175-218; *Béaloideas 4*, 449-53, *6*, 11-13.
22. For manuscripts, see Flower, 391-3. Text printed in Ua Ceallaigh, 25-38. Folklore versions, Ó Súilleabháin and Christiansen, Type 873; J. F. Campbell (1872), 9-16; Cameron, 161-2, 393-5; J. G. Campbell, 6-8.
23. Thurneysen (1935); Jackson (1964), 18-23.
24. J. F. Campbell (1872), 166-8.
25. Murphy (1953), 50-51; *Claidheamh* 25/4/1903, 2-3; IFC (see Catalogue); J. G. Campbell, 29-30, 49-51.
26. IFC 241:443-4; 242:73-4; and the references in notes 35 and 74 below.

27. For manuscripts, see Flower, 66. Texts printed in J. F. Campbell (1872), 151. Scottish folk versions in Stewart, 545; Mac Dougall (1889), 82-3; J. F. Campbell (1892), 46-9.
28. *Béaloideas 13*, 81.
29. Lists of oral versions in Bruford, 265. See also Neil Ross, 221-3.
30. Ibid., 70-76.
31. Skene, 458-60. Discussion in Gillies. See also John MacInnes, 120.
32. Byrne, 291, 297; Murphy (1933), 108; Céitinn, 354. The O'Brien propagandists also claimed that Fionn had foretold the rise to power of the sept, O Donnchadha, 98-9.
33. IFC 54:8; *Béaloideas* 7, 129.
34. Curtin (1943), 152; MacDougall (1891), 66-7; J. G. Campbell, 211-12; Curtin (1943), 148, 150; *Béaloideas 6*, 290.
35. Mac Giollarnáth, 66-7.
36. IFC 243:366.
37. Bruford, 215.
38. Ibid., 3-4, 115-16, 251-2.
39. Ibid., 117-18, 257-8.
40. Ibid., 116-17, 252.
41. Ibid., 118-20, 253.
42. References in Murphy (1953), liii. Murphy's interpretation of the motif in Irish lore is, however, hardly sustainable.
43. Krappe, 132-53; Bruford, 4, 253-4.
44. Ibid., 109-111, 266.
45. Ibid., 120, 262-3.
46. Ó Siochfhradha (1941), 74-80. Versions are in IFC from all four provinces.
47. Several versions in J. F. Campbell (1872), in Cameron, in J. G. Campbell, in Christiansen, in IFC, and in the notes to the relevant texts in Murphy (1953).
48. It was in standard form in Irish manuscripts of the eighteenth century, e.g. RIA 23 1 1:1-6, 23 B 27:183-9; British Museum, Egerton 155:120-122, Addendum 34119:34-5. Scottish oral versions in J. F. Campbell (1872), Cameron, and Young. Irish folk version in *An Stoc* 1/1930, 5.
49. See J. F. Campbell (1872), 165-6; *An Stoc* 9/1919, 2; IFC 136: 12-20.
50. J. F. Campbell (1872), 37, 178-80; J. G. Campbell, 165-71.
51. Ó Catháin (1985), 65-6, 84-5. Other versions in IFC Catalogue.
52. Several versions of the relevant stories in sources listed at note 47 above. For the Caoilte story in Manx lore, see Christiansen, 213-15.
53. Text edited and discussed and sources listed in Christiansen, 215-31, 359-71.
54. See Ó Súilleabháin (1942), 593-5; and Murphy (1953), 182-4. Many versions in IFC Catalogue.
55. Ó Gallchobhair, 22, 51; Brewer and Bullen, 2; Ó Siochfhradha (1941), 210; Ó Cadhlaigh, 198-9.
56. J. F. Campbell (1892), 413-14.

57. IFC 117:29.
58. *Irisleabhar 4*, 207; Ó Siochfhradha (1984), 37; Ó Máille *1*, 338-9. A Scottish saying has it that Fionn's worst ever strait was to be 'between refusing and want', Nicholson, 171.
59. *Béaloideas 4*, 426, 84.
60. J. F. Campbell (1892), 413.
61. IFC 478:675-82.
62. *An Stoc* 7-8/1919, 2. See also *Béaloideas 3*, 188, *6*, 40; and Nagy (1985), 88.
63. Ó Máille *2*, 228; *Béaloideas 4*, 83; IFC 227:116.
64. Neil Ross, 118.
65. See references to him in chapters 7 and 8. Also Ó Siochfhradha (1941), 26, 77, 105-7 etc.
66. *An Stoc* 6/1918, 3 and 6/1923, 6.
67. For the literature, see Ó Siochfhradha (1941), 18, 200, 266. For the folklore, see IFC 41:347, 52:181.
68. J. G. Campbell, 74.
69. *Béaloideas 6*, 84; J. G. Campbell, 73.
70. J. F. Campbell (1892), 414. Irish echoes in IFC *S*1051:303; Gregory, 70-71.
71. J. G. Campbell, 73-4; MacDonald, 135-6, 138; Nicolson, 53, 75, 96.
72. IFC 25:219.
73. J. F. Campbell (1892), 411; J. G. Campbell, 64.
74. J. F. Campbell (1872), 55.
75. de hÍde, 190-96.
76. IFC 1010:85-6.
77. See Ó hÓgáin (1988), 241-2.
78. *Irisleabhar 15*, 35; O Muirgheasa, 129. For Scottish and Manx versions of the seasons' saying, not attributed to Fionn, see Nicolson, 198. Donegal verse in IFC 102:228.
79. Hyde, 68; Ó Máille *1*, 338; Nicolson, 100; O'Rahilly (1921), 48; Ó Muirgheasa, 9; *Irisleabhar 16*, 198.
80. Nicolson, 347-8; Bergin and Marstrander, 43.
81. IFC 462:124.
82. *Béaloideas 11*, 61; IFC 462:123.
83. IFC 53:112-14; Ua Murchadha, 116; Ó Máille *1*, 27; *Irisleabhar 7*, 58; *Béaloideas 4*, 52; Nicolson, 341.
84. References in Ó hÓgáin (1988), 219. This idea that Fionn was once in dire want was found in Scottish lore also (see note 58 above) as was the idea that he and his men ate limpets (J. G. Campbell, 27, 75-6). This limpet [*bairneach*] imagery may have been suggested by the occurrence of similar sounding names like Bairnech, Báine, Muirne, Bran Bhoirne, in the literature, see indices in Stokes (1900), Ní Shéaghdha (1945), and Murphy (1953). See also *Béaloideas 3*, 188.
85. Murphy (1942), 3-5, 23-8.
86. Ibid., 5-23.

87. IFC 164:294; *Béaloideas 4*, 83; IFC 159:396; IFC 117:28-9.
88. J. F. Campbell (1892), 357.
89. Stokes (1900), 120-22 etc.
90. Ibid., 3, 58-9, 62-3. Also *Lia Fáil 1*, 98.
91. The source of this idea seems to be the mention in *Genesis* 6:4 of giants upon the earth in olden times, 'the mighty men of old, men of renown'. It is interesting to note the quite similar imagery connected with Arthur in post-mediaeval British landscape lore, see Glennie, *passim*, and Ashe, 149-54.
92. Bieler, 154; Mulchrone, 76-7.
93. Stokes (1900), 58-60, 62, 78.
94. Ibid., 72.
95. Boece, 418; Lyndsay *2*, 107; Dunbar, 103. See MacKillop, 72-4.
96. Céitinn, 330.
97. The origin is perhaps as early as the first Colloquy, see Stokes (1900), 54-5. Later examples, chapter 7, notes 22, 41, 43; Brewer and Bullen, 10-11.
98. References in *Béaloideas 2*, 227; Murphy (1953), xvi; Ó Súilleabháin and Christiansen, Type 1149; *Ulster Folklife 21*, 85-9.
99. See J. F. Campbell (1872), 7-8; Morrison, 45-9; and Broderick, 168-71 (original text in *Zeitschrift 38*, 169-71).
100. IFC 191:279.
101. Murphy (1953), xviii-xix; Broderick, 169; IFC 872:28-9, etc.
102. Murphy (1953), xix; IFC 84:357.
103. Lover, 11; Curtin (1894), 437.
104. Jones, 15, 89.
105. Colloquy mention in Stokes (1900), 181. Other references in Hogan 618; *Townlands*, 825; Máire MacNeill, 690; Comerford, 52; Herity and Eogan, 58; J. G. Campbell, 15; Waddell, 49; W. J. Watson, 243.
106. J. G. Campbell, 84.
107. IFC 156:129.
108. Irish references in Ó hÓgáin (1988), 212. Scottish instances in Glennie, 105; Neil Ross, 222; Waddell, 50-51, 77, 85-7.
109. Stokes (1900), 33, 43.
110. Borlase, *passim*; Ó Ríordáin, 57, 72-3, 84-5; Herity and Eogan, 85-93; Murphy (1953), xxxv. The designation 'Bed of Diarmaid' occurs also in Scotland, see Glennie, 102.
111. *Dublin University Magazine 34*, 424; Kennedy, 186; Croker, 52-7, Glennie, 101-5; J. G. Campbell, 14; IFC 815:5-6.
112. Ó Riordáin, 84.
113. J. G. Campbell, 14-15, 27, 55; MacKenzie, 252; Glennie, 104.
114. Thompson (1955-1958), Motif D1960.2. For references and discussion, see Ó hÓgáin (1985), 148, 335-6.
115. MacDougall (1891), 74-5; J. G. Campbell, 3-4; Nicolson, 28-9.
116. Ó hÓgáin (1985), 141-9; *Béaloideas 42-44*, 276.
117. *Dublin University Magazine 34*, 536; Murphy, xviii; Morrison,

15-16; IFC *S*635:74-5. Other examples in sources listed at notes 98-99 above.

118. Oral communication from Seán Ó Donagáin, a native of the area, 7/8/1986.

119. J. G. Campbell, 3.

CHAPTER 10 (pp. 311–322)

1. Céitinn, 324-34.
2. Holinshead, 39.
3. Brewer and Bullen, 1-15.
4. Ware, 47-63.
5. Camden, 1048.
6. Barbour, 43-4.
7. For Macpherson's influence see Ó Cadhlaigh, 407-24; MacKillop, 79-102; Tombo; Van Tieghem, and Montiel. For Napoleon, see Van Tieghem *2*, 3-13.
8. Scholarly investigations of Macpherson *vis-à-vis* Gaelic sources in Thomson (1951 and 1987).
9. O'Halloran, 57.
10. A valuable discussion of this in MacKillop, 128-33.
11. Heinrich Zimmer was the principal adherent of this theory, for which see Murphy (1953), 211. For its influence on Joyce, see MacKillop, 170.

Select Bibliography

Aarne, Antti and Thompson, Stith, *The Types of the Folktale*, Helsinki 1961

Adhalsteinsson, Jón H., *Under the Cloak*, Uppsala 1978

Almqvist, Bo; Ó Catháin, Séamus; and Ó Héalaí, Pádraig, (eds), *The Heroic Process*, Dublin 1987

Ashe, Geoffrey, *The Quest for Arthur's Britain*, London 1971

Barbour, John, *The Bruce*, W. W. Skeat (ed.), Edinburgh 1894

Baudiš, Josef, 'The Antiquity of the Kingship of Tara', in *Ériu 8*, 1916, 101-7

Baum, Paull Franklim, 'The Mediaeval Legend of Judas Iscariot', in *Publications of the Modern Language Association of America 31*, 1916, 481-632

Bergin, Osborne and Marstrander, Carl, *Miscellany Presented to Kuno Meyer*, Halle 1912

Best, Richard I. and Bergin, Osborn, *Lebor na hUidre*, Dublin 1929

Best, Richard I.; Bergin, Osborn; and O'Brien, Michael, *The Book of Leinster 1-5*, 1954-1967. See Anne O'Sullivan

Bieler, Ludwig, *The Patrician Texts in the Book of Armagh*, Dublin 1979

Binchy, Daniel A., 'The Saga of Fergus mac Léti', in *Ériu 16*, 1952, 33-48

'The Fair of Tailtiu and the Feast of Tara', in *Ériu 18*, 1958, 113-38

Corpus Iuris Hibernici 1-6, Dublin 1978

Boece [Boethius], Hector, *The Mar Lodge Translation of the History of Scotland*, George Watson (ed.), Edinburgh 1946

Borlase, William C., *The Dolmens of Ireland 1-3*, London 1897

Breathnach, Pádraic, *Maigh Cuilinn*, Dublin 1986

Bréhier, Louis and Aigrain, René, *Historie de l'Eglise 5*, Paris 1938

Brewer, J. S. and Bullen, W., *Calendar of the Carew Manuscripts 5*, London 1871

Broderick, George, 'Manx Stories and Reminiscences of Ned Beg Hom Ruy', in *Zeitschrift für celtische Philologie 39*, 1982, 117-94. Original Manx texts, ibid., *38*, 1981, 113-78

Bromwich, Rachel, *Trioedd Ynys Prydein*, Cardiff 1961

Bruford, Alan, *Gaelic Folk-Tales and Mediaeval Romances*, Dublin 1966

Budge, E. A. Wallis, *The Gods of the Egyptians 1*, London 1904
Bugge, Sophus, *Norroen Formkvædhi*, Christiania 1867.
Byrne, Francis J., *Irish Kings and High Kings*, London 1973
Camden, William, *Britannia*, London 1695
Cameron, Alexander, *Reliquiae Celticae 1*, Alexander Mac Bain and John Kennedy (eds), Inverness 1892
Campbell, John Francis, *Leabhar na Féinne*, London 1872
Popular Tales of the West Highlands 3, London 1892
Campbell, John Gregorson, *The Fians*, London 1891
Carey, John, 'Nodons in Britain and Ireland', in *Zeitschrift für celtische Philologie 40* 1984, 1-22
Carmichael, Alexander, *Carmina Gadelica 2*, Edinburgh 1928
Carney, James, *Studies in Irish Literature and History*, Dublin 1955
Medieval Irish Lyrics, Dublin 1967
Céitinn, Seathrún, *Foras Feasa ar Éirinn 2*, P. S. Dinneen (ed.), London 1908
Chadwick, Nora K., 'Imbas Forosnai', in *Scottish Gaelic Studies 4*, 1934, 97-135
Christiansen, Reidar, *The Vikings and the Viking Wars in Irish and Gaelic Tradition*, Oslo 1931
Colgrave, Bertram, *The Earliest Life of Gregory the Great*, Lawrence 1968
Comerford, M., *Kildare and Leighlin 2*, Dublin 1883
Croker, T. Crofton, *Legends of the Lakes*, London 1829
Cross, Tom Peete, 'The Gaelic "Ballad of the Mantle"', in *Modern Philology 16*, 1918-1919, 153-62
Motif-Index of Early Irish Literature, Bloomington 1952
Cubbon, William, *A Book of Manx Poetry*, Douglas 1913
Curtin, Jeremiah, *Myths and Folk-Lore of Ireland*, Boston 1890
Hero-Tales of Ireland, London 1894
Irish Folk-Tales, Séamus Ó Duilearga (ed.), Dublin 1943
de hÍde, Dubhglas, *An Sgeuluidhe Gaedhealach*, Dublin 1933
de Vries, Jan, 'Das Motiv des Vater-Sohn-Kampfes im Hildebrandslied', in *Germanisch-Romanische Monatsschrift 34*, 1953, 257-74
Keiltische Religion, Stuttgart 1961
Heroic Song and Heroic Legend, translated by B. J. Timmer, London 1963
Dillon, Myles, *The Cycles of the Kings*, London 1946
Early Irish Literature, Chicago 1948
Serglige Con Culainn, Dublin 1953
Lebor na Cert, Dublin 1962
Dillon, Myles and Chadwick, Nora K., *The Celtic Realms*, London 1973
Dobbs, Margaret E., 'A Note on Aidheda Forni do hUaislib Erenn and the Lost Legend of Ferdomon', in *Ériu 14*, 1946, 166-9
Dumézil, Georges, *Le Festin d'Immortalité*, Paris 1924
Dunbar, William, *The Droichis Part of the Play*, James Kinsley (ed.), Oxford 1958
Dunne, John, 'The Fenian Traditions of Sliabh na mBan', in *Journal*

of the Kilkenny Archaeological Society 1, 1849-1851, 333-62.
Dwelly, Edward, *The Illustrated Gaelic-English Dictionary*, Glasgow 1967
Eliade, Mircea, *Shamanism*, translated by Willard R. Trask, Princeton 1964
Zalmoxis the Vanishing God, translated by Willard R. Trask, Chicago 1972
Ellis/Ellis Davidson, Hilda R., 'Sigurd in the Art of the Viking Age', in *Antiquity 16*, 1942, 216-36
The Road to Hel, Cambridge 1943
Gods and Myths of Northern Europe, Middlesex 1964
Evans, J. Gwenogvryn, *The White Book Mabinogion*, Pwllheli 1907
Flower, Robin, *Catalogue of Irish Manuscripts in the British Museum 2*, London 1926
Ford, Patrick K., 'The Well of Nechtan and "La Gloire Lumineuse"', in Larson, 67-74
Foster, Idris L., 'Gwynn ap Nudd', in Murphy, 1953, 198-204
Frazer, Joseph G. (ed.), *Appollodorus: The Library 2*, London 1921
Gerstein, Mary R., 'Germanic Warg: The Outlaw as Werwolf', in Larson, 131-56
Gillies, William, 'Heroes and Ancestors', in Almqvist, Ó Catháin, and Ó Héalaí, 57-73
Glennie, J. Stuart, *Arthurian Localities*, Edinburgh 1869
Golther, Wolfgang, *Das Lied vom Hürnen Seyfrid*, Halle 1889
Gonda, Jan, *Notes on Brahman*, Utrecht 1950
The Vision of the Vedic Poets, The Hague 1963
Gougaud, Louis, *Christianity in Celtic Lands*, translated by Maud Joynt, London 1932
Gray, Elizabeth A., *Cath Maige Tuired*, Dublin 1982
Gregory, Augusta, *The Kiltartan History Book*, Dublin 1909
Gruffydd, W. J., *Math vab Mathonwy*, Cardiff 1928
Rhiannon, Cardiff 1953
Guyonvarc'h, Christian, 'Notes d'Étymologie et de Lexicographie Gauloises et Celtiques', in *Ogam 13*, 1961, 586-98
Gwynn, Edmund J., *The Metrical Dindshenchas 1-5*, Dublin 1903, 1906, 1913, 1924, 1935
Hartland, E. Sidney, *The Legend of Perseus 1*, London 1894
Henderson, George, *Fled Bricrend*, London 1898
Henry, Françoise, *Irish Art in the Early Christian Period*, London 1940
Herity, Michael and Eogan, George, *Ireland in Prehistory*, London 1977
Höfler, Otto, *Kültische Geheimbünde der Germanen 1*, Frankfurt 1934
Hogan, Edmund, *Onomasticon Goedelicum*, Dublin 1910
Holder, Alfred, *Alt-Celtischer Sprachschatz 1-3*, Leipzig 1896
Holinshead, Raphael, *Chronicles 4*, London 1808
Huizinga, Johan, *Homo Ludens*, London 1949
Hull, Vernam, 'Two Tales about Find', in *Speculum 16*, 1941, 322-33
Longes mac n-Uislenn, New York 1949
'A Rhetoric in "Finn and the Man in the Tree"', in *Zeitschrift für celtische Philologie 30* 1962, 17-20
Ions, Veronica, *Egyptian Mythology*, London 1965

Jackson, Kenneth Hurlstone, *Cath Maighe Léna*, Dublin 1938
The International Popular Tale and Early Welsh Tradition, Cardiff 1961
The Oldest Irish Tradition, Cambridge 1964
Jones, D. Gwenallt, *Yr Areithiau Pros*, Cardiff 1934
Jónsson, Finnur, *Edda Snorra Sturlusonar*, Kaupmannahöfn 1931
Joynt, Maud, *Feis Tighe Chonáin*, Dublin 1936
Jung, C. G. and Kerenyi, C., *Science of Mythology*, London 1985
Kennedy, Patrick, *Legendary Fictions of the Irish Celts*, London 1866
Knott, Eleanor, *Togail Bruidne Da Derga*, Dublin 1936
Kölbing, Eugen, *The Romance of Sir Beues of Hamtown 1-3*, London 1885-1894
Krappe, Alexander, *Balor with the Evil Eye*, Columbia 1927
Lang, James T., 'Sigurd and Weland in Pre-Conquest Carving from Northern England', in *The Yorkshire Archaeological Journal 48*, 1976, 83-89
Larson, Gerald James (ed.), *Myth in Indo-European Antiquity*, Berkeley 1974
Lee, S. L., *Duke Huon of Burdeux 1-2*, London 1882-1883
Le Roux, Françoise, 'Études sur le Festiare Celtique', in *Ogam 13*, 1961, 481-506.
Lewis, Charlton T. and Short, Charles, *A Latin Dictionary*, Oxford 1879
Lie, Hallvard, 'Sagnet om Lvorledes Sigvat ble skald', in *Maal og Minne*, 1946, 66-74.
Lincoln, Bruce, *Priests, Warriors, and Cattle*, Berkeley 1981
Loomis, Roger Sherman, *Wales and the Arthurian Legend*, Cardiff 1956
Lot, Ferdinand, *Nennius et l'Historia Brittonum*, Paris 1934
Lover, Samuel, *Legends and Stories of Ireland*, Dublin 1834
Lyndsay, David, *The Poetical Works 1-2*, David Laing (ed.) Edinburgh 1871
MacAlister, R. A. Stewart, *Lebor Gabála Érenn 4*, Dublin 1941
Mac Cana, Proinsias, *Branwen, Daughter of Llŷr*, Cardiff 1958
Celtic Mythology, London 1970
'Mongán mac Fiachna and Immram Brain', in *Ériu 23*, 1972, 102-42
The Learned Tales of Medieval Ireland, Dublin 1980
McCone, Kim, 'Hounds, Heroes and Hospitallers in Early Irish Myth', in *Ériu 35*, 1984, 1-30
MacDonald, T. D., *Gaelic Proverbs and Proverbial Sayings*, Stirling 1926
MacDougall, John, *Craignish Tales*, London 1889
Folk and Hero Tales, London 1891
Mac Eoin, Gearóid S., 'A Life of Cumaine Fota', in *Béaloideas 39-41*, 1971-1973, 192-205
Mac Giollarnáth, Seán, *Loinnir Mac Leabhair*, Dublin 1936
MacInnes, D., *Folk and Hero Tales*, London 1890
MacInnes, John, 'Recordings of Scottish Gaelic Heroic Ballads', in Almqvist, Ó Catháin, and Ó Héalaí, 101-30
MacKenzie, W. M., *The Book of Arran 2*, Glasgow 1914

MacKillop, James, *Fionn mac Cumhaill: Celtic Myth in English Literature*, New York 1986
MacNeill, Eoin, *Duanaire Finn 1*, Dublin 1908
MacNeill, Máire, *The Festival of Lughnasa*, Oxford 1962
Mac Niocaill, Gearóid, *Ireland before the Vikings*, Dublin 1972
Mac Piarais, Pádraig, *Bodach an Chóta Lachtna*, Dublin 1906
Bruidhean Chaorthainn, Dublin 1908
MacSpealáin, Gearóid, *Uí Cairbre Aobhdha*, Dublin 1960
Meid, Wolfgang, *Táin Bó Fraích*, Dublin 1967
Meyer, Kuno, *Cath Finntrágha*, Oxford 1885
Aislinge Meic Conglinne, London 1892
The Voyage of Bran 1, London 1895
Four Old-Irish Songs of Summer and Winter, London 1903
The Triads of Ireland, Dublin 1906
The Instructions of King Cormac mac Airt, Dublin 1909
Fianaigecht, Dublin 1910
Sanas Cormaic, Halle 1912 (= *Anecdota from Irish Manuscripts 4*)
Über die älteste Irische Dichtung, Berlin 1914
Moe, Moltke, *Samlede Skrifter 2*, Knut Liestol (ed.), Oslo 1926
Montiel, Isidoro, Ossián en España, Barcelona 1974
Morrison, Sophia, *Manx Fairy Tales*, Peel 1929
Mudrak, Edmund, *Die Deutsche Heldensage*, Berlin 1939
Mulchrone, Kathleen, *Bethu Phátraic*, Dublin 1939
Müller-Lisowski, Käte, 'Contributions to a Study in Irish Folklore: Traditions about Donn', in *Béaloideas 18*, 1948, 142-99
Murphy, Gerard, *Duanaire Finn 2*, London 1933
Duanaire Finn 3, London 1953
Early Irish Lyrics, Oxford 1962
The Ossianic Lore and Romantic Tales of Medieval Ireland, Cork 1971
Nagy, Joseph Falaky, 'Demne Mael', in *Celtica 14*, 1981, 8-14
The Wisdom of the Outlaw, Berkeley 1985
Nicolson, Alexander, *Gaelic Proverbs*, Malcolm MacInnes (ed.), Glasgow 1951
Nilsson, Martin P., *The Minoan-Mycenaean Religion*, Lund 1927
Opuscula Selecta 3, Lund 1952
Ní Mhuirgheasa, Máire, *Imtheacht an Dá Nónbhar agus Tóraigheacht Taise Taoibhghile*, Dublin 1954
Ní Mhuirgheasa, Máire and Ó Ceithearnaigh, Séamus, *Sgéalta Rómánsuíochta*, Dublin 1952
Ní Shéaghdha, Nessa, *Agallamh na Seanórach 1-2*, Dublin 1942; *3*, Dublin 1945
Tóruigheacht Dhiarmada agus Ghráinne, Dublin 1967
Ní Shéaghdha, Nessa and Ní Mhuirgheasa, Máire, *Trí Bruidhne*, Dublin 1941
Ó Briain, Pádruig, *Bláithfhleasg de Mhílseáinibh na Gaoidheilge*, Dublin 1893
O'Brien, Michael A., *Corpus Genealogiarum Hiberniae 1*, Dublin 1962

Ó Cadhlaigh, Cormac, *An Fhianuidheacht*, Dublin 1947
Ó Catháin, Séamas, *The Bedside Book of Irish Folklore*, Dublin 1980
Uair an Chloig cois Teallaigh, Dublin 1985
Ó Cathasaigh, Tomás, 'The Semantics of "Síd"', in *Éigse 17*, 1977-1978, 137-55
Ó Cuív, Brian, *Cath Muigh Tuireadh*, Dublin 1945
O'Daly, Máirín, *Cath Maige Mucrama*, Dublin 1975
Ó Donnchadha, Tadhg, *An Leabhar Muimhneach*, Dublin n.d.
O'Donovan, John, *Annála Ríoghachta Éireann 1-7*, Dublin 1848-1851
Ancient Laws of Ireland 1, Dublin 1865
O'Donovan, John and Stokes, Whitley, *Cormac's Glossary*, Calcutta 1868
Ó Duilearga, Séamus, *Leabhar Sheán Í Chonaill*, Dublin 1948
Ó Duilearga, Séamus and Ó hÓgáin, Dáithí, *Leabhar Stiofáin Uí Ealaoire*, Dublin 1980
Ó Gallchobhair, Tomás, ('Triúr Comhdhalta de Chuallacht Chuilm Cille'), *Gadaidhe Géar na Geamh-Oidhche*, Maynooth 1915
O'Grady, Standish H., *Silva Gadelica 1*, London 1892
Ó hAimhirgin, Osborn and Mac Néill, Eoin, *Eachtra Lomnochtáin*, Dublin 1901
O'Halloran, Sylvester, *The History and Antiquities of Ireland 3*, Dublin 1772
Ó hÓgáin, Dáithí, *Duanaire Osraíoch*, Dublin 1980
An File, Dublin 1982
The Hero in Irish Folk History, Dublin 1985
'Magic Attributes of the Hero in Fenian Lore', in Almqvist, Ó Catháin, and Ó Héalaí, 207-42
O'Kearney, Nicholas, *Feis Tighe Chonáin Chinn-Shléibhe*, Dublin 1855
O'Keeffe, J. G., *Buile Shuibhne*, Dublin 1931
O'Kelly, Michael J., 'Excavations and Experiments in Ancient Irish Cooking-Places', in *Journal of the Royal Society of Antiquaries of Ireland 84*, 1954, 105-55
O'Looney, Brian, *Laoidh Oisín ar Thír na n-Óg*, Dublin 1859
Ó Máille, Tomás S., *Sean-fhocla Chonnacht 1-2*, Dublin 1952
Ó Muirgheasa, Énrí ('F. Mac Róigh'), *Oidhche Áirneáil*, Dublin 1924
O'Rahilly, Cecile, *Cath Finntrágha*, Dublin 1962
Táin Bó Cúailnge: Recension 1, Dublin 1976
O'Rahilly, Thomas F., *A Miscellany of Irish Proverbs*, Dublin 1922
Early Irish History and Mythology, Dublin 1946
Ó Riain, Pádraig, *Cath Almaine*, Dublin 1978
Ó Ríordáin, Seán P., *Antiquities of the Irish Countryside*, London, 1965
Ó Siochfhradha, Pádraig ('An Seabhac'). *Tóraigheacht an Ghiolla Dheacair*, Dublin 1938
Laoithe na Féinne, Dublin 1941
Seanfhocail na Mumhan, Pádraig Ua Maoileoin (ed.) Dublin 1984
Ó Súilleabháin, Seán, *A Handbook of Irish Folklore*, Dublin 1942
O'Sullivan, Anne, *The Book of Leinster 6*, Dublin 1983
Paris, Gaston, *Histoire Poétique de Charlemagne*, Paris 1865

Patch, Howard Rollin, *The Tradition of Boethius*, New York 1935

Pernoud, Regina and Suard, François, *Histoire de Huon de Bordeaux*, Paris 1983

Pettazzoni, Raffaele, *The All-Knowing God*, translated by H. J. Rose, New York 1978

Plummer, Charles, *Vitae Sanctorum Hiberniae 1-2*, Oxford 1910
Bethada Náem nÉrenn 1-2, Oxford 1922

Pokorny, Julius, *Indogermanisches Etymologisches Wörterbuch*, Bern 1959

Potter, Murray Anthony, *Sohrab and Rustum*, London 1902

Powell, T. G. E., *The Celts*, London 1958

Power, Maura, 'Cnucha Cnoc os cionn Life', in *Zeitschrift für celtische Philologie 11*, 1917, 39-55

Power, Rosemary, '"An Óige, an Saol agus an Bás" – Feis Tighe Chonáin and Thorr's Visit to Útgardha-Loki', in *Béaloideas 53*, 1985, 217-94

Price, Liam, 'The Placenames of the Barony of Newcastle, County Wicklow', in *Proceedings of the Royal Irish Academy 44*, 1937-1938, Section C, 139-179

Rank, Otto, *The Myth of the Birth of the Hero*, translated by F. Robbins and S. E. Jelliffe, New York 1914

Rees, Alwyn and Rees, Brinley, *Celtic Heritage*, London 1961

Rhys, John, *Lectures on the Origin and Growth of Religion*, London 1888

RIA Dictionary: i.e. Royal Irish Academy, *Contributions to a Dictionary of the Irish Language*, Dublin 1913-1975

Robinson, F. N., *The Irish Lives of Guy of Warwick and Bevis of Hampton*, Halle 1907

Ross, Anne, *Pagan Celtic Britain*, London 1967

Ross, Neil, *Heroic Poetry from the Book of the Dean of Lismore*, Edinburgh 1939

Saintyves, P. (i.e. Émile Nourri), 'Le massacre des Innocents ou la persécution de l'Enfant predestiné', in P-L Couchoud, *Congrés d'histoire du Christianisme*, Paris 1928, 229-72

Schoepperle, Gertrude, *Tristan and Isolt*, London 1913

Scott, Robert D., *The Thumb of Knowledge*, New York 1930

Shah, Idries, *The Way of the Sufi*, Middlesex 1974

Sharpe, Richard, 'Hiberno-Latin *Laicus*, Irish *Láech* and the Devil's Men', in *Ériu 30*, 1979, 75-92

Sjoestedt, Marie-Louise, *Gods and Heroes of the Celts*, translated by Myles Dillon, London 1949

Skene, William F., *Celtic Scotland 3*, Edinburgh 1880

Smyth, Alfred P., 'The Húi Néill and the Leinstermen' 'Húi Failgi Relations with the Húi Néill', in *Études Celtiques 14*, 1974, 121-43; 503-23
Celtic Leinster, Dublin 1982

Stern, Ludwig C., 'Die Gaelische Ballade vom Mantel', in *Zeitschrift für celtische Philologie 1*, 1896, 294-326

Stewart, Alexander, *Works of the Highland Bards*, Edinburgh 1804

Stokes, Whitley, *Three Irish Glossaries*, London 1862

The Calendar of Oengus, Dublin 1880

The Tripartite Life of Patrick, London 1887

The Edinburgh Dinnshenchas, London 1893, reprinted from *Folklore 4*

Acallamh na Senórach, Leipzig 1900, i.e. *Irische Texte 4*

Stokes, Whitley and Strachan, John, *Thesaurus Palaeohibernicus 2*, Cambridge 1903

Tessier, Georges, *Le Baptême de Clovis*, Paris 1964

Thevenot, Émile, *Divinités et sanctuaires de la Gaule*, Paris 1968

Tierney, James J., 'The Celts and the Classical Authors', in Joseph Raftery, *The Celts*, Dublin 1964, 23-33

Thompson, Stith, *Motif-Index of Folk-Literature*, Bloomington 1955-1958

Thomson, Derick S., *The Gaelic Sources of Macpherson's 'Ossian'*, Edinburgh 1951

'Macpherson's "Ossian": Ballads to Epics', in Almqvist, Ó Cáthain, and Ó Héalaí, 243-64

Thurneysen, Rudolf, *Scéla Mucce Meic Dathó*, Dublin 1935

Tombo, Rudolf, *Ossian in Germany*, New York 1901

Towlands and Towns, Parishes and Baronies of Ireland, General Alphabetical Index to, Dublin 1851

Turville-Petre, E. O. G., *Myth and Religion of the North*, London 1964

Ua Ceallaigh, Seán, *Rudhraigheacht*, Dublin 1935

Ua Murchadha, Domhnall, *Sean-Aimsireacht*, Dublin 1939

Van Hamel, A. G., *Compert Con Culainn*, Dublin 1956

Van Tieghem, P., *Ossian en France*, Paris 1917

Vendryes, Joseph, *Airne Fíngein*, Dublin 1953

Von Sydow, C. W., 'Iriskt Inflytande på nordisk guda-och hjältesaga', in *Vetenskapssocietetens i Lund årsbok*, 1920

Waddell, P. Hately, *Ossian and the Clyde*, Glasgow 1875

Wagner, Heinrich, 'Studies in the Origins of Early Celtic Civilisation', in *Zeitschrift für celtische Philologie 31*, 1970, 1-58

'The Archaic Dind Ríg Poem and Related Problems', in *Ériu 28*, 1977, 1-16

Ware, James, *Ancient Irish Histories 2*, Dublin 1809

Watkins, Calvert, 'Language of Gods and Language of Men: Metalinguistic Traditions', in *Myth and Law among the Indo-Europeans*, Jaan Puhvel (ed.), Berkeley 1970

Watson, Seosamh, *Mac na Míchomhairle*, Dublin 1979

Watson, W. J., *Place-Names of Ross and Cromarty*, Inverness 1904

Weiser-Aall, Lily, *Altgermanische Jünglingsweihen und Mannerbünde*, Baden 1927

Weisweiler, Josef, 'Vorindogermanische Schichten der irischen Heldensage', in *Zeitschrift für celtische Philologie 24*, 1954, 10-55, 165-97

Wikander, Stig, *Der arische Männerbund*, Lund 1938

Williams, Ifor, *Pedeir Keinc y Mabinogi*, Cardiff 1930

Williams J. E. and Ní Mhuiríosa, Máirín, *Traidisiún Liteartha na nGael*, Dublin 1979

Young, Matthew, 'Ancient Gaelic Poems', in *Transactions of the Royal Irish Academy 1* (Antiquities), 1787, 45-119

IRISH AND CELTIC PERIODICALS

An Claidheamh Soluis, Dublin 1899-1932. Referred to as *Claidheamh*

An Lóchrann, Dublin 1907-1931

An Stoc, Dublin 1923-1930

Anecdota from Irish Manuscripts 1-5, Halle 1907-1913

Béaloideas: The Journal of the Folklore of Ireland Society, Dublin 1927-

Celtica, Dublin 1946-

Dublin University Magazine 1-74, 1833-1869

Éigse, Dublin 1939-

Ériu, Dublin 1904-

Irische Texte 1-4, Leipzig 1880-1909

Irish Texts 1-5, London 1931-1934

Irisleabhar na Gaedhilge: The Gaelic Journal 1-19, Dublin 1882-1909. Referred to as *Irisleabhar*

Lia Fáil 1-3, Dublin 1928-1930

Revue Celtique 1-55, Paris 1870-1934

Scottish Gaelic Studies, Edinburgh 1926-

Ulster Folklife, Belfast 1965-

Zeitschrift für celtische Philologie, Halle 1896-. Referred to as *Zeitschrift*

MANUSCRIPT SOURCES

BM Irish MSS collection in the British Museum, London

IFC Irish Folklore Collection in the Department of Irish Folklore, University College, Dublin. Card catalogue in that Department (*Fiannaigheacht*)

RIA Gaelic MSS collection in the Royal Irish Academy, Dublin

TCD Gaelic MSS collection in Trinity College, Dublin.

Index